Essay Index

THE POETS OF RUSSIA

1890–1930

THE POETS OF RUSSIA

1890-1930

By

RENATO POGGIOLI

HARVARD UNIVERSITY PRESS

Cambridge, Massachusetts

1960

Publication of this book has been aided by a grant from the Ford Foundation

Printed in the United States of America

Library of Congress Catalog Card Number 60–8000

To the Memory

of

GAETANO SALVEMINI

CESARE PAVESE

LEONE GINZBURG

CONTENTS

CONTENTS

CONTENTS

CHAPTER TEN: POETS OF TODAY

This book's main theme is the development in Russia of what is commonly designated as "modern" or "contemporary" poetry. A definition of these epithets will also help to explain the temporal limitations of my survey.

When applied to the noun "poetry" the attributes "modern" and "contemporary" are employed respectively in a restricted and in an expanded sense. The first indicates something less than the poetry of the moderns; the second, something more than the poetry of the generation still living. What we mean by them is simply that the poetry we call "modern" or "contemporary" is a new kind of poetry, the like of which has never existed before.

The chronology implied in either adjective differs according to countries, yet in all cases it refers only to the date of appearance. In short, it suggests different time sequences, each one with a variable *terminus ad quem*, while refusing to establish a *terminus post quem*, or even to admit its existence. It is, for instance, evident that "modern" poetry emerged in France earlier than anywhere else, with Mallarmé in the early 1880's, or even with Baudelaire in the late 1850's. And it is equally apparent that in all other countries, including Russia, the opening date can never be pushed farther back than the 1890's.

If there is no chronological problem for the closing date, it is only because "modern" poetry in the sense defined is the only kind of poetry still flourishing. It may be open to question whether this is an unmixed blessing. One may wonder whether the time will not soon come for another kind of poetry, less personal and suggestive, more objective and public. One may suspect, or even hope, that symbolistic mood and advance-guard taste, standardized as they have become, have already spent their creative force. All this, however, is but speculation or wishful thinking: when all has been said, "modern" poetry still remains the only mode vitally affecting Western verse.

There is a single exception to this rule, and that exception is Russia. Russia is the only country where a peculiar set of social, political, and cultural conditions has prevented the spontaneous development of "modern" poetry during the last quarter-century. This explains why I have assigned a closing date to this study and have pushed that date as far back as the thirties. After sketching the transitional *Kulturkampf* of the early revolutionary years, this survey stops abruptly at the very moment when the Soviet order submitted Russian intellectual life to a totalitarian *Gleichschaltung*.

This entails the exclusion of any figure that rose on the literary horizon after 1930, a rule confirmed, rather than denied, by the resolve to extend beyond that limit the *curriculum vitae* of any poet whose youth was nurtured in a freer atmosphere, and who in his maturity was able to cultivate almost privately the plant of modern poetry. Otherwise, except for mentioning, or discussing briefly, some early or belated poets, whether *neoteroi* or *epigones*, I have avoided considering Soviet verse, and failed to include its representatives among the masters of yesterday and today. This decision, even more than to my relative ignorance of the subject, was due to the conviction that the Soviet system has destroyed "modern" poetry in Russia, without allowing a newer one to be put in its place.

That there can be no history without judgment is a truism worth repeating. As for the history of poetry, like Shakespeare's Iago, it is nothing if not critical. In a survey of this kind the historical outlook should supply a broad view of the cultural background, while the critical insight should provide an appraisal of the works of art created against that background. Creative achievement, rather than historical significance, is thus the value which occupies the foreground of the picture, and this is why the title of this book speaks of "poets" rather than of "poetry."

The other reason for preferring that plural and concrete word over the abstract and singular one is the realization that any study of lyrical poetry, even when starting from a single poem, tends ultimately to reconstruct an entire poetic personality. By this I mean the poet's aesthetic rather than psychological temper; yet, while convinced that the former transcends the latter, I am far from believing that the one denies the other. Hence the joining, within the characterization of each poet, of his biographical sketch to his critical profile.

Being apparently built around a set of separate portraits, this book may at first look like a gallery of busts. Yet none of these poets, not even Aleksandr Blok, who seems, more than the others, to stand alone by virtue of having a full chapter to himself, is viewed in isolation from either group or milieu. Thus the book could be more properly likened to a landscape with figures.

The landscape itself expands within a frame rather large in scope. Thus Chapter One reviews the native tradition of Russian lyrical poetry, from its earliest Neoclassical representatives, who appeared in the Age of Enlightenment, to the great masters, classical in creation even if Romantic or realistic in spirit, of the nineteenth century. Chapter Two depicts the immediate environment within which the earliest of the poets of modern Russia flourished, and gives a vast panorama of that new culture, idealistic in philosophy, mystic in religion, and "aesthetic" in literature, which dominated Russian intellectual life from the *fin du siècle* to the first decade of the present century.

The reader may well grow impatient with all these lengthy preliminaries, wondering why should he wait so long before crossing the threshold of the mansion he has been asked to visit. Yet it is only through this gradual approach that the reader will appraise better the mansion as well as the figures that dwell within its walls. The same can be said of those special sections or passages dealing at the proper place with the literary currents that influenced Russian poetry from without, or rather imposed a common set of poetic ideas and attitudes on the whole of Western culture. Truly enough, the poets of Russia interpreted those ideas and shaped those attitudes in fashions of their own; and it is by emphasizing both analogies and divergences that this book tries to bring a partial contribution to the discipline now called comparative literature, even though the comparative method is used here primarily as a characterizing device.

For the sake of completeness I have treated these poets as more than just poets. It was only in the age of Pushkin that Russian literature witnessed a similar triumph of verse over prose. But, even more than the masters of Pushkin's age, the Russian poets of the twentieth century wrote novels, stories, and plays, as well as poems. Some of them are better remembered as writers of fiction, while others have left their mark also as authors of philosophical and critical essays. This explains the treatment of Blok's theater and of Belyj's fiction, to give only two examples, which will suffice to prove that these portraits would have been less truthful had I avoided referring in some detail to the outstanding contributions of their subjects to other fields than that of verse.

The obvious consequence of this is that a poet who was also a thinker or a critic, a novelist or a playwright, may loom larger than a figure of lesser range as man of letters but of greater depth as artist. This is why, in all the cases that so warranted, I have tried to compensate brevity of treatment with intensity of statement. It is only by failing to take this consideration into account that native connoisseurs of Russian poetry may protest that I devote more pages to such faded stars as Bal'mont, Brjusov, or Vjacheslav Ivanov than to Annenskij, Mandel'shtam, or Tsvetaeva, still vividly burning in the darkened sky of Russian poetry.

Some competent judges may object to the architecture of this book, which is functional in the sense that it serves primarily practical ends. I am willing to admit that other architects would have joined into a single block units that I have kept apart, while putting many statues into other niches than those I have assigned to them. Yet I believe that there are good as well as bad reasons for dividing the Decadent thread from the Symbolistic one, or for placing such figures as Annenskij, Kljuev, and Esenin precisely where I did. At any rate we must not forget that all ordering is convention and compromise; that any classification is but an attempt to square the circle, which ends by producing odd shapes of its own.

Many a critic may well question the relevance or pertinence of the many digressions of this book, such as those on the painters of the turn of the century, on the great men of the theater since Stanislavskij, and on the main thinkers of the idealistic camp, which together take up most of Chapter Two. "Extravagant" as they may look, I still think that these and other similar digressions help to recreate the atmosphere within which the poetry of modern Russia grew and flourished. Other and longer digressions are more obviously related to the main theme of the book: this is the case of the extended parallel, by way of comparison and contrast, between Russian and Western Symbolism, which fills almost the whole of Chapter Four.

The exclusion from the over-all picture of Soviet poetry as it developed from 1930 on may cast some doubt on the fitness of the vast *excursus* in Chapter Nine, which compares with each other on one hand the opposite types of the Soviet and of the Western writer, and on the other, the Soviet cultural situation and our own "popular arts" and "mass culture." This *excursus*, like the report on Pasternak's novel *Doctor Zhivago*, justifies its presence by the very need to explain the causes of that "twilight of poetry and art" now casting its shadow on the whole of the Communist world.

If the author of this book reads Russian poetry as a foreigner, it is also as a foreigner that he handles the language he writes in. It was a self-critical awareness of this fact that led me to solve negatively the vexing question of how to translate and to quote. Since I could not afford to put my non-native English to the acid test of metered speech, at first I thought of using liberally the many translations in verse available or extant. Soon enough, however, I realized that even the best of them were unsuited to my purpose. Thus I was left no other choice but to reduce my quotes to a minimum, selecting brief passages of peculiar importance, and of far greater significance in matters of content than of form. Thus, making a virtue of necessity, and with the single exception of the four lines from Pushkin which form the book's epigraph, I translated all verse passages into what I hope is an unobtrusive and unpretentious English prose.

Anyone writing in English about things Russian must take up

the challenge of how to transpose words originally written in the Cyrillic alphabet. I have faced this challenge squarely, by choosing the path of transliteration rather than that of transcription, and by adopting the only system which, while avoiding the use of diacritical signs, still satisfies the principle that a single Latin letter or English graph must correspond always and only to one and the same symbol of the Cyrillic alphabet. The reader who wishes to acquaint himself with such correspondences, and to learn the approximate phonetic value of each letter or graph within this system, should consult the table that immediately follows this foreword.

Convinced as I am that any other solution would have raised more problems without stirring fewer protests, I still realize that most readers will find it difficult to adjust themselves to the novel and strange spelling of many a name they were accustomed to see in variants less offensive to their sense of the English language. Yet I had no real alternative, since no other method, except the more exotic and complex one, entailing the use of special characters, might have been aptly employed in the bibliography and the index, which list hundreds of Russian titles in their original form.

For the sake of simplicity, I have avoided giving in the text all information which was not absolutely necessary. I have, for instance, not supplied the patronymic of each author in his biographical profile, yet I have provided that patronymic in the index, where it follows the author's surname and Christian name. It is likewise in the index alone that I have marked names, surnames, and patronymics with accents indicating the position of the tonic stress. While the text gives the titles of all Russian works cited only as rendered in English, the index, which lists all those titles alphabetically under the names of their respective authors, provides in each case the original titles as well.

The bibliography is classified according to a self-evident plan, which in the main follows the pattern of the book. Most of its listings are divided into the following series, each one of which forms a separate typographical unit: (1) critiques in Russian; (2) and (3) critiques and translations, respectively, into English,

French, Italian, and German. The bibliography is selective in the sense that it shows some preference for contributions of recent vintage. While not critical, it includes brief parenthetical remarks which may help the reader who wishes to pursue further the study of the subject.

After so many apologies, at least as many acknowledgments. I wish first of all to express publicly my gratitude to three Harvard friends and three colleagues from other institutions, who generously helped with suggestions, criticism, and advice. The three local friends were Roman Jakobson, Samuel Hazzard Cross Professor of Slavic Languages and Literatures; Professor Michael Karpovich, Curt Hugo Reisinger Professor of Slavic Languages and Literatures, Emeritus; and Professor Vsevolod Setschkareff, also a member of the Harvard Slavic Department. (Professor Karpovich died while these pages were being written, leaving a moral and intellectual legacy which the affection and admiration of all those who knew him will preserve for a long time to come.) The three colleagues from outside were Professor Gleb Struve of Berkeley, a world-known authority on Soviet literature; Professor George (Jurij) Ivask of the University of Kansas, a distinguished *émigré* man of letters; and Professor Vladimir Markov of UCLA, who, raised in Communist Russia, "chose freedom" after the war. Professor Markov read the section on Futurism and the few pages on the Soviet poets, while the others saw, although in different drafts, the whole manuscript. All these men have given me the benefit of their vast learning and experience in the field of Russian letters; their merit is as great as my demerit for all the errors of facts and mistakes of judgment a survey of this scope can hardly avoid.

For assistance in compiling the bibliography and the index, I am indebted to three former or current Harvard graduate students in Slavic, Messieurs Robin E. Steussy and Nicholas E. Alssen, and Mrs. Patricia Arant, who also helped with the proofs. I am equally indebted to the Harvard Foundation for Advanced Study and Research, which awarded me a grant to compensate their services. For the painstaking typing and retyping of the manuscript, I must thank three Harvard departmental secretaries: Miss Johanne Hirshson, Mrs. Beverly Moreau, and Mrs. Ruth Carpenter (especially the latter). I must pay a special tribute to the director and staff of Harvard University Press for their valuable and unassuming help in the hard task of preparing this volume for publication. My thanks must go also to the Librarian of the Houghton Library for allowing me to reproduce the vignette on the title page, taken from a copy of the original edition of Valerij Brjusov's *Urbi et Orbi* (Moscow 1903), which is part of that library's rich holdings in the field of Russian letters, as shown by the splendid catalogue, *The Kilgour Collection of Russian Literature* (Harvard University Press, 1959). I wish finally to express my gratitude to the editors and publishers concerned for permitting me to include in this book the pages on Pasternak and those on the Soviet cultural situation, which made their first appearance in *Partisan Review* and *The Yale Review*, respectively.

Before closing, I feel I must explain why I have inscribed this book to the memory of three Italian friends. The first, the great historian and freedom fighter Gaetano Salvemini, who taught at Harvard for over twenty years, died as an old man at the time I started working on this book. The second, Cesare Pavese, one of the outstanding Italian writers of his generation, discovered for his contemporaries the greatness of the American dream as expressed in American literature. Later he felt more attracted by the new Russian myth: and his disenchantment with that myth was one of the motives that led him in the end to a self-inflicted death. The third, Leone Ginzburg, born in a family of Russian *émigrés*, chose Russian literature as his scholarly field, while making the cause of Italian people his own, and it was as a leader of the Resistance that the Nazis executed him just before the liberation of Rome. The names of these three men seem a fitting inscription for a book like this, which is also an account of the eternal struggle between tyranny and liberty, even if limited to the poetic front. It is a sad sign of our predicament that that struggle may now affect even the republic of letters, once the freest of all commonwealths.

R. P.

TABLE OF TRANSLITERATION AND
PRONUNCIATION

CYRILLIC ALPHABET	TRANS- LITERATION	PRONUNCIATION (APPROXIMATE)
а	a	*a* in *father*
б	b	*b*
в	v	*v*
г	g	*g* in *garden*
е	e	*ye* (when accented, *yo*; in such case may be spelled and transliterated *ë*)
ж	zh	French *j*
з	z	*s* in *rose*
и	i	*i* in *little*
й	j	*y* in *day*
к	k	*k*
л	l	*l*
м	m	*m*
н	n	*n*
о	o	*o*
п	p	*p*
р	r	*r*
с	s	*s* in *son*
т	t	*t*
у	u	*ou* in *you*
ф	f	*f*
х	kh	German *ch*
ц	ts	*ts*
ч	ch	*ch*
ш	sh	*sh*
щ	shch	*shch*
ы	y	a low, guttural и
ь	'	(indicates palatization of preceding consonant)
э	è	*e* in *ebb*
ю	ju	*you*
я	ja	*ya* in *yard*

THE POETS OF RUSSIA

1 8 9 0 – 1 9 3 0

We were not born for barter or for strife,
For marketplaces or for battlegrounds;
To heed the Muses were we given life,
To pray and sing in harmony of sounds.
ALEKSANDR PUSHKIN

CHAPTER ONE

THE MASTERS OF THE PAST

I

PROLOGUE

In a cold and far-off country, both northern and eastern, there entered upon the scene between the beginning and the middle of the past century eight or ten heroic men who, virtually unaided, and almost against the will of fate, were to introduce a new tradition within the realm of world culture. The vast country where they were born was then called "The Empire of All the Russias," and the triumphant appearance of those great figures on the national and European scene seemed to compensate for many centuries of silence and obscurity, to reward what a historian of that Empire, Nikolaj Karamzin, had once called the "historical patience" of his people, and to bring to full life that great nation in which the thinker Petr Chaadaev had seen a land of the dead. Those men made it possible for the West to rediscover on its own account Russia as a new-found-land of the spirit; their words and deeds sufficed to add the voice of Russia to the chorus of world literature. Their shadows, and the dark mirage of their land, still occupy our mind and seduce our imagination. Those shadows and that mirage have obscured forever the dreamlands of our romantic grandparents, which were other countries of the North, the South, or the East; made us forget the Scandinavian fjords and the "mystic chasm" of Bayreuth, which were the lands of the heart's desire for our decadent parents; and replaced all this with a fabulous and almost unreal landscape, with a wasteland of the steppes, where, in poor villages or ghostly cities, there lived and suffered a strange and splendid people, which, at least in the tales of its writers, seemed to experience the human condition with an intensity and a significance not suspected before. This vision, which we may well call the Russian dream, will last as long as the modern world continues to ask, in its doubt and unrest, the questions which those men asked with a frequency and an urgency yet unknown to their Western masters. The memory of that dream is perhaps one of the noblest inheritances we shall leave behind us. Yet the figures who bequeathed us that marvelous legacy seem to remain in today's history (shaped in great part by Russia, often through the denial of the values affirmed by the very best of her sons) merely as a myth: the last great myth of Western culture, still alive, but already old, laden with heavy doubts and troubling enigmas, though it is scarcely fifty or a hundred years since that myth was begotten.

Indeed, no more than a third or a fourth of a century has elapsed since the civilized world celebrated the centenaries of the births of Dostoevskij and Tolstoj, who were the main heroes of that myth. Dostoevskij, who was perhaps the spiritual heir of Gogol', the oldest of all the great masters of Russian prose, died almost at the same time as his rival and enemy, Turgenev, the very year in which Alexander II, the Great Emancipator, fell the victim of a terrorist's bomb. Tolstoj lived instead to witness the two generations which followed his own, and saw broken or betrayed the tables of his law. Yet the future legend, ignoring or confusing dates, as legends do, will pronounce him dead at the same time as his lifelong rival and the first among his peers. The Russian mind looks at Dostoevskij and Tolstoj as if they were two prophets of the Old Testament; but the men of the ages to come will look at them as if they were the Aeschylus and the Sophocles of a new literature, at once Hellenic and barbaric, dominated equally by the spirit of Marsyas and that of Apollo.

As for Chekhov, posterity will perhaps consider him as the Euripides or Aristophanes who emerged at the decline of the tragic vision of his august predecessors. He turned his insight, as well as his humor and pathos, on the new men of the Russian intelligentsia, who wanted to lead their people and who brought to that task many petty vices and a few great virtues. Yet, although Chekhov, like so many other writers of his time, was himself one of those *homines novi*, he shared more than any other the glories of the dying past. The people who in 1904 carried his body to its resting place felt perhaps that they were burying the last member of a dynasty which had lost its throne and had left no prince on whom to bestow its crown.

What Chekhov carried to his grave was the great tradition of Russian nineteenth-century writing, which, at least for the West, seemed to be made up only of storytellers and novelists. Chekhov was the last classical master of Russian fiction; and, like all artists closing a series, he foreshadowed the shape of the things to come. Yet his death did indeed signify the end of an era. Before the close of the century, despite the simple and noble creations of Chekhov's talent, despite the last, brilliant flashes of Tolstoj's genius, the golden age of Russian literature had suddenly come to an end. What seemed to come to the fore in its stead was an age of bronze. The successors of Aksakov, Gogol', Goncharov, Dostoevskij, Tolstoj, Saltykov, Leskov, Nekrasov, and Ostrovskij (the last two, although respectively a poet and a playwright, belong by right to the school of the great masters of Russian realism) were, before, during, and after Chekhov's time, a galaxy of minor writers, provincial and sentimental, pathetic and picturesque, the best known of whom in the West are Garshin, Korolenko, Kuprin, Andreev, and Gor'kij. All of them, including the last, still extolled in Soviet Russia, were in a sense derivative artists, imitating the great writers of the past in everything except in their greatness. While the masters had created the tragic and heroic era of Russian literature, their disciples shaped instead its pathetic and comic period, reducing the glorious realism of the past to the anecdotal and the local, and replacing the study of man with the study of types and milieus.

That process of degeneration could be described as the triumph of the prosaic, and it was perhaps this triumph which in the end brought out a reaction against prose itself. Thus, starting with the turn of the century, there arose in Russia a new cultural and literary outlook, which dethroned prose and put poetry in its place. Thoughtless imitation gave way to conscious artistry; the moral and social preoccupations of the past yielded to the cult of beauty, and, at least in part, even to spiritual and religious concerns. The leaders of this movement did not attempt to restore the golden age just gone by, which could never return, nor did they try to establish a golden age of their own. For a while, to be sure, blinded by the glitter of the era they had helped to shape, they were led to believe that they were ushering in a great, new epoch; and once one of them, Merezhkovskij, claimed to see in that epoch another Renaissance. What that movement brought forth was, however, not another Renaissance, but merely a neoromantic Restoration; and its greatest merit or achievement was perhaps to cut short the age of bronze which was then threatening to engulf Russian letters, and to place in its stead an age of silver. Another of its merits was to bridge more fully than in the golden age the gap which seemed still to keep apart the Russian genius from the spirit of the West. "Never before," says the gifted *émigré* writer Vladimir Vejdle in his book *Russia Absent and Present*, "had cultured Russia such a sense of being naturally European, of being a nation with a natural place among the nations of Europe. Differences were recognized, but no longer regarded as irreconcilable."

Like all ages of silver, the literary period which opened with the turn of the century was composite in style, eclectic in thought, and syncretic in belief. Russia became not only a modern Alexandria, but also a new, if lesser, Byzantium. Like those Graeco-Roman poets who called themselves *neoteroi*, the literary artists who then flourished in two great centers of Russian life, Petersburg and Moscow, revived the Alexandrian spirit by reconciling tradition with novelty, by joining together alien genres and contrasting modes, by pursuing at once that showy pomp and that hidden elegance which respectively mark Asian and Attic taste. As thinkers, the leaders and the followers of the Russian modern movement felt the seduction of any moral, social, or philosophical idea, coming from either near or afar; and welcomed with enthusiasm, or accepted with resignation, the most contradictory tidings, which brought the men of their time fears or hopes, nightmares or daydreams. As believers, they seemed to be willing to test every dogma or religious tenet, and were ready to enter, for them-

selves and for their people, every road of the spirit, without knowing whether it would lead to damnation or bliss. All of them
searched for, and experimented with, all too many creeds, without
ever finding a steady faith, without ever building a single church;
and they erected all too many shrines to strange and lesser gods.
Apostles and heretics at once, they squandered the lofty heritage
of the past without raising anything new and valid in its stead.

In a sense, these men helped to prepare, unconsciously and unwillingly, the fate which finally destroyed their values and their
class. The existence of tsarist Russia was menaced by the swelling
revolt of the masses: and those men often sided with that revolt,
or rather, with the nihilistic protest of a radical and rootless intelligentsia, which tried to change Russian reality by utopian ideologies or by fits of terrorism. Thus the spiritual and political
leaders who had emerged at the beginning of the new century,
after failing to control the insurrection of 1905, which receded
almost by itself, were finally unable to stem the flood which submerged them in 1917. What the Futurist and Soviet poet Majakovskij was later to call "the tide of a second deluge" not only
destroyed their fortunes or persons, but brought to an end the
silver age of Russian culture; and cleared the ground not for another age of bronze, but for that iron age which now, more than
forty years later, still rules Russia and throws its shadow all over
the world.

It is the silver age of Russian literature, or rather its poetry,
which is the subject matter of this book. That age and its poetry
were important, although the latter seems to have left no trace
on the soil where it flowered for about two generations, and where
it withered more than one generation ago. If the Western observer
is at least partly able to appraise the fruits of a poetic tradition
from which he is doubly removed, in space as well as in time, it
is only because he still sees standing around him sprouts from the
same seed. But when that observer wishes to assess more fully the
local factors which first helped the plant of modern poetry to
blossom on Russian land, and then stunted its growth, he must leave
familiar ground, and enter an alien one. In brief, he must explore
the native habitat which favored and hindered the life of the tree.

This means in practice that this survey will end with the barren vista of Soviet culture, but will begin with the panorama of a greener poetic past. From its humble beginnings in the preceding century, Russian poetry reached its peak more than one hundred years ago: and it will be the task of this opening chapter to re-evoke all the old masters of whom the heroes of our story were but the distant offspring.

II

THE EARLY MASTERS OF RUSSIAN VERSE

The culture of Russia had no Renaissance; its medieval phase lasted, with neither break nor transition, up to the threshold of the modern era. As far as poetry is concerned, this means that Russia preserved longer than any other country two early medieval traditions: the tradition of ecclesiastical literature, transmitted through the written word, and as such a monopoly of the clergy, which was the only literate class; and the tradition of heroic poetry, transmitted by word of mouth, a privilege of the warlike nobility, or at least, of the singers of that class. These two traditions, which Slavic philology and Russian literary scholarship distinguish by the names of *pis'mennost'* (written literature) and *slovesnost'* or *ustnaja slovesnost'* (oral literature), merged in the highest poetic monument of the Russian Middle Ages, the *Lay of the Host of Igor'*, discovered at the end of the eighteenth century, but composed by an unknown poet, in rhythmic prose, probably shortly after 1187, to commemorate the raid of Prince Igor' against the Cumans, his bravery in defeat, and his daring flight from his pagan and barbaric enemies after he had fallen into their hands.

Russian oral literature developed from the Middle Ages on in both epic and lyric form. The epic tradition, which was less enduring than the lyric one, although in certain regions of Northern Russia it was still alive one hundred years ago, first developed in the so-called *byliny*, which celebrate the feats of legendary heroes against the background of pagan myths; and later in the so-called *stariny*, or in less fabulous evocations of great historical figures and events. The first collection of such mythical and historic songs,

6

which appeared in print as late as 1818 under the name of the fictitious Cossack Kirsha Danilov, performed during the Russian pre-romantic and romantic age the same function that Bishop Percy's *Reliques* had performed earlier for English literature. Even more lasting was the influence of the later collections of lyric folk song, conveying in simple accents such universal feelings as the joys or sorrows of love, or more particular experiences, such as those which found expression in brigand songs and sectarian chants.

In contrast with this exceptional survival — up to the threshold of the modern age — of popular poetry and oral composition, and of cultural forms which in the West had disappeared even from the memory of man, that kind of poetry which the Germans call "artistic," and which one could simply label as both secular and literary, was not destined to appear in Russia until the eighteenth century, although in most Western countries it had emerged as early as the thirteenth. Naturally enough, the first Russian practitioners of "artistic" poetry were chiefly imitators or adapters of foreign models, in regard to both content and form. Thus Antiokh Kantemir (1708–1744) wrote a series of satires à la Boileau, in the alien mold of Polish verse, which is syllabic in structure, while the pedantic grammarian Vasilij Tredjakovskij (1703–1769) composed conventional lyrics in simpler and more natural verse schemes. It was only in the later period of his life that Tredjakovskij adopted the tonico-syllabic pattern, which Lomonosov had already introduced, modeling it on the German example. That pattern was to last up to our time, when the loosening of the traditional prosodic shackles led Russian poetry back to the accentual rhythm of the folk song. If we forget, however, all the authors whose names are remembered only because of their technical contributions or historical importance, only two of the poets of eighteenth-century Russia, Lomonosov and Derzhavin, have any literary or artistic significance.

The great critic Belinskij depicted the erudite and encyclopedic Mikhail Lomonosov (1711–1765) as "the Peter the Great of Russian Literature," while Pushkin, who deserved that title himself, described Lomonosov more accurately, and not without a touch of irony, as "the first Russian university." A self-made man

7

(he was born the son of a fisherman, in the icebound North, not far from Archangel), Lomonosov mastered the most disparate disciplines. Like Goethe, he was attracted by the natural sciences, especially by physics and chemistry, to which he contributed discoveries of some relevance. He tried his hand at all branches of learning and all kinds of writing, including grammar and rhetoric. He was a child of the Enlightenment, which he understood as a massive attempt at self-education and self-improvement, the only manner in which a Russian of his time and milieu could conceive of that movement.

As an author, Lomonosov expressed the moral and scientific content of his culture primarily in terms of eloquence. His most important literary contributions are those of a technician and a theorist. He reformed Russian poetry in the light of Gottsched's poetics and of German prosody, yet, because of both the solemn magnificence of his style and the authority of his legislation and example, his place is rather that of a Russian Malherbe. He based his poetic diction on a judicious combination of colloquial, courtly, and Church-Slavonic elements, which he mixed in varying proportions, according to his theory of the "three styles," "high," "middle," and "low," respectively suited to genres of decreasing worth and dignity. More at home in the high style, he was tempted by the lofty muse of heroic poetry, but failed in his attempt to write an epic poem about Peter the Great. He was more successful in the field of didactic verse, so alien to our taste, but so fashionable in an age as interested in education and knowledge as the eighteenth century. Yet no historical consideration can mitigate his outright failure in the fields of satire and tragedy.

The compositions for which Lomonosov is still remembered are to be found among his lyrics. Practically all of them are solemn odes, often written as official panegyrics, either sacred or profane. The stiff classicism of their imagery, as well as their heavy mythological machinery, makes them typical manifestations of the pseudo-Pindarism which blighted the more pretentious poetry of the age. A few of his odes, however, stem from a freer and deeper inspiration: two of them are perhaps the best legacy he left to posterity. With titles which may well echo Young's *Night Thoughts*, they are respectively called "Morning" and "Evening Meditations on the Magnificence of the Godhead." The first evokes the splendid vision of sunrise; the second, a rarer and stranger natural spectacle, that of the aurora borealis. They fuse the most divergent aspects of Lomonosov's genius: his scientific insight and philosophic outlook merge with a feeling of cosmic awe, with a sense of the sacred. As for their style, it seems to reconcile within itself the extremes of Baroque pomp and of classical majesty.

Despite Lomonosov's merits, the first Russian poet who fully deserved posthumous glory was his great disciple and successor, Gavriil Derzhavin (1743–1816). Yet that glory was begrudged him for more than a century after his death. Critics and readers steeped in the three main fashions of modern literature, the romantic, the realistic, and the symbolistic, could not do justice to a poet like him. What was needed for this was a revival of interest in eighteenth-century taste, a reawakening of neoclassical attitudes in poetry as well as in criticism. As far as Russian culture is concerned, this happened only recently, primarily in *émigré* circles, and the first worthy monument erected to Derzhavin's memory was perhaps a monograph by the exiled poet Khodasevich, published about twenty years ago.

Partly a Tatar by blood, the humble scion of a family of the petty nobility, born and raised in a distant province, Derzhavin rose high enough in the civil service to become for a while Minister of Justice. Despite his scant learning (he knew well the language and literature of Germany, which offered him models in Haller and Klopstock, but was ignorant of Latin and French), he was endowed with enough literary flair to learn what he needed from the Slavic Bible and from modern versions of Horace and Anacreon. In many ways he simply proceeded farther on the path already opened by Lomonosov: without the latter's precedent he would not have written his famous ode "God," a powerful poetic statement of eighteenth-century deism, which was translated into all the languages of Europe. Derzhavin followed Lomonosov's example also in matters of versification and diction, yet his greater verbal gifts enabled him to solve better than his predecessor problems of style and of rhythm.

9

Derzhavin found the most genuine springs of his inspiration in his own temperament, which was a psychological blend of stoicism and epicureanism. He was a stoic in his manful acceptance of the human condition, ruled by the laws of nature and society, bound to death and suffering, as well as to duty and work. And he was an epicurean in his urge to savor life in all its joys and delights, whether coarse or refined, physical or spiritual, such as love and drink, or leisure and mirth. In Miltonic terms, he merged the mood of "L'Allegro" with that of "Il Penseroso." He was thus able to join lofty and humble strains in his *Felitsa* (or Felicia: a name by which he obviously meant "the happy one"), an allegorical and fabulous pageant celebrating the great Catherine in an orgy of exotic fancy, humorous familiarity, and good-natured fun. The originality of his personality permitted him to transcend the limits of imitation not only in his Horatian odes or anacreontics, but also in his funereal hymns or quasi-pastoral idylls. The most famous of the former are "On the Death of Prince Meshcherskij" and "The Cascade" (the latter written on the occasion of the sudden demise of the imperial favorite Potemkin). Its opening strophes, with the powerful vision of the waterfall, a huge power standing for both life and death, are among the highest peaks of Russian verse. As for his idylls, the most famous of them is *Life at Zvanka*, written as an epistle to a friend, to describe to him the poet's way of life in his rustic retreat. Here as elsewhere Derzhavin's inspiration is often faulty, and his manners uncouth, yet even such blemishes as these are but the vices of his virtues. Derzhavin was one of those rare literary artists who, while working within the limitations of neoclassical taste, avoided the elegant mannerisms and effeminate graces which are its bane and curse.

By the robust sweep of his talent (Belinskij called him a hero, or *bogatyr*, and praised the triumphal tone of his voice, even in its humblest songs), Derzhavin escaped the pitfalls of Rococo, which may be defined as a miniature parody, or an unconscious caricature, of neoclassicism. All the *poètes légers* and *petits maîtres* of the age wrote charming trifles in that style; and many of them, like the uncle of the greatest Russian poet of all time, Vasilij Pushkin (1767–1830), often chose the language of France as a vehicle for their frivolous exercises. The most felicitous practitioner of light verse was the Ukrainian Ippolit Bogdanovich (1743–1803), the author of the incredibly popular *Dushen'ka* (Animula), a free retelling in Russian disguise of the fable of Eros and Psyche, patterned not after Apuleius' ancient model but after the modern Gallic version of La Fontaine.

Nothing could be further from this kind of witty and mirthful verse writing than the earnest and melancholic inspiration of Vasilij Zhukovskij (1783–1837), whose life was as pathetic as his poetry. Born out of wedlock (his father was a landowner named Bunin, and his mother a Turkish slave), he was adopted by a relative, and grew up among a swarm of women, in a sentimental and mystical atmosphere. He took part in the Napoleonic wars, and was for many years the tutor of the crown prince (the future Alexander II). While in his youth he had suffered the pangs of a forbidden love for his niece, in his old age he happily married a girl forty years his junior, and spent the rest of his life in the country of his bride, in that Germany which had always been for him the promised land of the spirit.

Zhukovskij was essentially a poet of feeling, and as such he followed in the footsteps of Nikolaj Karamzin (1766–1826), who is better known to posterity as a historian, but who as a poet and a prose writer was perhaps the first Russian to find inspiration in the new sensibility. While abandoning in his lyrics the lofty modes of the ode for the humble one of the elegy, Karamzin also adopted in poetry a diction not too far removed from common speech, stirring, with his rejection of archaic and Slavonic forms, the indignation of the upholders of linguistic and literary purism. Zhukovskij followed Karamzin's example with a far greater refinement of both feeling and form, patterning his view of life after Schiller, while the early Karamzin had patterned his own after Rousseau.

From the very beginning of his career Zhukovskij felt the attraction of all the new literary genres and trends then emerging on the Western literary horizon, such as the poetry of graveyards and ruins, the Ossianic vogue, and the concern with folk tales and folk songs. He entered literature under the double influence of Gray and Bürger, with a free version of the former's "Elegy Written in a Country Churchyard," and with an even freer rendering of the latter's famous ballad "Lenore," which he transposed against a Slavic background, and renamed, after its Russian heroine, "Ljudmila." Henceforth almost the whole of his literary production consisted of translations, imitations, and adaptations, the main sources of which were the modern poets of England and Germany, who thus replaced the French and classical masters who up to that time had held sway over the Russian Parnassus. His main English models, besides Gray, were Thomson, Scott, Byron, and Southey; his chief German examples, besides Bürger and Schiller, were Goethe, Uhland, Hebel, Spiess, and even La Motte Fouqué, of whose prose tale *Undine* Zhukovskij produced a versified variant in Russian locale and costume. The poetry of Germany occupied in his Pantheon an even greater place than that of England, to the point that he used published or unpublished translations into German when in his late years he rewrote in splendid blank verse episodes from the *Mahabharata* and Firdusi, and produced a version in Russian hexameters of the *Odyssey*. As these examples well show, Zhukovskij's genius needed, as the poet said in his own words, the flint of an alien work to strike its own spark. In a more suitable image one could say that his genius acted like a filter or a retort, refining all foreign matter into a subtle substance, distilling even the heaviest liquid into a volatile fluid, into an exquisite quintessence.

Russian criticism has always found it difficult to place Zhukovskij historically, constantly wondering whether he should be considered a Romantic or not. Zhukovskij is, however, only a preromantic, in the sense that the new sensibility he conveys is not yet molded into a new aesthetic vision, or into a novel philosophical outlook. Nothing proves this better than his religious and metaphysical optimism, so typical of the mystical currents of the late eighteenth century. A preromanticism of this kind rejects the quasi-expressionistic trends of the *Sturm und Drang*, while it reconciles itself with the neoclassical revival and with its longings after *le beau idéal*. It was Schiller, Zhukovskij's beloved master, who had claimed that modern poetry could not be but sentimental: a truth which others were bound to take far more literally than Schiller ever did. Many writers of the same age chose other labels to state similar views: by praising the English poetry of the late eighteenth century as "philosophical," Madame de Staël meant to praise it for being melancholic and meditative. Chateaubriand himself, by recommending to the moderns what he called descriptive poetry, whether in verse or in prose, did recommend in reality the idealizing and idolizing contemplation of nature as a mirror of the self. Zhukovskij's verse is one of the most perfect and suave expressions of such moods as these, and it is not surprising that Aleksandr Blok, during the mystical revival of the beginning of this century, should turn toward some of Zhukovskij's lyrics as an inspiring precedent and as a suitable example.

Rather than to the "sweetness" of Northern poetry, Konstantin Batjushkov (1787–1855) chose to turn to the "light" of the poetry of the South. An officer in the Napoleonic wars, he served for a while as a diplomatic attaché at the Russian Embassy in Naples; like Hölderlin, he survived for thirty years in insanity the death of his poetry and his youth. An admirer of the Palatine Anthology and of the Latin elegy, as well as of Italian poetry from Petrarch to Tasso, he evoked with passionate frenzy the joys and pangs of love. The Russian representative of the *style Empire*, he tried, like Chénier, to write ancient verses on new thoughts, and revealed the modernity of his outlook in his famous "Dying Tasso," which conveys an almost Romantic view of the poet and of his destiny on earth.

Any survey of Russian poetry before the appearance of Pushkin cannot avoid mentioning Ivan Krylov (1768–1844), a polygrapher and a civil servant who only in his maturity found his real vocation, which was that of a fabulist. He spent all the rest of his life composing, revising, and publishing his fables, which, read by all, and translated everywhere, made of him the first Russian classic. Generally written after La Fontaine's real or ideal model, Krylov's fables are often novel in invention and sometimes replace humanized animals with animated objects. All of his Russian critics emphasize Krylov's originality, which they interpret in national, rather than in individual terms: a shrewd observer of life, Krylov was one of the first to open the gate of verse to a good-natured, and good-humored, satirical realism.

III

PUSHKIN

The greatest of all poets, and perhaps the highest of all the creators Russia ever produced, Aleksandr Pushkin, was born in Moscow in 1799, at the very eve of the century during which the Russian literary genius was destined to flourish and to reveal itself before the world. Pushkin's father was a penniless nobleman who had served in the Guards and who dabbled in verse; his mother was the granddaughter of Gannibal (or Annibal), the so-called "Moor of Peter the Great," an Ethiopian slave bought as a child in Constantinople by a Russian diplomat as a gift to the Emperor, who freed, educated, and raised his ward to the status of a gentleman, a general, and a landowner. Pushkin himself, no less than his biographers, attributed his hot blood, fiery temper, and vivid imagination to this black ancestor. When he was twelve, Pushkin entered the Imperial College which had just been founded under the name of Lyceum in Tsarskoe Selo, the Russian Versailles. It was there that he wrote his first French and Russian verses, earning public approval by no less a judge than Derzhavin. After graduation the poet accepted a modest ministerial post, but spent most of his time with older and younger literary friends, such as Karamzin, Zhukovskij, and Chaadaev among the former, and Vjazemskij, Del'vig, and Baratynskij among the latter.

Pushkin began his literary career with the publication of a light and fanciful narrative poem in eighteenth-century taste, partly patterned on the model of Ariosto, and entitled, after its hero and heroine, *Ruslan and Ljudmila* (1820). The poet was still enjoying its success when the writing of a political lampoon circulated in manuscript earned him banishment to Southern Russia. He was attached to the office of the governor of Ekaterinoslav, who allowed the poet to join a family of friends in a trip up to the Caucasus and Crimea: two regions which Pushkin himself was soon to change into the Spain and Greece of Russian Romanticism. At that time Pushkin had just discovered Byron, under whose influence he wrote his earliest verse tales, set against a Crimean or Caucasian background. Worthiest of mention among them is perhaps *The*

Fountain of Bakhchisaraj (1822), where the conventionality of characterization and plot is redeemed through the magic of verse. Shortly afterward, Pushkin was transferred first to Kishinev, capital of the recently annexed Bessarabia, where he played the role of a new Ovid, and later to Odessa, which was then one of the most exotic and cosmopolitan of Russian cities. His liberty of speech and behavior put him again in a bad light, but the scandal which ended forever his semiofficial career was supposedly the discovery of a letter to a friend, revealing the poet's leanings toward "pure atheism." Pushkin was placed under police supervision and confined without limit of time to Mikhajlovskoe, his mother's estate, in the province of Pskov.

The poet brought home the new fruits of his recent labors, including many lovely lyrics and another verse tale, inspired by his stay in Moldavia, *The Gypsies* (1824). This work, which according to Dostoevskij opens in Russian literature the problematics of man's fate, has been considered both a romantic and a realistic tale, a Byronian and an anti-Byronian poem. The misanthropic Aleko, who has left civilized life to join a band of gypsies and to marry the young and ardent Zemfira, is sent back to civilization as the only punishment for having killed his unfaithful bride, thus violating the customs and laws of the tribe, which proscribe revenge, while allowing free love. Notwithstanding the melodramatic quality of the theme, Pushkin transcended in that poem both Rousseauism and Byronism by taking the side of the social group against the proud and selfish outsider.

Despite the watch of the local authorities, Pushkin led at Mikhajlovskoe the normal life of a country squire, nursing his boredom as his Onegin does when confined in his little manor. Pushkin was, however, more fortunate than his hero, since inspiration visited his solitary hours. He found also the consolations of feminine friendship in a neighborly household, and enjoyed in his own the simple companionship of his old nurse Arina Rodionovna, who brought him back to the fresh springs of popular imagination and peasant speech. It was in Mikhajlovskoe that Pushkin wrote the most famous of his plays, the historical drama *Boris Godunov*, which he published in 1831 without immediate success. It was also there that he composed some of his loveliest poems, and drafted many of the cantos or "chapters" of his "novel in verse" *Evgenij Onegin*, at which he had been working since 1823.

His forced stay in Mikhajlovskoe saved Pushkin from the risk of sharing the fate of those of his friends who had taken part in the conspiracy of December 1825. By a paradoxical destiny, the ascent to the throne of the new Tsar marked the end of his house arrest. Nicholas I bestowed upon the poet the dubious grace of acting as his literary censor, while entrusting the chief of the gendarmerie with the more vulgar task of checking on the poet's political behavior and moral conduct. Pushkin spent most of the succeeding years in Moscow, where he met a vivacious beauty, the sixteen-year-old Natal'ja Goncharova. The poet fell in love with her and asked her hand, but was refused, and departed in despair on another journey to the Caucasus. Upon his return he renewed his offer, which this time was accepted. Pushkin spent the months preceding the wedding, which took place at the beginning of 1831, on his small estate of Boldino, making of this brief interlude one of the most creative seasons of his life. It was then and there that he finished *Onegin*, wrote almost all of his marvelous "little tragedies" or one-act verse plays, and composed a series of short stories which he collected under the title of *The Tales of Belkin*. The foremost of these tales, "The Station Master," joins with the novelette *The Queen of Spades* (1833) and the historical novel *The Captain's Daughter* to form the highest triptych of Pushkin's narrative prose.

The married couple settled in Petersburg, where the poet devoted most of his time to historical writing, as well as to an all-too-frivolous life, to which his vain and flirtatious wife felt attracted like a moth by the flame. The poet could hardly avoid going into the world, especially after 1834, when he was conferred the doubtful honor of being appointed court chamberlain. In 1833 Pushkin traveled to the eastern provinces of European Russia, to collect materials for his *History of the Pugachev Rebellion*, but on his way back he stopped again in Boldino, where he wrote *The Bronze Horseman* and some of his charming fairy tales. In 1836 he founded a literary journal, *The Contemporary*, in which he published *The*

Captain's Daughter. Yet during those years the work of the poet was affected by the ordeal of the man: Pushkin was losing his peace of mind under the impact of his wife's behavior, of the gossip of their circle, and of his own jealousy. It was to prevent an impending scandal, and to deny the public rumors of a supposed liaison with Madame Pushkin, that the Baron D'Anthès-Heeckeren, a French *émigré* who was the adopted son of the Dutch Ambassador, married the sister of Natal'ja, thus allaying the suspicions of her husband. But shortly after, upon receiving an anonymous lampoon listing his name among the members of the "order of the cuckolds," Pushkin dared his presumed rival to a duel without quarter, which took place the very day of the challenge. The poet fell mortally wounded, but was still able to shoot, and to hit, although not seriously, his adversary. After a long agony, Pushkin died bravely, at the dawn of January 29, 1837, when he was not yet 38 years old.

Seven years earlier, at the age of thirty, Pushkin had completed *Onegin* and opened its closing canto with a magnificent digression summing up in a few stanzas the whole of his literary career. Pushkin gave us there his own autobiography as a poet, and re-evoked the course of his creative life in the simple allegory of the apparitions, wanderings, and metamorphoses of his muse. That feminine being, the single, constant companion of his existence, appeared to him for the first time, says the poet, when, still a carefree boy, "*he* was flourishing in the garden of the Lyceum," chanting his "childish joys," "the glory of the Russian past," and "the trembling dreams of the heart": or, more simply, writing the pieces which in the canon of his work will be called "Lyceum poems." But as soon as the boy became a youth, he brought "*his* frolicking muse into the noise of banquets and stormy disputes, where she reveled like a Bacchante," an image by which the poet alludes to the *poésie légère*, bacchic and anacreontic, of his early manhood. Then, when the poet "fled afar," leaving forever the charmed circle of his rakish friends, his muse accompanied him on his travels into wild, distant provinces, helping him to discover the even more exotic lands of Romantic poetry. How often, says the poet, did the muse sweeten his gloomy journey with the charm of a mysterious tale! How often, on a Caucasian cliff, under the moon, she rode beside him like Bürger's Lenore! How often, on the shores of Tauris, she led him through night's darkness to hear the din of the sea, the chatty whisper of the Nereids, the deep, endless chorus of the waves! This passage obviously refers to that phase of Pushkin's career which is marked by the composition of both erotic idylls and historical legends or romantic ballads, by the joint influence of Chénier's neoclassicism and the Romantic lyricism of Byron, whom Pushkin imitated in his famous poem "To the Sea" and in other pieces. As for the passage that follows, it refers to *The Gypsies*, a verse tale à la Byron, and yet one of the first original products of Pushkin's genius. It was then, says the poet, that his muse visited in the heart of sad Moldavia the peaceable tents of nomadic tribes, growing wild among them, and forsaking the speech of the gods for a poor and strange tongue. Pushkin ends this splendid passage by conjuring up before us the final transformation of his muse, who, changing at the unforeseen change of everything around her, suddenly appears in his yard like a provincial maid, with a French book in her hands.

The provincial maid now personifying the poet's muse is undoubtedly Tatjana, the heroine of *Evgenij Onegin*. If the poet portrays her with a book in her hands, it is because the sentimental education of the main characters of that romance is shaped, for good or bad, by the literature they read. Onegin, an *enfant du siècle* and a city dandy, is fond of such modish and sophisticated literary products as *Childe Harold* and *Don Juan*, and likes to imitate their author and heroes if not in behavior, at least in pose. Lenskij, his friend and neighbor, who is a poet, admires the slightly less fashionable Goethe and Schiller, who inspire the reveries and speculations of his days, spent in noble dreams and lofty thoughts. Tatjana, born and raised in the countryside, finds instead her bible in *La Nouvelle Héloïse*, taking all too seriously its dated values, which are candor in passion and sincerity in love. The three characters represent thus the hold on imagination of English spleen, German idealism, and French *sensibilité*, while symbolizing in their persons three generations which coexist instead of following each other, owing to the cultural lag which marks the life of the provinces in contrast to that of the capital. This means that Onegin stands for the Byronism of the young, Lenskij for the Schillerism of their elders, and Tatjana for their forefathers' Rousseauism. The girl is the only one of the three who believes in what she reads, and this is why, as soon as she falls in love with Onegin, she dares, despite her trembling and fear, to write him a naïve letter declaring her feelings and baring her heart. At least on this occasion Onegin fails to act like a Byronian hero or a rake, and with thoughtless honesty lectures the girl about the dangers of her act. Onegin reacts, however, to the presumed ridicule of the situation by flirting all too ostensibly with the vain Ol'ga, who is Tatjana's sister and Lenskij's fiancée. Lenskij asks for an explanation, which Onegin, out of pride and prejudice, refuses to give. This incident thus leads inexorably the two friends to a duel, which ends with Lenskij's death. Onegin leaves to wander around, wearing not so much the badge of mourning as the mask of the fatal man. In the meantime Tatjana's family urges her to marry a middle-aged general rising fast in the world. Several years later, upon returning to Petersburg, Onegin is taken by a friend to a soirée, and there he recognizes Tatjana in a glamorous lady of the world. The glitter of worldly success makes him see in Tatjana the beauty and character he once failed to perceive. It is now his turn to fall in love, and to declare his passion, without fear of ridicule. But Tatjana will remain forever true to the vow that binds her to the man she married, and now it is her turn to refuse a devotion she cannot accept. She does so without moral sermons, but with a candid confession to Onegin that her girlish love is still alive in a heart no longer young.

The sad irony of this ending reveals the high morality of a story which Pushkin started as an imitation of Byron's *Beppo* or *Don Juan*, but which in the course of the creative process he turned into a rare mirror of wisdom and a unique wonder of art. It is not only here, but here more fully than anywhere else, that the writer becomes a classic, not in the literary or historical sense of the term but in the eternal and universal one. The author of this "novel in verse" resolves the conflict between the romantic and the realistic conceptions of poetry and life: more particularly, the contrast between the idealistic optimism of the German *Bildungsroman* and the pessimism of its French counterpart, so well exemplified in Flaubert's second *Education sentimentale*, where the title itself sounds like a mockery or parody. Through his denial of the naïve idealism of the first of these fictional forms, and of the utter cynicism of the other, Pushkin suggests in *Onegin* that the outcome of the pedagogy of living may be triumph as well as failure. By replacing the single protagonist of the Romantic novel (which Goethe called "a subjective epos") with a couple which is well-matched in art as ill-matched in life, Pushkin shows that at least his heroine is able to learn from the intimations of both reality and her inner being how to distinguish between truth and falsehood, which is precisely what neither she nor the hero were able to learn from literary attitudes or bookish dreams. Nothing is more significant in this regard than the visit Tatjana pays to the empty study of Onegin: an episode which seems to recall the scrutiny of Don Quixote's library by those two critical friends, the barber and the priest. The poet follows suit with an inquiry of his own, which takes the form of a series of questions concerning the character of his hero. Is Onegin, Pushkin wonders aloud, "an imitation or a vain phantasm, a Muscovite in Harold's cloak, a reflection of exotic fancies, or a glossary of modish words? . . . . or perhaps merely a parody?" Pushkin leaves these interrogations without reply, yet later he may supply the answer they require when he observes in passing that his Byronian hero is after all only "a good little chap, like you and me."

We know already that, like most romances in prose, this romance in verse is but the story of an unhappy love. Yet here the unhappiness is a double one, as if to show that it is wrong to look at that passion from the viewpoint of a single lover, whether man or woman. This dual perspective marks the extraordinary novelty of the work within its own tradition and epoch. Yet its deeper originality must be seen in the fact that it rejects both the romantic and the realistic solution of the love situation; and that it saves its heroine from the alternative implied in the second of those solutions, which is to turn her into either a Madame Bovary or an Anna Karenina. This is the reason why *Onegin* should be likened, rather than to *Werther*, *Adolphe*, or other equally passionate tales of the same age, to such an old-fashioned story of love and purity as *La Princesse de Clèves*.

Such a parallel points again to the classical quality of this work, a quality which is evident in its inspiration and vision as well as in its substance and structure. Pushkin's art consists here of a perfect blend of varying and discordant moods, of a steady balance of unruly and warring elements. While checking pathos with ethos in grave passages or serious scenes, he controls with wit all frivolous asides and light interludes. The best example to prove the second of these two cases may be found in the opening canto, with its description of a typical day of Onegin's life as a playboy in the limelight of the capital. Pushkin's pictures of *le beau monde* and his scenes of "high life" move gaily and freely between the opposite poles of sympathetic indulgence and amused irony. Pushkin produces the unique effect of a poetic comedy of manners by giving a clever artistic imitation, on the plane of style, of the fashionable elegance ruling the behavior of the society he both reflects and exposes. The art of the poet performs wonders which are no less dazzling than Pope's in *The Rape of the Lock*.

In other parts of the poem Pushkin works even greater aesthetic miracles by spinning in a single web pathos and wit, the opposite strands of his inspiration. Think, for instance, of Tatjana's nightmare: trying to flee faster from the pursuit of a monster haunting her, that modest maid must lift her skirt, and yet she blushes in her act, or rather, in her dream. Or think of the passage that follows the scene of the duel, which the poet has just closed by comparing Lenskij's fall to that of an avalanche, and his death to the premature withering of a lovely flower or to the sudden quenching of an altar fire. The poet attenuates immediately the pathetic effect of such images by a discursive speculation about the kind of man Lenskij would have become had he survived. For a while the author seems to think that Lenskij might have grown into the lofty poet he seemed to be born to become, but at the end Pushkin intimates that that promising and bright young man would have gone the way of all flesh, turning in his old age into a prosaic creature, into a "hollow man." Yet even this bitter wisdom fails to spoil the pity with which Pushkin looks at Lenskij's destiny and at the condition of man. This example may suffice to prove that the moral and imaginative resources of *Evgenij Onegin* are, within its limited scope, limitless; yet the foreign reader will fail to grasp its sovereign power and charm if he forgets that this novel is also a poem, composed in the closed form of a fixed stanza, joining together fourteen iambic tetrameters in an intricate rhyming pattern of masculine and feminine endings, in a constant wonder of sound and sense, of visions and words.

The reader seeking among Pushkin's nonlyrical production works which may deserve being compared in quality, if not in kind, to this magnificent "novel in verse" will find them in the very different poetic zones of the legendary, the dramatic, and the fabulous. There is no better proof of the versatility of Pushkin's genius than the immediacy of his responses to the varying challenges of a capricious, and yet exacting, muse. In a famous poem he likened the poet to an echo constantly and faithfully resounding all of nature's appeals. He may well have conceived of this metaphor as a specific reflection of his own creative personality, yet the emblem would still apply were the image extended from the sphere of nature to that of art. Pushkin heeded not only the calls of life, but also the summons of literature, although his voice made any old or strange utterance sound both familiar and new. Pushkin lent a willing ear also to the tidings of history, which inspired his two great poems on Peter the Great, *Poltava* (1823) and *The Bronze Horseman*. Even so, particularly in the second piece, the poet was able to transform history's pageant into a vision, and its nightmare into a legend.

The apparent protagonist of *The Bronze Horseman* is a simple Petersburg clerk who, like Onegin, calls himself Evgenij, and who loses his mind when one of the Neva's recurring floods submerges the frail houses of the poor and drowns his sweetheart. The real hero of this verse tale is, however, the great Emperor, who appears in a grandiose prelude, while laying plans for the splendid capital which his power and dream will call forth from the desert marshes of the North. The poem's theme is the everlasting conflict between history's will, and the sacrifices it imposes on the many and the weak for the glory of all or of the few. The many and the weak cannot be but the losers in such a struggle, and Pushkin symbolizes their destiny in the hallucination which haunts Evgenij in a sud-

den fit of madness. Looking at the famous Falconet statue of Peter
the Great, proudly sitting on his rearing mount, the bereaved victim
fancies that the bronze horseman descends from its pedestal and
pursues him in a wild gallop down the ravaged streets. The horror
of the apparition recalls the scene which closes the legend of Don
Juan; but the bronze horseman, unlike the stone guest, stands for
the tragedy and glory of history, not for the revenge or justice of
God. The novelty of the poem lies in its quasi-Goethean ambivalence, in the poet's merciful understanding that injustice is the price
of order, and that history is merciless.

Pushkin evoked history's course, both its bright and bleak moments, in the tapestrylike scenes of the oldest and most ambitious
of his plays, *Boris Godunov*, which he had written after the model
of Shakespeare's "histories," in the wake of the dramatic theories
of Western Romanticism. But in his later theatrical works, especially in the "little tragedies," his only concern was with man's inner
world, with his mind and spirit, with his will and heart. This is
particularly true of *The Covetous Knight*, where Pushkin gave
one of the earliest tragic versions of the type of the miser, traditionally molded into a comic or prosaic cast. The protagonist is an old
baron, who is the master rather than the slave of his treasure, since
he considers it a source of power, not merely a heap of gold. The
baron sacrifices everything to *auri sacra fames*; and in order to refuse his son his due, he does not hesitate to accuse him of attempted
parricide. The son calls the father a liar; the old knight challenges
his heir to a duel, and dies shouting, with words which would
sound comic if uttered on any other occasion, "My keys! my
keys!"

The most perfect jewel of Pushkin's dramatic art is, however,
another miniature tragedy, *Mozart and Salieri*, which deals with
the problem of grace, understood not as divine election but as
human exception, as genius rather than as sainthood. Pushkin
realized that there is no drama in grace: that in its context the only
tragic character is the one who, despite his merits, must avow that
he is not one of the chosen. Thus he made of Salieri both the protagonist and the antagonist, and turned the play into the tragedy of
envy. The old Salieri has sacrificed everything to his calling, ease

and health, love and happiness, life itself. Music is his religion, and he worships no other God than his craft. He believes that art should reward those of its devotees who labor and strive, performing day and night the services required by its cult. It is with heavy heart but unflinching hand that he finally poisons his younger friend and colleague, a thoughtless and careless angel working artistic portents in mirthful ease, with the blissful innocence of a playful child.

Pushkin himself revealed a Mozart-like gift in those *Fairy Tales* in verse he wrote, not from the viva-voce popular tradition, but after inferior literary models, including in one case Washington Irving. Even though most of their themes are the same as the Grimms', Pushkin replaced the somber world of the German *Märchen*, where sorcery itself is but an image of nature's darkest powers, with a toylike universe of his own making, a pure and gratuitous creation reflecting over its radiant surface all the lights and colors of a rainbowlike imagination. All these stories turn magic into wonder, and their loveliness is such that Prince Mirskij went so far as to claim that *The Fairy Tale of King Saltan* is the supreme achievement of Pushkin's poetry. Certainly there is nothing to which they may be compared in the European letters of the epoch: their whole forms a classical work, for which it would be wrong to speak of "romantic irony," since the poet wrote them not to prove his godlike power to fix and shape "airy nothings," but with the far more serious intention of amusing and pleasing the child within his and all men's hearts. Rather than a poet-nightingale Pushkin is here, to use the nickname given him as a boy by his schoolmates, a poet-cricket. It is the utter simplicity of compositions like these that explains why Pushkin's art loses its virtues when translated, thus disappointing most Western readers, who may well echo Flaubert's protest to Turgenev: *Mais il est plat, votre poète!* Pushkin's simplicity conceals the complex workings of a supreme artistic intelligence, wise enough to realize the truth the poet once uttered in a cry of the heart which we find written down in one of his letters: *La poésie, parbleu, doit être quelque peu bête.*

It is spontaneity of feeling and immediacy of statement that give Pushkin's lyrical poetry a unique sense of balance and ease, that bring into a single harmony its opposite strains, which are seriousness and nonchalance, insouciance and gravity. The highest and deepest of his secrets is a perfect spiritual equilibrium, that inner check which is the privilege of only the rarest talents, and which Dante named *il fren dell'arte*. This faculty is nowhere more visible than in Pushkin's lyricism. We see, for instance, that his art tends to enhance the tone of the poems dealing with the humble and intimate experiences of daily life, as in such famous pieces as "Winter Road" and "Winter Evening," "Elegy" and "Remembrance," or "Lines Written on a Sleepless Night." But we also see that he tends to tone down, or to transcribe into a lower key, the inspiration he draws from the spheres of the exalted and the sublime, as in the "Upas Tree" and "The Prophet," in "The Mob" and all the lyrics rehearsing the eternal theme of poetry and the poet. Through his power to control equally and evenly the moods of the soul and the modes of form, Pushkin is often able to express even the most Dionysian inspiration in Apollonian terms. This is what he did in "The President's Song," the only passage he added to *The Feast during the Plague*, a splendid and yet faithful rendering of a mediocre play by the obscure English poet John Wilson (Christopher North), where he turned into music even the horror of sickness and the terror of death.

While in his life Pushkin acted the part of Don Juan, in his art he behaved like a Faust who never forgets the beauty of Helen and the serenity of the classical world. When we take his work as a whole, we realize that among the moderns he is Goethe's only rival. And one could say of him what Friedrich Schlegel said of Goethe, that he was at once the Shakespeare and the Voltaire of his own nation and time. Like the great German poet, Pushkin merged within himself the traditions of two centuries, which in a sense were at war with each other. This and his temper made him play many other roles, including those of a Russian Pope and a Russian Wordsworth. Unassuming and unconcerned, he did not mind playing on his native literary stage even roguish parts and minor roles, like those of a Russian Parny or Earl of Rochester, as shown by the writing in his youth of such a Cavalier or libertine poem as the blasphemous *Gabrieliad*.

It was the range and the profundity of his creation which prevented Pushkin from exercising a lasting influence and from determining the future course of Russian poetry. Like Horace, he rightly claimed to have erected a monument *aere perennius*, which posterity admired with sacred awe but could imitate only in a few details, or lesser ornaments. This should not surprise us: such is the destiny of all great poets. What is remarkable in Pushkin's case is that not only his prose but also his poetry, and not *Onegin* alone, left a lasting mark on the creative imagination of the classic masters of Russian fiction, on Gogol' and Turgenev, on Dostoevskij and Tolstoj. As for the poets who followed him, they treated his work as more, or less, than a literary model or poetic example. They looked at it as if it were an oracle and a miracle, and at its creator as if he were not a master but a god: perhaps the only solar god ever to appear in the cloudy sky of the poetry of the North.

IV

ROMANTICISM: LERMONTOV AND TJUTCHEV

Pushkin was so radiant a sun that most poets of his time look like planets with no light of their own. No one seems to shine within the brilliance of his day; one must wait for the night to perceive the pale rays of those minor poets who followed lesser orbits than his. It is only in that shadow that we may see the flickering and moonlike halo of the poetry of Aleksej Kol'tsov (1809–1842). The self-taught son of a Voronezh cattle dealer, Kol'tsov found in poetry escape and respite from a hard and coarse existence. He wrote in two or three different manners, but he is remembered only for his lyrics of country life. He is a master of the literary folk song: yet in his case the adjective does not suggest an artificial imitation of the forms of popular poetry or a deliberate re-elaboration of its peculiar language and diction. In his best lyrics Kol'tsov tries to recapture the simple feelings which dictate peasant poetry. Many of them are written in the first person, and entitled after the characters who are supposed to sing them ("The Mower," "Plowman's Song"). They are generally composed in free series of five-syllable lines, with unrhymed masculine endings, and an even trochaic rhythm. The melancholy of their tone and mood is so overwhelming as to betray the subjective and personal quality of the sentiments they express. The rustic figures there complaining in melodic tunes of their miseries and hardships are but pathetic masks, hardly disguising the shy and tender self of the poet, which shoots through even in the pieces where he speaks with a feminine voice and plays the role of a poor country maid. This may suffice to prove how wrong are those critics who see in Kol'tsov a Russian Burns: he is a poet of shadows and dreams, lacking the robust vitality and the fiery passion of the Scottish bard. His importance for the history of Russian poetry is to be seen in his influence on the so-called "peasant poets" of the twenties, on Kljuev and especially Esenin, who found in Kol'tsov's poetry the moral archetype, if not the literary model, after which they patterned their own work.

Sunlike as he was, Pushkin was, however, but the major star of a constellation which literary historians like to designate as the Pushkinian "Pleiad." That Pleiad counts at least two poets who are not always fully eclipsed by Pushkin's sun. The first of them was Nikolaj Jazykov (1803–1846), who found his most felicitous vein in a series of bacchic songs, written in orgiastic rhythms and riotous words. The poet controls their wild musical frenzy through the firmness of the formal bond. His verbal fireworks, which remind sometimes of Derzhavin, made Jazykov the darling of some of the most conservative Futurists.

Far deeper in quality and broader in range, however, was the poetry of the worthiest of all Pushkin's competitors and friends, Evgenij Baratynskij (or Boratynskij: 1800–1844). In his youth he composed such verse tales as *Eda* (1828), the sentimental story of the seduction of a Finnish girl by a Russian officer, and *The Ball* (1829), which ends with the romantic suicide of a lady of the world betrayed by her fickle lover; both works were influenced by Byron as well as by Pushkin, and were written in a style trying to merge humor and feeling. In his maturity, especially in the lyrics of the collection *Evening Twilights* (1842), Baratynskij found a vision and an accent of his own. Russian criticism labels him a philosophical poet, and the label should be accepted in the sense that he was often able to translate his own contemplative musings into speculative insights. At his best, Baratynskij expressed such insights with an austere objectivity of statement and universality of outlook. His noblest poems convey with lucidity and gravity the grief of all created beings and the sublime consolation of art. Some of them are blighted, however, by "the sharp beam of thought"; and it was perhaps the awareness of this that made Baratynskij call happy the painter and the sculptor, who refuse to go beyond the limits marked by the pencil and the chisel, thus freeing themselves from the chain of intellect enslaving "the poor artist of the word." Through this conception Baratynskij anticipated the Romantic view of the poet as a being exiled from life, and yet exalted beyond it. Unlike the Romantics, however, he treated this theme without indulging in either self-pity or self-love. He generalized the theme and saw in the poet's plight our modern predicament, or the very condition of man. His vision of life was but a reflection of a cosmic pessimism, manly in temper and serene in mood, recalling Vigny and Leopardi rather than the gloomy and morbid poets of the German *Weltschmerz*. If the "The Last Death" and "The Last Poet" he sang respectively the ultimate doom of mankind and the final dissolution of the universe, in the poem he wrote "On Goethe's Death" he dreamed of a reconciliation between the human creature and God's creation, celebrating the German poet as the only man who could understand the voice of the rivers, hear the lament of the trees, converse with the waves, and read the book of the stars.

Baratynskij was generally viewed as a minor master, doing well a few of the many things which Pushkin had done far better than he. This prevented him from getting the recognition which is still his due. What was needed after Pushkin's sunset was, if not a new sun, at least a comet, shooting through the sky of Russian poetry like a novel portent. Such a comet was Mikhail Lermontov, a poet of genius, who represents in Russian the culmination of the Romantic spirit, then the sovereign ruler of the literatures of the West. Born in 1814 (his paternal family claimed noble origins from the Learmonts of Scotland and the Lermas of Spain, and at least the first claim seems to be founded in fact), Lermontov was raised by his maternal grandmother, who dreamed of a brilliant career for him. From his childhood he showed an amazing literary precocity and fecundity; the posthumous collections of his works are full of the productions he composed during his youthful apprenticeship. Such productions are generally immature and derivative, although they contain a few masterpieces, such as the famous poem "The Angel," which the poet wrote while still in his teens. The models he chose, besides Pushkin, were not the usual French *petits maîtres*, but the German Schiller, whom he imitated in his youthful dramas, and the English Scott, Moore, and Byron, whom he imitated in his early lyrics and verse tales. Byron was for a while his God: Byronism affected Lermontov's literary and sentimental education far more powerfully than it ever affected that of Pushkin. In a sense Byronism influenced Lermontov's psychological make-up even more than his poetic development. At the age of sixteen Lermontov composed a poem in which he claimed to carry the spirit of Byron within himself, and stated the wish to be granted a similar destiny; one year later he wrote another one, in which he said instead that he was not a second Byron, but a different, although equally "chosen being," with a Russian heart beating within his breast.

As soon as he became of age, Lermontov donned the prestigious uniform of a Hussar of the Guard, and played the role of a Byronic hero, living like a rake and a dandy in the glamorous showcase of the world. When he was twenty-three he revealed, however, his rare gift by writing a fiery poem, into which he poured his indignation at Pushkin's death, which he attributed to the intrigues of *le beau monde*, even to the parasites of the court. The poem, which circulated widely, although only in manuscript form, earned Lermontov a reduction in rank and a transfer to a line regiment fighting rebellious Moslem tribes on the Caucasian frontier. This experience opened to him new vistas, through the majesty of the mountainous landscape and the elemental simplicity of an existence ruled by hardship and death. There he had the opportunity to prove his mettle in battle and to find himself in meditation and solitude. Then his *Lehrjahre* ended, and his *Meisterjahre* began, to last only for a four-year period, culminating in a brief

29

homecoming, which made possible the publication in the year 1840 of the only collection of poems which appeared in Lermontov's lifetime, and of the novel *A Hero of Our Time*, the masterpiece of his prose. While his writings were freeing themselves from the last traces of the Byronian influence, his life was still dominated by stormy passions and Byronic attitudes, which led him to his second banishment to the Caucasus and to the duel where he met his death. It was in 1841, in the twenty-seventh year of his life, that, for having made a witless comrade the constant butt of his mockery, he fell the victim of no one but himself.

Lermontov is perhaps the most subjective of all Russian poets, the one most concerned with his own ego, with his own selfhood. In a private letter the poet once wrote: *moi, c'est la personne que je fréquente avec plus de plaisir*. The statement could be extended to his poetry, but not without qualifications; Lermontov's narcissism is more pathetic than hedonistic, and the poet himself viewed it not as a blessing, but as a blight. He knew that an excessive concern with the personal and the subjective may lead not to self-cultivation, but to self-destruction, changing the artist into a parasite of the man; since, as he said in an amusing epigram, *les poètes ressemblent aux ours qui se nourrissent en suçant leur patte*. Precisely because of this he was perhaps one of the first Russians to see in the poet's calling a predestination for suffering ("the poet's crown is a crown of thorns") and even for damnation itself. In this he went even beyond Byron and anticipated Baudelaire, who, by the way, mentioned Lermontov in his *Journal intime* as one of the few poets he would place in a select Pantheon of his own.

Lermontov, like Baudelaire, would have rejected Pascal's claim that man is *ni ange ni bête*. Both his view of the world and his way of life seem to rest on the idea that the angelic and the demonic principles are constantly at war against each other in man's heart and in God's universe. It is perhaps for this reason that his most popular compositions seem to be the early lyric "The Angel" and the long verse tale *The Demon*, which was the main, unfinished task of the last decade of his life. The former describes the descent of a young soul, in the arms of her guardian angel, into "this world of grief and tears," where she will never forget the blessed land she came from. The latter, influenced by Byron's *Cain* and Vigny's *Eloa*, tells the story of a sad and proud demon who seduces and destroys the Georgian maid Tamara, without fulfilling either his hatred or his love. While "The Angel" is a perfect little jewel, *The Demon* is a vast failure despite the splendor of its lyrical passages. Yet the one and the other have great significance as psychological documents, since they reflect the poet's conception of man as an exiled being, who finds his native habitat in other spheres than that of human existence, in a no-man's-land which may be either an Eden or a Hell. In another Byronic tale, *The Novice*, written against the same exotic, Caucasian background, Lermontov conveyed the sense of man's alienation from the life of this earth in the story of the escape from his monastery of a young Georgian monk, who dies in the ordeal of his flight, happy for having experienced, if only for a while, "the devouring fire of the sun of being."

Each one of these two verse tales is but a rhapsody of exalted monologues, which the poet utters through the transparent masks worn by their operatic and undramatic protagonists. Thus in a sense even in *The Demon* and *The Novice* Lermontov employs one of the favorite instruments of his lyrical inspiration, which he adopts most frequently in the poems of love. That instrument is the confession device, which in the lyricism of passion the poet uses simply and directly, as a truthful image of himself and his life, as a mirror of his guilt and shame, as well as a spring of hope and a well of repentance. This is another way of saying that Lermontov's mature lyrical poetry, unlike his early Schilleresque plays and late Byronic verse tales, succeeds in reconciling in human terms that conflict of the angelic and the demonic elements which was both the trauma of his art and the complex of his psyche. Lermontov achieved an even loftier resolution of that dualism in a few brief poetic utterances shaped like prayers, fusing in a new harmony the discordant tongues of sublimity and humility. Yet prayer, like confession, still remains a personal statement, even when not a subjective one; and Lermontov reached a higher degree of poetic objectivity in his discursive "meditations" (the title is perhaps patterned after Lamartine), which often have the noble gnomic quality of classical verse.

Lermontov felt, however, that his song should be "wild," and like most of the Romantics yielded to the passionate appeal of both indignation and enthusiasm. It was indignation that dictated his poem on Pushkin's death, as well as the many poems treating the theme of the reciprocal hostility between the artist and society, between the poet and the world. In such poems he chose the sharp and bitter language of invective and sarcasm, and spoke and acted like a real-life imitation of Chatskij, the unhappy, idealistic hero of Griboedov's *Woe from Wit*. It was enthusiasm that dictated the poems he devoted to the cult of Napoleon, as well as those he consecrated to his love for Russia, which he claimed, however, to love not for her glory, but "for the frozen stillness of her fields, the sigh of her daydreaming woods, and her rivers' floods, vast like seas." It was this love for Russia and her people, together with that eager curiosity for the primitive and the exotic which he shared with most of the Romantics, that led Lermontov to compose many first- and second-hand imitations of native and alien folk songs. It was after a famous example by Scott that he wrote his charming "Cossack Lullaby," and it was after Pushkin's *The Gypsies* that he wrote "The Rendezvous," the song of a jealous Cherkess lying in wait for murder and revenge. It was finally on the pattern of the *byliny* and *stariny* of the collection attributed to Kirsha Danilov that he composed the *Song of Tsar Ivan Vasil'evich, of his Guard Kiribeevich, and of the Brave Merchant Kalashnikov*, which tells the story of a Moscow merchant of the reign of Ivan the Terrible, whose wife has been insulted by a member of the Imperial Guard. The wronged husband kills the offender in a wrestling match held in the presence of the Tsar, thus saving his honor but losing his head on the scaffold.

Despite its almost perfect mimesis of the legendary and heroic tone of the old popular epos, which it reproduces in the accentual rhythm of its metrical pattern, the *Song* is a Romantic ballad, and it may well be the foremost *réussite* of European poetry in that genre. Yet the *Song* is also one of the best proofs that the late Lermontov was moving toward a more objective vision of art and life. Near the end of his all-too-short career, the poet felt the attraction both of the epic narrative in verse and of the realistic narrative in prose. In the same year he issued the *Song* (1837), he published also *Borodino*, a poem re-evoking the glorious chronicle of that battle as remembered and retold, in a homely and lively style, by an old veteran. Later the poet wrote a far more lucid and detached account of the realities of war in *Valerik*, "a letter in verse" which is the eyewitness report of an engagement between Russians and Cherkesses on the Caucasian river giving the poem its name. The most significant testimonial to the maturation of Lermontov's genius is, however, his short novel, *A Hero of Our Time*, built around five separate stories, which are related to each other through the person of the main character or his point of view. The protagonist, Pechorin, is patterned after Pushkin's Onegin, and it is through the portrayal of his hero that Lermontov, like Pushkin before him, transcends, both artistically and morally, his earlier Byronism. The sad lesson which both authors teach through those two heroes is the same as the one that Lermontov conveyed as a maxim in one of his poems: that "we hate and love by chance," rather than by our heart's desire. Lermontov's last lyrics reveal the same poetic wisdom, an equal mastery of beauty and of truth. In "The Angel" the childish poet had said that for a soul coming from on high to live and suffer among men no human tune could ever replace the divine melodies; yet, just before his all-too-early death, Lermontov proved himself able to turn into "heavenly sounds" even "the wearisome songs of the earth."

Lermontov's contemporaries considered him the only rival of Pushkin. For most of the nineteenth century few readers or critics challenged his right to occupy the second place in the Pantheon of Russian poetry. Our belated posterity is, however, inclined to feel that he must share this honor with Tjutchev: and there are many judges who consider the latter the one deserving the higher rank. Yet such a comparison of these two poets is not quite fair, since they hardly resemble each other, as their contrasting biographies easily show.

Born in 1803, on his family estate near Brjansk, in the Tula province, Fedor Tjutchev was less than twenty years old when he entered the diplomatic service, to spend abroad twenty years of his life, mainly in Munich, then capital of the kingdom of Bavaria.

On his return home, he resumed after a break his service in the Ministry of Foreign Affairs. Strongly impressed by the Revolution of 1848, which led him to write and publish in French three important political essays, he became with the passing of time more and more of a Slavophile, and even a Panslavist. Married twice (both his wives were German), he yielded in late middle life to a frenetic "last love," which ended only with the death of his younger partner, and which inspired some of the best among his later poems. In his last years he became a man of the world and a drawing-room wit, exhibiting a not-too-feigned indifference toward his literary work, which won him unsolicited, but restricted and intermittent, recognition in his lifetime. Tjutchev died in 1873, but his posthumous glory began at the end of the century with a famous article by Vladimir Solov'ev, which was to be followed by the universal acclaim of the modernists and the Symbolists.

Habent sua fata libelli; yet the destiny of the single book which contains the whole of Tjutchev's poetic heritage (including translations, a total of about 300 pieces, hardly averaging twenty lines in length) is almost unique. From the late twenties on he published scattered verse here and there, yet a score or more poems which appeared in 1838 in *The Contemporary* (they were entitled "Poems Sent from Germany," and signed only with the author's initials) passed largely unnoticed. In 1850 Nekrasov, then editor of the same journal, praised the poet highly, and four years later issued under *The Contemporary's* imprint the first collection in book form of Tjutchev's lyrics. The book was edited by Ivan Turgenev, who deserves great praise for the pains he took in this matter, but who revised and reworked the text so considerably as to make any exhaustive reconstruction of Tjutchev's canon almost impossible. It is true that that volume included only one third of Tjutchev's poetry, but much of that third was written in the poet's most creative period, the decade from 1830 to 1840. All too much of what Tjutchev composed after that date is made up of occasional patriotic pieces, interesting only as biographical documents or political pronouncements. Their literary significance, if any, may be seen in the fact that many of these poems deeply impressed Dostoevskij, who found in them confirmation of several of his ideas. Tjutchev was Dostoevskij's favorite poet, and the latter cited him frequently in his writings. The novelist's most usual quotation from Tjutchev's verse was the last stanza of a famous poem, with its closing vision of Christ passing through the poet's native countryside and blessing forever, under the weight of the cross, the bare squalor of Russia, of her nature, people, and way of life.

Despite its aspiration toward an objective and impersonal lyricism, Tjutchev's poetry may yet look closer to Lermontov's than to Pushkin's. This impression might also be due to Tjutchev's literary education, which was less classical and less French than that of Pushkin and which was, as in the case of Lermontov, primarily, if not exclusively, Romantic. Yet, while Lermontov found his real masters in England, Tjutchev went instead to the school of German thought and poetry. He was acquainted, and corresponded, with Schelling; he met Heine, whose works he translated along with those of Schiller and Goethe, and he wrote, upon the death of the latter, a poem as lovely as the one which Baratynskij composed on the same occasion and theme. Tjutchev replaced Lermontov's introspective visions and subjective intuitions with mystical and metaphysical insights, revealing a conception of nature very different from that which so many continental Romantics had inherited from Rousseau. He saw nature not as the idyllic and immanent mirror of the self, but as a transcendental power, annihilating any other force, overshadowing all reality. In German Romantic terms, one could say that Tjutchev is the poet of *die Nachtseite der Natur,* of "nature's nightly side." Yet this does not mean that he considers nature to be blind and brute instinct, or inarticulate and senseless matter. Vladimir Solov'ev was the first to claim that Tjutchev's poetry is an attempt to bare the chaotic and mystic roots of being. In Tjutchev's view nature is neither a mother nor a stepmother; we cannot blame her for ignoring creatures like ourselves, since, as the poet says, "man is merely nature's dream." Although incommensurably superior to any created thing, nature herself is a living and suffering organism, a complex being with not only a body, but also a mind, will, and soul of her own. "Nature is not what you fancy," said Tjutchev in a famous poem, "she is neither a copy nor a soulless face; in her there is spirit and freedom, passion and tongue." By spiritualizing nature, Tjutchev fails, however, to humanize her: he rather turns her into a universal oversoul, both divine and demonic in essence. Hence her immense distance from man, "a trivial dust," as the poet says, "not allowed to burn with godly fire."

Tjutchev views the universe as the stage of an enormous drama, a tragic conflict between the opposing forces of order and disorder, between the consoling illusion of life and the awful mystery of creation. The poet symbolizes this drama or conflict in a series of polarities or antitheses such as Chaos and Cosmos, Death and Sleep, Winter and Spring, Night and Day. The conflict is, however, more apparent than real: the drama is perhaps a mere play. Yet the struggle, if any, ends with the inexorable victory of what man deems to be the negative and destructive element, although it may well be the positive and constructive one. Creation is also annihilation: this is why Night is always bound to triumph over Day, which the poet describes as the veil which hides from man the secrets of being and not-being; ultimately Night will forever frown over the world "like a beast with a hundred eyes."

The poet's moral and psychological attitude toward the sublime objects of his mystical and metaphysical speculation is, however, complex, and even mixed; one could say that his sentiment accepts that vision less readily, and more doubtfully, than his imagination. It is the poet in him, or, in Tjutchev's words, his "prophetic soul," that feels in harmony with the universal symphony, while his more human faculties feel and fear that elemental discord of which man is but a passive witness and a powerless victim. Thus the poet is both ecstatically attracted and tragically awed by the wonders and terrors of the "sacred night." There is no better proof of this ambivalent attitude than his famous poem to the wind, an element in which Tjutchev saw, as Blok would see after him, the over-all symbol of all powers of destruction and metamorphosis. In his apostrophe to that element, Tjutchev implores the wind, with a negative imperative, "not to sing those awful chants of the native chaos."

The mind of Tjutchev was obviously unable to choose logically between the alternatives of a mystic pantheism and a cosmic nihilism. Yet he resolved the dualism of these two world views, irreconcilable in philosophical terms, by focusing his inspiration on the unbridgeable gulf between them. That gulf is but a reflection of the chasm which the poet constantly saw in the infinite space of the created universe; or perhaps it is a projection of the very abyss which Tjutchev, like Pascal, carried within himself. That abyss was never void, even though it became all too often a well of perplexity, or a source of that despair and doubt which inspired the poems of dejection and despondency of the second part of Tjutchev's life. Yet that abyss turns sometimes into a spring of life, bringing forth many poems of serene and detached contemplation, mostly in the form of seasonal landscapes, often seen against an autumnal background and made uncanny by the presence of a miraculous peace.

It was the poet's unique sense of spiritual privacy, his almost total surrender to the claims of inner life, that explain, more than Tjutchev's morbid sensitivity to any unfriendly criticism, his outright refusal to enter the literary arena and to peddle in public his poetic wares. It was also the unworldly aloofness of his poetry which inspired "Silentium," an apostrophe addressed to himself, closing with the singing words: "Listen to the song of your thoughts and visions, and keep silent." Despite its most famous line ("an uttered thought is but a lie"), that poem is but a reaffirmation of the Romantic disdain for the vulgarity of the multitude, and should not be read, as it was by many Symbolists, as an intimation of their paradoxical belief in the ineffability of that mystical experience in which they saw the single source of all the creations of art. Tjutchev paved the way for Symbolistic poetry more through his practice than through his theory: first by the utter simplicity and the august solemnity of his diction, which perfectly blends the colloquial and the literary element, often represented by Slavonicisms and archaisms; then by the melodic dissonance of his metrical counterpoint, by that interplay of rigidity and flexibility with which he treated his favorite lines, which were the iambic tetrameter and pentameter; and finally by the visionary power of his metaphors, by the mystical quality of his imagery.

REALISM: NEKRASOV AND FET

Most modern critics reduce the full development of Russian poetry during the second half of the nineteenth century to the achievements of two figures, supposedly representing the opposite trends of social realism and subjective lyricism. These two figures are Nekrasov and Fet. The judgment is aesthetically valid, yet, at least historically, such a view looks too simple. There is no doubt that in the eyes of their contemporaries those two poets did not always seem to be the lonely occupants of the whole field of Russian verse. This appears particularly true in the case of Fet, who had to share his glory with a group of poets who are traditionally and conventionally viewed as the native equivalents of the French "art for art's sake" movement. The productions of these poets, not untalented, but devoid of all sense of direction, unable to find a stable center, reflect the "cultural lag" then delaying the growth of Russian literature, especially in the domain of verse. They were at bottom belated Romantics, cultivating a dated and mannered idealism, vainly striving to serve at once beauty and truth, each one of which is a jealous and exacting mistress.

Indulgent readers may choose to praise these poets for their versatility; less indulgent ones, to blame them for their eclecticism. Both traits are equally present in the work of Count Aleksej Tolstoj (1817–1875), who was perhaps the main figure among the members of this group. Aleksej Tolstoj was not merely a lyrical poet: in his *Prince Serebrjanyj* (1862) and in his *Tsar Fedor* (1868), the second play in a famous trilogy, he may well have written respectively the best Russian historical novel after Pushkin's *The Captain's Daughter* and the best Russian historical drama after Pushkin's *Boris Godunov*. He began his literary career by perpetrating a successful literary hoax: with the help of his cousins, the Zhemzhuchnikov brothers, he created the fictitious figure of Kuz'ma Prutkov, a ridiculous and pompous bureaucrat. The inventors of that amusing and ridiculous character attributed to him various literary works of their own making, including a series of nonsensical and caricatural poems, satirical in substance and parodistic in form. It is quite significant that this and other of Tolstoj's humorous compositions still remain the most happily popular of all his writings. Yet his fame rests also on several ballads, more picturesque and sentimental than heroic or legendary, and on a few noble prayers and lofty lyrics which suggested to Maurice Baring a luminous parallel with the poetry of Tennyson.

The most famous of all his lesser companions and rivals, Apollon Majkov (1821–1897), brings to mind no English or Western poet of the same age, but rather such earlier figures as Walter Savage Landor and André Chénier. Trained as a painter and strongly attracted by the physical world, Majkov felt the fascination of antiquity, and took the conflict between paganism and Christianity as the theme of his main work, the ambitious dramatic poem *Two Worlds* (1882). Although he wrote widely in many veins, and on varied subjects, all too often historical and patriotic, he found his most felicitous vehicle in a series of sophisticated idylls, Alexandrian in taste and hedonistic in outlook. More popular than Majkov's, and at times even than Tolstoj's, was the poetry of Jakov Polonskij (1819–1898), who also all too frequently yielded to the cheap temptation of topical writing, but whose best lyrics, put to music by many Russian composers, seem to convey, like Schumann's *Lieder*, the wordless music of the soul.

It is worth remarking, not for social considerations alone, that all the members of this triad were active upholders of the tsarist regime, and that they served in official positions the powers that be. Tolstoj, a childhood friend of Alexander II, held many courtly posts; both Majkov and Polonskij worked, of all places, in the censor's bureau. The critic Mirskij may have taken this fact into account when he paradoxically labeled these poets "Russian Victorians," emphasizing so well their official respectability, their quiet acceptance of the social ethos and the political order. This, however, was not the case with another writer of strong nationalistic and conservative views, the gifted polemist and critic Apollon Grigor'ev (1822–1864), who befriended Dostoevskij and collaborated in the latter's ill-fated journalistic ventures. A free-lancer and a bohemian, Grigor'ev found and explored a poetic vein of his own in a cycle of "gypsy songs," strangely novel in the strains of their melody and the poignant melancholy of their moods. Those songs were destined to catch the fancy of Aleksandr Blok, the greatest Russian poet of the twentieth century, who first edited and collected them, in a volume published in 1916, almost seventy years after their author's death.

It was a congenital indifference to formal values, as well as a strong ideological bias, which prevented radical literary opinion, then the ruler of Russian thought, from doing justice to a poet like Grigor'ev, or later, to a far greater artist like Fet. That opinion cared little for art, and was often so iconoclastically inclined as to attack even Pushkin, the greatest of all Russian masters of the word. Yet that opinion chose to exalt one of the poets of that age, and to enshrine him in a sanctuary of its own. That poet was Nikolaj Nekrasov (1821–1878), the only writer of verse whose glory rivaled that of the classics of Russian prose. Nekrasov's canonization was in the making before his death, but was officially proclaimed during his funeral, when the crowd in attendance interrupted Dostoevskij's eulogistic address, protesting with loud cries of "Higher! higher!" the speaker's statement that his dead friend would hold a place next to Pushkin's and Lermontov's in all Russian hearts. The praise was exaggerated, and its premise wrong, yet Nekrasov's greatness is genuine, as less biased and better critics later avowed.

Nekrasov started his career, as Dostoevskij would have said, as a "proletarian of literature"; yet, without ever changing his set of values, and even by capitalizing on them, be became in his maturity a prosperous businessman as a purveyor of cultural goods. At the end of his life, he managed to recover from the bankruptcy of his enterprise, provoked by the suspension, by executive fiat, of *The Contemporary*, the journal founded by Pushkin, which the splendid, although partisan, editorship of Nekrasov had turned into a going concern and an organ of social protest, as well as into a source of both prestige and income.

Throughout his life, as a writer even more than as an editor, Nekrasov remained loyal to the literary preachings of Belinskij. He basically subordinated his own creation to an extra-aesthetic purpose. The cause he chose to serve had been predetermined by a programmatic criticism, committed to shaping literature rather than to appraising it. Critical leadership aimed at imposing on each writer the single-minded endeavor of satisfying social demands which the critic felt should be voiced on behalf of an audience at once captive and mute. Almost all the great Russian writers freed themselves, at least in part, from such influences and premises, especially from the rigorous tyranny of Pisarev and his followers, who wanted to reduce literature to the drab handmaid of a trivial and coarse utilitarianism. Yet Nekrasov felt always duty-bound to sacrifice his artistic calling to this missionary task. The doctrine which Nekrasov preached in words and deed was not new: it had already been stated in verse by Kondratij Ryleev (1795–1826), a lesser Romantic whose celebrity was mainly due to the martyrdom he underwent in the cause of freedom, when he was hanged for the part he had taken in the Decembrist revolt. Nekrasov rephrased Ryleev's creed in two lines no less ugly than famous: "You may be allowed not to be a poet, but you cannot avoid being a citizen."

All the main writers of Nekrasov's age claimed to be realists, and he was the only poet who fully accepted their creed. Nekrasov's realism was all too often pathetic and topical, yet not infrequently it raised itself to the level of a visionary insight. Far more than many of his fellow prose writers, Nekrasov kept faith with the realistic ideal as understood by Belinskij. The latter had stated that ideal in the formula of "natural school," by which he traced not only the current trends, but even the future course, of Russian fiction. The task of that school was for Belinskij the representation of Russian life in its inner and outer truth, as well as the transformation of that life into a better existence. The instruments of such transformation were to be not only love and pity, but also indignation and scorn. In brief, realism should be shaped by both compassion and protest. In their reforming bent, both Belinskij and Nekrasov pushed compassion and protest far beyond the limits Gogol' had marked in his motto of "laughter through tears." In Nekrasov the laughter becomes a sneer, while the tears dry up, embittering rather than relieving the heart. Nekrasov's soul seems indeed to heed solely, in the poet's words, "the muse of grief and wrath." Such tension often had adverse effects on his art, producing jarring notes that spoil even the purest music with sounds which Merezhkovskij described as "scratchings of glass."

Nekrasov's inspiration found its outlet not only in versified eloquence, but also in the poetic equivalents of genre painting and the comedy of manners, such as sermons and apologues, true stories and fables with an all-too-obvious moral. Yet his imagination was frequently able to transcend such forms and materials, ascending to the sphere of prophecy and vision, of legend and myth. The old saying *facit indignatio versum* is rarely as well suited to anyone as to him; yet his wrathful zeal is so extreme and intense that it prevents his poetry from calming down into the skeptical smile of worldly sarcasm. The ethos and pathos of his poetry are not satirical, but lyrical in temper. Thus they find their most natural avenues in the invective and the complaint; their most congenial vehicles in the elegy and the iamb. Ultimately Nekrasov's passion reaches its own catharsis in a tragic and yet serene contemplation of the elemental existence of the Russian peasantry, slowly unfolding within the fixed cycle of the seasons, with their recurring labors and hardships, ruled by malady and death. Thus this ideological poet becomes a mythmaker: breaking from the confines of description and narration, from the bane of propaganda and rhetoric, his poetry enters freely and boldly into the unknown realms of the primeval and the fabulous. When this happens, Nekrasov turns even his popular fancies into vivid allegories, at once national and universal in scope, as in the poem *Vlas* (1856), where the poor farmer by that name becomes the eternal archetype of the peasant, singing in choral notes the plight of the Russian Everyman; or even better in the polyphonic suite *Red-Nosed Frost* (1863), which is at once a naïve fairy tale of Russian winter and a cosmic vision of the sorcery and magic of nature, of its secret and sacred witchcraft. It was such compositions that led Rozanov to claim that in Nekrasov's poetry "there is more national spirit than in the whole of Tolstoj. . . . A fifth or so of his poems are an everlasting treasure of Russian letters, and will never die. . . . Nekrasov knew how to find novel strains in both rhythm and speech. . . ." It is the legendary and visionary quality of his imagination, as well as the strange novelty of his dissonant music, that saved Nekrasov's literary heritage from that neglect to which it seemed natural that the new poetic generations should condemn it. Yet the Symbolists paid him not only a critical tribute but also an artistic one, sedulously imitating his attempt to make poetry out of the prose of life, to find a bewitching melody even in the discord of the world. Blok followed his example by turning into song the howl of the wind, while Belyj patterned on Nekrasov those "drunken ditties" by which he tried to distill a bittersweet potion from reality's dregs.

All Russian critics, whether of the Right or the Left, see the antagonist of Nekrasov in Afanasij Shenshin (1820–1892), better known under his mother's German name, which was Fet (Foeth). Conventional literary historians consider him, even more than Aleksej Tolstoj, as the genuine Russian representative of the "art for art's sake" school. In the West, however, that formula implies more than the simple belief that art must serve no other purpose than that of art itself. Its practitioners lean almost always toward either bohemianism or aestheticism, which are two different ways of confusing life and art. Yet Fet was neither a Parnassian nor an aesthete; he avoided not only nonliterary commitments, but also literary ones. He kept art and life rigorously separated: in his work poetry and biography never mix. His case seems to prove Pushkin's claim that there is no hollower or shallower creature than the poet when the muse does not visit him. After having published, starting with the early 1840's, a few volumes of verse which earned him, along with the friendship and admiration of Turgenev and Tolstoj, the coarse sneers of the radical critics, Fet abandoned literature and lived the existence of a hardheaded and hardfisted landowner, thinking only of his well-being and profit. Yet twenty years later, in a slightly more favorable atmosphere, he went back to poetry, and published from 1883 to 1891 a series of small collections of poems under the general title of *Evening Fires*.

Except for a visible progress in matters of craft, the poetry of Fet's maturity does not differ appreciably from that of his youth. In both stages, it represented a revival, rather than a mere survival, of the Romantic spirit. If Aleksej Tolstoj and his peers were but late Romantics, Fet was instead a neoromantic, in the recent German

43

meaning of that term. For this very reason he foreshadowed the Symbolists, in vision as well as in form. Of all the Russian poets of his time he was the one who sacrificed least to decoration, as well as to pathos and eloquence; his supreme ruler was the spirit of music, which flooded his poetry with effusive, and yet elusive, streams.

Fet found his inspiration not in the eventful climaxes and crises of life, but in the fantasies and vagaries of sentiment, or in those flashes of insight making memorable even the most aimless musings and broodings of the soul. Fet captures the most inarticulate states, the most fleeting motions of the spirit, and fixes them into images shadowy yet not formless, which seem to preserve the fluid spontaneity and the vibrant vitality of the labile experience which shaped the original mood. The mood itself becomes a *Stimmung*: one thus could say that both the raw material and the finished product of his poetry are but psychic quintessences.

Even when Fet's imagination is possessed by fiercer and loftier passions, such as the ecstasies of love, a mystical longing for the Divine, a sense of awe before the mystery of the universe, he controls the emotional tension of his spirit, which he reflects in the deep and dark water of contemplation, in the quiet and even mirror of eternity. The uncanny sorcery of an art seemingly able to convey the symbolic generality and the vivid concreteness of a unique and irrevocable sensation, of a vague transport of the soul or of a sudden trembling of the heart, turns many of his lyrics into occasional poems in the manner of Goethe, although Fet treats this kind of inspiration less lucidly and more subjectively, and fails sometimes to master the objective substance of his vision and to trace fully its moral contours. This may also be due to his deep-seated conviction that poetry and language are congenitally unable to express the richness of experience and the fullness of existence. In this view Fet is Tjutchev's follower and Blok's forerunner. Yet if he thinks that poetry and language are restricted, it is because he thinks that life and nature are limitless. If he finds art wanting ("all poetry is falsehood"), it is because he feels overwhelmed by the ineffable wonder, rather than by the unspeakable horror, of being. He claims that "the soul should speak without

44

words," and maintains that the loveliest poems are unwritten, since he feels that there is poetry even in silence, since he hears the "wordless chant" that "throbs in *his* heart like a wingless bird."

Fet learned many of his lessons not only from Tjutchev, but also from the German poets to whom both went to school. Fet, who translated widely from German literature (not only a vast selection of Romantic lyrics, but also Schopenhauer's masterpiece), became the equal of his own masters, rivaling Heine, whose works he rendered into Russian verse. Like Heine's loveliest *Lieder*, Fet's best lyrics will sparkle forever in the darkness of time, if not like stars, at least like will-o'-the-wisps. It hardly matters that they may lack the tragic and cosmic breadth of Tjutchev's poems, that they simply re-evoke a private world of impressions and dreams, or, as the poet says, "the obscure ravings of the soul and the confused aroma of the grass." Fet was aware of the untimeliness and loneliness of his creation, and expressed that awareness in the beautiful lines where he described himself as a humble and forgotten creature kneeling in the shadow to rekindle the fire in what was the vesper hour of his life, and of Russian poetry as well. Yet he was also conscious of the magical power of his gift: he well knew that his poetry, even if it was only "a dry leaf fallen from the limb," would shine again "in the lasting gold" of its songs.

CHAPTER TWO

MODERNISM AND DECADENCE

I

THE HISTORICAL BACKGROUND

Nicholas I (1825–1855), the Tsar of the age of Pushkin and Gogol', had started his reign by repressing the conspiracy of the Decembrists and had remained to the end of his life a ruthless upholder of the autocratic regime. The reign of his son Alexander II (1855–1881), which was adorned by such luminaries as Dostoevskij and the early Tolstoj, opened upon the aftermath of Russia's defeat in the Crimean War (1854–1856) and was marked at its beginnings by a series of great social and political reforms, the most important of which was the emancipation of the serfs (1861). But later, in the wake of the Polish uprising (1863), the Tsar swung back to reaction, thus reawakening the dormant radical movement. In 1881 an underground organization named "The People's Will" decided to take its revenge upon the Tsar, who fell under a terrorist's bomb.

The tragic event which closed Alexander II's reign inspired his heir and son Alexander III (1881–1894) with a fanatic zeal, with an iron will to destroy the revolutionary forces root and branch. One of the students hanged in 1887 for preparing an attempt against the life of the sovereign was Aleksandr Ul'janov; a brother of his, then a schoolboy in Simbirsk, was destined to avenge him and to become the nemesis of Russian autocracy under the name of Vladimir Lenin. By repressing the revolutionary movement, Alexander III repressed also the moderate aspirations of the

46

educated classes for a greater freedom of opinion and expression
in the field of thought, thus forcing many of their best minds to
join the radical camp. In his intransigent obscurantism the Tsar
showed himself to be a faithful disciple of his tutor, Konstantin
Pobedonostsev, a former professor of law at the University of
Moscow, who was later appointed to the office of Procurator of
the Holy Synod, and who will be remembered in Russian literary
history as the scornful protector of Dostoevskij and the excom-
municator of Tolstoj. A cynic and a die-hard, Pobedonostsev was
the real ruler of Russia during the reign of his pupil, as well as for
part of his successor's.

The reign of Nicholas II (1894–1917) coincided with the main
phase of the literary period which is the theme of this book. The
modern movement started with the beginning of his rule, and was
destined to survive for only a few years after his abdication,
which marked the end of the Romanov dynasty and of Russian
tsardom. The execution of the imperial family in the distant city
of Ekaterinburg (1918) closed a reign which had always been
haunted by blood and death. The final tragedy had been foreshadowed by the catastrophe of Khodynka, when, during the coro-
nation festivities of 1896, three thousand men, women, and children were stampeded to death by the populace mobbing the tribune
in the expectation of a distribution of free gifts; by the "Red Sun-
day" of January 22, 1905, when the workers of Petersburg, carry-
ing crosses and led by the *pop* Gapon, came to the Winter Palace
to submit their grievances to their "little father" the Tsar, were welcomed by lead and fire, and left on the pavement more than a
thousand dead; finally, on Christmas Eve of 1916, by the murder
by a few court aristocrats of the "monk" Rasputin, who, by claiming to heal the hemophilia of the heir apparent, had gained the ear
of the Empress and had become the corrupter of the court.

Yet the reign of Nicholas II had not been devoid, at least at
its beginnings, of a splendor of its own. The most important of the
progressive transformations of Russian life which took place at that
time was the belated, and yet meteoric, rise of industrialism and
capitalism. While city-dwellers witnessed with both pride and dis-
may the rapid proliferation of huge factories in new slums or old

47

suburbs, villagers and nomads watched with wonder and awe the discovery of rich mining fields in the midst of their lands, or the sudden appearance, even in steppes or deserts, of modern railroads. For the great scientist Dmitrij Mendeleev, aware of the unlimited resources hidden in Russia's boundless hinterland, this spectacle opened the vistas of a bright future, the promises of immense material progress. Even his son-in-law, the poet Aleksandr Blok, who was rather a visionary of the spirit, was haunted by the same dream, and celebrated Russia, in one of his poems, as a "new America." The industrial revolution was, however, not accompanied by doubly needed social reforms. Although one of the spokesmen of Russia's ruling class, Aleksej Suvorin, who founded and edited the semiofficial *New Times*, the outstanding Russian newspaper of that period, saw the best hope of the conservative cause in its alliance with technological advance and economic progress, in effect such a fateful combination of material expansion and political backwardness created new problems without solving old ones. The most fatal consequences of the process were the further alienation of the peasantry from the body politic, and the formation of a new class, both rootless and dispossessed, the urban proletariat.

The intelligentsia failed to respond to the challenge of the changing times, and avoided facing a crisis which, for the first time in Russian history, was perhaps not without a solution. It thus refused to control the new course by providing it with leaders and managers risen from its ranks. At first, it sought both hope and escape in Tolstoj's evangelical anarchism; later it found an avenue of protest in new forms of political activism, thus reawakening the revolutionary spirit, which had lain dormant for a decade or so. All thinking Russians felt rejected by the centers of influence and power, although some of the best writers at that time were not blind to the positive aspects of the acquisitive drive which was shaking their backward country from her inertia and sleep. Gor'kij, who was a self-made man himself, showed a surprising understanding of the character of the new Russian entrepreneur, merging the traits of the robber baron with those of the hardfisted and boorish merchants of yore. Chekhov saw, without regret but not without misgivings, the fading away of the charming, parasitic gentry before a new race of men, ruled only by the profit motive; and symbolized this event in the felling of the cherry trees at the end of his play *The Cherry Orchard*.

Yet Russian society remained backward in thought as well as in deed; and this is the reason why tsarist Russia hardly knew a party of reaction as such. Even the so-called "Black Hundreds," a group of activists who tried to save the regime with illegal means, were little more than hooligan bands with official support. What took the place of a conservative party was the whole of Russia's officialdom, from the bureaucratic nobility to the petty civil servants, a social group in the main devoid of a moral code, with no other concern than its corporate interests. The authority of the ruling class rested not only on the power of the state, but also on the prestige of the Church, which was the main pillar of the regime and fell with it.

The upholders and representatives of autocracy and orthodoxy felt no need to justify their principles or rationalize their institutions through a doctrine of tradition or theory of conservatism. The rulers of tsarist Russia neglected, or even despised, their most brilliant ideologists, from the early Slavophiles to Dostoevskij, from Konstantin Leont'ev to Vasilij Rozanov. And they failed to realize that, by enslaving the university and muzzling the press, by persecuting intelligence and silencing public opinion, they helped rather than hindered the changes they feared, and even far more radical transformations of Russian society. By using censorship, martial law, and penal colonies as normal instruments of government, by employing in emergencies such extraordinary means as police provocation, charging Cossacks, and even semiofficial *pogroms*, the regime dug its own grave rather than that of its foes.

During its death throes, the tsarist order produced only two statesmen endowed with some daring and vision. These two statesmen were Vitte (Witte) and Stolypin. Vitte acted as the midwife of Russian capitalism; his highest merit was to extend to all corners of the empire the lifeline of a modern state, the railroad. Stolypin tried to consolidate the newly won economic conquests by dividing the land among its toilers, thus transforming at least part of the peasantry into a conservative class, ready to support a social system from which it could benefit. Vitte the builder failed, however, to prevent the tragic adventure of the war with Japan, which was started as a political diversion and to serve private interests. As for Stolypin, his program of agrarian reform survived by only a few years his death (1911) by a terrorist's bullet.

The war with Japan (1904–1905) ended in shame and defeat. The national pride of Russia was broken, and its ruling class was perhaps unable to learn from that lesson as much as it had learned, half a century earlier, from the Crimean War. The defeat brought in its wake a new "time of troubles," the "little revolution" of 1905, which seriously threatened the foundations of the Russian state and which Lenin later considered a "dress rehearsal" for the great Revolution of 1917. That brief, unsuccessful upheaval was destined to impress the imagination of many artists and writers of the following generation, such as the film director Èjzenshtejn and the poet Pasternak, both of whom saw the most significant episode of 1905 in the mutiny by the crew of the *Potemkin*, a Black Sea battleship.

In order to calm the storm, the regime was forced to grant sweeping concessions, which failed, however, to become a gradual and consistent reforming process. Thus those concessions were taken as signs of bad faith and ill will and hastened the fall of tsarism rather than postponed it. The most important of them were the abolition of censorship and the establishment of the Duma, the first and last Russian parliament. The institution of that body, which had limited power and was subject to recall, failed to change tsarism into a constitutional monarchy on the English model, although it gave a brief lease of life to the intermittent and anemic tradition of Russian liberalism. For the first time Russian liberal opinion could rally in the open, around a lawful opposition party of its own. Its members called themselves Constitutional Democrats, and chose as their leader the historian Pavel Miljukov. The appearance of this short-lived party on the stage of Russian history represented perhaps the climax of the Westernizing trend, which that party tried both to express and to control. The leading Constitutional Democrats kept allegiance to the philosophy of positivism, but replaced the social radicalism of the old faith with a moderate reformism and with a less moderate nationalism. For this and other reasons the party always had a limited following, restricted to the enlightened nobility and to the most prosperous members of the professional class.

From the 1890's on, the Left had been traditionally divided into two factions, one deriving from the old Populist creed and the other from the new doctrine of Marxism. It was from the first faction that the Social Revolutionary Party was finally founded, with the aim of basing the palingenesis of Russia on the cornerstone of the peasantry. Less naïve than the Populists, the Social Revolutionaries did not idealize the tillers of the soil as much as their predecessors had done. They knew, for instance, that the Russian peasant had to be educated if Russia were to take the place they felt she deserved to hold in the community of nations. Yet they failed to work effectively toward this goal, as well as toward other practical ends. Notwithstanding their militancy, they were dreamers rather than doers, indulging in abstract theorizing and in political wishful thinking, completely unable to understand the historical crisis of their time. They attracted both the intellectual elite and the classless intelligentsia precisely because, despite their agrarian ideology, they were a party without a strong tie to any class.

In the long run the Marxists, unfriendly as they were to the agrarian cause, showed themselves far better able to understand the peasant question than Populists old and new; and this is why after February 1917 they could exploit for their political ends the peasant soldier's yearning for both peace and land. Yet the development of Marxism was connected, even in Russia, with the rise of industrialism and the formation of the working class. From its very beginning Russian Marxism was a strongly knit organization, centered around brilliant leaders, from the older Georgij Plekhanov to the younger Vladimir Lenin. While their congenital centrifugal tendencies prevented the Social Revolutionaries from reshaping the formless body of their party into an effective political organ, Russian Marxism seemed able to profit even from its own rifts. The division of the Marxist party, the Social Democrats, into an orthodox majority and a heretic minority, which took place in

1903 (the names Bolsheviks and Mensheviks did not mean originally "maximalists" and "minimalists," as it is often believed, but simply the "bigger" and the "lesser" fraction), led to the expulsion of the weaker, moderate grouping, and submitted the party to the rule of a hierarchical centralism. At once doctrinaire and opportunistic, both ruthless and fearless, constantly training their small but loyal following through direct action, as well as through organization and propaganda work, the Bolsheviks were the only party able to act when the hour struck.

As for the Social Revolutionaries, it was their idealistic outlook which made them enter the blind alley of political adventurism and yield to the temptation of individual terrorism. One of the leaders of their "Fighting Organization" was the incredible Boris Savinkov, whom Lenin defined as "a petty bourgeois with a bomb in his pocket," and who was the prime mover of the political murders of the Minister of Interior Pleve (1904) and of the Grand Duke Sergej (1905). Exploits like these inflamed the minds and hearts of the young, but soon enough terrorism and the entire revolutionary movement fell into disrepute because of their inability to achieve political results, and perhaps also because of the sudden discovery that some of their more popular heroes, like *pop* Gapon and Evno Azef, the Social Revolutionary leader, were *agents provocateurs*, or spies in the pay of the political police. As for Savinkov himself, who escaped the consequences of Azef's betrayal, he belongs to the cultural and literary history of his nation and time, within which he played the role, both tragic and pathetic, of the decadent activist. In 1909, under the pseudonym Vsevolod Ropshin, Savinkov published *The Pale Horse*, a terrorist's diary in fictional form, which he wrote under the moral and literary influence of the Merezhkovskijs and their circle. After 1917, when he was for a while a member of Kerenskij's government, Savinkov conspired against the Reds from abroad; arrested during a secret mission in Russia, he was put to trial and killed himself in a Soviet jail (1925).

It was a widespread sense of disappointment with what seemed to be the hopeless failure of the revolutionary movement that shaped the mood of both the elite and the intelligentsia in the years between the defeat of Russia in the Far East and the explosion of the First World War. The main manifestations of that mood were negative and morbid in temper, such as the preaching, in 1906–1907, on the part of a few men of letters, of the doctrine which went under the fancy name of "mystical anarchism," while being in reality nothing more than a fashionable version of decadent immoralism and aesthetic individualism. A parallel and even more nihilistic trend was that naïve and pretentious sexual egotism which ruled the imagination of the young generation from 1910 on. The gospel of that creed was *Sanin*, a cheap best-selling novel by the popular writer Mikhail Artsybashev, which appeared in 1907. While Sanin, a Nero of the boudoir, was but a vulgar and bourgeois variant of Nietzsche's Superman, what was to be called Saninism, or the tendency to imitate the example of that fictional hero in real life, was but an unconscious parody of decadent hedonism. As for what one might name "the failure of nerve" of the Russian intelligentsia in the years between the "little revolution" and the great one, it found its literary expression in a popular and mediocre writer, Leonid Andreev, whose stories and plays convey a dual mood of shallow pathos and crude despair, combining reality and allegory in a mixture which looks like an involuntary parody of both the old and the new.

Despite their disenchantment with the progressive or the radical ideal, despite their escape into the more or less occult worship of strange gods, or their public profession of the secular religions of Eros and art, most of the Russian men of letters of that age remained ideologically or sentimentally loyal to what then seemed to be the lost cause of the political Left. From this viewpoint the idealistic and aristocratic innovators of art and literature failed to distinguish themselves from the belated practitioners of "civic poetry," or from the surviving preachers of nineteenth-century materialism and positivism. In this regard, both the "mystics" and the "aesthetes" of the new Russian culture differed greatly from their Western brethren, most of whom were staunch upholders of the cause of reaction, and flirted all too often with backward-looking political sects. Perhaps only in Russia could the teachings of such foreign thinkers as Schopenhauer and Nietzsche, or of such national masters as Solov'ev and Dostoevskij, lead toward a revolutionary utopia rather than toward a counter-revolutionary one.

This simply means that no Russian writer of that time, without excepting even the few who, like Rozanov, took the opposite political side, could approve of the *status quo*. All of them felt that Russian life was still a "lie," as Turgenev had once said it was, and took their stand on this view. Only a few guessed that there was a great danger, or simply a great error, in such a stand. So, for instance, Petr Struve, a former Marxist who had turned into a conservative liberal, published in 1909, with the collaboration of such thinkers and writers as Sergej Bulgakov, Nikolaj Berdjaev, and Mikhail Gershenzon, the collective testimonial of *Guideposts*, a series of essays condemning the irresponsibility of the intelligentsia and its inability to appraise such values as those of nation, religion, and liberty. This indictment failed to produce any lasting effect, precisely because Russian opinion was then strongly anticonservative, even when deeply moral and religious in spirit.

From the nineteenth century on the Russian mind had been far more protesting than reforming in temper. This may explain why so many Russian writers of the twentieth century could not resist the attraction of the idealistic radicalism of the Social Revolutionaries. Only a minority heeded the appeal of Marxian, or so-called "scientific," socialism. (The outstanding member of this group was Gor'kij, who in his best works represented, however, the neoromantic anarchism of the tramp and the merchant's "rugged individualism.") All this may also explain why most of them saluted with frenetic enthusiasm the upheaval ushered in by the revolution of February, but recoiled in indignation and disgust when the Bolsheviks stormed the Winter Palace, dispersed the Constituent Assembly, and subjected to their rule a sixth of the earth. In short, they failed to understand a general historical truth: that the Girondins pave the ground for the Jacobins, or, in the terms of their own experience, that the Lenins and the Trotskijs take over after the failure of the Kerenskijs and the Miljukovs. February always foreshadows October, and even prepares for it. We who have survived the ordeal of our Russian brethren have been learning better than they another historical lesson, which the

Russian tragedy represents in a fashion at once exemplary and unique. There are countries where what Dostoevskij called "the fast road" of social and political changes is easier to take than the slow one. The paradox of modern Russia is that there moderate liberalism and gradual reform appeared to be but an unreal dream. As Berdjaev said in *The Origins of Russian Communism*, "in Russia it was not a Communist revolution but a liberal and bourgeois one that turned out to be utopian." Yet the utopia that succeeded seems to have built a world less "brave" and less "new" than the one which the utopia that failed had dreamed of and hoped for. No other outcome was perhaps to be expected, since the iron law of revolution seems to be that it cannot achieve its task without the help of its antithesis, which is involution rather than evolution.

II

THE MODERN MOVEMENT IN LITERATURE

The external history of the modern movement in Russian literature may be briefly outlined by a survey of its chief circles and cenacles, and above all, of its main presses and reviews. What such a survey makes immediately evident is that the organized movement first took shape in Petersburg. Its earliest conscious beginnings must probably be seen in the campaign which a Petersburg periodical, *The Northern Herald*, founded in 1882 as the mouthpiece of a moderate political liberalism, waged during the last years of its life in behalf of what was to be called "the struggle for idealism." The man who led and named that struggle was the Jewish critic Akim Flekser (1865–1926), better known under his pen name, A. L. Volynskij, who for almost a decade, from the late eighties to the late nineties, contributed to *The Northern Herald* a series of articles championing the cause of the young. The campaign ceased abruptly in 1898, when the journal, after valiantly resisting the harassments of censorship, died because of financial hardships. The new trends, however, survived the failure of their first organ, growing in influence and strength and calling forth better instruments and younger leaders who pushed the frontier of the new culture far beyond the limits reached by its first pioneer.

The merit of Volynskij's contribution is not lessened by the consideration that his work was mainly exploratory and often primarily polemical in character. He was, after all, one of the first men of letters who re-evaluated in full the spiritual heritage of Dostoevskij, and who condemned with authority Belinskij's degenerate offspring, that swarm of radical critics who had been ruling the Russian mind from the middle of the century on and who were still influential in the eighties and even later, under the effective leadership of Nikolaj Mikhajlovskij.

After the disappearance of *The Northern Herald*, the flag passed for a while to *The World of Art*, a periodical to be discussed in another context, since it was mainly concerned with the visual arts. It deserves being mentioned here because its pages were quite hospitable to young writers, especially to the prophets of the new idealism, such as Rozanov, Shestov, and Merezhkovskij. Merezhkovskij, after abandoning the pure aestheticism of his youth, gathered around himself many of those who were to be called "God-seekers," and found a more congenial organ for the ideas of his group in a journal which took the symbolic heading of *The New Road* (1903–1904). Those among the "God-seekers" who felt the attraction of Christian communalism, and who shared, in a mystical way of their own, the concern of the radical intelligentsia with social and political issues, published instead, under the editorship of the poet Georgij Chulkov but under the moral guidance of the theologian Sergej Bulgakov and the philosopher Nikolaj Berdjaev, another journal, significantly entitled *Questions of Life* (1905–1906).

In a sense, none of the periodicals and groups which from the nineties on expressed the intellectual life of the capital was primarily devoted to literature per se. The task of founding the publishing house and the literary journal destined to represent the new aesthetic outlook fell, almost a decade later, upon the old capital: a fact which many observers took as a further proof of the traditional myth of the spiritual cleavage between Moscow and Petersburg. Yet that fact, were it at all meaningful, should have been interpreted as a denial of the myth, or at least, as a reversal of its terms. According to a generalization very fashionable at the time,

the two groups of men of letters then representing the cultural life
of the newer and of the older metropolis were made up respectively
of "mystics" and "aesthetes." Since the "mystics" were supposed
to be primarily concerned with the traditional spirituality of the
Russian mind, while the "aesthetes" were by definition enthusiastic followers of the new artistic culture preached and practiced in
the West, the paradoxical inference to be drawn from that generalization was that for the first time the Slavophiles of Russian
literature were centered in Petersburg, and its Westernizers in
Moscow.

Many an actor and many a spectator of the Russian literary
scene reaffirmed the doubtful truth of this paradox, which they
complicated further with the claim that the elites of the two cities
stood for contrasting literary trends as well as for divergent lines
of thought. This meant in practice viewing Moscow as the home
of Decadence, and Petersburg as the abode of Symbolism. Such a
distinction has no greater validity than the previous one, as a few
examples may easily prove. There is no reason to say that the poet
Annenskij, then considered an "aesthete," was less representative
of the literary culture of Petersburg than the prose writer Merezhkovskij, a "mystic" par excellence. If Russian Decadence had its
first conscious master in Valerij Brjusov, the leading literary figure
of the old capital, later it found its most accomplished artist in
Fedor Sologub, who settled in the new one. Andrej Belyj, who as
a youth had founded in his native city the student club of the
"Argonauts," seeking wisdom as well as beauty in the lore of the
West, was likewise able to turn Moscow into a center of Symbolism no less effective than the Petersburg of Aleksandr Blok. As
for one of the most influential masters of that time, Vjacheslav
Ivanov, who acted at once as a "mystic" and as an "aesthete," or as
a Decadent and as a Symbolist, who felt the attraction of both East
and West and worshipped equally art as religion and the religion
of art, he preached his creed and served his cult both in Petersburg,
which adopted him as a son, and in his native Moscow, to which
he chose to return.

Yet, when all this is said, it remains true that for a while Moscow
became the focal center of Russian literary aestheticism. A group

of youthful writers, led by Valerij Brjusov, who had already raised the banner of Symbolism (then understood in a sense very different from the one it was to take later in other hands), founded there in 1900 the "Scorpion" Press. The members of this group, whose views sharply differed from those of Belyj's "Argonauts," were later to be called "Scorpions" after the name of their press. Although handsomely supported by the financial contributions of a rich literary amateur, at first they published only a few books. It was only later that, under the prompting of their leader, the "Scorpions" undertook the monthly publication of *The Scales*, which lasted from 1905 until 1909, with Brjusov as the *de facto* editor-in-chief.

The Scales, which had originally taken the *Mercure de France* as its model, started as an organ of literary information and criticism, turning its main attention toward Paris, where it had as regular contributors and correspondents a French and a Russian poet, René Ghil and Maksimilian Voloshin. Yet soon enough *The Scales* found another center of attraction in Brussels, or rather in that group of Franco-Belgian writers who gathered around such reviews as *La Wallonie* and *La Jeune Belgique*. Shortly after its foundation *The Scales* opened its pages to creative writing, whether original or translated, performing for new Russian poetry the same function Stefan George's *Blätter für die Kunst* had been performing for the new poetry of Germany. *The Scales* published drama and fiction as well as poetry, finally becoming, through the breadth of its interests and the variety of its taste, one of the foremost European literary journals of its time. Its pages presented to the Russian reader the best which was being written not only in Russia and in France, but in the whole of the West, often in the form of direct contributions from such outstanding foreign figures as Maurice Maeterlinck, Rémy de Gourmont, Jean Moréas, Emile Verhaeren, Giovanni Papini, and many others.

With the passing of time the undertaking, as successful as most such enterprises can be, proved to be all too expensive, and the "Scorpions" decided to terminate the publication of *The Scales* at the end of its fifth year of life. Yet they did so with the calm assurance that the review had fulfilled its task and won its battle.

The battle itself, carried on officially under the flag of Symbolism, had been fought for the more general cause of modern poetry and in behalf of the liberty of art. The sense that the cause was won despite the defeat of one of its main instruments is evident in Brjusov's farewell address, which appeared in the last issue (December 1909). The writer concluded his editorial apology with this proud declaration: "Through the triumph of the ideas of Symbolism, namely, that the new art carries within itself the best energies for spiritual life on earth, and that art itself is therefore the revelation through which mankind may some day reach the ultimate truth . . . , the review has become unnecessary, since it has achieved its purpose, thus making superfluous its means."

Many of Brjusov's literary colleagues felt otherwise, because they held different views about Symbolism or because they wanted to preach other creeds. It was to give expression to a new, short-lived trend, that Georgij Chulkov founded and edited in Moscow, with the financial support of a wealthy merchant, *The Golden Fleece* (1905–1906). This trend, which, after the title of a book by Chulkov, took the name of "mystical anarchism," was an offshoot of the sense of failure which followed the repression of the "little revolution" of 1905. A few literary figures, with Vjacheslav Ivanov at their head, embraced that doctrine, which could be defined as a kind of spiritual libertarianism, or even libertinism. Following the examples of the "Scorpions," who had been issuing regularly the miscellany *Northern Flowers* (1901–1911), so entitled after a similar organ of Pushkin's "Pleiad," the members of *The Golden Fleece* group, which counted Aleksandr Blok among their sympathizers, published a yearbook of their own, *The Torches* (1906–1907). In contrast to publications like these, pleading special causes or representing small coteries, one should cite at this stage the splendid example set by a periodical of the old school, one of those which the Russians used to call "fat journals," being broad in size as well as in scope, and dealing with all sorts of problems and issues. That periodical was the Muscovite *Russian Thought*, which from 1910 to 1917, under the editorship of Petr Struve, opened its literary pages to the best writers of the time, both old and young.

In the last decade before the revolution the proliferation of journals and presses publishing the new literature was so rapid and intense that it is impossible to keep track of all of them. The most important of these presses were perhaps the "Griffin" of Moscow and the "Wild Rose" of Petersburg, respectively issuing the year-books by the same names (1907–1914 and 1907–1917). In addition, one should probably mention such other firms or concerns as "Musagetes" of Moscow, which published a periodical by the same title, and two later Petersburg presses with the mythic names of *Sirin* (Siren) and *Alkonost'* (a fabulous bird with a woman's face). The appearance of so many vehicles of publishing was perhaps a sign less of vitality than of confusion, while the discontinuance of both *The Scales* and *The Golden Fleece* contributed to a mood of uncertainty and perplexity. Many contemporary witnesses read all this as a symptom of the progressive disintegration of both Decadence and Symbolism. Others felt that the place left empty by trends which seemed to have run their course could be occupied with stability only by something really different and new.

The attempt to fill this void, and to guide Russian letters on to fresher paths, was undertaken in 1909 by the Petersburg journal *Apollo*, edited by the poet Sergej Makovskij, now still living in Paris as an *émigré*. The new journal's avowed intent was to voice the protest of the younger generation against the literary theories and poetic practice of their elders. Yet it offered generous hospitality to the masters of the old generation, and asked them to contribute to a debate on Symbolism, in which they took a rather defensive attitude. Soon enough *Apollo* became the official organ of newly rising Parnassian tendencies, publishing between 1910 and 1913 the manifestoes of the so-called Clarists and Acmeists. The impact of the First World War, however, frustrated *Apollo's* determined attempt to establish in Russia a school of poetry primarily intent on problems of craft. After surviving briefly the death of its cause, the review disappeared in the storm of 1917.

Strangely enough, Symbolism seemed to find a new lease on life in the apocalyptic atmosphere of that upheaval. One proof of this is the appearance of the miscellany *The Scythians* (1917–1918), edited by a mystical left-winger, Ivanov-Razumnik, who rallied Blok, Belyj, and Esenin to the banner of "Scythianism," a doctrine viewing the Russian masses as the barbaric creators of new spiritual and social values. Another proof is Belyj's irregular but rather prolonged publication of an almost personal journal, *Notebooks of Daydreamers*, which lasted from 1919 to 1922. It was in those very years that the literary situation underwent a radical change, which found expression, before the final advent of an official literary doctrine imposed from above, in a series of trends novel in spirit and strange in form. At least for a brief spell the task previously performed by modernism was taken over by the advance guard, while Decadence, Symbolism, and Acmeism were replaced by Futurism, Imaginism, and Constructivism. But the story of these schools, even more ephemeral than those which had preceded them, is part of another chapter in the cultural history of twentieth-century Russia and will be told in another portion of this book.

No account of the activities or manifestations of Russian literary modernism would be fair or complete without mentioning and crediting its outstanding contribution to the aesthetic and cultural education of the Russian public. All the leaders of the movement were not only poets, but also scholars, or at least men of letters; the range of their learning was wide and varied, often extending to exotic traditions and strange lores. Cosmopolitan in outlook, catholic in taste, often universal in interests, they constantly supplemented their creative activities by working as translators and interpreters. They reshaped into Russian words or thoughts all sorts of foreign writing, ancient or modern, verse or prose, "literature of knowledge" as well as "literature of power." By taking full advantage, with consummate skill, of the inborn virtues of the Russian language, which are assimilation and flexibility, they were able to reproduce foreign poems through Russian equivalents of their native metrical structures, and to introduce foreign ideas in quasi-familiar garb, in clothing which would please rather than shock, and never surprise. In this task they were helped on one hand by a host of enlightened patrons and open-minded publishers, on the other by the cultivation and dedication of a loyal, and not too limited, audience. They neglected no foreign classic, from Homer to Vergil, from Dante to Cervantes, from Racine to Shakespeare or Goethe, but nonetheless devoted the best and most of their efforts to the poets and thinkers of modern Europe, from the early Romantics to their contemporaries. They enriched Russian literature with translations and interpretations of Novalis and Kleist, of Byron, Shelley, Coleridge, and Poe; but chiefly, of all the poets of modern France, from Gautier to Baudelaire, from Mallarmé to Rimbaud, from Verlaine to Verhaeren. They paid attention also to newer, odder, or more fashionable writers, such as Wilde, Walt Whitman, D'Annunzio, Maeterlinck, Hamsun, and Kipling. They paid particular tribute to such thinkers as Schopenhauer and Nietzsche, and to playwrights like Ibsen and Strindberg, all of whom they installed for a while in the Pantheon of Russian letters where, although adopted, they were worshipped as tutelary deities.

III

THE ARTS AND THE THEATER

The culture of modern Russia achieved its greatest triumphs in the realms of the idea and the word. Despite all their merits, the visual artists of the first and second half of the past century, whether Romantics like Brjullov and Ivanov, or realists like Vereshchagin and Repin, look like pale copies when compared to Pushkin and Gogol', or to Dostoevskij and Tolstoj. The tradition they established in the art of painting, the most central of all figurative arts, lacked the vital power of the lofty inheritance which the classical masters of Russian literature bequeathed to Russia and the world.

That renovation of taste which the upholders of the "new currents" preached and enacted in the field of letters at the turn of the century was even more overdue in the domain of the arts. The single instrument of this revival was a periodical already mentioned, *The World of Art*, which appeared in Petersburg, splendidly printed and lavishly illustrated, from 1899 to 1904. That journal educated the Russian public to a new sense of plastic values as much as *The Scales* was to educate it to a new sense of literary ones. Such a publication could hardly be a profit-making enterprise, and it seems that on occasions even the Tsar's private purse contributed to its support. Yet its main "angel" was Savva Mamontov, one of

62

those merchant princes who were at that time the most generous patrons of Russian letters and arts. Along with Mamontov, who chose to support the legitimate theater as well as the opera and the ballet, the best known of such merchant princes were Shchukin and Morozov, who had the vision to enrich the private and public galleries of Russia with priceless masterpieces by the great Impressionists, as well as with early works by Picasso, then an obscure figure in Paris, the Mecca of modern art.

The editor of *The World of Art*, as well as the leader of the critics and artists who grouped around it, was Sergej Djagilev, who was destined to become one of the greatest artistic promoters of the first quarter of this century, in Europe as well as in his homeland. Djagilev edited the review with the help of many gifted collaborators, headed by Alexander Benua (1870), an artist of French descent, as indicated by his name (Benois). An old man now, living and working in France, Benua is still remembered not only as a graceful and quaint painter, as delicate as Raoul Dufy, but also as an art critic and art historian of great distinction. Besides reawakening the interest of his contemporaries in French Neoclassicism and Rococo, Benua helped them to rediscover the beauty of Petersburg, fashioned by the genius of the great Italian architects Quarenghi and Rastrelli. Yet the most important accomplishment of Benua, Djagilev, and their collaborators was the fostering of an enlightened curiosity about the new art of the West, as well as an intelligent re-evaluation of the painting and architecture of ancient Russia. Last but not least, they led the Russian public to a sympathetic appreciation of the best of their "moderns." Among the living Russian artists to whom *The World of Art* gave critical support, one should mention Isaak Levitan (1861–1900), the author of many landscapes without figures reinterpreting Russian nature with a poetic truth akin to that achieved by the masters of the Barbizon school; Valentin Serov (1865–1911), perhaps the greatest Russian portraitist of his age; and finally, Mikhail Vrubel' (1856–1910).

All these painters may well look rather academic and conventional to a sophisticated observer of our time. The last of them, mystical and visionary, succeeded perhaps better than the others in expressing in plastic terms the literary spirit of the age. Vrubel's obsession with both the cosmic and the supernatural, which led him to paint Pan, and to try to recapture in vain the foul charms of Lermontov's Demon, made of him the aptest interpreter of both decadent aestheticism and mystical symbolism in visual form. Often compared to Blake, with whom he shared an interest in the graphic arts, Vrubel' was rather a Russian Gustave Moreau or Aubrey Beardsley; like the latter, he frequently illustrated the books of his literary contemporaries. Despite a recent renewal of interest in Vrubel' among the *émigrés*, he and the other artists of his generation and breed are now forgotten in both Russia and the West. Soviet official taste finds that their fanciful artiness hardly conforms to the canons of Socialist Realism; as for Western connoisseurs, they view as far better exponents of Russian art such painters as Vasilij Kandinskij and Mark Shagal (Chagall), who developed their native gifts by joining, the one in Munich, and the other in Paris, two of the mainstreams of European modernism.

Benua and other painters of his generation became Djagilev's collaborators in the most glorious and lasting of the latter's achievements, the so-called *Ballets Russes*, which conquered Paris in 1909 and 1910, and, after Paris, the whole world. No other man was ever able to attract and inspire so much talent as Djagilev did. All the great choreographers, ballet masters, and dancers of our age went to his school and were his creatures, even more than his pupils: Fokin, Masin, Lifar, Pavlova, Karsavina, and the supreme wonder, Nizhinskij. Among painters, Djagilev commanded the collaboration of Lev (Léon) Bakst (1866–1925), who designed the costumes and décor for so many of his ballets and became the most accomplished master of that eclectic and ornamental manner which the Russians named "stylization" (*stilizatsija*), the Germans, *Jugendstil*, and the French, *art nouveau*. Among composers, Djagilev's favorites were the last two of the great Russian "five," Borodin and Rimskij-Korsakov, and, among the young, the newly discovered Igor' Stravinskij and Sergej Prokof'ev. Among foreign artists, old and new, he enlisted the collaboration of the composer Debussy, the painter Picasso, the poet Cocteau.

All Europe was seduced by the Russian Ballets, especially by its

masterpieces, which were Borodin's *Prince Igor'*; Rimskij-Korsakov's *Shéhérazade, Sadko,* and *The Golden Cockerel;* Debussy's
Après-midi d'un faune; and Stravinskij's *Petrushka* and *Firebird.*
The performances revealed to the West a splendid syncretic creation, uniquely merging in a complex artistic unity the musical, the
pictorial, and the mimetic elements, blending in the splendor of a
single artistic vision the modern and the barbaric, the popular and
the exotic, the Slavic and the Byzantine. Had he been able to add
to his sorceries the witchcraft of the word, Djagilev might have
given us the illusion of the ultimate realization of the Wagnerian
dream of an "art of the future," of a *Gesamtkunstwerk* joining
within itself, under the supremacy of the spirit of dance, all divers
arts.

It was primarily through choreographic and operatic manifestations, the latter highlighted by such an artist as Fedor Shaljapin,
that Russian culture revealed to the West the histrionic mastery it
was equally able to achieve on the legitimate stage. Yet the story
to be told deals less with authors and performers, and more with
directors and producers. Thus, despite the contributions of such
uneven and yet successful playwrights as Chekhov, Gor'kij and
Andreev, and of such popular performers as Ivan Moskvin, Vasilij
Kachalov, and Ol'ga Knipper (Chekhov's wife), the real rulers of
the modern Russian theater were its directors. This was true even at
the beginning, when the stage manager still acknowledged the
primacy of the playwright, and ranked only as *primus inter pares*
among his various interpreters. It was even truer at a later phase,
which, despite a short revival of poetic drama, coincided with that
growing exhaustion of dramatic creativity affecting Russian literature since early Symbolism. In the Soviet period, which closes the
process, we finally witness the establishment of the totalitarian
dictatorship of the director, who submits author and text, even in
the case of the classics, to a double yoke: on one side to the official
ideology of the regime, and on the other to the arbitrary singleness
of his own artistic purpose.

The central, nay, the Olympian figure of the modern Russian
theater is its earliest master, Konstantin Alekseev (1863–1938), the
son of a Moscow merchant, better known under the art-name of

Stanislavskij. He began his career as an actor, and in 1898 founded in his native city, in collaboration with the playwright Vladimir Nemirovich-Danchenko, that famous Art Theater which was bound to become, even beyond Europe, the wellspring of all modern stagecraft. Even though he appeared on the cultural scene when Russia's literary golden age was already on the wane, Stanislavskij was destined to represent in the world of the theater, for more than a quarter of a century, the most magnificent traditions of Russian classical realism. This made the Art Theater the shrine of the intelligentsia, rather than of the artistic elite. The founder and leader of the Art Theater was in a sense the Tolstoj of the Russian stage: he believed with that great master that art should be based on objective and subjective truth, and that it should reflect human experience not through the realism of the mind, but through the realism of the heart.

Stanislavskij changed the theatrical outlook as much as Tolstoj had transformed the moral and psychological one. While Tolstoj had debunked the romantic hero and celebrated the uniqueness of every human being, particularly of the common man, Stanislavskij imposed the same views on the stage by banning the great performer and the scene stealer, the virtuoso and the star, and replacing them with players willing to accept with religious fervor the bonds of a common devotion and of a democratic discipline. By following the vision, rather than the will, of their director, Stanislavskij's troupers became both the dedicated servants and the stern masters of their craft. Whereas Tolstoj had envisaged literature as the writing down of the utterances of one's inner voice, which he felt were in harmony with the universal demands of human feeling, Stanislavskij taught his actors, through the training which was later to be dubbed his "method" or "system," to reach slowly but surely that state of total psychological identification with their part which can make even the smallest role meaningful and unique. Only by an almost mystical submission of their real personalities to the fictitious ones of their characters could those actors succeed, through a process of double empathy, in imparting to their audience that infection of feeling to which Tolstoj reduced the whole magic of art.

MODERNISM AND DECADENCE

Like Tolstoj, Stanislavskij preferred a few outstanding and established modern masters to either classics or innovators and iconoclasts, and shared his liking for prose over verse, for observation and introspection over fancies and dreams. He felt more at home in the present than in the past, with real men and women than with fairies and ghosts, with commonly and shabbily dressed characters than with personages donning gorgeous costumes or wearing strange masks. Thus the mainstays of his repertory were Ostrovskij, Ibsen, Gor'kij, and Tolstoj himself, but above all, Chekhov, the author of *Three Sisters* and *The Cherry Orchard*. Fittingly enough, it was first the failure, and then the success, of Chekhov's early play *The Gull* which provided the Art Theater with the emblematic bird that was to become its coat of arms.

From the viewpoint of props and décor, Stanislavskij's art reached its high point, or rather its ultimate excess, in the performance of Gor'kij's *Lower Depths*, where the obsession with lifelike detail went beyond every limit. The perfection of Stanislavskij's "imitation" inspired legends similar to those which the ancients used to tell to praise the mimetic powers of their painters, such as the story of the bird vainly trying to peck a seed from a bunch of grapes so well painted as to look real. The most frequently told of such legends is the one claiming that his troupe once had rehearsed so well a Gor'kij play in a provincial town where a *pogrom* had just taken place that the sudden irruption of a few fictitious Cossacks on the stage caused the audience to flee, in a fit of terror, from the house. Yet the naturalism of Stanislavskij, as Tolstoj said once of Chekhov's, was impressionistic: his sense of reality was less plastic than picturesque, and had a quasi-lyrical quality. He envisaged the theatrical illusion in terms of genre painting, as one of his most striking conventions seems to hint: that the players should act as if the space left open by the rising curtain were filled by a "fourth wall." The "fourth wall" notwithstanding, the Art Theater was always able to establish a sense of communion with its audience, making a bridge of the gap dividing orchestra and proscenium, which is indeed, even though in a different sense from Wagner's, a "mystical chasm."

The two directors who tried, as they claimed, to "liberate" the

Russian stage from the deadly grip of Stanislavskij's reform, which in the hands of his disciples was degenerating into academic mannerism, were Evgenij Vakhtangov and Aleksandr Tairov. The former was a neoromantic, in love with the poetic and fantastic drama, with the "fairy tales" of Gozzi and the "romantic comedies" of Shakespeare. With the help of a troupe of young actors, whom he trained to cultivate a sense of style and of creative caprice rather than mimetic skills, and with the collaboration of such new decorative artists as the young painters Mikhail Larionov and Natal'ja Goncharova, who designed the fanciful and suggestive settings his style required, Vakhtangov produced plays which instead of re-creating the illusion of life tended to create a life of pure illusion, novel and fresh. At the end of his career he transcended, however, the limits of his taste by shaping into an effective artistic concern the majestic and mystical "Habima" Theater, which was founded in the early 1920's by a group of Jewish actors with the aim of replacing the Yiddish demotic comedy with a national and religious drama in Hebrew.

Both Vakhtangov and Tairov were for a while influenced by Nikolaj Evreinov, the theorist of the "theatrical theater," or of the drama as pure spectacle. Tairov replaced Vakhtangov's sense of the poetic and the picturesque with the architectonic and the plastic, and enforced a manner of acting at once emphatic and stylized, almost expressionistic. If Vakhtangov was neoromantic, Tairov was neoclassic, and expressed on the stage a taste which found its literary embodiment in such a poet as Mandel'shtam. The parallel is the more fitting since Tairov's neoclassicism, like the neoromanticism of Vakhtangov, moved within a limited range and worked at its best within the scope of closet drama. The literary critics of that time often discussed what they called, on the analogy of chamber music, "cameral" art; if Vakhtangov paid his tribute to this concept in deeds, Tairov did so also in words, calling his troupe the "Chamber Theater." The concept of "camerality" (*kamernost'*) has remained alive even in Soviet culture, where it is, however, being used with a belittling connotation, to designate the tendency to cultivate a minor and private sort of artistic creation, in contrast with the "social command," and the civic mission, of Marxist art.

Even Vsevolod Mejerkhol'd, who from the Revolution up to the time when he disappeared forever, a victim of the great Stalinist purges, was destined to become the leader of the Soviet stage, as uncontested in his field as Majakovskij in poetry's realm, had begun his career as a "cameral" artist. A disciple of Stanislavskij, he started on his path by reacting against the problem play and stage naturalism, and founded a theater of his own, centered around the great actress Vera Komissarzhevskaja and choosing as its chief vehicles the lyrical dramas of Maeterlinck and Blok. Later he became the leading figure of the theatrical advance guard, presenting modernistic shows against a décorless stage, with actors dressed only in over-alls, schooled by what he called "biomechanics," a body training not too different from that developed by dancers and athletes.

Unlike Stanislavskij, who had always shown some catholicity of taste and great respect for the playwright's work, Vakhtangov and Tairov preferred a limited and specialized repertory affording better opportunity to their poetic fancies and artistic whims. Without rejecting or reshaping the text, they turned it into a mere pretext. Mejerkhol'd went further, advocating and initiating that "rejuvenation of the classics" which he based in theory on the ideological demands of the new order, but developed in practice as a technique enabling him to put into effect his view of the theater as pure showmanship. If the endeavor was in any sense successful, then Mejerkhol'd's supreme attainment was his reinterpretation of *The Inspector General*, which reduced that glorious comedy to an absurd farce, and treated Gogol's text as if it were merely a script. While transcending the limitations of the closet theater and "cameral" art, even the later Mejerkhol'd failed to sway an audience as large as that which Stanislavskij had held under his spell. He attempted to create a theater of the masses but succeeded only in lowering the drama to the level of the circus: an art form which one may disparage with the very words the Formalist critic Shklovskij chose to praise it: "the circus, thank God, does not need beauty; it is difficulty which is its real object." No other statement could better suggest that process of degeneration which Russian culture underwent from its age of silver to its age of bronze and iron, in the theater as well as in other aesthetic domains, for taking as its own standards those of the mass media and the popular arts.

Mejerkhol'd was a highly representative figure in more senses than one, but above all because he brought to its most radical consequences a new conception of the actor's role. Even before him other directors had reacted against Stanislavskij's system, and had tried to restore that view of the actor's task which Diderot had expressed in his *Paradoxe du comédien*. According to Diderot, the best player is the one who most feigns and least feels. It was in the light of that theory that the actor was first changed from an active interpreter of pathos and character to the passive executor of the director's will. For Vakhtangov the actor was to be a *maschera* or stock character in the sense of the Italian *commedia dell'arte*; for Tairov, a mime; for Mejerkhol'd, a marionette, according to an ideal hypothesis already suggested by Gordon Craig. In effect Mejerkhol'd handled the actor as if he were an inarticulate acrobat, or a blind performing machine. This last of all such reinterpretations of the role of the player, which were not always effective in practice, might stand as an allegory of that dehumanization and mechanization of life which was to be an effect of the Soviet order; and it may well be that Mejerkhol'd was made to pay with his life for this unconscious insight.

One may also advance the far less doubtful claim that the mighty band of these theatrical innovators symbolizes that series of changes of style, taste, and fashion which the culture of their homeland underwent from the nineties on. If Stanislavskij may be seen as a belated stage representative of the realistic tradition, Djagilev must certainly be viewed as the outstanding representative of the decadent revolt in the ballet, as well as in many other fields. While Vakhtangov and Tairov may be considered respectively the neoromantic and the neoclassical adapters to the domain of the performing arts of the tenets of such schools as Clarism and Acmeism, Mejerkhol'd may well be viewed as a Symbolist of the theater in the first phase of his career, and as a Futurist in the next. As for such a late literary advance guard as that exemplified by the Constructivist group, it appears that it found its equivalents on the screen rather than on the stage. But this is a story to be told against the background of early revolutionary culture, which expressed itself at its best through the black and white of the moving pictures, through the vivid eloquence of the silent film.

IV

NEW TRENDS OF THOUGHT

The "new currents" were not exclusively artistic or literary, and the development of Russian poetry during the period treated in this book cannot be fully understood without reference to those trends of thought which were part of the same general movement. All those trends, taken singly or as a whole, found their most typical representatives in three or four outstanding figures; and there is perhaps no better way to summarize the ideas that conveyed the spirit of the time than to draw the profiles of a few of its intellectual leaders.

The first of these leaders, the only one among them who worked and acted in the foreground of the modern movement, was Dmitrij Merezhkovskij. Born in Petersburg in 1865, Merezhkovskij started his career as a poet and as a literary polemist, with contributions to be appraised in another context. He gained his literary ascendancy primarily as a philosophical critic, asserting new values in the realm of thought. At first he preached the gospel of decadent aestheticism, which he later replaced, or rather merged, with a strange religious messianism of his own. This messianism was based on the expectation that world history would soon enter its third or last stage, the reign of the Holy Ghost. According to Merezhkovskij, the triumph of the religion of the Holy Ghost would forever reconcile the religion of the Father and the religion of the Son, joining in a higher epiphany pagan and Christian truth, the faith of the flesh and the faith of the spirit. Yet, being perhaps more of a Manichaean than a Gnostic, Merezhkovskij was led to emphasize not so much the future, final stage of fusion and harmony, as the phase, whether past or present, of cleavage and rift. In brief, Merezhkovskij paid less attention to the single triad which in the end will resolve all contradiction into a new unity, than to that endless series of diads which turn into an everlasting strife history itself. This is true of

7 I

even the best of his books, *Tolstoj and Dostoevskij* (1901), where the parallel criticism of their personalities, works, and beliefs unfolds into the metaphysical duel of two opposite archetypes. After having reduced the first of those two masters to a "visionary of the flesh" and the other to a "visionary of the spirit," Merezhkovskij refused to reconcile in any way an antagonism which was rooted in his own mind rather than in its objects. One could say in Hegelian terms that Merezhkovskij was far more interested in the purely negative dialectic of thesis and antithesis than in the positive solution, by means of their synthesis, of the conflict of the two. Thought itself was for him an antithetic process: an equation of contrasting ideas, or rather, abstractions, such as God and Satan, Hellenism and Hebraism, spirit and flesh, good and evil, or what Merezhkovskij used to call by the Heraclitean terms of "abyss from above" and "abyss from below."

The most important of these antinomies was that of Christ and Antichrist, on which Merezhkovskij based his philosophy of history, and which in its turn inspired all too many of his works. The genre to which such works belong could be defined as "historical fiction," in all the meanings of this term. With them Merezhkovskij turned his messianism toward the past, changing himself into a "retrospective prophet" in a far more literal sense than Friedrich Schlegel meant when he defined the historian and his task by that term. The method by which Merezhkovskij reconstructed and reinterpreted the historical past could be termed metaphysical hindsight; this is particularly true of his first trilogy, a series of historical novels published successively under the general title *Christ and Antichrist*. The first volume of the sequence, *Julian the Apostate* (1896), deals with "the death of the gods" of pagan antiquity and with the vain attempt by that late Roman Emperor to revive and to restore the deities which Christianity had overthrown. The gist of the story is that Julian the Apostate came too late, while the gist of its sequel, *Leonardo da Vinci* (1901), is that that great mind came too early, when the world was not yet ready for "the resurrection of the gods," for the reconciliation of religion with art and science, for the acceptance, on the part of Christianity, of worldly beauty and earthly love. The philosophical and historical antithesis on which the third and last novel of the series is based is a different one. This novel, *Peter and Alexis* (1905), develops a specifically Russian version of the selfsame struggle. The two adversaries are the great Emperor, a doer in the secular spirit of the West, and his heir and son, a dreamer in the mystic spirit of Holy Russia and the Eastern Church. Here, following a popular tradition and the Slavophile view, Merezhkovskij saw the Antichrist in Peter the Great; while in a succeeding historical trilogy, consisting of the drama *Paul I* (1909) and the novels *Alexander I* (1911) and *The Fourteenth of December* (1913), the author took a far more liberal and traditional stand, viewing the incarnation of the Antichrist in that tsardom which was both State and Church, and treating as harbingers of a new era those who, like the Decembrists, had fought for the freedom of the human spirit.

With these and other books, as well as with the periodicals he inspired and the activities he promoted, Merezhkovskij was able to affect the thinking and feeling of his contemporaries in a manner certainly out of proportion to the merits of his ideas and the quality of his work. What he succeeded in creating was but a system of empty generalizations, which impressed the Russian mind, always eager to wrestle with abstract issues, with those which were generally called the "accursed questions" of good and evil, of the Tower of Babel and of the City of God. The influence of the metaphysical problematics of Merezhkovskij decreased gradually but constantly in the years between the first revolution, which he saluted with both enthusiasm and awe, and the second one, which he rejected with revulsion and horror. Many of his writings after October 1917 were vehement anti-Communist tracts, but from the early 1920's, when he settled in Paris, until the time of his death, he repeated and vulgarized for the benefit of his Western readers, in a series of books which were translated into several languages, the same historiosophic doctrines he had preached for more than a quarter of a century in the land of his birth.

A less broad but more solid international reputation was ultimately the lot of a contemporary of Merezhkovskij, endowed with far greater philosophical and literary gifts. This man was Lev Shestov, who was born in Kiev in 1866 with the surname of

Shvartsman, and died in Paris in 1938, after seeing his exile sweetened at its end by his recognition as one of the masters of French Existentialism. Within Russian culture Shestov represented a strange fusion of spiritualism and immoralism. He came to the fore in 1900 with an essay, *The Good in the Teachings of Tolstoj and Nietzsche*, in which he took the German philosopher's side in the controversy about morality, denying any spiritual validity to the ethos of compassion and brotherhood, and quoting at the end Nietzsche's warning: "Woe to all those . . . who know no love higher than pity." Shestov's denial implied, however, a "transvaluation of values" different from the one recommended by Nietzsche, as shown by a warning of his own, which he added to that of his German master, and by which he closed that book: "We must seek for what is above pity, above the Good: we must seek for God." This work was the first of Shestov's many tracts against idealism, by which he meant moralism in practical life, rationalism in philosophy, and sentimentalism in religion, or, more simply, all those modes of thought and behavior presupposing the belief that ours is the best of all possible worlds. Shestov protested against such naïve optimism, and claimed that "we should treat pessimism and skepticism not as enemies, but as friends not recognized before."

It was his pessimism or skepticism that led Shestov to see the power of mystical revelations in those crises and ordeals of the spirit which had forced such men as Pascal, Nietzsche, and Dostoevskij to enter what Shestov himself called the "region of tragedy." Such was the very theme of the essay *Dostoevskij and Nietzsche: The Philosophy of Tragedy* (1901), where self-knowledge is considered a mystical experience which involves Tobias' fight with the angel, or man's lonely struggle with his soul. This is what Shestov meant with the affirmation that "the thousand-year-long kingdom of reason and conscience is now over for man; a new era is about to begin, the era of psychology, which here in Russia was first opened by Dostoevskij." In the next work, which he entitled *The Apotheosis of Groundlessness* (1905) and defined as "an essay in adogmatic thinking," Shestov used the aphoristic form of expression and the devices of contradiction and paradox to criticize logical thought and to affirm his own irrational and subjective conception of truth. In 1916 he published *Potestas Clavium*, foreshadowing his later antithesis between Athens and Jerusalem, and contrasting the Hellenistic tendency of Christianity, according to which the keys of life are in the hands of man, with the Hebraistic one, which, on the authority of the prophets and St. Augustine, of Luther and Calvin, claims that that power lies in the hands of God. After the Revolution, Shestov published in France a series of essays on Dostoevskij and Tolstoj, on Pascal and Kierkegaard, besides several philosophical works, where he restated his views with a classical clarity and a trenchant wit which helped to gain for his work the sympathetic interest of the French literary elite.

Similar attention was given not only in France, but also in America and in England, to the late work of another exiled Russian philosopher, Nikolaj Berdjaev, who like Shestov was born in Kiev (1874) and died in Paris (1948). Berdjaev started as a Marxist, but later helped to edit the periodicals of the Merezhkovskijs and other "God-seekers," and contributed to that critical assessment of the intelligentsia and its ideology which found its document in the miscellany *Guideposts*. During his maturity Berdjaev developed a philosophy of personality based on the one hand on liberty and creation, and on the other, on morality and religion. The books which became the cornerstones of his system are *The Philosophy of Liberty* (1911) and *The Sense of Creation* (1917). The Revolution led him to meditate about the past and the future of both Russia and the West, and to write two works which made him famous in Europe: *The World-View of Dostoevskij* (1922) and *The New Middle Ages* (1924). In the latter he prophesied the transformation of our modern civilization into a novel kind of technological barbarism. A strong opponent of what he called the "lie" of Communism (by which he meant its denial of liberty and religion), Berdjaev showed in his late years more sympathy than any other *émigré* of his generation toward its "truth," by which he meant the idea of social justice. At the end of his life Berdjaev published "an essay in philosophical autobiography," *Self-Knowledge* (1940), which, among other things, is an important reinterpretation of the movements of ideas which ruled Russian intellectual life during the first two decades of the century.

Their international reputation, whether deserved or not, has saved the names of Merezhkovskij, Shestov, and Berdjaev from oblivion and their works from neglect. The same cannot be said of one of their contemporaries, whose memory and cult are being preserved only by a few surviving admirers in the thinning ranks of the oldest émigrés. Yet future historians may well consider him one of the most brilliant and original literary figures of his time. This man was Vasilij Rozanov. Born in Vetluga in 1856, Rozanov spent many years of his life as a teacher of history and geography in provincial high schools. He started his literary career in the mid-eighties with an antipositivistic tract, but his first important work was a monograph on *The Legend of the Grand Inquisitor* (1890), which is still held a landmark in Dostoevskian criticism. In the 1890's he settled in Petersburg, and became a regular contributor to Suvorin's conservative daily *The New Times*, where he wrote anti-Semitic articles and approved of Tolstoj's excommunication by the Holy Synod. Practically all the books he published in the first decade of the century were collections of articles originally written for that daily or for the periodical press.

The main theme of these books, the most important of which were *Around the Walls of the Temple* (1906), *The Dark Visage* (1911), and *Moonlight People* (1913), was Christianity or Orthodoxy, religion or the Church. Their chief aim, however, was to attack that asceticism and spiritualism in which Rozanov saw a denial not just of man's most vital instincts but of the moral and social order, even of religion itself. Believing that marriage is the highest of all sacraments, and that procreation is a holy task, Rozanov in these and other books contrasted the warm, fecund, and healthy faiths of primitive, classical, and Biblical antiquity with the cold, sterile, and morbid faith of the New Testament. Jesus, the Son, is for Rozanov the enemy of His Father, as well as of all solar gods: His "dark visage" seems to eclipse the sun in the universe, while His most loyal followers, "the moonlight people," as Rozanov calls the monks, seem to extinguish all light and delight from this world. Nothing shows better Rozanov's peculiar position within the culture of his time than his simple- and single-minded concern with the mystique of sex. In this he greatly differed from Merezhkovskij, who, while claiming to value equally the spirit and the flesh, in reality subordinated the latter to the former, as shown especially in the book on Dostoevskij and Tolstoj, where the parallel of those two great writers ends in an invidious comparison, to the damage of the second. As for Rozanov, he rejected any dualism, and replaced it with a monism of his own, assigning all positive values to the flesh, and all negative ones to the spirit. This made of him not a cheap immoralist, but rather a mystical worshipper of life, who saw in the perpetuation of the species the only token of man's immortality.

This may explain why at the end of his life this prophet of sex became a prophet of the self. The self of which he was the announcer, however, was not the ego of the aesthete, but the prosaic and yet all-too-human "I" of the common man. What Rozanov celebrated was private life, the intimacy of the nest, the innermost quiverings of the soul. "All religions will pass," said he, "but this will remain — simply sitting on a chair, and looking afar." As a writer, he became the transcriber of all the musings and broodings, all the spontaneous intuitions which suddenly lighten the psyche like will-o'-the-wisps. His chosen medium for such transcriptions was brief notations, impressionistic in style and subjective in form and content. In a famous passage Rozanov thus described the psychic *Erlebnis* which became the mainspring of his art: "The wind blows at midnight and carries away leaves. . . . So also life in fleeting time tears off from our soul exclamations, sighs, half-thoughts, half-feelings. . . . These fragments of sound . . . come straight from the soul, without elaboration, without purpose, without premeditation, without anything eternal. . . ."

The last three, and the most important, of all Rozanov's books were but repositories of such fragmentary utterances, feelings, and thoughts, often assuming the aspect of an informal diary, or rather, of a series of impressions reported in chronological sequence. The first of these books was *Solitaria* (1912), which was followed in 1913 and 1915 by a first and second "basket" of *Fallen Leaves*. The third and last of these works, *The Apocalypse of Our Times* (1918), which Rozanov wrote and published in installments in the monastery town of Sergiev-Posad, where he had found shelter and refuge, was less rhapsodic in form and content, because it dealt with a single theme, with the great historical event of the Revolution, which the writer interpreted with the same "pathos of subjectivity" which had inspired his previous works. It was in that town, while working at another installment of the *Apocalypse*, that he died in 1919.

As already hinted, Rozanov shared with many of his contemporaries that worship of Dostoevskij which was one of the outstanding traits of the epoch. The apostle of this cult had been a man of the earlier generation, the philosopher Vladimir Solov'ev, who after his death was exalted as the prophet of Russian Symbolism. Solov'ev's *Three Addresses in Commemoration of Dostoevskij* (1881–1883) was the first apotheosis of that master, who at the end of his life had befriended the young philosopher and had presumably portrayed him in the character of Alesha Karamazov. Solov'ev's pioneering work opened a long series of great Dostoevskian commentaries, predominantly religious and philosophical in inspiration and content. The series included among its outstanding items a few works already mentioned, having been contributed by the thinkers and writers already treated in this chapter, such as Rozanov's *Legend of the Grand Inquisitor*, Merezhkovskij's *Tolstoj and Dostoevskij*, Shestov's *Dostoevskij and Nietzsche*, and Berdjaev's *The World-View of Dostoevskij*. To them one should add a few more titles, both older and newer, such as Volynskij's *Book of the Great Wrath* (1904), a study of *The Devils*; Belyj's more formalistic *Tragedy of Creation: Dostoevskij and Tolstoj* (1911); and finally many essays by Vjacheslav Ivanov, no less concerned with the mysteries of Dostoevskij's vision than with the secrets of his form, as shown by the very title he gave to his German monograph: *Dostoiewskij: Tragödie, Mythos, Mystik* (1932). Besides adding an interesting chapter to the history of Russian criticism, all these apologetic and hagiographic commentaries contributed to the formation of the Dostoevskij legend or myth: to the transformation of that figure into a mighty cultural hero, embodying the Russian genius and blowing the wind of the spirit over the wastelands of the modern world.

DECADENCE

In the mid-eighties, although apparently triumphant, the golden age of Russian prose had already entered its phase of decline. At the end of the following decade Lev Tolstoj wrote his iconoclastic book *What is Art?* (1897), which was, among other things, a strong attack against poetry in general, and against modern poetry in particular. On a famous page of that book, Tolstoj chose as his own target the very epithet "poetic," condemning under that heading what other critics, or other times, would have instead preferred to condemn under such labels as "conventional" and "literary." "Thus, in our circle," said Tolstoj, "all sorts of legends, sagas, and ancient traditions are considered poetic subjects. Among poetic people and things we reckon maidens, warriors, shepherds, hermits, angels, devils of all sorts, moonlight, thunder, mountains, the sea, precipices, flowers, long hair, lions, lambs, doves, and nightingales." After asserting that "in general all those objects are considered poetic which have most frequently been used by former artists in their productions," the great prose writer concluded: "poetic means borrowed." While on that page Tolstoj made use of the very notion of poetry for the purpose of defining "falsity in art," in another section of the same book he exemplified that falsity in the works of the new poets then emerging in France, such as Verlaine and Mallarmé. Yet the ultimate task of the new generation, which was then already rising on the literary horizon, was precisely to rehabilitate the adjective "poetic" and to restore to Russian literature all the values for which that adjective stood. The men who undertook to perform this task could not have achieved it without studying what the artists of other nations and times had been doing before them; thus the young Russian writers of the end of the century had no alternative but to go to the school of the same French poets whom Tolstoj had singled out for special sarcasm.

If Tolstoj's statement is a faithful indication of the atmosphere dominating Russian literature at the end of its most glorious period, it is hardly surprising that the few writers of the eighties and the early nineties who indulged in verse writing were often treated like, and even considered themselves to be, literary outcasts. Poetry was then a handmaid of prose, and all the poets of that time seemed to be fated to either mediocrity or obscurity, or both. The most significant document of this state of mind is the late poetry of a very minor figure, Semen Nadson, a writer of partly Jewish descent, who was born in 1862 and died very young in 1887. Following a first phase of "civic" inspiration, Nadson wrote a series of poems, querulous and sentimental, in which the complaint of the poet about his lot often turns into a complaint about the destiny of poetry itself: "The flowers are withered, the fires quenched; yet a chord still quivers from the broken strings." If that quivering note stands for the poet's voice, soon to be muted by death, then the broken instrument may stand for Russian verse, which was then in a sorry plight.

The muse of Nadson, while a muse of decay, was not yet, however, a muse of Decadence. Many years later, in an exchange of letters with the critic Mikhail Gershenzon, which appeared after the Revolution under the title of *A Correspondence from One Corner to Another*, the Symbolist poet Vjacheslav Ivanov properly and suggestively defined Decadence as "the sense, both oppressive and exalting, of being the last of a series." In Nadson's poetry there is a sense of oppression, but there is no sense of exaltation, since no feeling of hope tempers his mood of despair. The cultural phenomenon which in modern literature takes the name of Decadence is possible only when the vision of the impending catastrophe merges with the expectation that another culture will be built on its ruin. That expectation may be only an illusion: yet the modern idea of Decadence is based on such a dialectic. An old, tired, and sophisticated society may at least in part turn the very objects of its fears into objects of hope. The last heirs of a dying tradition may be willing to prepare the ground for the builders of another cultural order, who will be at once their successors and destroyers; the representatives of the series already closing may even delude themselves that they may become the first representatives of the series not yet begun. In brief, modern Decadence derives its essence and meaning from the antinomy of such contrasting concepts as civilization and barbarism, from the very antithesis of the ideas of decay and rebirth. This implies the fusion, as well as the cleavage, of the old and the new: the final outcome of such a rift is the reconciliation within the Decadent outlook of two extremes which at first sight seem to deny equally the Decadent principle, even though from contrary ends. These two extremes are the opposite cultural polarities generally named primitivism and modernism. Even the earliest leaders of the Russian Decadent movement were fully aware of this paradox, which they never tired of restating, since it was their *raison d'être*, the cornerstone of the shrine they wanted to build.

The paradox itself had been vaguely anticipated by another Jewish poet of Nadson's generation, Nikolaj Vilenkin, born in 1855, and better known in literature under the pen name of Minskij. If we look deeply enough, we do not find a great difference in inspiration and quality between the poetry of the two; like Nadson, Minskij started his career as a "civic" poet, and in a sense always kept faith with the ideals of his youth. He left Russia in the wake of the "little revolution," after having written for Lenin's *Pravda* (Truth) a workers' hymn versifying in its first line the Marxist slogan "Workers of the world, unite!" He spent the rest of his life as an exile in France, where he died in 1927, and whence he protested against the great Revolution from the standpoint of humanitarian socialism. Yet in the late eighties Minskij had been seduced by Nietzsche, the thinker who understood better than anyone else the problematics of Decadence and who felt equally attracted by the ambiguous vision of a cultural agony which could be also a rebirth. Minskij gave his own version of Nietzsche's ideas in a pretentious tract, *In the Light of Conscience* (1890); and he preached in the dull prose of that work, as well as in the heavy rhythms of his verse, the good new tidings of individualism, immoralism, and aestheticism. While in one of his poems Minskij proudly claimed that he was forging a new poetry by destroying all ties with the past: "I break old chains, and sing new prayers," in another piece he sadly acknowledged that the new poets were but the shadows of a world of which they were no longer part: "we, the twilight of another sun, the weary evening of an alien day, the cold ashes of an alien fire. . . ." The vagueness of Minskij's anticipation of the idea of Decadence derived from his inability to understand the ambivalence of its fundamental dualism; he simply failed to recognize that in the dimness of the historical sky the signs of sunset could be the same as those of dawn.

Minskij had started his career as a camp follower, and he ended it as a straggler rather than as a pioneer. His generation found its pathfinders not in poets like him, but in such critics as Volynskij and Merezhkovskij, who paved the ground for the new literature by indicting the false values of the present as well as of the past. It is true that Merezhkovskij was a poet as well as a critic, and that in a sense he had already announced the poetry to come in a collection of quasi-modernistic lyrics influenced by Poe and Baudelaire, which he had published in 1892 under the fashionable title of *Symbols*. Yet the book by which he opened the new era was the polemical pamphlet *On the Causes of the Decline and on the New Currents of Contemporary Russian Literature*, written earlier but published later (1893), just one year before the appearance of Valerij Brjusov's *Russian Symbolists* and Konstantin Bal'mont's *Under the Northern Sky*, the two books which marked the sudden emergence in Russia of what we call modern poetry.

Merezhkovskij's pamphlet is more of a psychological and historical document than a literary program: the novel style which the writer recommends in its pages may well imply the use of a symbolic imagery but amounts to hardly more than a sort of poetic impressionism. While it would be wrong to treat this pamphlet as the first manifesto of Russian Symbolism (even if the term is taken in its broadest sense), we must certainly treat it as the most eloquent testimonial of the decadent mood. Its title emphasizes the interconnection of the old and the new: it is by the juxtaposition of such opposite notions as "decline" and "new currents" that Merezhkovskij turned the simple concept of decay into the complex idea of decadence. While aiming his most telling blows, like his senior, Volynskij, at the target of sociological and utilitarian criticism, the young writer claimed that some of the roots of cultural decay were to be found within Russian literature, rather than outside it: in its failure to appraise the very values which Merezhkovskij himself was later to foster and preach, and which, for lack of a better name, may be labeled as a "new idealism." Merezhkovskij saw another aspect of that decay in the spiritual crisis of the age, which he represented at once in the agony of the old generation and in the anguish of the new. The author described the state of mind by which the new generation was confronting its task as being one of fear and trembling, of terror and awe: "There are no more barriers! We are lonely and free. . . . The horror of this feeling is unheard of. Never before did man feel in his heart such a wish to believe, nor was so aware of his own inability to do so."

Merezhkovskij conveyed a similar mood in his verse, of which he published many volumes, up to the *Collected Poems* of 1910. The most typical of all his early poems is perhaps "Before the Dawn," where, speaking in the first person plural for his generation, the author defines himself and his own contemporaries as "children of the night," who are eagerly waiting for the dawn, although they know that at sunrise, being only shadows, they will vanish from the face of the earth. The very image suggests what one might call the agonic phase of the Decadent state of mind, while the metaphor defining the task of the young generation as that of *being* (not *making*) "a path over the void" conveys another phase of the same state of mind, the one related to the cultural concept of transition. The idea that the present generation was bound to act at once as a break and a link, both dividing and joining the past and the future, was to be shared by most of Merezhkovskij's contemporaries. Even Bal'mont, a pure poet less concerned with doctrine than any of Merezhkovskij's contemporaries, defined his own epoch as one where "thinking man stands between two ages." As for Merezhkovskij himself, he went further than this, reinterpreting the notion of transition in a tragic sense, and assigning to the generation which appears at the peak of a historical and cultural crisis the duty to sacrifice itself for the sake of a generation still to come and yet unseen. And it was in another line of the poem cited above, where he claimed that the "laments" of the men of his age and milieu were also their "hymns," that Merezhkovskij almost anticipated Vjacheslav Ivanov's statement that the Decadent attitude is made of the awareness, both "oppressive and exalting," that one may die only for others to be born. A clear or obscure sense of this truth was fated to dominate the culture of Russia for all that period of time which we have called the silver age of its literature. From all available instances we may choose as a single example the lines by which Fedor Sologub later described the historical destiny of himself and his peers: "Wanderers in a starless sky, seekers after a somber paradise, we trusted in our path, and dreamed of the lights of heaven. Yet we stopped at the threshold, heavy with shame and anguish. . . ."

The psychology of Decadence is certainly not limited to its own historical myth, which could be defined as the attempt to turn the impending apocalypse into an unexpected palingenesis, or to find ecstasy within agony itself. The components of the Decadent state of mind are many and manifold; and the first and foremost among them is the tendency which takes the name of aestheticism. Aestheticism implies the supremacy of art, on the one hand over nature, and on the other, over life. In the first case, aestheticism produces artificiality, or, more generally, an art which finds its inspiration not in observation and in experience, but in the fancies of the brain, or in the whims of the will. In the second case, aestheticism leads the artist to treat life as if it were only a passive matter, the raw material for aesthetic creation; or even to fashion life itself after the pattern of art. The effects of these two attitudes are nihilism and hedonism. The former, with its rejection of ethos and conscience, leads to indifference and apathy, to what Brjusov called, after the Parnassians, "impassivity" (*bezstrastie*); the latter, with its exaltation of pathos and the senses, leads to the triumph of passion, to what Bal'mont named, all too romantically, "transport" (*vostorg*). The Russian Decadents sinned in either one of these two directions, or even in both, at least as grievously as their Western brethren; yet they understood from the very beginning that the idolatry of art would lead, as all idolatries do, to the denial of any other ideal, value, or norm. They realized that aestheticism is naturally bound to become immoralism, and they accepted such an outcome. The idea that there is a tie between beauty and evil, especially when beauty is strange and new, was constantly and consistently preached, in few variations but in numberless versions, by the Russian poets of the late years of the nineteenth century and the early ones of the twentieth. All statements to this purpose repeated, like an echo, what Merezhkovskij had already announced in "Before the Dawn": "On behalf of New Beauty, we break all commandments, we transgress every limit."

Aestheticism and immoralism join naturally together in an extreme individualism, which the Russian Decadents learned primarily from Nietzsche, and which led them, like their Western colleagues, not merely to a heretical, and yet spiritual, religion of the creative personality, but also to a vulgar worship of an all-too-human Ego, in the manner of Barrès' *culte du moi*. Sologub raised to the level of an apotheosis this coarse worship of the self: "I am perfect, I am the only God." Zinaida Gippius turned the same cult into a blasphemous narcissism: "I adore myself like God." Bal'mont finally reduced self-adoration to common selfishness or outright egotism: "I do not love all others as I do myself." Aesthetic individualism reacted in its turn against immoralism (which after all is but a negative recognition of the very values which it is bent on destroying), by changing it into amoralism, into an attitude of absolute indifference toward all ethical issues. Immoralism implies the acceptance of vice and the rejection of virtue, but amoralism refuses to choose between foul and fair. The Decadent artist or poet refrains from making this choice on the ground that as a man he must explore all realms of life, experiencing the bliss of Paradise as well as the tortures of Hell. The Western poet who brought this idea to its extreme consequence was Rimbaud, who considered the ordeal of living, the odyssey of both body and spirit, as a process of initiation at the end of which the poet becomes a *voyant*. Merezhkovskij, who also wanted to become a seer, preached the same doctrine, affirming repeatedly that there is no difference between the road of good and the road of evil, between the upward and the downward path; that the thinker and the poet will find the highest knowledge by pursuing jointly the revelations of the spirit and the revelations of the flesh; that mankind itself will learn wisdom through the mysteries of both Christianity and paganism. Brjusov continuously reaffirmed similar views, preaching equality of love and sin, singing hymns to all idols, pledging allegiance to both Satan and God.

85

Such an amoralism or immoralism found its most frequent and intense expression in the realm of sex. Eroticism is one of the main sources of inspiration for Decadent art, which treats that theme in all its variations, from the pole of an innocent, paganlike sensuality to that of perversion and morbidity. When shifting from the collective to the individual field, Decadent culture translates its own historical and sociological concerns into biological and psychological equivalents, and replaces its interest in the process of decay and corruption of the body social or politic with a curiosity for physical and spiritual ailments, for the process of degeneration which man undergoes either as a person or as an organism. This is why the Decadent Eros is primarily the Eros of senility; its sensuality, vicarious and vicious, constantly wavers between perversion and impotence, or between sadism and masochism. This kind of Eros, which is so frequently frustrated, seems often to find fruition in the violation of all measure and norm: and its connection with Satanism leads it all too often to perform "black masses," and to pretend that its orgies are agapes, or holy rites. Nobody was more willing to combine sacred and profane love than a Symbolist poet, Vjacheslav Ivanov, who was far more strongly affected than his brethren by the Decadent strain, and who dared to tread the path of obscenity in that pseudomystical celebration of the varieties of the sexual act which he entitled "Veneris figurae" (the term *figura*, understood in such a sense, is taken from Ovid). A poet of the following generation, Mikhail Kuzmin, who succeeded in the attempt to express his unhealthy, Decadent inspiration in a minor, but perfect, neoclassical mold, went even further than Ivanov and advocated, with shameless innocence, the cause of homosexual love.

At least secondarily, the Eros of Decadence is also an Eros of exhaustion and fatigue, a fever of the brain leading to a spiritualized kind of sensualism. One of the main paradoxes of the Decadent spirit must be seen in the very attempt to impose a mystical vision on material reality itself. Nothing is more paradoxical, for instance, than the extreme idealism often preached by the most sensuous poet of the Russian Decadence, Konstantin Bal'mont, who once claimed that truth may be reached only by denying the testimony of our senses and defined the latter as "avenues of falsehood." In reality that very idealism became for the Decadents the road that led them toward the sentimental falsities and romantic fallacies which are the nemesis of Decadence itself. It was from that naïve and subjective idealism that Bal'mont derived his exaltation of the "moment" (*mig*), and his claim that every fleeting instant is not only an "atom," but also a "diamond," shining with the light of revelation, with the supreme splendor of an absolute value; and it was on that shaky foundation that he based his expectation that miracles and wonders would happen for his own benefit.

The decadent dream of the impossible found perhaps its most typical expression in Bal'mont's half-childish, half-Neronian outcry "I want buildings afire!" But even the Russian Decadents, like all men, lived after all in buildings of brick or stone; and their best poetry was often inspired by the realization of this. Such a realization does not imply, however, an acceptance on their part of our all-too-human world, or an attitude of resignation to the failure of their dream. The Decadent poet remains alone in his misery, as he was in his glory, precisely because he is deprived of a sense of human fellowship. Zinaida Gippius expressed this feeling of alienation by confessing: "I cannot live with human beings." Sologub, like so many artists of his time, whether Russian or foreign, saw in this condition both a curse and blessing, a mission as well as a destiny. He expressed this view by addressing to the poet the two-line sentence: "In mute solitude — live, dream, and die," sounding at once like a curse and a warning, reading like both an epigram and an epitaph.

For the Decadents art is a hardship and sacrifice: a hardship which may not even be worthwhile, a sacrifice which may fail to reap commensurate rewards. Brjusov acknowledged that from a poet's creation, costing him so much suffering and labor, posterity, or, as he says, eternity, "may save seven or eight lines alone." This very awareness, however, spurred those poets to take infinite pains with their work. They paid great attention to problems of technique and style, diction and rhythm. By doing so they revitalized Russian verse, which at the end of the century had degenerated into a kind of metered prose; and they restored standards of craftsmanship which, with the exception of Fet, Russian poets seemed to have irreparably lost after the age of Pushkin, Lermontov, and Tjutchev. As soon as they appeared in print, Bal'mont's and Brjusov's early pieces made the sentimental and conventional tunes of such older poets as the popular Nadson and the fashionable Apukhtin look quaint, awkward, and obsolete. The latter two had gained an undeserved reputation with unshapely compositions and prosaic songs; it was in reaction against the artless mannerisms of the last practitioners of nineteenth-century poetry that Bal'mont and Brjusov set an example that no poet who came after them could disregard without risk.

The masters of Russian Decadence renewed poetry not only by creating new patterns of sound, but also by changing the poet's vision of things. They replaced worn-out similes with new, daring metaphors, and created an imagery of their own, often representing reality with all the magnificent colors of the rainbow. Frequently, however, in tune with their Decadent mood, they replaced those colors with paler hues, and chose to represent with them the ages, seasons, or hours which better symbolize the passing of time, as well as of men and things. Thus they celebrated the stages of maturity and decline, changing poetry into a song of evening, into a poem of autumn, or even into a hymn of death. The lasting charm of that song was due to its verbal magic, rather than to any other form of artistic witchcraft. The poetry of every Alexandrian epoch tends essentially to what a poet of the early Italian Renaissance chose to call *portenta verborum*, and the literary creators of the Russian silver age were primarily poets of the word, of a word which was flesh rather than spirit. Even in this they fulfilled the task of Decadence, which was to be not a denial of culture, but a culture of negation, a flower of both evil and ill.

CHAPTER THREE

THE DECADENTS

I

KONSTANTIN BAL'MONT

Konstantin bal'mont was born in 1867 in the province of Vladimir, on the ancestral estate of his family, which like Lermontov's claimed remote Scottish origins. As a boy and a youth he was attracted by the revolutionary movement, and his political activities earned him an expulsion from the Gymnasium and a brief spell of jail and banishment while he was a student of law at the University of Moscow. Shortly afterward he began his literary career with the private publication of a booklet which he simply and proudly entitled *A Collection of Poems* (1890), but which he later repudiated as unworthy of himself. From that time on Bal'mont devoted all his energies to his literary work, except during the Revolution of 1905, which stirred again the radical leanings of his youth. On that occasion he briefly joined the Social Democratic Party, fled abroad to avoid new and more serious persecutions, and finally wrote and published in Paris a series of political invectives in verse, which he called *Songs of an Avenger* (1907). After that experience he again took up toward life a bohemian attitude and an aesthete's pose. From that time up to the First World War he traveled to the four corners of the world, visiting Europe and Mexico, Egypt and the islands of the South Seas. Despite his youthful allegiance to Marxism, he refused to accept the Revolution of 1917, and three or four years later he chose the path of exile. He settled in France, spending most of his time in Brittany, to die there in 1943 after a long mental illness.

Bal'mont was primarily a poet, and his prose, which includes fiction, travel sketches, the critiques collected in the book *Mountain Peaks* (1904), and a few theoretical pieces (the most important of the latter is *Poetry as Magic*, which appeared in pamphlet form in 1915), has all the defects of his verse but none of its merits. All the collections of poems for which he will be remembered appeared during a brief span of time, that ten- or twelve-year period which formed the only phase of Bal'mont's life marked by creativity, and not by fecundity alone. The production of those years opened with the threefold series of *Under the Northern Sky* (1894), *In the Boundless* (1895), and *Stillness* (1898); and closed with another threefold series, *Buildings Afire* (1900), *Let Us Be like the Sun* (1903), and *Nothing but Love* (1903). *Let Us Be like the Sun*, to which the poet gave the subtitle "A Book of Symbols," won the acclaim of the critics as Bal'mont's highest achievement, even though it is merely the most typical, as well as the most popular, of his works. Keener judges feel, however, that Bal'mont's poetry reached its peak in *Nothing but Love*, and already saw a falling off of his powers in *The Liturgy of Beauty* (1905), with which Bal'mont's good season came to an end. The many volumes which appeared up to the time of the poet's departure from Russia, and the fewer and slighter ones which he published in the first decade of his exile, are hardly worthy of being mentioned and well deserve the oblivion which was their immediate lot. With rare and random exceptions, the production of the late Bal'mont reveals the decline of his talent into mediocrity and mannerism.

The main body of Bal'mont's literary output is taken up by his translations, many of which are in prose, including not only plays by Ibsen, Hauptmann, Wilde, and Maeterlinck, or tales by Hoffmann and Hamsun, but even biographical and scholarly works. Yet the most and the best of them are verse renderings of works of poetry, which almost consistently follow the rhythmical structure of the original texts. Bal'mont's poetic versions include a collection of Spanish folk songs; five plays of Calderón; a large selection of Walt Whitman's *Leaves of Grass*; Wilde's *Ballad of Reading Gaol*; a vast anthology of primitive, archaic, exotic poems, which the translator himself collected under the title *Appeals from Antiquity*

(1908); many renderings of the works of the great Romantic Slowacki and of other modern masters of Polish, Czech, Bulgarian, and Lithuanian verse; and finally, an endless series of translations from modern lyrical poets of the West (Goethe, Heine, Coleridge, Wordsworth, Byron, Rossetti, Tennyson, Baudelaire, Leopardi, Espronceda, and so on), some of which the poet included in *From World Poetry*, an anthology published in Berlin in 1921.

From the viewpoint of their scope, timeliness, and influence, this author's most important translations are, however, those of the complete poetic writings of Shelley and Poe, which seem to typify in an extreme manner all the virtues and vices of Bal'mont as an interpreter and an adapter of another poet's work. For better or worse, Bal'mont transformed Shelley's "The Sensitive Plant" and "The Skylark," and Poe's "The Raven" and "Ulalume" into Russian poems, or rather into poems of his own, although critics and scholars have different views concerning the merits of his performance in either case or in both. In his renderings of those two poets, as he was always wont to do, Bal'mont vastly expanded the original, intensifying as much as possible its rhythmical and phonetic effects. While all judges agree that he failed with Shelley, a few insist that he succeeded, at least in part, with Poe. If this is true, then Bal'mont's relative success in this case may well be explained by the greater opportunity which the American's poems seem to offer to a translator intent on displaying all his verbal fireworks. There is no better example of Bal'mont's inborn virtuosity, as well as of his translating practice, unchecked by any inhibition or restraint, than his rewriting of "The Bells," where, by enlarging and stressing the sound pattern of the refrain, he changed the tinkling rattle of Poe's sledge bells into a deafening din.

Modesty was not one of Bal'mont's virtues, and he felt no compunction in praising emphatically his own contribution to the renovation of Russian verse. "I have shown what can be done for Russian poetry by a poet who loves music," he proudly stated in one of his prefaces. In an autobiographical note composed in 1907, he proclaimed: "I affirm with calm assurance that before me no one knew how to write sonorous verses in Russian. . . . In me there is a sense of eternal youth. People maintain that *Let Us Be like the*

Sun is the best of my books. This is absurd. I am in a state of per-petual motion: such is my nature. . . ." In a poem of that book, after declaring that he had found "the contours of dreams never revealed before," he concluded: "I broke the glass of sound." Later, in one of the most famous lyrics he ever wrote, to which he gave the form of a prosopopoeia with the personification of his poetry speaking on his behalf, he defined himself as "the exquisite flower of the slow Russian speech"; asserted that all the poets who had come before him had been mere "precursors"; boasted that he had been the first to discover the curves of his native idiom; and finally ended by saying: "I am the perfect verse." There is no doubt that Bal'mont had an exaggerated opinion of his own merits, yet it re-mains true that he accomplished almost single-handedly a genuine rhythmical revolution, which sounded the death knell of late nine-teenth-century Russian verse. Bal'mont, said Maksimilian Voloshin, "found the Russian verse weary and frozen. He softened it, and because of him, it will always ring with a new sound."

The analysis of a single stanza, taken from a poem where the poet compares himself to the wind, will suffice to give an idea of Bal'mont's technique and craftsmanship. The meaning of its four lines may be literally rendered with the following words, where the reader will notice the overpowering presence of the pronoun "I," or rather, since the Russian verb allows the omission of pro-nouns, of verbal forms in the first person: "I am the free wind, I always blow; I stir the waves, I fondle the willows; I sigh amid leaves, silently I sigh; I lull the grasses, I lull the crops." The orig-inal reads thus:

> *Ja vol'nyj veter, ja vechno veju,*
> *volnuju volny, laskaju ivy,*
> *v vetvyakh vzdykhaju, vzdokhnuv nemeju,*
> *leleju travy, leleju nivy.*

Even a reader unacquainted with the Russian tongue may recognize some of the elements forming the sound pattern of these lines: the rich alliterations *vol'-nyj, vol-nuju, vol-ny*; the alliterative repeti-tion *vzdykh-aju, vzdokh-nuv*; the simple repetition *leleju, leleju*; the anaphorical endings *v-eju, voln-uju, lask-aju*; the identical end-ings *nem-eju, lel-eju*; the consonance between the words *travy* and *nivy*, the one placed at the caesura, and the other at the end, of the last line. To this one must add the absolute symmetry of the structure: every line is divided into two parts, each one of which consists of a double iamb with a feminine ending. Finally, if we except the first line of this quatrain, and fail to count in the others the double appearance of a monosyllabic pronoun and the presence of a preposition consisting of a single consonant, we shall see that every hemistich is formed by two words of either two or three syllables, the one being a verb, and the other a noun.

The passage quoted reveals at once the positive and negative qualities of Bal'mont's diction and style, and suggests why his art was bound to degenerate, by an excess of virtuosity, into the vice which the critic Kornej Chukovskij was later to call by a Russian term which sounds more like "bal'montitis" than like "bal'mont-ism." This degeneration led to the triumph of an empty sonority, which denied by itself the poet's claim of his own "musicality." It is obvious that what we term the melody or the harmony of verse is something very different from the melody or harmony of a musical composition. Thus, when we speak of the music of poetry, we must realize that we are doing so only metaphorically, and we must also refuse to reduce that music, as well as music in general, to the materiality of its sounds. In poetry rhyme should agree with reason, and this is why one could repeat for Bal'mont what T. S. Eliot said of a poet whom the Russian resembles on many grounds: "What we get in Swinburne is an expression of sound, which could not possibly associate itself with music." In Bal'mont as well as in Swinburne language and the object which it should represent "are identified solely because the object has ceased to exist, because the meaning is merely the hallucination of meaning. . . ."

It is not only this aspect of his work that separates Bal'mont from the better among his contemporaries, who were, like Brjusov, more controlled, or, like Sologub, far more conscious craftsmen. What distinguishes Bal'mont from them, as well as from the poets of the following generation, is on the one hand the vitality and exuberance of his talent, and on the other, his lack of self-consciousness and self-restraint. He is the only Russian poet of his time who could sometimes indulge in a panic enthusiasm recalling

93

D'Annunzio, or in a cosmic optimism which reminds one of Walt Whitman. Thus, at least psychologically, Bal'mont is far from being a Decadent, although the term reacquires its validity if used as a merely literary label, as a summary description of his literary experiences. By nature a neoromantic, Bal'mont becomes a Decadent by choice or by pose; but, unlike D'Annunzio, he fails to develop the dialectics of Decadence, which implies a paradoxical sympathy for the primitive and the barbaric.

Like D'Annunzio, however, Bal'mont sings the praises of life, understood as the triumph of nature and the feast of the senses. This is especially true of the work of his maturity, when he was tempted by more vital lands and warmer climates, and went, in words as well as in deeds, "from the northern sky to the bright South." Bal'mont was often able to evoke the charms of winter and the subdued beauty of the melancholic landscapes of his native land, the "languid tenderness" of the Russian countryside, as he did in a poem entitled with an abstract word of his coinage, which reads in English like "Ineffability"; and once he went as far as to proclaim: "lovelier than Egypt is our North." Yet, all this notwithstanding, he will be primarily remembered as the poet of summer. Like the early Belyj, Bal'mont is the singer of the sun, which, however, he celebrates as a cosmic power rather than as a symbol of the godhead. Life is for him a solar experience. One of his most famous poems opens with the proclamation: "I came into this world to see the sun and the blue horizon," and ends with the announcement: "I shall sing of the sun in the hour before death." At least three of his books, *Let Us Be like the Sun*, *Buildings Afire*, and *The Firebird* (1907), indicate by their very titles his worship of heat and light, his obsession with the sun as reality and myth. It is in the sun that he personifies himself, both as a man and as a poet, and Boris Zajtsev was right when he said that Bal'mont's poetry reflected, or even embodied, "the face of Helios."

Yet, like D'Annunzio, Bal'mont celebrated not only Helios, but all the elemental powers of nature, identifying himself with each of them. In the poem "The Gospel of Being" he preached the imitation not only of the sun, but also of the wind and the sea, enjoining all men to heed the commands he had received from those

94

elements: from the wind, to be volatile; from the sea, to be ever-changing; from the sun, to burn. As this threefold command easily proves, Bal'mont's poetry does not limit itself to the expression of the joy of being, although it is there that it achieves its highest feats. Some of the better poems of his later years evoke those moments of our experience when the fever of life seems to subside, when "the unpurged images of day recede" and give place to the night of the soul. Two good examples of such a shift of mood are two simple, allegorical poems, "The Gull" and "The Swan," which take up again the romantic theme of the poet as a heavenly spirit exiled to this earth, but which express with calm resignation his all-too-human doubts and griefs.

Bal'mont's originality lies in two factors, both of which operate at the margins, rather than at the center, of his work. The first one is psychological, and has to do with his temperament, which seems not to differ too much from that of many modern poets of the West, but looks rather singular when compared with the personality types most frequently occurring in the history of Russian poetry. The second factor is technical, and concerns his exceptional virtuosity, which is an almost monstrous phenomenon, precisely because it works spontaneously and flows endlessly, led by no conscious aim, unchecked by any critical insight. In brief, we have to do with an originality founded on passivity: and this is why one could use as an emblem for Bal'mont's art Pushkin's lovely poem likening the poet to an echo responding to any call. Unfortunately, Bal'mont's poetry is incapable of responding to the appeals of life and reality with the simple and natural fidelity of an echo or of an Aeolian harp: it alters and reforms the sounds it hears, almost without listening to them; and it sends them back, magnificent, magnified, and magniloquent, with romantic reverberations, from the resounding cave of the poet's soul. Each one of Bal'mont's poems seems to grow hypertrophically, by assimilation and diffusion, rather than by evolving slowly from its own seed. This explains why this poet devoted so much of his creative activity to translation; this may even suggest that he behaved as a translator even when composing works of his own.

The implication that Bal'mont is a translator even as an original poet has nothing to do with the Romantic conception of *Poesie der Poesie*, according to which the poet gives voice to the mute and passive poetry hidden in the bosom of nature, nor with the Symbolistic view of the poet as a decipherer and interpreter of the mystical riddles of the universe. Bal'mont is a translator in the sense that he imitates nature and life without conscious artificiality, but with approximate and exaggerated images, where he mirrors himself even more than his objects. His genius is in substance that of an *improvvisatore*, as Bal'mont avowed in the poem where he defined himself as "the exquisite flower of the slow Russian speech." "I grasp all, I take all, depriving others," said the poet in another line of the same poem, with the selfish, uncritical pride which is characteristic of every virtuoso. In another piece he described with a naïve ostentation his own creative method, which is no method at all, as this passage may easily show: "Suddenly my strophe is born, another rises without hesitation; already a third shines from afar; smilingly, a fourth joins the race; whence and how many I never know. . . ." And the poet concludes, blissfully unaware of the implications of his statement: "Truly I never compose. . . ." In the poem where he claimed to be born into this world to see the sun, Bal'mont asked the rhetorical question: "Who is my equal in singing power?" and answered it simply: "No one, no one." Ultimately the improviser is but a performer; and Bal'mont may have failed to realize that his self-appraisal as a peerless singer was perhaps more than a flowery metaphor. Posterity may well take that definition literally, and view him as a maestro of *bel canto*, as the greatest tenor of Russian poetry.

II

VALERIJ BRJUSOV

Valerij Brjusov was born in 1873 in a family of prosperous Moscow traders. He felt the call of the muses when he was still in his teens, and acted from the very beginning not as an amateur, but as a professional man of letters. He planned early his future career, part of which was to be devoted, as he said later, to "the initiation of young Russian writers into the French poetry of the nineteenth century." Brjusov made this statement in the preface he penned for Jean Chuzeville's French anthology of Russian twentieth-century verse, while on another occasion, when asked to write a short autobiographical sketch, he willingly defined himself as a pupil of the very teachers he had set as examples for his younger colleagues: "I began to write poetry very young, but it was only at the age of thirteen that I felt myself truly a poet. In the early nineties I became familiar with the poetry of Verlaine and Mallarmé, and a little later with Baudelaire's. Thus I discovered a new world. The first poems I published were composed under the influence of my readings in French literature. . . ."

When he was hardly more than twenty years of age, Brjusov had already translated Maeterlinck's *Pelléas et Mélisande* and Verlaine's *Romances sans paroles*, and had gathered around himself a group of youthful enthusiasts of the new poetry. In 1894, with some help on the part of his friends, he edited and published the pamphlet *Russian Symbolists*, which contained versions from a few French masters (Baudelaire, Verlaine, Mallarmé, Rimbaud, Maeterlinck), and original, although derivative, poems, mainly signed by himself. This first pamphlet, and the two which followed suit, had a *succès de scandale*. The daily and the periodical press treated Brjusov and his companions like knaves and fools, and chose as main objects of their scorn some of Brjusov's most daring images, like the one projecting "violet hands on an enameled wall," and especially a single-line poem of his, reading simply: "Oh cover your pale legs." Vladimir Solov'ev himself mockingly reviewed the three issues, and closed the review of the last with a series of felicitous parodies which sounded almost like replicas of the samples of new poetry presented in Brjusov's pamphlets.

Those samples shocked public opinion by offending not only its standards of taste, but also its ethical norms, and for a while Brjusov was treated as a public enemy of both morality and art. The young poet took all this in his stride, and challenged even further his elders and all the upholders of respectability and tradition by entitling as *Chefs d'oeuvre* (1895) the first collection of poems which appeared under his name. In the preface he added to the boastful insolence of that title by making assertions as outrageous as these: "In its present shape, this seems to me a perfect book. I never felt as sure of myself as I feel now, while bestowing it upon eternity." *Chefs d'oeuvre* was followed by *Me eum esse* (1897) and *Tertia Vigilia* (1900), but it was only after the turn of the century that Brjusov published his two masterpieces, *Urbi et Orbi* (1903) and *Stéphanos — Wreath* (1906). While Brjusov's earlier books had been primarily influenced by the usual French models, Baudelaire, Mallarmé, and especially Maeterlinck, the poetry of his maturity found its formal ideals in Gautier, the Parnassians, and even in Pushkin, from whom he learned how to master pathos and to control words. From the viewpoint of thematic novelty, the later Brjusov was one of the first to follow the example of a more recent and lesser poet in French, who was a Belgian like Maeterlinck, and who was then heading the so-called Flemish Renaissance. That poet was Emile Verhaeren, whose works Brjusov translated into Russian, and whom he imitated, perhaps with greater success than the original model, in the attempt to celebrate in urban terms what Baudelaire had called *l'esprit de la vie moderne.*

Urbi et Orbi, and especially *Stéphanos*, gained for Brjusov that recognition by the world at large which he richly deserved, and which up to then had been denied him. Within the circle of his peers he was already respected as a master and followed as a leader. Endowed as he was with remarkable practical abilities and with great promotional and organizational gifts, he had been from its very beginning the prime mover of all activities connected with the "Scorpion" publishing firm. From 1904 to 1909, as we already know, he held the *de facto* if not *de jure* editorship of the *The Scales*, the magnificent review issued by that press. This leading editorial position made Brjusov the dictator of Russian literary life at the very time when his importance, if not his reputation, as a poet was already on the wane. If *Roads and Crossroads*, a revised and selected edition of all his previous poetry, which appeared in 1908, confirmed his standing without adding anything to his fame, the following collections, *All Melodies* (1910) and *The Mirror of Shadows* (1912), already marked the decline of Brjusov's creative powers.

Brjusov was not only a poet, but also a storyteller and a playwright. In 1907–1908 he published his important novel, *The Fiery Angel*, from which the composer Sergej Prokof'ev was later to take the libretto for the opera by the same name. The place and time of the novel is the Germany of the early Reformation; the narrator is a mercenary soldier with humanistic leanings, in whom Brjusov mirrored himself, as he reflected in the story a rather unsavory episode of his life, his rivalry with Andrej Belyj for the love of a strange, hysterical woman, who reappears in the novel in the shape of a witch. The plot itself deals with a case of witchcraft, evoked in an aura of reality and fancy, of history and legend. In the background of the novel there appear such shadowlike figures as Cornelius Agrippa and Doctor Faustus. Beautifully written, *The Fiery Angel* is not so much a historical novel as an archaeological tableau in the manner of Flaubert's *Salammbô*. The same can be said of another novel, *The Altar of Victory* (1913), set in the Rome of the fourth century; while *The Republic of the Southern Cross* (1910) is a political fantasy not too different in spirit from the play *The Earth*, a verse drama written in 1905. In both of them the utopia of the future is treated as a nightmare, rather than as a dream.

Except for several stories, some of which are tales of horror and wonder in the manner of Edgar Allan Poe, the rest of Brjusov's literary heritage is taken up by translations and criticism. The translations, besides the items already mentioned, include versions of two Decadent tragedies, D'Annunzio's *Francesca da Rimini* and Wilde's *The Duchess of Padua*, as well as a late anthology of Armenian poetry, published in 1916. His outstanding contribution in this field is, however, a version of the *Aeneid*. Most of Brjusov's critical essays, the best of which are perhaps those on Pushkin and Tjutchev, were collected by him in *Far and Near Ones* (1911). Among his critical writings one should, however, also mention his reinterpretation of Gogol', strangely entitled *Man Burnt to Ashes* (1908); the aesthetic manifesto "Key of Mysteries," originally published in *The Scales* (1904); and, finally, many technical studies about the structure of verse and rhyme, of meter and rhythm.

Brjusov composed most of these technical studies after the end of his creative period, which closed with 1917. In 1914 he had been one of several Russian poets who saluted the war; in 1917 and after he was the only writer of his generation who not only welcomed the Revolution, but collaborated freely and willingly with the Soviet regime. He even joined the Communist Party, and accepted a position in the Commissariat (Ministry) of Education. Yet his ready compliance with the new order failed to restore Brjusov to that position of influence and prestige which could give him a sense of security and self-respect. What later enabled him to stand the horrors of Soviet life was perhaps his exclusive and inalterable devotion to the cause of culture and art. He served that cause by lecturing on poetry at the University of Moscow, by instructing in verse-craft a group of proletarian apprentices, by continuing his activities as a translator and as a critic, and, finally, by composing a series of technical and metrical exercises, which he published in 1919 under the proper heading of *Experiments*. After issuing another collection of poems, sadly entitled *Last Dreams* (1921), Brjusov died in his native city in 1924, hardly more than fifty years of age, but already an old man, sick in body and spirit.

It is claimed that Brjusov could give his allegiance to the Red state only because no faith of any kind, whether religious or political, had ever attracted him. This is true; yet his decision to accept the new faith may have been dictated also by a sense of historical fatalism. If he bowed to the dictatorship of the proletariat, it was perhaps because his prophetic insight had anticipated it. He had done so at the time of the Russo-Japanese War and the Revolution of 1905, in one of the poems of *Stéphanos*, "The Coming Huns," an apocalyptic vision announcing the imminent irruption from the East of a new barbaric horde. The poet foresaw that the invading conquerors would free the enslaved masses, and that the latter would show their joy by making bonfires of books. Then scholars and artists would save their treasures in caves and catacombs, knowing that sooner or later those treasures would be destroyed by the barbarians, but wondering whether chance would ultimately preserve any of their labors for posterity's benefit. Yet, speaking in the first person for all his peers, and sharing their terrors and doubts, Brjusov concluded his prophecy in the spirit of what the ancients called *amor fati*, greeting the coming Huns "with a hosanna and a hymn."

If Brjusov could thus salute the new barbarians destined to bring destruction and ruin to his world, it was perhaps because he was a barbarian himself, although a regenerated one. Brjusov had mastered the cultural experience of modern Europe with the aggressive spirit of a Scythian taking possession of the learning and wisdom of Greece; or with the singleness of purpose of a rude man of the North, coming down to Renaissance Italy to rediscover the mystery of ancient beauty, and to unveil again the Graces and the Muses. Some of Brjusov's contemporaries, remembering that he came from a merchant's family, compared him to a tradesman's son, bringing home from Europe's emporia not only commodities but also *objets d'art*. Brjusov, however, was not a mere acquirer of culture, but a conqueror too. It was this aspect of his character that earned him the nickname of "little Napoleon," although he was rather a Peter the Great in miniature, who almost single-handedly westernized Russian poetry anew. He reduced this process of westernization almost exclusively to the reshaping of Russian literary culture after the pattern of French modernism, although he preferred to symbolize that process under the transparent mask of the frequent Latin titles (*Me eum esse, Tertia Vigilia, Urbi et Orbi*) which he chose for his works. Once he selected a Greek title in Greek characters, followed by its Russian equivalent (Στέφανος — *Venok*); and he dared to entitle his first collection of poems (*Shedevry — Chefs d'oeuvre*) with a glaring Gallicism. It is true that Brjusov often wandered in other spiritual regions than that of *doulce France;* yet, by turning toward such writers as Poe, Wilde, and D'Annunzio, he again paid a tribute to the French spirit, since those authors had become part of France's literary empire. Thus it is only fair to compare the task which Brjusov fulfilled in his own nation and time to that which Horace had accomplished for the poetry of classical Rome, and of which he had boasted in "Exegi monumentum": like the Roman poet, who had transposed the song of Greece into Latin modes, Brjusov gave a Russian voice to the poetry of France.

This was perhaps Brjusov's highest achievement: a fact obviously implying that for him formal values claimed precedence over all other ideals or concerns. One could almost say that he failed to take seriously any problems except those of form. He avowed as much in the poem "I," where he proudly stated that his spirit had never languished "in the haze of contradictions": a not-too-oblique reference to the tendency of too many of his contemporaries to lose lucidity of vision and firmness of hand in the clouds of metaphysical speculation. In another poem he directly apostrophized the "God-seekers" of his age, telling them that he felt estranged from their controversies about God and Satan, Christ and the Antichrist. Elsewhere he described this estrangement in terms of universality and open-mindedness, such as the desire to sail with the boat of his poetry on any sea, and to celebrate at once Jehovah and Lucifer. In "I" he expressed the same view, and painted himself as a spirit endowed with a gift for total understanding, with a many-sided ability to experience and feel everything: "I love all dreams, I hold dear all tongues, I consecrate one line to every god." Such an indiscriminate sympathy for all creeds is but the effect of a fundamental indifference to any form of belief, and the poet hastens to acknowledge, with great honesty, that he was born to play not the role of an apostle or teacher of truth, but merely of a student, eager to learn from his betters the secrets of thought and form: "I visited the groves of Lyceus and Academe, marking on wax the sayings of the wise; a faithful disciple, I was loved by all, while loving only the conjunctions of words."

Brjusov must have held very dear this closing formula, since he repeated it in "To the Poet," a piece which is an *ars poetica* in a psychological key, and in imperative terms. The repetition occurs in the passage where Brjusov claims that life is but a pretext for the composition of resounding rhymes, and where he enjoins the poet to seek forever "the conjunctions of words." Among the other commands which Brjusov addresses there to the poet are those to be as proud as a flag and as sharp as a blade, and, above all, to follow Dante's example, by letting "the underground flame" burn one's cheek. Here Brjusov speaks with the voice of Baudelaire and Rimbaud: by the poet's duty to go through hell-fire he means that he must search for *paradis artificiels*, that he must strive after *le dérèglement de tous les sens*. In brief, Brjusov maintains that the artist must taste the fruit of the tree of knowledge, in order to experience good and evil, and thus to become an angel and a demon, a superman and a demigod. Yet in the following stanza Brjusov speaks rather with the voice of Flaubert, preaching on one side the gospel of artistic impassibility: "contemplate everything, but be a cold witness of all," and, on the other, the related and contradictory doctrine of the artist's sacrifice and martyrdom: "that your virtue be a readiness to climb the pyre where you will burn." The poem ends on this note, with the assertion that the secret wreath of the poet is but a crown of thorns.

Some of these views are but replicas of the literary commonplaces of the time (as shown by the morbid poem where, reshaping in decadent terms a Christian myth, Brjusov compares the sufferings of his soul to Saint Sebastian's martyrdom); and yet this does not mean that Brjusov restates them in a spirit of fashionable imitation or pose. If this poet ever believed in anything, it was in the ideas connected with aestheticism, which has already been defined as the attempt to lower existence to the status of the raw material of poetry and to reduce life to the condition of art. For Brjusov, it is not experience that determines creation, but creation that determines experience: the poet must go through a novel ordeal only in order to create a new form of art. All of Brjusov's psychological metamorphoses were due not to moral conversions or spiritual crises, but to the shifts of his own aesthetic interests, to the desire to carry out a rare experiment, to develop a theme still untouched.

It is quite significant that Brjusov achieved his most successful artistic effects at the opposite ends of his thematic range, by working on subject matters challenging him to become either as ancient or as modern as possible. In the first case we have to do with the cycle of poems which he collected in *Stéphanos* under the heading of "The Everlasting Truth of the Idols," or more generally, with all the pieces he wrote on classical scenes or pagan myths. We find among them perhaps some of Brjusov's highest poetic feats, for instance, "The Last Supper," which does not deal with Christ's passion, despite its title, but with the suicide of an old and tired Roman couple, who choose to die after an orgy, while their drunken guests are asleep. Other poems of this kind are "Achilles at the Altar," depicting the Greek hero waiting for his fatal wedding with Polyxena; "Medea," representing that barbarian heroine while she flees the scene of her crimes on her dragon-driven chariot; "Orpheus and Eurydice," which, like many other of such pieces, is written in dialogue form. It was this group of poems, hammered or chiseled out of a hard and noble matter, that earned for Brjusov the label of "poet of marble and bronze" which Belyj awarded him.

When he followed, however, the example of Verhaeren's *Villes tentaculaires*, and wrote poems celebrating the throbbing life of the great modern centers in a spirit already anticipating Futurism itself, Brjusov worked instead, to use the words he employed in his poem "To the City," in "steel, brick, and glass." Yet, unlike the Futurists, he used only rarely the new medium of free verse and preferred to sing of the beauty and horror of urban life in traditional meters. The most important of his urban poems are perhaps "To the City" and "Eventide," both of which are written in regular rhythms. In the former Brjusov evoked the modern metropolis in a vision of fabulous realism, as a machinelike monster, devouring everything, and yet generating from its very entrails the poisons which will be the cause of its death. In "Eventide" (or, more literally, "The Flow of Evening") Brjusov painted the gold and tinsel of the metropolis at dusk, with the crude light of its lampposts and shopwindows, with the "sheaves of fire" and "blue lightnings" flung by its autos and streetcars; and closed the poem with a hymn to the real ruler of our urban civilization, "Her Majesty the Dust." If in his city poems Brjusov became for a while the poet of industrialism and capitalism, in his "factory songs" he sought instead to express the self-consciousness of the urban proletariat, of those masses building a civilization of which they were the slaves rather than the masters. Yet what led Brjusov to write these pieces was not a sense of sympathy for the working class, but perhaps the simple desire to attune the accents of modern poetry to the strains of the Russian folk song.

All this seems to suggest that the real muse of Brjusov was deliberation itself. Nothing better proves this truth than the lyric where, speaking in the first person, the poet compares himself to a plowman, and addresses his "dream" as his "faithful ox." Man and animal plod abreast along the field, toiling without rest or relief; and when the poet-plowman feels that his oxlike dream is failing in its effort, he incites it with his voice and excites it with his goad. This parable is almost symbolic of Brjusov's art, which is based on strenuous exertion, and on a constant will: a will ruling even over imagination or inspiration, which is what the poet here means by the word "dream." It was this quality of Brjusov's genius that led the critic Julij Ajkhenval'd to compare him to the protagonist of Pushkin's *Mozart and Salieri*, to that Salieri who had sacrificed all, with supreme devotion, to the art of music, and who could not comprehend why God had graced with an effortless creative power such a simple and naïve being as Mozart, unable to take seriously even his divine gift. Yet, precisely because he resembled Salieri, Brjusov felt the overpowering seduction of the Mozart-like wonders of Pushkin's art, up to the point of trying to complete a tale in verse and prose, *The Egyptian Nights*, which Pushkin had left unfinished. Brjusov did not do this to compete with the greatest of all Russian poets, but only to pay a tribute to his greatness, as a token of admiration and a sign of worship. The man who once said of himself, "I would rather not be Valerij Brjusov," sacrificed even his ego for the sake of his art. He never thought of himself as a god of poetry, but as one of its priests; he acted more like the servant than the master of his craft. Posterity may deny him lasting fame, but it will always respect his name at least for what Mallarmé, in his "Toast funèbre" to the memory of Théophile Gautier, called *la gloire ardente du métier*.

III

FEDOR SOLOGUB

Bal'mont and Brjusov are the most significant examples of the Decadent movement in Russia, even though they chose to call themselves Symbolists. This is not very surprising: after all, even in France, there had been only a small group of insignificant writers, for the most part bohemians and social outcasts, who had dared to label themselves as *Décadents*. Thus in Russian literary history the terms "decadence" and "decadent," never displayed in any literary manifesto or program, belong almost exclusively to the critical vocabulary, and sometimes to the polemical one. The literary historians themselves preferred to speak of "decadence" in the abstract, or of "decadents" in general, rather than to speak, individually and concretely, of a "decadent" writer or work. This is, after all, the best way to proceed; it is only what the poets of that time have in common that the label presumes to define, at least in simplified and abridged form. The very fact that it is used only in order to suggest a historical condition deprives the label of its sting, and reduces it, at least up to a point, to a neutral, descriptive term. This gives the historian the right to gather under that heading writers who preferred to call themselves otherwise, for instance, Symbolists; or who refused to accept either label; or who seemed to stand apart from both groups.

It is my contention that none of the poets who emerged in Russia from the closing years of the past century to the end of the first decade of the present one was able to transcend in full the decadent genius of the culture within which each one of them acted both as seed and fruit: and this is no less true of those whom I define as Symbolists in the narrow sense of the term. Thus, without fear of contradiction or unfairness, I shall consider in the remainder of this chapter three authors who, despite their different stands toward, or even against, some of the trends of the epoch, still represent the spirit of their age, even if they do so, at least in one case, against their own conscious intent. All of them were affected in different degrees by at least one or two of the main components of *fin du siècle* culture, which were a morbid dualism in the sphere of morality and religion, a double allegiance to the traditional and the fashionable in the field of style, and the alternate tendencies to subordinate either art to life, or life to art. In brief, these authors were either mystics or immoralists, either modernists or aesthetes: in more than one case, they were perhaps all these things at once. The two oldest belonged to the same generation; as for the youngest, he seemed to belong to a different breed. The main literary trait they share is that all of them were not only poets, but also, and even primarily, storytellers and novelists. This is one of the reasons why they may appear less typical figures than many of their contemporaries, since the spirit of the age seemed to find a far more vocal and effective expression in the field of verse than in that of prose.

The oldest and foremost of these poet-novelists was Fedor Teternikov, better known under the pseudonym Sologub. The same surname, in a slightly different spelling, had adorned Russian letters in the middle of the nineteenth century, through the works of a popular narrator, Count Vladimir Sollogub. Unlike his namesake, Teternikov-Sologub was, however, a commoner: he was perhaps the only author of plebeian origins among all the Russian writers of his age group. Born in Petersburg in 1863, he soon lost his artisan father and was raised in the household where his mother worked as a domestic servant, thus sharing the early destiny of Strindberg, who was, like him, a "chambermaid's son." His mother's masters helped the youth to graduate from a teachers college. For many years a provincial schoolmaster, and later, an inspector of grammar schools, Sologub was finally transferred to the capital and remained connected with elementary education up to the time when he finally won wide literary recognition and material success. This happened more than ten years after he had published, in 1896, his first three books, a volume of verse, *Poems;* a collection of tales, which included also a few lyrics, *Shadows;* and the novel *Bad Dreams.* The latter describes the vegetative and yet tortured existence of a schoolmaster lost in the rut and routine of life. In 1904 Sologub published a volume of *Collected Poems,* followed later by his two best books of verse, *The Circle of Fire* (1908) and *Pearly Stars* (1913). After ten years of labor and five of waiting, in 1907 he was finally able to publish his masterpiece as a writer of fiction, the novel *A Petty Devil,* which won greater acclaim than any other Russian novel of that time. Its hero, Peredonov, is another provincial schoolmaster, representing not only the mire of life, but also the filth of the soul. The suggestive power of that characterization impressed readers and critics so much that Peredonov entered the ideal gallery of Russian literary types, to occupy there an almost unique place. The moral disease of which Sologub's book seemed to be the diagnosis was universally designated as

Peredonovism, a term which became as popular as Oblomovism or Saninism.

Peredonov, who is finally led to murder by the hallucinations and nightmares engendered in his sick mind by an obsessive persecution complex (he is constantly haunted by a mischievous feminine phantom, the so-called "Untouchable One" or *Nedotykomka*, one of the most original creations of Sologub's fancy), embodies evil as a senseless abomination, as an aberration without object. Against Peredonov, in whom evil is a revolting psychic ailment, a monstrous leprosy of the spirit, Sologub places a handsome couple of lovers, the boy Sasha and the older girl Ljudmila, his crafty and ruthless seducer. Their love has often been described as an idyll, but, if this is true, the idyll is a perverse one. Their wanton voluptuousness, which implies an ambiguous adoration of the beauty of the flesh, almost beyond the barrier of the sexes (Ljudmila, for instance, is fond of dressing Sasha like a girl), reflects the narcissism of the writer, and ends by conveying a view of life no less morbid and wicked than the one suggested by Peredonov's spiritual and physical ugliness.

Sologub produced many other narrative works after *A Petty Devil*, but none of comparable significance, except perhaps a few short stories. His most ambitious undertaking as a writer of fiction remains, however, the three-volume novel *A Legend in the Making* (1908–1912), which tells the complicated story of the revolutionary Trirodov, a nihilist who leaves reactionary Russia to become the king of a Mediterranean archipelago, which is dominated by a volcano, a symbol of perdition and ruin. If we add to all this a few more novels and tales, lesser collections of poems, a cycle of political satires in the form of fables, a translation of Kleist's *Penthesilea*, excellent versions of modern French poetry, and, finally, a series of plays, some of which are patterned after Hauptmann or Maeterlinck, we have practically the whole of Sologub's literary output. After the Revolution he withdrew from the foreground of the literary scene, although he issued two other collections of poems, and probably produced much which has been lost or left unpublished. Life under the Soviet regime was hell for Sologub, and in 1921 he and his wife were granted passports to go abroad. Shortly before their departure, in the fall of that year, Madame Sologub drowned herself in a fit of despair, and her body was recovered from the Neva only after the spring thaw. Sologub remained in Russia, and died in 1927 in Leningrad, after having for a few years survived his wife and himself, like a ghost.

Sologub's fame will rest primarily on *A Petty Devil*; yet, had he written only that, he would be remembered merely as a Russian Barbey d'Aurevilly, or at most, as a Russian Villiers de l'Isle-Adam. His name will, however, be recommended to posterity by his lyrics, which have earned their author a place of his own within the poetry of his time. Sologub's verse, no less than his prose, is ruled by a negative vision of life, expressed in terse images and sober speech. Here the "bad dreams" of his fiction become clear and lucid as objective visions; and one could fairly say that Sologub was better able than any of his Decadent brethren to fix languid and morbid moods into classic molds. His temperament was neurotic, but there was no hysteria in his art. The material of his inspiration is unhealthy; yet, unlike his peers, all too naturally led to express the sickly and the perverse in allusive and elusive terms, he always controls his frenzy and submits his own pathos to the severe ethos of form.

The Satanism of many other Decadent poets, not excluding Bal'mont and Brjusov, is often hardly more than a pose; and, as such, it is merely the reverse of Romantic sentimentalism. Sologub's Satanism is, however, a genuine reflection of his view of human life. Existence, especially that of modern man, seems to him a kind of nonexistence. Man goes through the limbo of being like a living corpse. Life is demonic not merely because it denies God, but also because God denies life, or, as the poet says, "God does not want life, and life does not want God." By identifying the human and the earthly with the demonic, Sologub lowers the human to the level of the subhuman and sinks the earthly underground. The demonic obsesses Sologub's imagination as much as that of Gogol' and Dostoevskij, yet the evil spirits he conjures resemble more the impish sprites of Gogol' than the black angels of Dostoevskij. Dostoevskij's devils are the projection of man's intellectual pride, the nemesis of what the great novelist called "the disloyalty of intelligence." Nothing could better explain their genesis than the profound caption of a famous etching by Goya: "The sleep of reason engenders monsters." It was perhaps from Dostoevskij that Sologub took the idea, and even the title, of his main novel; yet there are no "petty devils" in the work of that master, while the fiction of Gogol' and the poetry of Sologub are full of them. The regions or elements producing those perverse creatures are fancy and superstition; and this origin, while depriving them of symbolic power, strengthens their psychological significance, and endows them with a sense of reality which is at once eerie and grotesque. Sologub's mean demons may not be the evil geniuses of the soul, but they certainly are the malicious trolls of the psyche. Perhaps this is the reason why the poet treats them with the familiarity which one reserves for one's intimates or friends. Once he calls Satan his father, and considers all his minions as man's companions and helpmates, even if wicked ones. In the "Devil's Swing," the poet describes life as a swing: it is man who sits there, but it is the Devil who pushes him high and far, without pause or rest, waiting for the rope's break and the victim's downfall. This little, almost naïve, parable clearly reveals Sologub's tendency to reduce diabolism to the level of devilry, to a mischief even more cruel than outright Satanism.

Even more than in the Devil, Sologub believes in black magic. A sorcerer, rather than a wonderworker, he practices his witchcraft in the dim halfway region between death and life, in the no-man's-land of the spirit: "Far away from men, clad in blue silence, I work my spells." It was perhaps through one such spell that he produced the cycle of poems entitled "Masks of Experiences." This cycle deals with the theme of the successive incarnations of the soul in lower beings, and reaches its climax in the strangely beautiful song of a bitch, howling and whining at the full moon. In Sologub's poetry, human beings are rarely as lively and vocal as that poor brute, unless they are not yet grown up. The poet feels indeed that "only children are alive," while adults "have been dead for long." This is why his inspiration found its most moving strains in such a poem as "Simple Song," a lament in lullaby tunes, complaining over a boy killed by a stray bullet during the quelling of a riot. This lyric is as chaste and graceful as a funeral urn; one could say that all of Sologub's best poems are as light and shapely as an ancient vase, pure in form, even when impure in content. That Sologub must have been aware of this quality of his creation is shown by the poem "Amphora," in which he chose to describe his art as a beautiful vessel which a slave carries on his shoulder in perfect equilibrium, to prevent the liquid it holds from being spilled, since that liquid is not a drink but a poison. This ethical awareness redeems Sologub's poetry from the cheap and vulgar immoralism which stains such a large body of Decadent writing, and, along with his formal mastery, saves his work from neglect. It was not the vanity of an aesthete, but a lucid self-criticism, which led him to claim in one of his lyrics that all his sins as a man and as a poet would be remitted and forgiven because of a single merit, which was the purity of his craft. Sologub was right in this expectation: his name will be spared by the judgment of posterity; his poetry will escape that oblivion which is the nemesis of all artists who sin against their calling by bad faith, even more than by bad works.

IV

ZINAIDA GIPPIUS

The second of the authors to be discussed in this context is a woman, who belonged to the same generation as Sologub, who like him was a writer of both fiction and poetry, and who, while devoting only scant attention to the latter, except at the beginning of her career, was finally bound to gain far greater eminence, if not reputation, in the field of verse than in the field of prose. This woman is Zinaida Gippius, the lifelong companion of Dmitrij Merezhkovskij, of whom she was not only the wife, but also the Nymph Egeria. Born in Petersburg in 1869 to a family of Swedish descent, after her marriage she became the uncrowned queen of the literary life of the capital, making her home a more lasting center of attraction than even Vjacheslav Ivanov's "tower." Clever and beautiful (Rozanov and Blok suggestively described her as a "witch" and as a "water sprite"), she acted not only as the Sibyl but also as the Sylphide of the philosophical and religious circle that formed around her husband and herself. With the devotion of a disciple, but with a far greater literary intelligence than her husband's, she preached all her life Merezhkovskij's creed; and when the latter took the road to Damascus, which led him far away from aesthetic paths, she phrased the spiritual command of Merezhkovskij's conversion in two lines patterned on the slogan by which Nekrasov had once proclaimed the priority of civic duty over poetry itself: "You may be allowed not to be a poet, but you cannot avoid being a citizen."

Gippius' most important work of fiction is a novel, *The Devil's Puppet* (1911). Its literary importance is not great; yet it proves that even as a novelist Gippius was more gifted than her husband. The story conveys a tragic vision in the manner of Dostoevskij's *The Devils*. Like the latter it is a political novel, even though it is written from a different ideological standpoint. Its theme is the fatal failure, on the part of the political and spiritual leaders of the Russian Left, to help to build, during the ordeal of 1905, the new society and the new church of which they had been dreaming and preaching for so long. It is this failure that makes of those would-be angels and apostles not tragic "demons" but pathetic "devil's puppets."

The novel now has hardly more than historical interest, and there is perhaps more lasting merit in Gippius' lesser pieces of fiction, where she often shows a keen insight into the psychology of her sex. Her prose reaches its high point, however, in her excellent, although too subjective, critical essays, which are mainly psychological profiles and individual critiques, always lucid and often acid, for which she chose the masculine pen name Anton Krajnij ("Anthony the Extreme"), and which she collected in a two-volume work significantly entitled *Living Faces*. This work appeared abroad in 1925, since, after their disappointment with 1905, the Merezhkovskijs had refused to accept 1917 and its aftermath, and had gone together into exile, where Zinaida Gippius died in 1945, four years after her husband.

The best of Gippius' poetry is included in *Collected Poems*, published as early as 1904. In these lyrics, as well as in those written later, the poetess handles the commonplaces of the poetry of her time, generally suggested by a pessimistic conception of life and by an idealistic vision of the world. The central fable of her poetry is the ordeal of the spirit in its attempts to break away from the jail of reality, and to fly heavenward. Gippius treats this motif with great originality, but in impersonal accents, and with a kind of detached serenity. Naturally enough, she succeeds better when she describes the defeat of the spirit rather than its triumphs; not so much the soul's flight as its downfall. It is with repelling metaphors and drastic words that she depicts the vulgarity of daily life, the prosaic coarseness of our existence on earth. Nothing is more significant in this regard than the poem "Psyche," where she develops for her own purposes the image of the little, dark, empty room, with only cobwebs in its corners, by which Svidrigajlov, in Dostoevskij's *Crime and Punishment*, conveys his own nihilistic notion of the idea of eternity. The poem reveals Gippius' ability to express her own experience in terms of an abstract, cerebral wisdom, and to suggest her view of life in aphoristic and epigrammatic form. She converts images into ideas, and ideas into images, with no effort, almost at will. A perfect example of this is the poem "Electricity," where, by metaphorically using the scientific terminology connected with the phenomena of electric polarity, she translates the mechanical antitheses of her husband's nebulous metaphysics into a popular allegory, into a familiar myth.

v

IVAN BUNIN

The third and last of these poet-novelists is Ivan Bunin, who like the other two, is far better known, especially abroad, as a narrative writer. This is only fair in his case: while Sologub's poetry is at least as good as his fiction, and Gippius' verse is clearly superior to her prose, Bunin's lyrics can be hardly compared, from the viewpoint of both quantity and quality, to his novels and tales. Born in 1877 in Voronezh, to a decayed family of the landed gentry, counting among its ancestors the great Zhukovskij and Anna Bunina, a minor poetess of the early nineteenth century, Ivan

113

Bunin gained his first literary success with his translations from Byron, and especially with his masterful rendering of Longfellow's *Song of Hiawatha*. He earned, however, a more deserved and lasting fame with several collections of tales, the most important of which is named, from its title piece, *The Gentleman from San Francisco* (1916). Bunin published his early narrative works under the sponsorship of the publishing group *Knowledge*, headed by Maksim Gor'kij as an organ for those young realistic writers who wished to continue the great tradition of nineteenth-century Russian literature, with its concern for social reality and moral truth. As a writer of both prose and verse, Bunin took a disdainful attitude toward the modern movement, and proudly proclaimed himself a faithful disciple of the glorious masters of Russian realism. Yet as a novelist and a storyteller he seems to be not only the heir of Goncharov and Tolstoj, or the peer of Chekhov and Gor'kij, but also a belated follower (maybe the only one in the whole of Russian literature) of such French writers as Flaubert and the Goncourts, who took, or claimed to take, an attitude of poetic detachment toward the human and social realities they chose to represent.

It is perhaps this Western quality of his writing that in 1933 gained for Bunin the Nobel Prize, an honor never bestowed on any other Russian author before him. Yet this late Russian practitioner of *écriture artiste* was affected by the modern Russian movement far more than he cared to admit. While the tale which is his supreme masterpiece as a storyteller, "The Gentleman from San Francisco," is a perfect expression of the Flaubertian attempt to transcend life and to conquer death by fixing them forever in the enduring beauty of a marble-like form, his novel *The Village* (1910) is more than a matter-of-fact representation of Russian country life at the beginning of the century, since its realistic outlook is affected by an almost decadent sense of impending disaster. As for the novelette *Dry Valley* (1912), which occupies an exceptional, or rather, unique, place in the canon of Bunin's work, and which was written almost like a musical composition or a long prose poem, it may be considered the only genuine masterpiece which Russian Symbolism produced in narrative form.

Strangely enough, Bunin looks far more like a traditional realist in his verse than in his prose. His poetic production, limited in scope and narrow in range, must have appeared secondary and derivative even to Bunin himself. Description, which is one of the main staples of his fiction, is also one of the mainstays of his poetry, in which, however, it is used with greater taste and discretion. His verse is far more direct and laconic, far less heavy and ornamental than his prose, and this may be the reason why Vladimir Nabokov, an *émigré* author of great distinction, who was destined to become a successful writer in English, once said (perhaps with his tongue in his cheek) that Bunin the poet should be preferred to Bunin the writer of fiction. Short and simple, Bunin's lyrics draw with somber precision lucid landscapes and vivid scenes, which often have the significance of a neat allegory or of a plain parable. It is a pity that Bunin, who went into exile after the Revolution and died in France in 1954, as the grand old man of the Russian literary emigration, did not cultivate more the writing of verse: inferior as they are to his fictional works, the poems of this outstanding storyteller often reveal a good will toward life which is conspicuously absent from the stern and stark world of his prose.

CHAPTER FOUR

SYMBOLISM

I

THE LEGACY OF VLADIMIR SOLOV'EV

Out of the midst of Russian culture as it had matured from the end of the nineteenth century, there appeared at the beginning of the twentieth three men who, after having developed in isolation and silence, proclaimed themselves the prophets of a new faith, the harbingers of a new truth. For their creed or message they took the old name of Symbolism, an abstract term which the poets of the preceding generation had used less frequently than the more concrete Symbolist or Symbolists, and which the new men understood in other ways than their elders had. Yet the very fact that these three new poets, and all those who joined them, called themselves by the same label seems to imply that, while aware of being the announcers of a new tiding, they still felt themselves to be the heirs of the poets who had immediately preceded them. This is why it fell not upon the poets of either generation, whom the contemporary observers distinguished merely as old and new Symbolists, but to later critics to differentiate them sharply enough to designate the newcomers as Symbolists, and their predecessors as Decadents. The new group assigned itself the task of reinterpreting Symbolism in terms both more national and more universal: its three leaders, who were Vjacheslav Ivanov, Andrej Belyj, and Aleksandr Blok, made the bold attempt to supply Russian Symbolism with that mystical intuition and metaphysical insight which, all their theoretical declarations notwithstanding, earlier Symbolists both Russian and Western, perhaps with the exception of Baudelaire, had conspicuously lacked.

These three men, who grew and ripened at first without knowing each other — Ivanov in Germany, Belyj in Moscow, Blok in Petersburg — drew their doctrines from many, varied sources. Ivanov, the oldest of the three, had learned some of his lessons from Nietzsche; but later, like his two younger colleagues, he turned to a nearer, and perhaps fresher, spring: to the theological speculations of a Russian thinker of the end of the century, Vladimir Solov'ev. Brjusov and his school had already shifted the attention of Russian poetry toward the recent French example, and, although in lesser measure, toward other modern European experiences, but these new Symbolists spread their nets deeper and farther and drew their inspiration also from the poets of nineteenth-century Germany, especially from such early Romantics as Novalis. Poetry was their main, but not exclusive, concern, precisely because they placed it at the center of all cultural activity and considered it not the handmaid, but the sister, of theology. This is why, through or beyond the ways of poetry, they turned to all sorts of religious experience, in its cultivated as well as in its uncultivated forms, showing sympathy, interest, or at least curiosity for the strange and wild beliefs of the Russian dissenters, as well as for the Neoplatonic tradition or medieval mysticism. From the heretical eschatology of both sectarians and mystics they developed a messianism or a millenarianism of their own, conceiving the hope, both fanatic and vague, that they would witness in their own lifetime a Second Coming, or a New Advent.

From all these complex and perplexing doctrines they wrung an oppressing and obsessive sense of the haunting presence of supernatural powers, either good or evil, even in the world of everyday reality; and they viewed poetry both as a passive, almost mediumistic instrument, registering the emanation or irradiation of that presence, and as an active spiritual force, liturgical and theurgical in essence, producing epiphanies and portents. For them, poetic inspiration could derive only from religious initiation and ecstatic vision; this is why they conceived of their group as if it were a monastic order or a mystical sect rather than a literary school. Since they came at the right time, when idealism and spiritualism were again becoming fashionable, when a large section of the Russian intelligentsia felt perplexed and bewildered, longing not so much for a revival of the ancestral faith as for sentimental consolations and emotional thrills, they found an audience ready to listen to their siren voices and to be seduced by them. Their novelty surprised and impressed even those among their elders who could not change their ways and follow them or their new path; Brjusov himself greeted the new poets as "seers," although he considered them, to use the double title of one of his volumes of collected essays, as being both "near" to, and "distant" from, himself.

Brjusov would certainly have been unable to accept the creed of the new poets, whose gospel has often been summed up, by themselves and their critics, in the closing lines of Goethe's *Faust*:

Alles Vergängliche
ist nur ein Gleichniss;
das Unzulängliche
hier wird's Ereigniss;
das Unbeschreibliche
hier ist's getan;
das Ewig-Weibliche
zieht uns hinan.

It is indeed true that Ivanov, Belyj, and Blok started with the belief that even a passing phenomenon may be understood as a noumenon, or as a highly significant symbol; that the unreal, or, as they would have said, the ideal, may become act or deed; that even the ineffable may find, especially in poetry, voice and speech; and, above all, that through the mediation and the contemplation of the principle of love, of the Eternal Feminine, man may ascend to high heaven from this low world. The last of these beliefs was, as a matter of fact, the cornerstone of their faith; yet they drew it not so much from Goethe as from other poetic and mystical precedents, the most immediate and influential of which were the visions and the fantasies of Vladimir Solov'ev, the only modern Russian whom, along with Dostoevskij, they considered their apostle and master.

The brief span of Vladimir Solov'ev's life occupied less than the whole of the second half of the nineteenth century, since he was born in 1853 and died in 1900. Thus he practically belonged to the same generation as Chekhov, although the latter, in thought as well as in deed, represented that generation far more typically than Solov'ev. While Chekhov lived in the present, as a man of his own time and a child of the earth, Solov'ev lived either in the past or in the future, as a surviving ghost or as an untimely prophet. His great merit, or, more simply, his natural task, which endeared him forever to the Symbolists, was that of denying the main cultural trends of his own positivistic and ideological age, and of standing almost alone for the very spiritual values which both the leaders and the camp followers of Russian late-nineteenth-century thought had stood against. Even his adversaries were willing to recognize that Solov'ev was perhaps the first Russian thinker who was also a philosopher in the technical sense of the term, and that he had shaped a system as consistent and compact as any of the constructions of Western speculative thought. The Symbolists, however, did not admire and praise him for this, but rather for his extravagant mystical temper, for the transcendental digressions of his mind from the rational path. They paid tribute to him for having replaced nineteenth-century utilitarianism and materialism with a new idealism, not philosophical, but visionary and apocalyptic in temper. Solov'ev had indeed broken the tradition which had made philosophy the handmaid of politics and sociology, to make it again the handmaid of theology, although in a new and different sense. In so doing, Solov'ev had not only prepared the ground for Russian Symbolism, but had also laid the foundation for a school of religious thinkers which, like a new Platonic Academy, survived the downfall of Holy Russia and of the tsarist empire, by finding a new abode in the West and flourishing even in exile.

All of Solov'ev's disciples, whether avowed or not, followed his example in making the City of God the main object of their speculative concern. Like their master, and like their Symbolist brethren, they refused, however, to believe that no reconciliation is possible between the City of God and the City of Man; and in the messianic spirit of the Russian tradition, a spirit which they shared with their godless adversaries, with all those who believed in the secular religions of either revolution or progress, they still held fast to the hope that an ideal or heavenly order would sooner or later rule even the world of man. As we already know, some of them developed this hope into what they called "the religion of the Holy Ghost," which consisted in the apocalyptic expectation of the imminent advent of a third and final phase in human and sacred history: a phase to be ruled by the third person of the Trinity as the previous ones, the Biblical and the evangelical, had been ruled by the other two. This expectation was often tied to the old myth of Moscow as the Third Rome, to the belief that Russia was to become the last of the three kingdoms of the spirit. It may not be amiss to recall at this point that the first Russian who developed that myth, the early sixteenth-century cleric Filofej of Pskov, had derived the idea of the three Romes from the heterodox doctrines of an Italian mystic of the twelfth century, Joachim of Flora, who, like Solov'ev and his poetic disciples, had prophesied that the third person of the Trinity would sway the last age of the world in womanly form. All too many of Solov'ev's followers treated that incarnation as an allegory of Holy Russia, thus falling back on the Slavophile idealization of Orthodoxy, on a national messianism as narrow-minded as Dostoevskij's. When understood in this restricted sense, the religion of the Holy Ghost represented at least a partial deviation from the teachings of its master, who conceived the future mission of Russia in cosmopolitan terms, dreaming of the reunion of all Christian churches, and revealing outright Catholic sympathies just before his death. The only writer who was to follow, up to its final issue, the same path, was Vjacheslav Ivanov, whose ultimate conversion to the faith of Rome, determined as it was by the shattering impact of the Revolution and its aftermath, must still be viewed as the logical consequence of the dream of a really ecumenical church.

It was the same religious universalism, as well as a sane mistrust in the reactionary and nationalistic belief that the Russians were the only "god-bearing people" on earth, that had led Solov'ev to write the poem significantly entitled *Ex Oriente Lux*, ending with

the famous question whether the Russia of the future would conquer the West with the sword or with the cross, or, in the poet's
words, whether she would represent the East of Xerxes or the
East of Christ. If Solov'ev was perhaps still willing to give that
question an answer of doubtful hope, Aleksandr Blok would later
give instead the reply of despair, when in the revolutionary poem
The Scythians he proclaimed that Red Russia, seeing that the West
was unwilling to join hands with her, had no alternative but to
ruin Western civilization by opening the gates defending Europe
from Asiatic barbarism.

All the mystical and idealistic writers of the beginning of the
century found in Solov'ev's writings not only their Gospel, but
also their Apocalypse. Thus, for instance, the strange work he entitled *Three Conversations on War, Progress, and the End of
World History* (1899–1900) is but a prophecy of the imminent
coming of the Antichrist, which was to be literally accepted by
Dmitrij Merezhkovskij, who based on that prophecy his own absurd
philosophy of history. Others sought in Solov'ev's work a justification for their attempt to build a learned, syncretic religion,
grounded on the hypothesis that Christianity had been foreshadowed in the faiths of many nations and ages, especially of Oriental
antiquity. As for the Symbolists, particularly if they aspired to a
prophetic role, like Vjacheslav Ivanov, they were mainly attracted
by the two main utopias of Solov'ev's thought. The first of them,
which took the name of "free theosophy," consisted in the belief
that the mind could and should unify all fields of knowledge and
establish a synthesis of science, philosophy, and theology. The
other, which took the name of "free theocracy," was but a projection of the hope that human society could and should change into
a mystical commonwealth, under the suzerainty of the Holy Ghost.
Yet, even more than by Solov'ev's intellectual and moral utopias,
the Symbolists were influenced by his mystical and erotic myths.

The most important of these myths is that of the corporality
of the spirit, within which Solov'ev included such different notions as the Christian dogma of the double nature of Jesus, as "son
of man" and "son of God"; the worship of His Mother; and the
allegory of the Church as the bride, or the body, of Christ. It was

within the framework of this myth that Solov'ev introduced his own version of the Dostoevskian antithesis between the "god-man" and the "man-god." It is not the person but the human race which will redeem again the world once redeemed by the sacrifice of the man-god. The advent of what Solov'ev called "god-mankind" was for him the Second Coming, or another incarnation of the God-head; and it was on the expectation of this reincarnation, of this return of the dove of the spirit, that he based the chiliastic utopia of his own "free theocracy." In brief, Solov'ev founded both his evangelical and his apocalyptic beliefs on the cornerstone of the famous utterance in the Gospel of St. John: "and the Word was made flesh."

Solov'ev was not only the philosopher or the theologian of the Incarnation, but its mystic or seer. As such, he went beyond the letter and the spirit of that dogma and unfolded from it the hypothesis that the whole of creation is ruled by a single, all-embracing feminine principle. It was through that principle that Solov'ev introduced within the abstract scheme of his all-too-idealistic system of thought the intuition of the universal presence of the vital power of love, which generates life and conquers death. According to the spontaneous contradictions of his thought, Solov'ev now would consider that power as pure nature, as the energetic matter which the Greeks named ὕλη; and now would spiritualize and personify it into a mystical and divine feminine being, to which he gave the Gnostic name of Sophia. Sophia was for him what the mystics of Neoplatonism would have called the World-Soul: Solov'ev sometimes treated her as if she were another incarnation of the Holy Ghost, or even a hypostasy of the Mother of God; and he raised her, in his own version of Marian worship, almost to the status of a fourth person of the Godhead. At any rate, Solov'ev built around the figure or person of Sophia a theogonic and cosmogonic conception, which was but another variant of his doctrine of the identity of Word and World, of his notion of the spirituality of matter and of the materiality of the spirit.

The cult of Sophia was bound to become the main motif of Solov'ev's poetry, and, after him, of Russian Symbolism. His poetry is but a constant invocation of her name or a persistent evocation of her image. In his poems he depicts Sophia after the "woman clothed with sun" of the Book of Revelation, exalting her mystical presence in man's and life's nether world. The poet, who calls her the Eternal Friend, seems at times to believe that she is already on her way to bless mankind forever with her advent: "Know that now the Eternal Feminine here descends in a body incorruptible." Solov'ev celebrated Sophia not only in his lyrics, but also in his letters, as well as in other literary works, the most important of which is perhaps the narrative poem *Three Meetings* (1899). Here he reported the three apparitions of Sophia, as they had taken place within his own mystical experience, or rather, within the objective reality of his life. Solov'ev boasted of the same mystical precocity as Dante (who was nine years old when he had the first physical and spiritual revelation of his Beatrice), and claimed to have witnessed Sophia's earliest visitation when, still a child, he had recognized her image over the altar of a Moscow church. Her second appearance occurred, of all places, in the library of the British Museum; the third and last, in the Egyptian desert, near the Pyramids. Yet *Three Meetings* is not merely a transcription of three ecstatic visions or moments of grace; it is also a strange document of their very opposite, as well as of the nihilistic side of Solov'ev's enigmatic character. There and elsewhere Solov'ev revealed the tendency to put his own mystical insight to the acid test not only of a skeptical incredulity, but even of a blasphemous cynicism. In this, too, Solov'ev anticipated that sense of revulsion which Blok was later to feel for the object of his worship, and which led him to replace adoration with mockery, and idolatry with iconoclasm.

Solov'ev's poetry helped the Russian Symbolists not only to build the religion of their sect, but also to develop the poetics of their school. In this sense, its influence fully coincided with the literary theories of the foreign poets whom the earlier Russian Symbolists had taken as their own masters. Independently from them, and with greater literalness and emphasis, Solov'ev had stated in verse the view that poetry is the highest of all instruments of vision. Poetry was for him both the vessel and the vehicle of that "prophetic dream" which he viewed as the only means "to discover eternal truth." Only such a dream could help man to reconcile into a new harmony all the contrasting aspects of reality, or, in the poet's words, "to marry the white lily to the crimson rose." Solov'ev held the revelations of poetry to be both possible and necessary precisely because he believed that our perceptions of the physical world, even if only as dim reflections in a dark mirror, foreshadow a higher spiritual reality which we could not reach merely by means of our senses or our thoughts. Dear Friend, asks Solov'ev rhetorically in one of his poems, don't you see that all which appears to us is but a shadow of what escapes our sight? Don't you know that the visible is but a ray of the invisible, that the wordless dialogue of two hearts is but an expression of the ineffable? It is evident that such a mystical and poetic doctrine implied the use of that vague device which many others, before and after him, defined by the term "symbol," even though Solov'ev hardly used that word.

The modern reader of Solov'ev's poetry fails to be deeply impressed by it, and may find all too obsessive the conventional, Nordic background of his poems, perennially oppressed by the whiteness of their clouds, mists, and snowstorms; constantly haunted by the presence of too many phantoms or ghosts; all too feebly illuminated by the gemlike flicker of dying embers which give neither light nor heat. Yet the lover of Russian verse will recognize in them the anticipations of the elemental landscapes and of the ecstatic imagery which are such a great part of the poetry of the early Blok. Still, despite the varied manifestations of Solov'ev's influence, nothing was bound to affect the poets of Russian Symbolism as much as the enigmatic feminine being which had inhabited the wastelands of his imagination. The figure whom Solov'ev had called the Eternal Friend would reappear in Blok's early work under the name of the Beautiful Lady. Blok, Belyj, and Ivanov would make her not only the subject of their poetry, but also the object of their worship. And it was more than a coincidence that the youngest of all the members of the new cenacle, who was to join hands with Blok and Belyj, forming with them another triad, was the nephew of the philosopher and his spiritual heir, Sergej Solov'ev. The latter heeded more fully than the master or any other disciple the mystical call, and after having written a beautiful biography of his uncle and two charming books of poems, left forever the career of letters for the vocation of the priesthood.

II

THE SYMBOLIST MOVEMENT IN RUSSIA

It was not the first time in literary history, from the Provençal "courts of love" and Dante's *fedeli d'amore* to Novalis or to the Pre-Raphaelite Brotherhood, that poetry had turned into an apotheosis of womanhood, and that poets had acted as if they were the sacred servants of that cult. The poetry of erotic mysticism, which may be viewed as an offshoot of both Christian dogmas and Eastern heresies, whether understood allegorically or not, had always tended to shape itself into schools which were also sects. The reason for this may well be seen in those Gnostic or Manichaean doctrines and attitudes which in his book *L'Amour et l'Occident* Denis de Rougemont considers the original springs of the poetry of the troubadours, of the medieval romances, and of the modern mystique of passion and love. Still, among the poets of our time, none took the ritual of initiation and the liturgy of revelation so seriously as the founders of Russian Symbolism. They undertook their task with such single-minded devotion and simple-minded literalness that every one of them deserves being called a "knight-monk," to use the label which Blok was later to coin for their master Solov'ev. Yet the definition applies particularly well to Aleksandr Blok himself, who, in the naïveté of his youthful idealism, seemed to many also a reincarnation of the hero of a famous poem by Pushkin, the "poor knight" symbolizing that poverty and purity of spirit without which no quest after the Holy Grail can succeed. Dostoevskij had used Pushkin's "poor knight" as an emblem for the protagonist of *The Idiot*, the quixotic and Christ-like Prince Myshkin, and Blok resembled that character also, being like him endowed with a visionary gift while devoid of any power to redeem or to heal.

If Blok was the "seer" of the new faith, Belyj was the theologian who formulated its dogmas, and Sergej Solov'ev the priest who per-

125

formed its rites. When Blok married Ljubov' Mendeleeva, whose first name means "love" (and who, as her surname indicates, was the daughter of the great Russian scientist who founded modern chemistry, the discoverer of the periodic law and the framer of the periodic table of the elements), Belyj interpreted that private event in symbolic and mythical terms, as the alliance of poetry with the religion of love and with the magic of science. Blok's friends read her patronymic, Dmitrievna, as if it meant daughter of Demetra, instead of daughter of Dmitrij, and they saw in this the token of another spiritual harmony, joining poetry with the earth spirit, and pledging a new cosmic order.

The early Russian Symbolists were attracted not only by religious and metaphysical hopes, but also by less unworldly promises. They really believed that the return of the dove of the spirit would announce the emergence of a new human world from the receding waters of history's deluge. Blok expressed this expectation by hailing the "dawns" (*Zori*) of a new era, all the mystical signs which seemed to forebode the ascent of a brighter sun, the coming of a day without clouds. Yet the "dawns" of Blok were bound to be as imaginary and deceitful as the far more modest and personal dreams haunting the imagination of some of Chekhov's characters, and which Chekhov himself had called "mirages." From their provincial isolation, Chekhov's "three sisters" dream simply of a richer existence for people like themselves, which could include the possibility of a journey to Moscow, or the certainty of a change for the better in the near future. But the three sisters realize that even such simple hopes will remain forever mere "mirages," and content themselves with thinking that "life will be better three hundred years from now."

The fanciful "dawns" of those three Symbolist spiritual brothers, as a matter of fact, showed themselves to be even far more human, sentimental, and private "mirages." One could even say that what the poets of Russian Symbolism took as dawns, as the announcement of daybreak, were instead, as they later realized, twilights, revealing the agony of a moribund hour. Yet at first Blok, Belyj, and Sergej Solov'ev mistook the sunset for the sunrise; at least for a while they deeply believed in their own apocalyptic and eschatological dreams, without ever doubting that the hoped-for palingenesis was at hand. Like early Christians, they expected to see the Kingdom of God in their lifetime. In the approaching descent upon earth of the feminine incarnation of the cosmic and divine order, they anticipated a radical renewal of Russian life, the conversion, or even the rebirth, of the Russian soul, the transformation of Russia into the Zion of a new world.

The political and religious reaction which followed in the wake of the "little revolution" of 1905, which was in its turn stirred by the defeat of tsarist Russia in the war with Japan, was destined, however, to shatter this dream. Blok, with his almost mediumistic sense of the invisible forces which were changing the world around him, had started losing his faith earlier, partly under the influence of personal and private factors, or, more simply, of his marriage to Ljubov' Mendeleeva, in whom he now saw a real woman, rather than the incarnation of the Eternal Feminine which his friends still insisted on seeing. For this reason, Sergej Solov'ev and Andrej Belyj had considered him a traitor, and yet Belyj was destined a few years later to follow his former friend on the path of despair and disbelief. Belyj was, however, the first of the two to try to bring back the religion of their youth, by replacing the spiritual worship of the heavenly Sophia with a more earthly and humble cult, which found its object in the feminine personification of an all-sinful and all-suffering mother — Russia. In this, naturally and spontaneously, Blok was to follow Belyj's lead; and, several years later, after the upheaval of 1917, both of them found for a while in the Revolution a resurrection of their old dreams.

Of the three masters of Russian Symbolism, Vjacheslav Ivanov was the only one who, while often changing attitude or outlook, succeeded in keeping faith, if not in the religion of Sophia at least in the Symbolist ideal. At the end of his life, as we already know, he saved that ideal and all the hopes connected with it by a return to traditional religion and by a conversion to the Roman Church. Even before that return and that conversion, he had succeeded in preserving the bond between poetry and religion, precisely because he conceived of that bond in less literal and immediate terms than the other members of his sect. In brief, he saw in poetry not so much a mystical or speculative instrument, able to do religion's work by itself, as a special mirror reflecting religious experience in emblematic images and allegorical visions. Thus Russian Symbolism, in both theory and practice, survived only with Ivanov and went into exile with him. Even as an old *émigré* Ivanov cultivated the theoretical and artistic heritage of the school, integrating it with the metaphysical traditions of the past, thus acting as the only religious humanist of his sect.

Belyj too went abroad, where for a while he thought he had found anew the verities he sought. Yet what he brought back after his return to the land of the Soviets was but the ghost of Russian Symbolism: the poetic and literary ideal he tried to keep alive was a Symbolism of his own, interpreted, so to say, almost in surrealistic terms. As for Blok, who was destined to remain in his native land and to die all too young, he was the only one of the three who accepted with lucid despair the defeat of the dreams of his youth. He did so precisely because nature had endowed him with a higher prophetic vision and with greater poetic gifts. In his last years he heeded the lessons of reality and life, and turned his art from an instrument of revelation into a mirror of truth. Unlike Ivanov and Belyj, he refused to whiten the sepulcher, or to embalm the corpse, of Symbolism. The dark grace of his genius allowed him, almost against his will, to save from the ruins of his faith that poetry which he, like his brethren, had once placed on the single cornerstone of belief.

III

RUSSIAN AND WESTERN SYMBOLISM

Despite Blok's final denial, the emphatic claim that poetry and religion are one remains the most characteristic of all the original tenets of Russian Symbolism. Yet Russian Symbolism, especially if we neglect or de-emphasize that claim, will in the long run appear to the cultural historian but a peculiar variant of the general European movement by the same name. The main difference between the Russian and other local brands of the same product is one of tradition and orientation, as is shown by the fact that the Russian

Symbolists learned their craft not only from their immediate foreign predecessors, who were mainly French, but also from the poets
of German Romanticism, as well as from their Russian disciples,
who had kept the memory of German poetry alive during the whole
of the nineteenth century, and who include such glorious names as
Zhukovskij, Tjutchev, and Fet. It was from Romantic Germany
that Solov'ev had drawn the images, as well as the ideas, of his own
poetry, while Blok was bound to begin his career as a modern and
original disciple of Zhukovskij. In this direct connection with the
Romantic tradition Russian Symbolism differed strongly from its
French counterpart. Baudelaire and all his near and distant followers, from Mallarmé to Valéry, accepted as valid the impatient
reaction which took place in French poetry, from Gautier's "art
for art's sake" school to the Parnassian movement, against Romantic poetry, which in France had sinned too much in the direction of impassioned eloquence and emotional subjectivism.

In this regard the modern poets of England and America seem
to have adopted, unlike their Russian brethren, the antiromantic
stand of their French predecessors. Their sense of hostility or aloofness toward the Romantic heritage was and still is chiefly due to a
conception of poetry which is based on the premise of impersonality, and which requires the rejection of any kind of autobiographical pathos or subjective lyricism. The modern poets of
Germany and Austria, who had learned their lessons from the
same French masters, failed, however, to feel a similar compulsion,
and considered themselves the continuers of the great German
poets of the early nineteenth century, especially of Novalis and
Hölderlin. What motivated this attitude was also the fact that
German Romantic poetry, more intensely than the English and to
a far higher degree than the French, had been full of anticipations
of Symbolism; this is the reason why the modern poetic movement
in Germany and Austria took the very apt name of *Neuro-
mantik*. From this viewpoint, Blok, Ivanov, and Belyj are far nearer
to George, Rilke, and Hofmannsthal than to any of the other
groups of poets of the same time. It is perhaps for this reason that
the literary historian Semen Vengerov labeled the whole of Russian
Symbolism, broadly considered, and including all the Decadent

and neoidealistic trends which emerged at the end of the century, a "neoromantic movement."

Despite this, Blok, Belyj, and Ivanov conceived of poetry in a way which diverged only in part from that of the leaders of French Symbolism, and of their followers in all other European countries. And, at least at first, they based that conception, even more consistently and persistently than their foreign masters or their fellow disciples from abroad, on a dualistic view of man's life and of God's universe. Following old religious and mystical notions, Poe and Baudelaire had distinguished between a higher and a lower world. Man, who lives "down here," cannot enter into communication with "up there" other than by way of "symbols." According to an established mystical view, what we call a "symbol" is the one device by which the human mind may not only express, but even discover, a relationship which it could not fathom by itself. Only "symbols" are supposed to bridge the gap which separates heaven and earth, the human and the divine, the temporal and the eternal, the material and the spiritual. By using a method made up in part of mystical foresight, and in part of Platonic "reminiscence," the poet is thus deemed able to link a series of symbols in a chain or a ladder, through which he and the reader may ascend, if only briefly, from the world of things to the world of ideas, thus reestablishing a precarious equilibrium, a fragmentary or temporary harmony, between the two conflicting spheres of human experience.

In mystical literature the "symbol" is called "correspondence." But, from a famous sonnet by Baudelaire where the latter term is used in a slightly different sense, "correspondence" has come to mean a particular device, expressing the connection existing between divers kinds of symbols. Whereas the symbol establishes a kind of vertical relationship between the lower and higher sphere, thus transcending the fundamental duality of the real and the ideal, the "correspondence" establishes a horizontal relationship and affirms the existence of a parallelism, symmetry, and even identity, between symbols belonging to different forms of expression. In brief, the "correspondence" presupposes a semantic analogy between different sense perceptions, as well as between different art media and linguistic techniques. In practice, the "correspondence" implies that there may be an equivalence in suggestion and meaning between a verbal symbol and a visual or musical one. This means not only that the human mind may reach the same revelation through a pattern of words as through a pattern of colors or a pattern of sounds, but also that each one of those patterns is translatable into any one of the other two. It is on the presupposition of such a double relationship, on the basis of what Baudelaire, following Swedenborg, called the "universal analogy," that the Symbolist poet endeavors to perform his set task, which, according to Blok's definition, consists of trying "to catch, through snatches of words, the confused march of other worlds."

The French Symbolists, who followed in many ways the example set by the Parnassians, often paid more than lip service to the notion that poetry must be impersonal and objective, and that it can express as well as painting or sculpture a formal ideal primarily plastic in essence. This is what Baudelaire himself tried to do, especially when he attempted to reshape verbal symbols into a visual key, or to transfer a pictorial or sculptural work of art into a poem, replacing other artists' colors and lines with sounds and words of his own. Similar attempts were made by some minor modern Russian poets, but not by the greater and more genuine Symbolists. Thus, in an even more extreme form than its French counterpart, Russian Symbolism primarily represents, among the main trends of modern poetry, the one which aims at fashioning its own formal ideal after the pattern of the musical one.

That ideal had first been formulated in the West, and originally had not been limited to poetry alone, as Baudelaire demonstrated as a critic of painting when he analyzed the effects of Delacroix' art in musical terms; or as Walter Pater sensed when he stated that in the modern aesthetic situation all arts seemed to tend toward "the condition of music." Yet in the West itself that tendency or trend was bound to reach its climax in the art of verse. This is proved by the fact that the two most important attempts to define the new poetry as it developed in France were based more on the theory of music than on the practice of symbolism. Mallarmé once declared that the paramount intent of himself and his colleagues had been *de tout réprendre à la musique*, "to take everything back from music," and his great disciple Valéry was later to paraphrase and limit his master's statement by maintaining that the common aim of the French Symbolists had been *de réprendre à la musique leur bien*, "to reclaim from music their own," or to recover from the latter a native gift properly and originally belonging to poetry alone. If we compare these with similar attempts by the Russian Symbolists to define the doctrine of their school, we shall see that they too single out music as the poetic principle for excellence, but attribute to music a higher power and a larger domain than Mallarmé or Valéry ever did. Thus, for instance, Andrej Belyj claims in one breath the identity of poetry, music, and symbolism when he says: "Music ideally expresses symbols; the symbol is always musical." Yet, when read in the context of his theories, these words obviously imply the precedence of the musical sense over symbolic insight. As for Blok, his exaltation of what he called after Nietzsche "the spirit of music" entails the notion that the spirit itself is but music. For Blok the latter is not merely the root of poetry, but the source of all power and vision, as he suggested when he proclaimed, rephrasing the opening sentence of St. John's Gospel, that "in the beginning was music," rather than "the Word."

The very excess of their metaphysical claims prevents the literary historian or critic from using such pronouncements as reliable indications, if not of the aims the Russian Symbolists sought to achieve, at least of the directions toward which they tended to move. Their visionary outlook ruled their minds a posteriori as well as a priori, and determined even their evaluation of Russian Symbolism as a historical fact. In brief, we cannot take at its face value even their posthumous appraisal, because it often tends to assume, as in Blok's case, too negative a bias. Strangely enough, we may assess better the contributions of European Symbolism in general, and of Russian Symbolism in particular, by using as a starting point the belated post-mortem report which Paul Valéry wrote on French Symbolism itself.

That report took the form of a retrospective manifesto, which Valéry drafted in 1920 as a preface to a book by a fellow poet. Of particular interest to us is that in those pages Valéry singled out the attempt to recapture the "spirit of music" as the very mission of the school he had joined in his youth. After stating that the poetic principle of Symbolism was a musical one, Valéry treats all of its manifestations as corollaries of that postulate: "The obscurities and peculiarities Symbolism was so often blamed for . . . the syntactical disorder, the irregular rhythms, the oddities of vocabulary . . . , the constant imagery . . . , all this may be easily inferred, once the principle is acknowledged." Valéry was aware that the attempt had led to divergent, and even negative, aesthetic effects; after all, as he said of the poets of his own generation and tongue, "some would cherish Wagner, others Schumann." Yet one should not forget that what Valéry had in mind in those pages were the intentions rather than the achievements of the Symbolist school: hence the unavoidable conclusion, at least on the part of the reader, that the view that poetry and symbol are, either potentially or actually, musical in essence, is hardly more than a metaphor, expressing an artistic ideal which was never to be realized in practice, and which individual poets would treat at most as either an exalted abstraction or a vague program. Yet that view is significant as the symptom of an aspiration which was both genuine and inborn, and the tendency so revealed is peculiar and important enough to be taken into account by the student endeavoring to understand the difference between modern Symbolism, or Symbolism with a capital S, and eternal symbolism, or symbolism with a small initial.

If modern Symbolism, of which Russian Symbolism is but an integral part, envisages its operations under the guise of a musical analogy, medieval symbology, which is perhaps the most typical manifestation of universal or recurring symbolism, views its own products in graphic, or better, emblematic, terms. The modern Symbolist poet may glimpse with his mind, or rather sense with his heart, a hidden truth or a higher reality; yet, being unable to contemplate that truth with clarity, and to express that reality in its fullness, he will be satisfied with merely suggesting it. But the medieval symbolist does not content himself with guesses or hints, and wishes to communicate as completely as possible, with the means at his disposal, his own mystical experience. Thus his aim is to visualize and represent: or, more precisely, to give the objective image of a reality which cannot be perceived through the senses.

It has been said that modern Symbolism is dynamic, and medieval symbolism is static, by which is generally meant that the former is more interested in the psychological process of revelation, and the other, in its speculative results. At any rate, precisely because it is the reflection of a consistent and systematic world view, medieval symbolism is often able to tie its emblems together and to raise a series of emblems to the level of what the early painters of Christendom used to call a "story." Modern Symbolist poets, however, use their symbols as if they were separate images, which they cannot relate to any pattern except that of their mood. This is another way to say that symbolism may at best reappear or survive in modern culture only as a paradox or as an exception, and that it will manifest itself only in rhapsodic fashion and fragmentary form.

Thus medieval culture was able to treat each symbol as part of a whole, as a link in the chain which took the name and shape of allegory. Modern Symbolism has, however, fully divorced itself from allegory; and it has done so not as a matter of choice, as is generally believed, but as a matter of necessity. It is the sense of such a necessity, felt even by those who are not conscious of it, which motivates that antithesis between symbol and allegory of which the modern mind seems to be so inordinately fond. Separating the two, or opposing the one to the other, is an operation of dubious validity if we look at symbolism *sub specie aeternitatis*: yet it becomes justified from the standpoint of historical Symbolism. Allegory is, after all, incompatible with a poetry based on melos and pathos alone, or reduced only to the lyrical mode, which modern culture considers the whole of poetry, or at least its most perfect and absolute form. But allegory has no place in modern poetry for reasons more substantive than this. Allegory is both possible and necessary in those cultures where the poet shares with his community, or at least with a considerable body of the faithful, a set of solid and concrete beliefs, which he is able to express with the objectivity of contemplation, rather than with introspective lyricism. This is certainly not the case with modern poetry, and with modern Symbolism in particular. What makes the latter's position highly paradoxical is that modern Symbolism starts, at least ideally, from the presupposition of a bond between religion and poetry, although in practice it ends by preaching no other religion than that of poetry itself, thus replacing the deification of the Logos with the idolization of the Word.

Modern Symbolism derives that presupposition from Romantic idealism, rather than from the Christian tradition, which refuses to identify religion and poetry, since it submits the latter to the former, or even to philosophy, which it views in its turn as but the handmaid of theology. Yet, despite this, perhaps only in order to assign to poetry a lofty spiritual task, modern Symbolism accepts for a time, and only problematically and hypothetically, the philosophical foundations of Christian dualism, and treats poetry as if it were a kind of mystical ladder, bridging the gap between a lower reality and a higher one. It is according to a similar aesthetic mysticism, which was already part of the metaphysical speculation of Northern Romanticism, that Kierkegaard gave his suggestive definition of the poet as "a spy of God." The formula is quite significant, since it seems to imply that the poet tries to discover the secrets of Heaven by stealth, and almost against God's will. What is even truer is that the modern poet looks at God from perspectives through which God cannot be seen. These perspectives, which the modern poet does not choose by himself, but simply accepts as imposed by the historical condition or cultural situation of which, whether willingly or unwillingly, he is a part, are those of either a monistic idealism or an equally monistic materialism, or even that skeptical or scientific pluralism which is perhaps the dominant trait of modern culture. All these tendencies have deprived modern man of the sense of the sacred, have reduced the divine to a daydream or a wishful thought. Symbolism started as the poetry of an illusion, rather than of a hope; one could say that no Symbolist poet ever tried to become a "seer," but was at best, and only intermittently, a "spy of God."

The idealism and the spiritualism of the early French Symbolists were essentially negative in character; they were primarily an outright denial of that positivism and materialism which from the middle of the nineteenth century on had become the salient traits of the culture of the West. Yet one could extend to the whole of European Symbolism, with slight qualifications and reservations, what Valéry rightly said of all the poets who, like him, had learned their lesson from the direct example of Mallarmé: "A young and rather stern generation rejected the scientific dogma, which tended to be no longer fashionable, without adopting the religious dogma, which was not yet so." It was precisely because they had appeared on the literary horizon a little later, that so many of the Symbolists who wrote in other languages than French felt far more attracted than their French predecessors by those religious or mystical creeds which in the meantime had become fashionable again. Yet even in their case we can hardly speak of a return to established dogmas or traditional beliefs.

If in view of this consideration we classify all the major poets of European Symbolism into different groups according to the quality and substance of their faith, we shall see that all of them fall into the following categories. The first one is that of the non-believers, of those who refuse the ideas of both religion and God, and fail to see in the cosmos any other order than a mental or poetic harmony of their own, which they often project on frivolous and even profane objects. This category is an important one, since it includes such outstanding representatives as the highest-ranking poet of French Symbolism, Stéphane Mallarmé, as well as some of his most skillful disciples in France and abroad, from Paul Valéry to Wallace Stevens. The second category is made of those who waver continuously between doubt and faith, or who base their poetry not so much on faith as on doubt. Some of them, like Baudelaire, seem to believe more in disorder than in order, in sin than in redemption, and are often of the Devil's party, whether they know it or not. Others, like T. S. Eliot, are far more effective as critics of the City of Man than as upholders of the City of God; the real theme of their verse is the denial of present-day reality rather than the affirmation of a higher and permanent realm of being. The third category is formed by all those poets, so well represented by Rilke and George in Germany and by Yeats in the English-speaking world, who have built the edifice of their poetry on the shaky foundations of arbitrary creeds and personal beliefs. Some of them, like Yeats, who is perhaps the greatest of this band, have tended to replace Christian dogmas with non-Christian myths;

and all these poets, as well as the poets belonging to the other groups, have replaced parables with fairy tales, and public allegory with private symbolism.

One could say that while none of the leaders of Russian Symbolism finds a place within the first of these categories, all of them rightly and naturally belong to either the second or the third, or even better, to both of them at once, according to the varying tendencies of their temperament, or to changing phases of their career. Generally they fit better within the second category qua poets, from the viewpoint of their concrete achievements, as will be easily shown in their individual profiles and through the analysis of their work; while they fit better within the third qua prophets, from the viewpoint of their abstract attitudes or self-conscious poses. Thus, for instance, Belyj was, of the three leaders of Russian Symbolism, the one who, in a sense, chose a solution similar to Yeats', clinging, as a means of keeping his faith, to the arbitrary beliefs of strange and occult sects. Blok leaned toward the solution of Rilke, which was to make poetry not only out of faith but out of anguish as well. Ivanov took the same path as Stefan George and acted always as if he were a high priest of poetry, in whom the religious habit could survive even the loss of faith in God. Yet, precisely because of the rigid consistency of his creed, if not the absolute constancy of his devotion, the last of these figures may be considered the most systematic theorist of the three; and this may well justify the attempt to summarize the poetics of Russian Symbolism through the particular perspective of his views.

From beginning to end Vjacheslav Ivanov insisted on the tie between Symbolism and mysticism, and saw the cornerstone of the new poetry in man's faith that a divine order rules equally the physical and the spiritual world. It was from this postulate that he drew as a corollary the tenet that "the poetic image is a microcosm reflecting the macrocosm." Ivanov's outlook implied that art is, or should be, related to religion, to a religion which he, however, understood more as theurgy than as theology: "A genuine symbolic art attains the religious sphere, insofar as religion itself is primarily an act, the act of perceiving the tie between the sense of life and all that exists." It was this conception that led the early

Ivanov to understate the differences, and to overemphasize the similarities, between the modern or historical variant of Symbolism and its archetypal forms: "Symbolism seems to be within the new poetry but a reminiscence of the holy language of the ancient sages, who had given to the words of common speech a special, secret meaning, which was known to them alone, thanks to their knowledge of the connections between the sphere of the sacred and the experience of the senses."

It was on this supposed dependence of the new poetry from that eternal symbolism after which the religious spirit of humankind seemed to be constantly yearning, that Ivanov based his claim of the independence of Russian Symbolism from its French counterpart: "The study of the work produced by our Symbolist school will show how superficial was the Western influence on us; how little we thought out what we borrowed and imitated; how those borrowings and imitations were in the long run unproductive; finally, how much deeper are the roots reattaching to its native soil what in our poetry is genuine and vital." And it is quite significant that Ivanov saw the most distinctive quality of the school or movement of which he was a leading member in the very fact that "Russian Symbolism could not be, and did not want to be, merely art."

All the poets of the second generation of Russian Symbolism, who were the only Symbolists in the proper sense of the term, fully agreed with this view, differing in this from the poets of the older generation, who here are called Decadents. Thus Valerij Brjusov, the most influential and representative of the latter, was the one who most consistently claimed that Symbolism was primarily, and even exclusively, art. As late as 1910, at the time of the controversy raised in the review *Apollo* by the poets of a third generation who condemned at once Decadents and Symbolists, Brjusov defined Symbolism purely and simply as an "artistic method," the discovery of which had been the particular merit of the poets of the two older generations, all of whom were of "the so-called Symbolistic school." Brjusov felt, however, that that method was neither particular nor exclusive, but inclusive and general: he saw in it not *an* artistic method, but *the* artistic method par excellence, which found its distinction not within, but outside, itself: "It is this method that spells the difference between art and that rational knowledge of the universe which is characteristic of science, as well as between art and that endeavor to penetrate the occult by irrational means which is characteristic of mysticism. Art is autonomous: it has its own method and mission."

Brjusov's proud belief in the autonomy of art implied a recognition of its limits, and the relative moderation of his views becomes more apparent when they are compared with Ivanov's ambitious claim that the whole of the life of the spirit is the poet's province. It is such a claim which marks the difference that separates not only Ivanov's generation from Brjusov's, but, more generally, Russian from French Symbolism. Even Poe, Baudelaire, and Rimbaud had asserted their belief that poetry should become an instrument of universal revelation only in tentative or hypothetical terms. Later on, speaking in retrospect, and bringing to their logical conclusion not only his ideas, but also those of his master Mallarmé, Valéry found a paradoxical merit in the fact that, at least within French Symbolism, philosophy, and even ethics, tended to shun poetic creation and "to dwell only among the reflections preceding the actual works." How skeptical this statement sounds when contrasted with Ivanov's oracular utterance that "the function of Symbolism is to express the parallelism of the phenomenal and the noumenal!" And it is on the strength of such philosophical pretensions and metaphysical ambitions that Ivanov was finally led to affirm not only the independence, but even the superiority, of Russian Symbolism, in regard to its French counterpart: "What Mallarmé wanted was simply that our thought, after completing its circle, would redescend to the very point the poet had prescribed it should stop. For us Symbolism is instead an energy which frees itself from the boundaries of the given world, launching the soul on the motion of a spiral shooting upward."

Despite this evident allusion to the Mallarmean image of poetry as a hyperbola, Ivanov here seems to fail to realize that even the poetic ideal of his own generation was a curve fatally bound to return to the plane of the earth. Only experience could teach him later to recognize this harsh truth. The very range of his vision allowed him to understand better than his fellow poets that "crisis" of Russian Symbolism, which was so widely discussed in the years between 1905 and the war. Ivanov succeeded in doing so because he was able to view it as the reflection of a broader and older crisis, that of modern Symbolism itself. Ivanov stated his views in this regard in an essay which he wrote in 1907 under the title of "Art and Symbolism." In that essay Ivanov acknowledged that the modern artist is paradoxically led to Symbolism by his own extreme subjectivity: "The artist pushes so far the isolation of his own intimate experience and independent creation that ultimately he severs himself from the crowd, and tragically realizes the reciprocal incommunicability of the souls, each one of which remains enclosed within the shell of its own solitude. The language of things, circumscribed by separate concepts, must be replaced by allusive references, by a suggestive and fluid imagery: and this is what we mean by the ancient term 'symbol.' This is how subjective symbolism is created, and its aim is to mediate between lonely spirits."

It would be difficult to express better the limits of modern Symbolism, as well as the singularity of its task; and Ivanov is here fully aware of how much it differs, in scope as well as in function, from medieval or eternal symbolism. Yet, almost against his better judgment, he persisted in believing that a reconciliation of the two is not only possible, but even imminent: "Besides and beyond this newfangled Symbolism, and at first, as in Baudelaire's case, in improper combination with it, another and older kind of symbolism may arise. Its norm, through Novalis and Goethe, brings us back to the great anagogic poetry of Dante and of his predecessors, or to a symbology which has nothing to do with subjective idealism, being exclusively intent on revealing within the objects it represents their full ontological significance and the seal of their value. Here, and only here, the word 'symbol' reacquires its genuine meaning, and suggests a contemplation of reality through the perspective of its connection or analogy with a higher or truer reality. This type of objective representation implies an ascent *a realibus ad realiora*." The passage, however, concludes with the implied acknowledgment that a return to objective symbolism would involve a reversal of the cultural foundations of the modern world, and a revaluation of all its values: "Such a view of Symbolism is an outright denial of the analytical and relativistic principle of our modern, critical culture, while subjective symbolism is but a reaffirmation of that culture."

Precisely because of this the attempt to restore objective symbolism within a modern cultural framework could not succeed. Ivanov himself had described elsewhere the symbol as "the cryptogram of the ineffable": an ideal definition of its traditional function, which was to convey an ecstatic or mystical vision that normal human language could not express. Any mystical vision is a transcendental, even if temporary, victory of the soul over the self. Only through that victory may the personal soul momentarily attain the divine, or join with the world soul. As for what we call ecstasy, it is but the liberation of the spirit from the bonds which chain it to either the psyche or the mind, or to both. Only by means of symbols may the mystic or spiritual seer be able to communicate a unique and universal experience to his fellow men. But at best the modern spirit treats symbols as hieroglyphics, which, far from revealing the ineffable, suggest merely the occult; or, at worst, only vaguely and obscurely hint at the poet's private being and inner world. Goethe once said that "in a true symbol the particular represents the universal, not as a dream or shadow, but as the living and instantaneous revelation of the unfathomable." If this definition is right, then we must acknowledge that modern poetry has produced symbols which represent the particular alone, and as dream and shadow at that.

IV

THE NEMESIS OF SYMBOLISM

In brief, modern Symbolism leads to one of two blind alleys, intellectualism or irrationalism. The second alternative is the more frequent. By being made a vessel of the irrational, the symbol turns into a microcosm reflecting another microcosm, thus becoming something not too different from what Freud means by that very word: a symptom of spiritual trouble and psychic disorder, the distorted mirror of the artist's neurosis, of the poet's narcissism.

Belyj unintentionally avowed as much in a passage where he praised modern Symbolism as the attempt to express "the deepest layer of our consciousness" by means of images which are symbols insofar as they suggest the "inner perceptions" of that consciousness. Such a statement tends to imply, beyond the terms used and the meaning intended, that symbols are but spontaneous or even automatic expressions of that unconscious which is the scientific object of "depth psychology."

Symbolism so understood ends by becoming unwillingly a kind of glorified expressionism. If this is true, how slight its achievements look when compared with the pretensions of its practitioners! For instance Valerij Brjusov, the great master of Russian Decadence, or of the earliest stage of Russian Symbolism, went so far as to affirm, in his famous essay "Key of Mysteries," which he wrote for *The Scales* in 1904, that Symbolism was the culminating phase in the process of development of modern art, a process which he described as a progressive liberation from the chains of intellectualism. "The history of the new art is above all the history of its deliverance. Romanticism, Realism, and Symbolism are but three stages in the artist's struggle for freedom." As for Belyj, he went even further, maintaining that Symbolism was not simply the culmination of a gradual evolution, but a synthesis of all previous traditions, not only of Romanticism and Realism, but of Classicism as well: "Symbolism is at once Classicism, Romanticism, and Realism: it is Realism insofar as it reflects reality; it is Romanticism insofar as it is a vision corrected by experience; it is Classicism for unifying form and content."

Of all these sweeping generalizations the only one still acceptable is the one which relates Symbolism to Romanticism, since the former was obviously the latter's offspring. As for the preposterous assertion that Symbolism includes even Classicism itself, it may be easily rejected on the grounds of the principle which T. S. Eliot stated in his essay on Baudelaire, that "a poet in a romantic age cannot be a 'classical' poet except in tendency." Notwithstanding all claims to the contrary, this principle is valid for the whole tradition of modern poetry, from Baudelaire to Eliot himself, and applies even more fully to the Russian poets of Belyj's generation, who, unlike their French masters and English colleagues, failed to take seriously the ideal which Eliot was to express in such a definitive way in "Tradition and the Individual Talent": "Poetry is not a turning loose of emotion, but an escape from emotion; it is not the expression of personality, but an escape from personality." It was because of their refusal to make their own, at least up to a point, the Parnassian tenets of the impersonality of art and of the artist's *impassibilité*, that the Russian Symbolists, along with their German brethren, deserved and welcomed that neoromantic label which all their other Western peers refused to accept.

It is from a special viewpoint that one must consider Belyj's affirmation that Symbolism allied itself with even the most obvious of its literary opposites, at least in historical terms. That opposite was Realism, then still alive as a parallel line of aesthetic development, as well as a noble precedent, and the supreme tradition of Russian literature. The Russian Symbolists had to take a stand toward that tradition, through which the Russian genius had already manifested itself; and their stand, at least in generalities and principles, could not be but a negative one. Any attempt to reconcile these two opposites was bound to end in disaster, or with the bloodless victory of the stronger of the two. Blok was the only one who understood that the duality of those two outlooks could not be resolved; that chaining the two together would bring about the destruction of the weaker link. Yet he not only faced the challenge and accepted his own defeat, but acknowledged that defeat as both natural and just.

Being the least critically minded of the poets of his nation and time, disdainfully indifferent to literary problems as such, Blok saw that duality not as a conflict between Symbolism and Realism, but as the duel between imagination and truth. First he doubted, and then denied, the ultimate validity of the artistic and religious creeds of his generation when confronted with the prose of life, with man's daily existence in a profane world. It was in his letters and diaries, rather than in his essays, that he confided his misgivings about the poetic sect which had made him one of its patron saints: "Symbolism, the 'correspondences,' the 'moments,' all these things are childish trifles." It was there that he repudiated mysticism not

143

only as an error, but also as a moral flaw: "We need reality. Nothing in the world is more awful than mysticism." By reality Blok meant a deep ethical experience, a keen understanding of both outer and inner truth: "We must show our fellow men our true, said, human face, not the mask of a literary school which does not exist."

That literary school did, however, effectively exist, even though it had ultimately to come to terms with the cultural reality of which it was historically a part. It was the naturalistic temper of modern culture which led that school to sever the bonds which, at least ideally, still seemed to tie it to medieval symbolism. By doing so the new poetry ended by denying its very doctrine of the word. Medieval symbolism had been an offshoot of what the historians of philosophy designate as medieval realism, which is the very opposite of modern philosophical Realism. Medieval realism maintained that words are not vain sounds, but the proper names of things, which in their turn are but earthly reflections of eternal and absolute archetypes. In brief, each word was thought to be the objective, although shadowy, symbol of a metaphysical idea. Modern Realism claims instead that art must mirror things as things, as objects which are enclosed within a purely physical space, and which we perceive only through our senses. Literary realism uses words just as visual and plastic realism uses colors and volumes: as external stimuli which reproduce in our minds the material image of things. In brief, even in the most abstract forms, modern art tends toward sensory illusions, which are highly subjective in character, and which differ only in degree from what the Symbolist poet calls "symbols."

There is no need to challenge the validity of the term symbol as it is being used in connection with modern poetry, precisely because it may mean nothing and everything, as Valéry remarked in a passage full of insight: "In vain did those who watched these experiments, and even those who put them into practice, attack the poor word itself. It means only what one wants it to; if someone fastens his hopes upon it, he will find them there!" The task of the historian of literature, and of the critic of poetry, is to point out that the modern poet uses words as symbols not in the religious sense, as metaphysical visions or mystical emblems, but in the semantic sense, as verbal icons. Potebnja, a Russian philologist and literary theorist of the late nineteenth century, had already put this principle in a nutshell by stating that "a symbol is a mere metaphor," and nothing more.

Thus for a modern poet the noun "rose" stands for either *a* rose or his own mood. If such a verbal sign acts within the structure of the poem as a "guidepost word," to employ a formula of which the Russian Symbolists were very fond, it is precisely because that sign points, through or beyond the objects, to the subject, or to the poet's self. But for the medieval poet a rose is *the* rose, while being at the same time the allegory of love, whether sacred or profane. This means that for the medieval symbolist the thing is the vessel of the idea, and the idea the substance of the thing. Hence the belief that the spirit may be understood through the letter, and the letter through the spirit. Thus the obscurity of the letter is but a veil, which both conceals and reveals. It was Carlyle who attributed to the symbol the double requisite of "concealment" and "revelation." The mystical tradition claims that the symbol, although occult to the uninitiated eye, is evident to the initiated one. The modern Symbolist seems, however, to conceive of the symbol as a chiaroscuro, as an interplay, even within the poet's mind, of darkness and light. Thus, instead of becoming the custodian of a mystery, he simply remains the watchman of the Sphinx, of its enigmas and riddles.

Such was the paradoxical outcome of the central doctrine of Symbolism, from which that movement took its name and flag. No less paradoxical was the outcome of the other of its main theories, which is perhaps more crucial than the first: the one according to which music is the ideal condition of all art. As we already know, the Russian Symbolists took that principle both more seriously and more broadly than their French masters and Western colleagues, and did not hesitate to extend it to the whole domain of the spirit, beyond the realms of words and forms. Thus Andrej Belyj held that music is not only "the substratum of poetry," but also the power which helps man to realize that "the visible world is but a veil over an abyss." In such a definition the idea of music is changed from a literary metaphor or an aesthetic analogy into a philosophical myth. There is no need to recall that Belyj drew the very image of the veil over the abyss from a famous Tjutchev poem to realize that the myth is a catastrophic one, that music is for Belyj not an echo of the harmony of the spheres but the prophetic din of that "last cataclysm" which will destroy creation itself. For Blok music was the voice of chaos, suddenly breaking loose in the natural and the social world: the wild song of the elements, or of the masses in revolt. It was such a worship of the "spirit of music," no less than the belief that "the world" is "idea and representation," that ultimately led the Russian Symbolists to follow the path already taken by their beloved Schopenhauer, and to end their vain search with the surrender of their hopes to a sort of cosmic nihilism.

At least consciously, the surrender was never total, and allowed temporary restorations of the faith lost through despair and disbelief. Even Blok, at such a late date as 1910, when he was left with few illusions, reasserted against the enemies of Symbolism the claim of his youth, and maintained that the poet is "the lonely keeper of a mysterious treasure, although there are around him others who know of the treasure. . . . Hence, we, the few knowing ones, are the Symbolists. . . ." In reality the Symbolists did not know the treasure, but merely knew *of* it; or rather, dreamed of its existence all too vividly, and never found it when they sought it. One could even say that while some good Symbolist poetry was written in the illusion that the Holy Grail was within reach, far better poetry was written out of the fear that the quest would fail, or even the realization that it led to a dead end. There is no doubt that the Symbolist attitude bore better fruit when dealing with the psychic states which precede or follow the ecstatic trance, rather than with the mystical experience itself. The moods which the poets of Symbolism expressed most successfully were expectation and hope, especially when mixed with hesitation and doubt, or disenchantment and loss of faith, with the attendant falling back of the soul from what Mallarmé called *azur* to what he named *ici-bas*. Thus the main muses of Symbolism were the muse of escape, which led the poet to seek refuge, in the title of one of Baudelaire's poems, "anywhere out of the world"; and the muse of failure and despair, which brought him back to an unholy earth and to an all-too-human world. In either case Symbolist poetry turned into a forward- or backward-looking yearning for an impossible Symbolism.

Truly enough, many of the noblest monuments of that poetry were erected on other pedestals than these. Some of the poets chose as their ground either a relative acceptance or an outright denial of the inner dialectics of Symbolism. In their awareness that the modern mind was unable to solve the conflict between the ideal and the real, or to transcend the ego as well as the world, a few poets, for instance Yeats, made great poetry out of the dialogue or debate of the soul with the self. Others, like Mallarmé and Valéry, renounced the view of poetry as experience of the infinite, and reduced it to an exacting and yet futile exercise within the finite world of form. Exceptional as they were, even these eccentric solutions tend to prove that all the highest achievements of Symbolism were attained in a state of tension within its own system of belief: in a kind of antagonistic reaction against its very creed. Thus Symbolism ended in a symbolism of negation, in an allegory of failure, in a chant of nothingness.

V

SYMBOLISM VERSUS DECADENCE

It was such nihilism that led so many Symbolist poets to an escape into the aesthetic cult. One could extend to the whole of modern Symbolism, as well as to its Russian variant, the conclusion which Valéry drew for the French school: "In the profound and scrupulous worship of the arts as a whole, it thought it had found an unequivocal discipline or even a truth. A sort of religion was very nearly established." Also in Russia that sort of religion had already been established in the climate of Decadence, and this may help to see how closely the Russian Symbolists of the second generation were connected with their predecessors. There is no doubt that from a broad historical viewpoint Decadence and Symbolism must be considered as different branches of the same tree. It is equally evident that they share many outstanding traits, besides their common leaning toward aestheticism, toward the self-adoration of the poet and the idolatry of art. Here it may suffice to cite, as a single example, the tendency on the part of the genuine Symbolists to yield no less supinely than their Decadent brethren to the temptations of the demonic and the seductions of Satanism, to the superstitious worship of the blind and dark forces of the underworld.

Yet, despite this, one must never forget that the relationship between the two is a dialectical one. This is so true that no less a Marxist than Lev Trotskij refused to throw together these two variants of modern literature under the single label of bourgeois Decadence, or Decadent Bohemia, as the critics of the Left usually do. Trotskij differentiated between the two trends by means of distinctions which others had already made before him, such as those separating the younger from the older generation and the "mystics" from the "aesthetes." This is what Trotskij had to say in a penetrating page of his book *Literature and Revolution*: "The Decadent school, which preceded Symbolism, sought the solution of all artistic problems in the personal experiences of sex, death, and the like, or rather, in nothing else but sex and death. . . . Hence . . . the need to find a higher sanction to individual demands, feelings, and moods, thus enriching and elevating them. Symbolism . . . seemed to the intelligentsia to be an artistic bridge toward mysticism. In this concrete, sociological meaning . . . , Symbolism was not merely a method of artistic technique, but an escape for the intelligentsia from reality, its means to build a new world. . . ."

Despite his distaste for both schools, at least here even Trotskij betrays or displays a relative preference for Symbolism. Thus he follows the general rule according to which all such parallels work without exception to the disadvantage of Decadence and the profit of Symbolism. So, for instance, such an early observer as Volynskij contrasted the two tendencies so as to imply that Symbolism was mainly positive and Decadence mainly negative in character. While defining Decadence as the temptation to yield to that "wicked, devilish beauty" which attracts the soul from below, Volynskij defined Symbolism as the lofty attempt to mediate between the human world of appearances and the divine world of the occult.

Later a critic who was at once a socialist and a mystic, Ivanov-Razumnik, brought that invidious comparison to the extreme point when he stated, paraphrasing Horace, that Decadents *fiunt* or "are made," while Symbolists *nascuntur* or "are born." Although willing to admit that the soil of Decadence was poetically less fertile than that of Symbolism, the impartial literary historian must reject the partisan claim that the two movements were unrelated in tendency, opposed in direction, and incommensurate in artistic value. In reality Decadence and Symbolism were but different faces of the same coin, or parallel variants of the same historical situation. As a matter of fact, if asked to designate that situation by a single term rather than with both, one should choose Decadence, which, albeit less attractive, is certainly the more inclusive, and perhaps also the more honest, of the two. One might even maintain, reversing Ivanov-Razumnik's statement, that all the Russian and Western poets of that age were born Decadents, although many of them made themselves into Symbolists (one could even claim that not a few of the latter reverted to Decadence, at least in part). Certainly this view, if accepted, would disentangle the web of the whole problem, and solve all terminological confusion, with a simple rule: that there were Decadents who were not Symbolists, but that there was no Symbolist who was not a Decadent as well.

It was the outlook of Decadence that fashioned even the social and political attitudes of the Russian Symbolists, as it fashioned those of their Western peers. True enough, among the latter all too many refused to take any political stand, flaunting their scornful indifference to any social issue or civic concern; or, when willing to take sides, they chose all too often to ally themselves with the parties of the extreme Right, while most of their Russian brethren joined those of the extreme Left. Although differing in stand, all such attitudes stemmed from the same root: the modern artist's radical dislike for that bourgeois society within which he lives, on the claim, half true and half false, that he is no part of it. It matters little whether his protest leads him to withdraw from the political arena, or to embrace either one of the two ideologies of subversion, the reactionary or the revolutionary. If the Russian Symbolists showed a marked preference for the latter alternative, it was because they were affected even more than their Western brethren by that sense of doom which is the core of the Decadent spirit. They felt the morbid attraction of the impending disaster and tried to change even the dark forebodings of their personal ruin into the radiant hope that the catastrophe would bring about a new society and a new world.

Symbolist art and poetry tended always toward a tone of "high seriousness," although the Decadent spirit all too often infected them with that gloom which was its most fashionable mood. Being far more naïve and less skeptical than their Western colleagues, easily swayed by the seduction of hope as well as the temptation of despair, the Russian Symbolists denied themselves the opportunity to release their minds from the hold of perplexity through the practice of irony and jest. Modern art as a whole neglects the lowly but effective purgation of laughter and ignores the therapeutic virtues of comic relief. Decadents and Symbolists were particularly devoid of a sense of humor; yet even French Symbolism indulged in the bitter banter of a Tristan Corbière or in those sophisticated drolleries to which Jules Laforgue gave the name of *fumisteries*. The almost fanatic frenzy of their inspiration led the Russian Symbolists to vent their spleen in blasphemy and sacrilege rather than mockery and farce.

It was the ultimate degradation of their ideal that made the Russian Symbolists deeply aware of what they called the "crisis," or even the "breakdown," of Symbolism. Yet, at least outside of Russia, many refused to hold such a pessimistic view. Thus for instance Valéry never saw a failure in the fact that Mallarmé, who had started to write poetry as a means for "the orphic explanation of the earth," had closed his career by avowing that not even the "throw of dice" of thought and art could abolish chance and its whims. Valéry admitted that Symbolism could be either a "spiritual illusion" or an ideal truth, but a truth which was, as he said, "a frontier of the world," on which man could not settle for long. He also acknowledged that "the overenlightened zeal" of the Symbolist outlook might have "resulted in an inhuman state," yet he never felt that such a state had been unproductive, even if it bore other fruits than the ones dreamed of.

The tree of theory is gray, but the tree of life is of another color, although it may well not be green. Even Baudelaire, who once affirmed that "prosodies and poetics proceed from the very structure of the spiritual being," could mock without fear of contradiction his beloved Poe for pretending to have written "The Raven" after a pre-established plan. As Baudelaire said on that occasion, poetics is one thing and poetry is another, and the second is never written after the pattern laid down by the first. This truth fits particularly well the case of Symbolism. Yet, despite all appearances to the contrary, the poetics of Symbolism was in its own way as influential as the poetry itself. There is no doubt that we must see in that poetics the root of all those literary and artistic movements which appeared later, with the avowed intention of destroying the shrines and denying the sacraments of Symbolism. What Surrealism tried to achieve, for instance, was merely to replace the daydreams of the soul with the nightmares of the psyche, thus acting as an inverted Symbolism. Like the Decadents, and like the heretics and renegades of Symbolism, the Surrealists sought refuge in a reality darker and lower than what one might call the realism of daylight, which, despite the label of their choice, they replaced, as Ortega y Gasset was the first to remark, with a kind of "infrarealism." In painting, the heritage of Symbolism is to be seen not only in post-Impressionism, as is generally believed, but also in Cubism and abstract art, which on the one hand act as visual and plastic equivalents of "pure poetry," and on the other, develop to extremes the iconoclastic tendencies of later Symbolism. Futurism is in its turn but an agonized attempt to transcend both Decadence and Symbolism, to project the present into the future, to replace the divine order with a man-made and machinelike world.

In the light of history Symbolism must then be considered not a heresy or a fallacy, but rather a paradox. The paradox lies in the fact that it paved the ground for the advance-guard while trying to restore the dream of a poetry belonging to another time as well as to another world. This is the reason why the Symbolist attitude remains even now, although under different names and forms, a standard aesthetic attitude, one of the main constants of Western poetry and art. Using as apt formulae the titles of two books in which the English scholar and critic C. M. Bowra assessed the contributions of the last two generations of European poets, one could say that even "the creative experiment" of the post- and anti-Symbolists is but one of the many variables of "the heritage of Symbolism." It matters little that Symbolism failed both as a spiritual quest and as a literary method; or that this sect or school carried the seeds of perdition within itself. What really matters is that despite all this it was a highly seminal movement. In the long run its nemesis turned into a catharsis: it is true that its sancta sanctorum changed into a Pandora's box, but it is equally true that the latter became in its turn a horn of plenty, full of rich and novel fruits.

Notwithstanding the claims to the contrary made by many of its Western representatives, Symbolism was both the offspring and the heir of Romanticism; and no less than Romanticism it succeeded in affecting the future development of Western verse, of which, directly or indirectly, it became the supreme and almost the single norm. From this viewpoint Symbolism has been performing for contemporary poetry a task similar to that which Petrarchism and Platonism fulfilled for the lyrical poetry of the Renaissance, with the difference that the lyrical poets of the Renaissance treated Petrarchism and Platonism as formal or abstract ideals, so removed from life that they could never enter into conflict with it. It is its own conflict with life which finally destroyed the Symbolist movement as a going concern. Yet, precisely because no other vital movement has arisen to take its place, Western poetry is still haunted by its ghost. Through the unique but eloquent example of Boris Pasternak that ghost may well haunt even the poetry of today's Russia, despite the powerful exorcisms by which Soviet culture has tried to conjure away the phantoms still left abroad by the vanished idealism of the past.

CHAPTER FIVE

SYMBOLISTS AND OTHERS

I

ANDREJ BELYJ

Boris BUGAEV, better known in literature as Andrej Belyj, was born in Moscow in 1880. The son of a famous mathematician, he followed at first in his father's footsteps, and studied natural sciences at the University of Moscow, where the elder Bugaev was a professor. It was an interest in philosophy, and especially the reading of Schopenhauer and Nietzsche, which made the youth first realize that his mind was made for other fetters than those of scientific thought. A common curiosity for the new trends affecting the culture of the West led him and other students of the School of Sciences to found at the beginning of the century the Moscow circle which took the name of "Argonauts," as if its members were seekers of a new "golden fleece." Yet the influence which finally led him to enter the career of letters was a more personal one: his friendship with the family of Mikhail Solov'ev, who was the brother of the philosopher and a highly cultivated man. His wife Ol'ga was a painter and a writer, and their son Sergej, then still a boy, was destined to form later a mystical brotherhood with his older friend Boris, and with his Petersburg second cousin, Aleksandr Blok. It was Mikhail Solov'ev who acquainted his young neighbor with the philosophy and the poetry of his own brother; who encouraged him to publish his earliest literary composition; and who chose for him the pen name Andrej Belyj, which means "Andrew the White."

153

Belyj began his literary career as a poet, but a poet in prose, and one can say that he remained practically the only poet in prose of Russian Symbolism. His prose poems, however, unlike those of Baudelaire and Mallarmé, are not merely short lyrics in nonmetrical speech. Far more ambitious in scope and far more complex in texture, they are based on a loose narrative web, the threads of which reappear intermittently in the shape of refrains and leitmotivs. The models on which Belyj shaped the style of his prose poems were the Nietzsche of *Also sprach Zarathustra* and the Gogol' of the most nightmarish and visionary pages of *Dead Souls*; while he patterned their structure on the principle of musical composition, with phonetic and rhythmical effects so elaborate and ornamental as to transcend the limits of even the most sonorous and cadenced prose, thus justifying the name of "symphonies" which Belyj himself gave them. The earliest of these compositions was the *Dramatic Symphony* (1902), a prophetic vision of Vladimir Solov'ev's Sophia and her imminent coming among men. Blok, who was then writing his *Poems on the Beautiful Lady*, saluted that vision enthusiastically in a review closing with the words "I have dreamed this dream." The *Dramatic Symphony* was soon followed by the *Northern Symphony* (*Heroic*) (1903), which in the complete series was to precede the earlier one, and by the third, entitled *Return* (1905), which deals with the Nietzschean idea of "the eternal recurrence." The fourth and last, *The Goblet of Blizzards*, appeared after a slightly longer interval (1908). Belyj filled this closing piece with the sound and fury of the Russian winter, as well as the grief and wrath of his soul, at that time chagrined by a hopeless love for Blok's wife and enraged by the aloof indifference of his former friend.

Belyj would not be remembered as a poet if he had left us only these prose poems. Written in a cloudy and heavy style, full of pretension and bad taste, they are now unreadable and deservedly forgotten. Immediately after his first two "symphonies," Belyj published, however, his earliest collection of verse, *Gold in Azure* (1904). The main theme of these lyrics is the same as that of the *Dramatic Symphony*, as well as of the poetry of the youthful Blok. Yet here Belyj utters his own mystical announcements with a clarion voice, and symbolizes the spiritual presence of Sophia not in the vague paleness of Blok's morning or evening twilight, but, as the title suggests, in a flood of gorgeous colors, in the radiance of noon or the glow of sunset. The poems of this book fall brightly and noisily like cascades of pearls and jewels, like torrents or precious stones. This impression of flow, which overwhelms the fixity of Belyj's imagery and compensates for the heaviness of his verbal matter, is produced almost exclusively by the surprising fluidity of the rhythmical stream. Starting with this book Belyj introduced into Russian versification an equivalent of Verlaine's *vers libéré*, a less rigid treatment of the traditional prosody, emphasizing tonic values at the expense of the syllabic scheme.

This quality of Belyj's rhythm also pervades the poems of his second collection, *Ashes*, which appeared in 1909. In this volume the poet replaces the ecstatic and orgiastic inspiration of *Gold in Azure* with a convulsive pathos and a hopeless woe. His muse now lays down her bright sacramental garments and dons the coarse garb of a rustic mourner, chanting her grief in simple, monotonous tunes. Here the poet's master and model is no longer Solov'ev, but Nekrasov, the realistic painter of Russian country life, which he reflected in the mirror of truth, and of which he sang with a voice full of both pity and wrath. Belyj's peasantry and countryside represent Russia herself, personified as a monstrous feminine figure, miserable and wicked, with "yellow eyes" made by the lamps of her "crazy taverns." Instead of hymns, the poet now utters curses and plaints: "Enough, don't wait, don't hope," he says once to the Russian people, with the calm resignation of a lucid grief; "disappear into space, disappear," he cries another time to Russia, in an outburst of rage and despair. The extreme emotional tension of *Ashes* is relaxed in the following collection, reflective in tone and philosophical in temper, which Belyj entitled *Urn* (1909), as if to indicate the intention of embalming in a shapely vessel the ashes left in his heart by the spent fire of life. "Search not for peace, since no peace exists": these words seem to be the most fitting epigraph for this book, which closes for all purposes (except for a few minor, and belated, collections) the lyrical phase of Belyj's work.

In the following decade Belyj abandoned lyricism for fiction and poetry for prose. In 1910 he published his first novel, *The Silver Dove*. Its protagonist, Darjalskij, is an intellectual who joins a peasant sect of sex-worshippers practicing promiscuous sexual intercourse as the only mystery and sacrament of their cult. They deify free love and symbolize it by the bird which gives a name to their sect and a title to this book. The story ends with the murder of the neophyte, condemned to death as a traitor by the White Doves, when he tries to break away from their bond and to return to a world ruled by the spirit rather than by the flesh. The novel allegorizes the erotic dialectic of Russian Symbolism, and emphasizes the darker side of the religion of the Eternal Feminine, embodying here the *Erdgeist*, the genius of the earth.

In 1912 Belyj published another novel, which is perhaps the highest accomplishment of his literary career. Entitled *Petersburg*, this novel is based on an even broader moral and philosophical conflict than the one adumbrated in *The Silver Dove*. In this second work of fiction Belyj develops with obsessive insistence the historical and political myth of Petersburg, created jointly by the ominous superstitions of the Russian people and by the tragic imagination of its thinkers and poets. That splendid, artificial capital had been built on the bones of thousands of serfs in the frozen marshlands of the North, as the fruit of a despot's monstrous whim, as a challenge to nature and even to history itself; this is why the Russian peasantry had seen in Peter the Great an incarnation of the Antichrist, and was still prophesying that Piter, or the new Babel he had built, would be destroyed not merely by one of the Neva's periodic floods, but by the waters of a new deluge. Not all the great poets of Russia shared this apocalyptic interpretation of the Petersburg legend, which affected most those who were under the conscious or unconscious influence of the Slavophile view. Yet even Pushkin, while celebrating in *The Bronze Horseman* the founding of Petersburg as a heroic deed, lamented the human sacrifice entailed by that historical feat. The Gogol' of the so-called "Petersburg tales," and the Dostoevskij of *The Double* and *White Nights*, of *Notes from Underground* and *Crime and Punishment*, transposed that myth into the key of a fantastic and visionary realism, and saw in that weird city the eerie abode of hallucinated creatures, obsessed by frustrations and fixations, by brain fevers and heartbreaks.

It was through the mediation of those two great storytellers that Blok and Belyj inherited and made their own the Petersburg myth. It is true that through Pushkin other variants of the same legend equally affected the imagination of some of their contemporaries, such as Merezhkovskij, Gippius, and Annenskij. Yet Belyj's treatment of the theme is a highly original one, even though the novel reveals its Dostoevskian legacy in both spirit and structure, being at once an ideological novel and a sensational thriller. In Belyj's narrative, as in the fiction of Dostoevskij, thesis and theme merge in a perfect fusion of plot and atmosphere. Despite its political overtones, the intrigue looks like that of a mystery story, and it is built on both horror and suspense, as if it were a Gothic tale. It is with morbid fascination that the reader of *Petersburg* follows the crowded and pressing march of the events. As in Dostoevskij's fiction, the action is concentrated on the crisis, both short and intense, that precedes the final catastrophe. The plot deals with the attempt by the young terrorist Ableukhov to kill with a time bomb his own father, a functionary who symbolizes that mixture of an alien civilization and native barbarism which is the Russian state. In appearance, the son plays the role of the protagonist, and the father that of the antagonist, but in practice the roles are reversed. It has been observed that the old and the young Ableukhovs, cursed by the same Tatar blood, end by representing but two different aspects of Russian nihilism. This is true; and it is no less true that that nihilism is shared by the author himself. While working structurally after the pattern of Dostoevskij, from the viewpoint of imagery and style the author of *Petersburg* followed primarily Gogol's example. There as elsewhere he imitated that master in his uncanny sorcery, in his ability to catch the ugliness and the filth of reality within the artful spider web of a splendid form. It is this quality, rather than any superficial or insubstantial similarities, that up to a point justifies the parallel, often made by Western critics, between Belyj's fiction and the art of Franz Kafka or James Joyce. At any rate, whether the parallel is convincing or not, *Petersburg* remains a masterpiece. (The same cannot be said of its belated sequel, *Moscow*, published in 1926.) As a sad comment on the state of American publishing, one must remark at this point that the manuscript of the English version of *Petersburg* had to wait almost thirty years before a sponsor was found willing to present it to an Anglo-American audience.

In 1910 Belyj went abroad with Asja Turgenev, a painter and supposedly a descendant of the great novelist. In 1914 they settled at Dornach in Switzerland, to join the confraternity established there by the German mystic Rudolf Steiner. Steiner was the founder of "anthroposophy," which, despite its name, was a variant of "theosophy," preaching like the latter an occult lore derived from the Western mystical tradition as well as from the spiritualism of the East. What "anthroposophy" tried to teach in practice was a gradual disembodiment of personality, which would finally enable the soul to contemplate a truth no longer veiled by the senses or obscured by the passions of the self.

Belyj's enthusiasm for the way of life of the Steinerian brotherhood soon waned, yet he remained in Dornach for some time after the beginning of the First World War, and returned to Russia in 1916. His infatuation with Steiner's doctrine survived for a while, however, after his return, inspiring in part the writing of *Kotik Letaev* (1917–1918), which, after his two great novels, is perhaps Belyj's most important narrative work. *Kotik Letaev* is a poetic self-portrait of the writer as a child. The autobiographical character of the story is evident even in the name of the protagonist, since "Letaev" is coined after "Bugaev," and *Kotik*, or "kitten," was the nickname by which the writer had been called as a child. The vivid freshness of this evocation of childhood is not fully spoiled even by Belyj's attempt to express the experiences of early life, from infancy to boyhood, within an "anthroposophic" framework, and to project the phases of a child's growth into a ponderous analogy with the spiritual progress of the world soul.

Belyj returned to poetry immediately after the Revolution, perhaps because he felt that only verse could express the renewal of his hope and the revival of his faith. He saluted both February and October with frenetic enthusiasm, and in 1917 he rewrote the ending lines of one of the most famous poems of *Urn*, changing the blasphemous curse of the closing cry: "Disappear into space, disappear, O Russia, O Russia of mine!" into an almost blissful hallelujah: "O Russia, O Russia, O Russia, Messiah of the days still to come!" In 1918, he fell, like Blok, under the influence of Ivanov-Razumnik, the member of a left-wing faction of the Social Revolutionaries which allied itself with the Bolsheviks, and the prophet of Scythianism. It was under that spell that Belyj wrote and published a long narrative poem composed in that kind of free verse which the Russians call *dol'nik*. The poem, entitled *Christ Is Risen* (from the ritual words of greeting which Russian believers exchange on Easter Day), attempts a reinterpretation of the Revolution in charismatic terms; yet Belyj's Red hallelujah is far inferior to, and far more superficial than, Blok's Red hosanna; the ending of Blok's *The Twelve*, with the appearance of Christ among a band of Red Guards, seems to imply the awareness that the Revolution will redeem Russia's sins with the baptism of blood. Far more important than *Christ Is Risen* is Belyj's last outstanding poetic work: the narrative poem *First Meeting* (1921), inspired partly by Pushkin and even more by Solov'ev. In this composition Belyj tried, like Blok in his *Retribution*, to recreate, in a mixture of autobiography and fantasy, in a brilliant display of pathos and wit, the spiritual atmosphere and the cultural environment of his youth. With good reason many reliable critics view this poem as Belyj's highest achievement in the medium of verse.

In 1921, the poet took refuge in Berlin, where he tried to escape from the nightmare of the Revolution, as well as from its hardships. For two years he lived and worked there as an *émigré* writer, but in 1923 he could not stand exile any longer and returned to Russia, where he tried to adjust to the new order, and where he died in 1934. Although he produced other poems, and many other novels, still chiefly philosophical and autobiographical in character, one could say that Belyj's creative gift hardly survived the Revolution itself. Yet he devoted the best part of the last decade of his life to literary theory and criticism, and, even more, to the composition of his literary reminiscences, as both a continuation and a rewriting of the splendid *Recollections of Aleksandr Blok*, which he had published in the Berlin review *Epopée* in 1922–1923. This rewriting, or rather remaking, was dictated by the sharpening of a chronic resentment, the effect of which was to increase the distortions of the earlier version, and to change them into outright falsifications. The full series of Belyj's memoirs, which he was unable to complete, includes in chronological order the following volumes, the last of which appeared posthumously and in unfinished form: *On the Border of Two Centuries* (1929), *The Beginning of the Century* (1933), and *Between Two Revolutions* (1936–1937). It is obvious that these memoirs have less and more than mere documentary importance: biased and inexact as they are, they will remain in Russian literature as a masterful account, always interesting and often appealing, of those strange men and circles, currents and events, which dominated Russian culture from the end of the nineteenth century up to the First World War. Even though quite different in tone, scope, and content, they may be compared to Gertsen's *Past and Thoughts*, if for no other reason than that Belyj, no less than Gertsen, ended by becoming a mocking critic and a severe judge of the very world of which he had been a part.

Belyj's criticism too has more than a passing importance. Many of his outstanding contributions in this field belong to the earliest period of his career, and most of them are gathered in the collections entitled *Symbolism* (1910), *The Green Meadow* (1910), and *Arabesques* (1911). The first of these is particularly significant, especially in the two essays where Belyj studies Symbolist poetry from the viewpoint of verse and technique. These two essays form a personal and controversial treatise on Russian versification, in which, by distinguishing between "meter," or the abstract verse scheme, and "rhythm," or the actual sound pattern of the line, Belyj anticipates some of the theories of the critical school of the Formalists, concerning what the latter were to call the "melodics" and the "instrumentation" of verse. The most important critical works he wrote in his late years are the monograph *Rhythm as Dialectic and the "Bronze Horseman"* (1929), a splendid metrical analysis of that masterpiece; and *The Craftsmanship of Gogol'* (1929), a complex and often arbitrary study of that master, which influenced the theory and practice of many young Soviet writers. Thus one could say that, despite his own feeling of alienation from

Soviet reality, Belyj made his presence felt in Red Russia more than as a mere survivor of a distant past.

During the years of the civil war and of War Communism Belyj had edited in Petrograd a periodical already mentioned elsewhere, *Notebooks of Daydreamers* (1919–1922), while during his brief exile he started writing an autobiographical narrative entitled *A Moscow Crank* (1922–1926). If I cite these two titles it is because I find them highly significant: Belyj was indeed a crank and a daydreamer, as well as a seeker of God, who, like many other God-seekers, worshipped too many idols, one after the other. Although a far lesser poet than Blok, the very variety of his religious, literary, and psychological experiences marks him as the most representative figure of Russian Symbolism. In his continuous pursuit of new faiths and new creeds, Belyj unconsciously served, better than anybody else, the hidden historical task of that movement, which was at once to conceal and to reveal the cultural crisis of the epoch. If Belyj refused to see the crisis of Symbolism, it is perhaps because he embodied that crisis in his person, as well as in his work.

II

VJACHESLAV IVANOV

If the later Belyj replaced the cult of the Eternal Feminine with Rudolph Steiner's "anthroposophy," the early Vjacheslav Ivanov joined the teachings of an older and far greater German master, Friedrich Nietzsche, with the preachings of Vladimir Solov'ev. From Nietzsche he drew the conception of the tragic as a Dionysian ecstasy or frenzy, directly expressing "the spirit of music," and the view that any kind of creative trance is a sort of sacred disease. Far more of a mystic than Nietzsche, he transformed the latter's notion of the philosopher as a "physician of culture" into his own notion of the poet or thinker as the keeper or interpreter of an esoteric lore and a mystical wisdom. From Solov'ev, or, more generally, from the recent idealistic tradition of his own nation and time, he took the idea of the man of letters or the man of culture as a mediator between the values of eternity and those of history, as well as

161

between the demands of the collective and the individual spirit, between what Solov'ev had called *kelejnost'*, or "religion of the cell," and *sobornost'*, or "religion of the congregation." On one side he reattempted, in a spirit far different from Matthew Arnold's, and far closer to similar attempts by some of the men of the early Italian Renaissance, to ally the Biblical and the classical, to re-establish a reconciliation between the Hebraic spirit and the Hellenic genius; on the other side, after having learned from the early Nietzsche and from later students of Greek religion the agonic interpretation of the Bacchic ritual and sacrifice, he tried to adapt it to the metaphysical and syncretic Christianity of Solov'ev, suggesting a symbolic and mystical identity between Jesus and Dionysus.

This gifted and complex personality started from different cultural and intellectual premises, and had a slower maturation, than his two younger brethren, Belyj and Blok. Born in Moscow in 1866 (his family had belonged for a long time to the clerical class, and his father was a minor government official), Vjacheslav Ivanov early trained for a scholarly career rather than a literary one. He studied classical philology at the University of Moscow and later at the University of Berlin, where he worked under Mommsen, and from which he graduated with a thesis in Latin dealing with a highly technical problem in the field of Roman antiquities. Yet Ivanov was bound to abandon soon philology and archaeology, as well as a brilliant scholarly career, for the far more attractive and insecure callings of philosophy and poetry. What led him on this new path was the example of Nietzsche, to whom he had turned because of his interest in the cult of Dionysus. Before the end of the century he wrote his first poems and earned the praise of Solov'ev, who saw them in manuscript. Yet it was not until he had crossed the threshold of middle age that Ivanov published his first collection of verse, *Pilot Stars* (1903), which surprised the literary circles, especially with a cycle of poems devoted to the Dionysian myth. That book, and a brief personal appearance, earned him an enthusiastic reception on the part of the Symbolists, who welcomed him as one of themselves. His second collection of verse, *Translucency* (1906), confirmed his recognition as a master.

One year later he returned home and settled in Petersburg with his wife, Lidija Zinov'eva-Annibal, a minor writer and a distant descendant of "the moor of Peter the Great," as Pushkin had named his maternal ancestor. The Ivanovs opened their "tower" (a penthouse apartment on Tauride Street) to weekly gatherings which attracted the best and most brilliant minds of that time. Their "Wednesdays," which were as important for the Russian cultural life of those years as Mallarmé's "Tuesdays" had been for the French literary life of one generation before, became a center of influence and prestige, made more effective by Ivanov's intellectual authority, as well as by his personal magnetism. In 1905 and 1906 Ivanov published *The Hellenic Religion of the Suffering God*, his earliest version of a series of studies about the Dionysian cult, in which he saw a foreshadowing of Christianity and the sacrifice of the Son of God. At the same time, in the wake of the failure of the Revolution of 1905, he embraced the cause of "mystical anarchism," which had been originally preached by the minor poet Georgij Chulkov, but of which Ivanov became the main prophet and apostle. The "mystical anarchists" had made their own the formula of Ivan Karamazov, who claims to reject not God, but God's creation, and they had developed from that formula the theory of the "inacceptability of the world." Their protest against a reality to which they could not consent led them to take not the hard way out of contemplation and renunciation, but the easy path of a license denying any moral authority or legal bond.

It was Ivanov's mystical anarchism, as well as the publication of another collection of poems, *Eros* (1907), which, as the title indicates, tended to confuse cosmic and spiritual love with eroticism and sex, that led him first to clash with Belyj and then to break with him. Ivanov's example, along with the moral crisis which dominated Russian society after 1905, encouraged many minor writers to exalt sexual license in pseudo-mystical terms, and to produce a long series of vulgar and pretentious pornographic works. In *Self-Knowledge*, which has been mentioned earlier as an important testimonial of the spirit of the age, the philosopher Berdjaev, who had been sympathetic to "mystical anarchism," strongly condemned the tendency on the part of Ivanov and his followers

163

to degenerate from spiritual seers into sensuous and voluptuous voyeurs: "Eros would decidedly prevail over the Logos," says Berdjaev: "it was the flesh that would become word, rather than the word, flesh. . . ." As far as Ivanov is concerned, this tendency subsided after the death of his wife in 1907, which inspired the poems of *Cor Ardens*. This book, the poet's most accomplished work, may be viewed as Ivanov's *In Memoriam*, since it expresses not only his grief at the loss of his life companion, but also his faith in the immortality and the reincarnation of the soul, as well as his belief in the possibility of a daily moral communion and spiritual intercourse between the living and the dead.

In the following years the influence of Ivanov declined, and the final sign of this decline was the end of his "Wednesdays," which took place in 1912, when the poet moved to Moscow. Yet in the decade which preceded the Revolution, Ivanov published, besides the tragedy *Prometheus* (1916), another important collection of poems, *The Sweet Secret* (1912), the message of which, as proclaimed in its title piece, was that "mystery is sweet." Yet the best production of this period of his life is less creative than critical, and includes all his important collections of essays, *By the Stars* (1909), *Furrows and Boundaries* (1916), and *Things Native and Universal* (1917). During the war Ivanov returned home from a stay abroad and settled in Moscow. He saluted the Revolution with an attitude of his own, consisting of detached sympathy. In 1920, when he became a guest in a rest home which the new regime had opened for older intellectuals, he argued in writing the meaning of that great historical event with his roommate, the liberal critic and cultural historian Mikhail Gershenzon (1869–1928). This brief exchange of letters, published the same year under the title *A Correspondence from One Corner to Another*, is one of the greatest and noblest documents of the time. While Gershenzon, following in the footsteps of Tolstoj and Rousseau, takes a radical standpoint and welcomes the Revolution as a social and moral palingenesis, as the attempt by man to reject the oppressive burden of the faiths and ideologies of the past, Ivanov holds fast to his own Goethean and Nietzschean humanism, and to the belief that no revolution is valid unless it is a spiritual and moral renaissance. In the end he places the Revolution itself squarely on the foundations of those traditional values, both religious and cultural, which forge the history of man.

The *Correspondence* shows that Ivanov's attitude toward the Revolution, although still remaining, at least in comparison to the attitude of other writers, almost Olympian in temper, had changed; and a document of that change is to be seen in one of his highest poetic works, a series of twelve sonnets written according to the Italian metrical pattern, which appeared under the title of *Winter Sonnets* in an anthology of "revolutionary poetry" published in 1921 at Berlin by Il'ja Èrenburg. There the Revolution is seen not as a historical but as an elemental event, symbolized by snow and ice, by the cruel indifference of nature toward man, exposed to cold and hunger, searching for fire and lair, for food and shelter. It was indeed the pressure of need which forced Ivanov to become again a scholar and a teacher, and to spend three years as professor of classical philology at the newly founded University of Baku, on the shores of the Caspian Sea, where he ended a new version of his *magnum opus* on the Dionysian religion, while feeling exiled as Ovid in barbaric Thrace. In 1924 he left Russia and settled in Italy, chiefly in Rome, teaching Greek for a few years at the University of Pavia, and publishing once in a while in German and Italian, two tongues he could handle with almost the skill of a native. In 1926 he became a convert to Catholicism and gave a poetic account of that conversion in another sonnet cycle entitled *Roman Sonnets* (1926).

For almost a quarter of a century, up to his death in 1949, Ivanov continued working, revising his old writings and composing new things, the most important of which seems to be a long verse diary that he drafted in the year 1944. One of the few sizable items the poet was able to publish during the decline of his life was the lyrico-philosophical cycle *Man*, fragments of which had appeared in print during the First World War, and which for the most part had been written before he left his homeland. A full edition of that cycle was issued in Paris in 1939, at the beginning of another world conflict, thus escaping the attention of even the literary circles of the Russian emigration.

Ivanov's posthumous publications have been equally scant; most of them (in the main reprints) appeared in separate issues of *Oxford Slavonic Papers*, from 1955 to 1957. The Clarendon Press has been promising for years to publish the collection *Light of Evening*, containing both old and new pieces, but up to now the promise has not been kept. *Habent sua fata libelli*: yet there is no reason to doubt that posterity will recover Ivanov's literary heritage from the obscurity where it still lies, as a treasure buried by the historical destiny of the generation to which he belonged, and of which he was the last survivor.

It was natural for a poet like Ivanov to turn his attention toward broader and older traditions, beyond the immediate example of the European poetry of his own time. The modern classics he most admired were Dante and Goethe, whose names are frequently mentioned in his critical writings, and in whom he saw the two guides of the human mind, one leading it toward the mystery of God, the other, toward the riddles of nature. To other foreign masters he paid the highest tribute a poet can pay, by giving them a new voice in his tongue and style. From among the great writers of ancient Greece he quite naturally chose to translate the sublime tragedies of Aeschylus (his version of *Agamemnon* is a masterpiece) and Pindar's magnificent odes, although he gave perfect renderings of other choral and melic poets, including Bacchilis, Sappho, and Alcaeus. Among the lyric poets of Christendom, his preferences as a translator went equally to Petrarch and Novalis. To all these predilections we must add his admiration for Nietzsche, which never subsided; his love for Tjutchev's poetry, with which, being philosophical in temper, and oriented toward the Romantic idealism of the German tradition, he always felt great congeniality; and finally, his enthusiasm for Dostoevskij, who he considered a seer and prophet, and whose insights (unlike those of Solov'ev) he never doubted. One could even say that all of Ivanov's cultural ideals are summed up in the subtitle which he gave as late as 1932 to the German version of his studies of that great Russian master: *Dostoiewskij: Tragödie, Mythos, Mystik.*

Ivanov's threefold concern with the tragic, the mythic, and the mystical suggests his conception of poetry. Poetry is for him essentially a religious search, and he views the poet as, if not a priest, at least an initiate. Ivanov himself, however, was not only a poet, but also a scholar: a seeker of knowledge, as well as of wisdom. This means that he was as attracted by the quaintness and complexity of his own lore as by the truth hidden within it. Thus, like every connoisseur or specialist, he often became a pedant, flaunting his learning and showing off his erudition. He did so by supplying his poems with exegetical notes and bibliographical references, a critical apparatus better suited for a philological paper, as if he were afraid that the complexity of his allusions would escape not only the understanding, but even the attention, of his reader.

Poetry of this kind naturally requires a special idiom. Ivanov's verse may be rightly considered the highest and most extreme manifestation in the history of Russian poetry of both "poetic diction" and "grand style." The very fact that Ivanov is the most typical Russian representative of a type of poetic language which in other literatures is mainly a Renaissance or post-Renaissance phenomenon is a proof of the uniqueness of the development of Russian poetry. Maurice Baring, limiting his consideration to the nineteenth century, and focusing his attention on Pushkin, compared Russian to Greek lyrical poetry, failing to realize that at least in part such eighteenth-century poets as Lomonosov and Derzhavin had indulged in neoclassical fashions and pseudoclassical mannerisms. Yet it is true that, in its main tradition, Russian poetry follows the Wordsworthian ideal of "common speech"; and it is equally true that only such a modern poet as Ivanov fulfills there the task accomplished in other traditions by such figures as Malherbe or Milton. Despite the fact that he was a Greek scholar by trade, Ivanov represents within the poetry of Russia the same tendency that in English literature is often defined by such epithets as "Latinate" and "Italianate." It is not merely coincidental that Lev Shestov gave Ivanov (not without irony) an appellative which was originally given to a great figure of the Italian Renaissance, and called him "Vjacheslav the Magnificent."

It is in the spirit of the Italian Renaissance that Ivanov spiritualized pagan themes and paganized Christian ones; and it matters very little that the hieratic pomp of his lines is achieved through the use of both Grecianisms and archaisms, the latter taken chiefly from Church Slavonic, in a manner which suggests an attempted reconciliation of Byzantine and classical taste. Such an art demands the almost exclusive practice of closed forms, primarily ancient or medieval in origin, which the poet treats with flawless perfection, controlling rigorously not only rhyme and rhythm, but also diction and syntax. With Pushkin, Ivanov was one of the few Russian practitioners of the Italian sonnet, and he handled that medium with such skill that he was once able, by solving with the mastery of a virtuoso the difficulty involved in repeated *enjambements*, to compose a sonnet made of a single sentence. In medieval fashion, he often treated the same verse form, which is normally limited to a single, self-sufficient poem, as if it were a stanza, one of the many flowers woven into what in ancient Italian poetry was termed a "crown" or "garland" of sonnets: and it was into such a "garland" that he shaped one of his masterpieces.

All this tends to prove that Ivanov's poetry leans all too deliberately toward an abstract compositional symmetry, that too many of his lyrics are written after a premeditated design. This is particularly true of the cycle *Man*, which is divided into two complicated, polimetric parts. The components of both sections are wrought in an identical series of different metrical molds, which in each case follow each other in reverse order. Since the poet fashioned each half after the scheme of the Pindaric ode, one may say with his own words that the first part proceeds from strophe to antistrophe, and the second, from antistrophe to strophe. To help the reader recognize this pattern of inversion and parallelism, the poet marked with the same letters the pieces occupying corresponding points on the twin criss-cross lines forming the geometry of his plan.

The inspiration of *Man* is Christian, and although its formal repertory contains two sapphic odes, most of its meters (such as the sonnet and the *ottava*) are taken from the literary tradition of the Catholic West, from the poetic storehouse of medieval Italy. Yet it is noteworthy that the poet chose to order that cycle according to one of the most elaborate Greek metrical structures. This may well indicate that even when treating Christian themes and Latinate forms, he still viewed the poetry of Greece as the supreme aesthetic ideal. Yet even within Greek poetry what he admires most is not the simple melos of monodic verse, but the complex choral music of the ode, the hymn, or the dithyramb. In his Hellenism the Dionysian urge overwhelms all Apollonian restraint; his muse always behaves like a Bacchante (see the poem "The Maenad"), even when she assumes the pose of a Sybil. The orgiastic temper of his poetry is not affected even by shifts of outlook, taste, or technique; and the poet often introduces a morbid aura of decadent Christianity even into the poems dealing with the most classical subjects. At once a pagan and a mystic, he seems to worship both Astarte and the Madonna. Speaking in the terms of ancient mythology, one could say that he sacrifices impartially to Venus Urania and to earthly Aphrodite; or, if we prefer a Christian metaphor, that he is all too often ready to impose the ritual garments of Sacred Love over the nude body of Eros.

It was perhaps this aspect of Ivanov's thought and work that led Prince Mirskij to label him a splendid sophist. Yet his philosophical and aesthetic conceptions are better understood through such terms as eclecticism and syncretism. In religion, he tried to join together dogma and myth, to reconcile the canonic tradition and the apocryphal one, to marry the holy with the unholy, or at least with profane cults. In culture, he sought a synthesis of knowledge and faith, and dreamed of an alliance between Christianity and humanism. In poetry, he attempted to merge the modern and the archaic, the classical and the primitive. Yet both as a poet and a thinker he looks more like an Alexandrian or a Byzantine than like a Hellene.

It is not for me to judge whether Ivanov purified his religious sophisms through his conversion to Roman Catholicism, toward which he had moved even before the Revolution, and which he had almost foreshadowed in his poem "The Road to Emmaus." Nor is this the place to discuss whether in his debate with Gershenzon he really succeeded in the attempt to bring together art and faith, Hebraism and Hellenism. All too often this master acted like a pompous hierophant or a ponderous mystagogue. Yet the man who was finally forced to avow, for himself and his brethren, "none of us is a true Symbolist," was able once in a while to express his view of life and the world in visions and transfigurations of his own.

This is certainly the case with one of the poems of *Man*: a poem which must be understood as an allegory of the spirit's liberation from the shackles of the self. The poem's theme is a death scene: a passer-by glimpses through an open door a priest keeping vigil over a dead old woman. To express the epiphany of death, the poet speaks to the reader in the three voices of the passer-by, the priest, and the deceased. The same visionary power triumphs in Ivanov's masterpiece, in those *Winter Sonnets* which convey the tragedy of the Revolution through the clear and simple images of an archaic, universal experience, still haunting the memory of the race. As we already know, the poems of that sequence symbolize the trials and the hardships of the present ordeal in man's ancestral struggle for physical and moral survival against the horrors and terrors of the primordial way of life. It is with a sense of both piety and awe that the author of that cycle reflects history's nightmare within the nightmare of prehistory, touching the heart and the mind of the reader by an immediacy of vision and a simplicity of statement all too rare in his poetry.

III

INNOKENTIJ ANNENSKIJ

The poet to be discussed here and now was not only the senior of Vjacheslav Ivanov, who was himself older than the other members of the new Symbolist group: he had been born a few years earlier than even Sologub and Merezhkovskij, the two oldest of all the masters of Russian modernism. Yet this poet bared his own rare gift to himself and to others all too late and too briefly, just before his own death; and that revelation coincided with what at the time seemed to be the "crisis," or even the "agony," of Russian Symbolism. He conveyed the decadent mood with such genuineness of feeling as to change it into a personal experience; and if he used for the purpose the visionary imagery and suggestive music of the

Symbolists, it was only because he found those media the expressive vehicles most congenial to his psyche. This is but one of the reasons why many readers of keen taste, as well as many critics of deep insight, consider him a lyricist of the first rank; and some of them do not hesitate to place him, within the gallery of the Russian poetry of his time, in a place second only to Blok's.

This poet is Innokentij Annenskij, who was born in a remote Siberian city, Omsk, in the distant year 1858. Trained as a classicist, he taught ancient languages in secondary schools, rising to the positions of headmaster of the Gymnasium of Tsarskoe Selo and of school inspector in Petersburg, where he died when he was hardly more than fifty years old. For a long time he was known only as a classical scholar and a translator of Euripides. He also imitated the Greek dramatist in a few tragedies of his own. His posthumous "satyr play," *Thamyras Cytharede* (it was performed by the Tairov troupe in 1916, and published in 1919), dealt, however, with a fable supposedly treated by Sophocles in one of his lost plays: that of the proud harpist Thamyras, who dared to challenge Apollo to a contest of musical skill and was punished for his presumption by the loss of his sight. As we know already, Annenskij entered the literary arena, both as a lyricist and a critic of the new poetry, at the end of middle age, when his short life was almost over. He was about forty-five when he published his first book of poems, under the strange pseudonym *Nik. T. O.*, a partial anagram of his Christian name, forming the Russian word meaning "no one." The choice of that pseudonym, obviously patterned after the Οὖτις by which Homer's Ulysses cunningly names himself to Polyphemus, reflects the author's awareness of his own obscurity. That first book, *Still Songs* (1904), half of which was taken up by very personal translations, mainly from modern French verse, passed almost unnoticed, but the poems which appeared later in many periodicals were enthusiastically received. Annenskij died shortly before 1910, when his masterpiece, *The Cypress Chest*, was published. The rest of his literary heritage is made up of verse fragments and minor pieces, collected, under the title *Posthumous Poems*, as late as 1923; and of two volumes of sensitive and well-written critiques: *A Book of Reflections* and *A Second Book of*

Reflections, published respectively in 1906 and 1909, the last the very year of the poet's death.

The whole lyrical output of Annenskij amounts to about a hundred pieces, rarely consisting of more than three or four stanzas each. At first impression it seems that his poetry tends to move in an atmosphere similar to that of Verlaine. This is particularly true of his earlier poems, where, like that French poet at his best, Annenskij tries to catch vague impressions and to convey indefinite feelings, to fix transitory experiences or to shape impalpable things. The most frequent background of such poems is a garden, painted in the chiaroscuro of twilight rather than in the *plein air* of midday. That garden may well symbolize Annenskij's spiritual and physical world, which is indeed a *hortus conclusus*, preserving the faded flowers of being, while his heart might in turn be compared to a smaller, private shrine, or to use the image of one of his titles, to a quaint coffer or "cypress chest" embalming the relics of feeling.

Yet, if we look deeper, we shall see that if Annenskij is a Verlaine, he is a Verlaine in a saturnine mood. His voice sounds so intimate and discreet, his tone so unassuming and subdued, that it seems his poetry should be called, as Verlaine named his own, a *chanson grise*. As for the tender musicality of his tunes it is so fluid and vague that his lyrics should be likewise defined with the Verlainian title of *romances sans paroles*. Annenskij himself must have been aware of this, since he entitled the first of his collections *Still Songs*. Yet at second glance that "stillness" reveals the feverish and electric quality of this poet's inspirations, and we discover that the "songs without words" are in reality wordless plaints, that the *chanson grise* is in reality a mournful and wailing chant. Thus, while looking at first like a Russian Verlaine, Annenskij turns out to be the only poet of his nation and time whose temper and vision could be compared, in quality if not in degree, to those of Baudelaire.

Annenskij's landscapes, being *états d'âme* in the most literal sense of the term, cannot be simply interpreted as the emblems of a timid and petty decadence, mirroring itself in the twilights or glimmers of late autumn. As Baudelaire said of himself, Annenskij is a painter working not with light but with darkness. His palette neglects all bright and wholesome colors for vanishing shades or fading hues. Yet it is through such shadows and nuances that he succeeds in depicting the purgatory of life and the hell of the world. Thus in substance all his landscapes are but imaginative projections of the innermost experiences of his psyche; one could say that few modern poets ever turned the pathetic fallacy to a better advantage, by sharing with nature at large the shame of the self and the pain of life. Annenskij resembles Baudelaire also in his tendency to see sin and evil even in the most lovely flowers of the earth. All his poetry is in essence but the pathetic revery or morbid fancy of the sense of being, full of a poignant melancholy intoxicating the soul. Annenskij himself saw the spring of his inspiration in "the subtle poison of remembrance," by which he meant a reminiscence mixing loathing and disgust with longing and regret. And it was the poet's awareness of the wicked charm of his craft that led him to avow that he loved his verses "as only a mother can adore her sick children."

In brief, like Baudelaire, Annenskij transformed the mystic dreams of Symbolism into the nightmares of the self. The poet of insomnia and ennui, he conveyed his obsessive and yet lucid vision with direct simplicity of utterance, in almost colloquial speech. Mirskij saw a splendid paradox in the fact that this classical scholar, unlike his colleague Vjacheslav Ivanov, always refused to be tempted by that grand style and lofty diction which are the nemesis of modern classicism. Of all the dimensions of form, the ones for which Annenskij showed greatest concern were meter and rhythm. He was no innovator in that field; all he sought was to recapture in his verse that trancelike music which may be found in the best of the Romantics. His own is but "chamber music," yet the quality of his poetry may be likened, more fairly than to that of his contemporaries, to the most quintessential lyrics of Tjutchev and even Pushkin: in the case of the latter, especially to such a brief piece as "Lines Written on a Sleepless Night," with its uncanny sense of all the perceptions and hallucinations which may haunt a brain morbidly awake, from "the Parque's stammering gossip" to "the mouselike rustlings" of daily life.

MAKSIMILIAN VOLOSHIN AND JURGIS BALTRUSHAJTIS

This is perhaps the place to discuss two poets who might otherwise be hard to classify. The first of them is Maksimilian Voloshin, a lonely and eccentric figure, although he was connected with the Symbolists, or at least with Vjacheslav Ivanov and his "tower." Of all the Russian poets of his time, Voloshin is perhaps the most derivative, the one who imitated most faithfully the rather minor and belated French masters whom he acknowledged as his models. Yet it was his peculiarly Russian frame of mind which at the end of his career led Voloshin to write a series of poems that gained him a small niche in the gallery of Russian poetry. Born in Kiev in 1877, he spent his youth in Paris, where he had gone to study painting and where he remained almost constantly up to the beginning of the First World War. His interest in the visual arts, and his intention to follow Baudelaire's and the Parnassians' example by giving verbal transcriptions of pictorial or sculptural works, are apparent in the long poem he devoted to the glass windows of the Rouen cathedral, which can be read in his first collection, simply entitled *Poems* (1910). His love for France and her culture is equally evident in his imitations and translations of several French writers, especially Barbey d'Aurevilly, and in his suggestive profiles and critiques, most of which he wrote originally as the Parisian correspondent of *The Scales*, and which he later collected in the volume *The Effigy of Creation* (1914).

The poetry of this long-term expatriate, who returned to his native Southern Russia only to find a haven on the warm shores of the Crimea, the Riviera of the Black Sea, is full of Latin splendor and pomp. Yet Voloshin's is a cold and heavy pomp, almost metallic, which recalls the art not so much of his favorite poet, Henri de Régnier, as of the late Parnassian José-Maria de Hérédia. Like Hérédia, Voloshin chisels and engraves, producing a long series of medal-like representations, impeccable in form and painstakingly minute in detail, of figures and scenes taken from the most different ages of world history. To representations of this kind, which Hérédia had called "trophies," Voloshin chose to give the name of "mirrors," as if to emphasize the impassioned objectivity of his vision. That vision is both lifelike and lifeless, since it fixes all lines and colors in the Byzantine rigidity of a geometrical composition, of an artificial form. Voloshin freezes his motionless and passionless figures in the glassy fixation of an unseeing gaze, making them mummylike rather than marblelike, and changing Parnassian immobility and impassability into ataraxy and apathy. His formal ideal seems to be fully expressed by the two lines which Beauty utters in Baudelaire's sonnet:

> *Je hais le mouvement qui déplace les lignes,*
> *et jamais je ne pleure et jamais je ne ris.*

It was with far less indifference that after the impact of the Revolution Voloshin turned his attention to the tragedy of Russian history, which inspired the collection he entitled *Deaf-and-Dumb Demons* with a phrase taken from a famous Tjutchev poem (1919). Voloshin reflected indirectly the same experience in the cycle *Poems on the Terror* (1924), a series of tableaux re-evoking some of the most famous and cruel episodes of Robespierre's dictatorship. The cycle was written to suggest a parallel between the French and the Russian Revolutions, between Jacobins and Bolsheviks, between the bloodbath of 1793 and the slaughter of 1918; yet the suggestion remains a silent hint. It is highly characteristic of Voloshin that he could not give direct representation of the worldshaking events he had personally witnessed, and that he would depict those events only at a double remove, by transferring them to another place and time.

One could then say that Voloshin tried to express and reinterpret the catastrophe he was witnessing in the light of a tragic and passive historical view, in scenes or visions from the national past, reflecting or projecting almost emblematically the present nemesis. Despite his attempt to achieve an attitude of contemplative serenity, controlling hope and despair, even in his last poems Voloshin yielded to his cosmic pessimism and nihilism: the only feeling which still seemed to quicken the cold blood of this poet was the morbid sorcery of mortality, the lugubrious charms of the tomb. In both Holy and Unholy Russia he saw, with fascinated eyes, only the triumph of death. He was certainly not the only poet of his kind whose brain was constantly inhabited by the all-conquering worm. Yet there are few moderns who felt more strongly the attraction of nothingness, who were more obsessed by the mystique of negation, who yielded more willingly to those diseases of the soul to which other ages alluded with such phrases as *tedium vitae* and *cupio dissolvi*. Perhaps this is the reason why Voloshin chose to remain in Soviet Russia, where he was allowed to live in his Crimean retreat up to his death (1932), abandoned but not persecuted, as if he were only a superannuated aesthete or a harmless crank.

Another poet who deserves interest is Jurgis Baltrushajtis, who had nothing in common with Voloshin except the equal sadness of their end. Nothing, indeed, contrasts more with the Southern pomp of Voloshin than the bareness of this son of the North, since, as his name indicates, Baltrushajtis was of Lithuanian descent. In his youth he was an active but nonvocal member of early Symbolism, and the discreet detachment of his position may well explain why he was able to echo the accents of later Symbolist poetry in a lower key, yet with a voice of his own. Like almost all the men of letters of his time, he paid due tribute to foreign writing by translating Byron, many of the great Scandinavian novelists and playwrights, and the Italian poet Gabriele D'Annunzio. His poetic work is almost completely collected in two volumes, *Steps of Earth* (1911) and *The Mountain Path* (1912). As these titles seem to suggest, the main source of Baltrushajtis' inspiration is a sense of closeness to nature, a nature stern and austere, teaching man the lessons of duty, sorrow, and toil. Through the contemplation of nature, Baltrushajtis achieves spiritual vision and moral wisdom.

This poet, born in Catholic Lithuania and raised in Orthodox Russia, conveys the sense of a calm and solemn devotion with an almost Lutheran gravity of tone and simplicity of speech. His landscapes, homely and familiar, portray the cold and rigid nature of the North, while all his poems seem to suggest, not in hidden and allusive symbols, but in clear and plain figures, the pathos of life and the nobility of suffering. The philosophical severity of his thought recalls the poetry of Baratynskij, but his style and imagery bear a certain affinity to the grave simplicity of the mature Blok. Baltrushajtis is, however, far less inspired and visionary than the latter, more inclined to a resignation made of both serenity and quiet. He bows before sorrow with an attitude of humble and taciturn consent, as can be seen in one of his most beautiful lyrics, "The Testament of Grief," in which the poet addresses his soul with the simple command: "Accept your hard hour as a blessing."

Baltrushajtis' sober and measured poetry is perhaps too colorless and a little stiff; his rhythmical stresses fall all too often with the monotonous regularity of the grains of sand in that hourglass which is the subject of one of his best pieces, and perhaps the emblem of his art. Il'ja Èrenburg compared Baltrushajtis' poems to woodcuts, and certainly that poet worked with the rude and heavy hand of a woodcarver, placing, against the background of his flat and desolate skylines, trees that stand like crucifixes, and thickets which look like crowns of thorns. This quality is to be seen even in his late verse, gathered in the volume *The Lily and the Sickle*, as well as in a collection of Lithuanian poems, both of which appeared posthumously, in Paris and Boston respectively, five years after his death (1948). Baltrushajtis had turned his hand to composing poetry in his native speech even before the establishment of the Lithuanian Republic, which he represented as envoy to Moscow from after the Revolution to shortly before the last war. When the Soviets overran the little Baltic state, the poet took refuge in France, and died there in 1943, in solitude and distress, as if he were unable to survive the annihilation of his homeland.

V

TRANSITIONAL POETS

The panorama of Russian poetry at the turn of the century cannot be complete unless we mention two Muscovite poets, who were both befriended by Valerij Brjusov, and were slightly younger than he, but who disappeared early, one by death, the other by an act of renunciation which, although dictated by opposite motives, recalls that of Rimbaud. The first is Ivan Oreus, born in 1877 to a family of Baltic origins, who died by drowning in 1901 when he

177

was only twenty-four. Most of his literary heritage was published posthumously by Brjusov, with the title *Verse and Prose* (1904), under the author's chosen pen name, Ivan Konevskoj. The second poet is Aleksandr Dobroljubov, born in 1876, who, after a brief literary career (he published two booklets, the earlier of which had appeared in 1895 under the Spinozian title *Natura Naturans-Natura Naturata*), disappeared as a wandering God-seeker in the vastness of the Russian land, where he seems to have died at the time of the Civil War. In 1905 Brjusov published the third and most important work of Dobroljubov's pen, *From the Book Invisible*, a medley of lyrical poems and rhapsodies in prose. Both Konevskoj and Dobroljubov are mystical pantheists. The former expresses his view of life and the world in tight language and closed forms, and yet with accents so moving and discordant as to recall the poetry of Gerard Manley Hopkins. Dobroljubov reminds us instead of William Blake. His poetry, more suggestive and obscure, flows with great technical freedom, shaping vague images and chanting subtle rhythms. Dobroljubov's favorite medium, which was the prose poem, prevented his work from affecting in any appreciable way the course of Russian poetry. The example of Konevskoj, which briefly influenced even Brjusov, was destined to become an effective poetic precedent for two of the most creative minds of the Russian literary advance guard, Velimir Khlebnikov and Boris Pasternak. Yet both Dobroljubov and Konevskoj represent but different aspects of the same transition or crisis: their relative aloofness from the fashions which most seduced their contemporaries makes of them two significant links in the modern tradition of Russian poetry, which, at least up to the Soviet period, is an unbroken chain.

CHAPTER SIX

ALEKSANDR BLOK

I

BLOK'S LIFE AND MINOR WORKS

THE new sensibility which was to imbue and to shape the arts and letters of the Russian silver age found its highest interpreter in a man who was born a poet in the most authentic sense of the term, and who, through the priceless contribution of his artistic and moral insight, was destined to transcend the limits of the aesthetic and cultural movement to which he was originally bound. That man was Aleksandr Blok, who represented a new culmination in the history of Russian lyrical poetry, three quarters of a century after Pushkin, Lermontov, and Tjutchev, and who opened new paths for the future. Blok was the most highly creative figure of his age; and the originality of his work, the peculiar appeal of his personality, the moving strangeness of his life, make necessary a detailed study not only of his poetry but also of his biography.

Aleksandr Blok was born in 1880 in a building of the University of Petersburg, to a family of distant German descent. His father was a jurist, who later taught public law at the University of Warsaw; his mother was one of the daughters of the famous botanist Beketov, who was also rector of the University of Petersburg. The father, intelligent and gifted, had a violent temper and an unbalanced mind, and soon after their marriage his wife divorced him. From his childhood up to the threshold of his maturity, Aleksandr lived with his mother and his mother's family, within a circle of women relatives, all sensitive and cultivated; and such a long seclusion in an exclusively feminine environment, a little morbid and unnatural, had a powerful and lasting influence on the poet's psychology. Only in his maturity was he able to free himself from that charmed circle: in his reaction against it, he felt in tune with the misogynism of Strindberg, once confessing in verse, without thinking primarily of sexual love: "All too often was I in women's rosy chains. . . ."

As a child and a youth, "Sasha" used to spend his summers at the Beketov country house in Shakhmatovo, not far from Moscow. In Moscow, the Bloks were related to the family of Mikhail Solov'ev, the philosopher's brother, who had married a cousin of the poet's mother. Blok was thus a second cousin of Mikhail Solov'ev's son, Sergej, who was five years his junior. Yet it was only in 1900, shortly after his discovery of the poetry of Vladimir Solov'ev, that Sasha befriended the precocious "Serezha," who seemed to have inherited the mystical tendencies of his famous uncle. It was the Solov'ev family that put Blok in touch with another promising youth, equally interested in mysticism and poetry, Boris Bugaev, son of a professor of mathematics at the University of Moscow, and destined to become well known in the annals of Russian letters under the pen name of Andrej Belyj. When in 1903 Aleksandr Blok and Boris Bugaev wrote their first letters to each other on the same day, the two correspondents considered that strange coincidence as a sign of election and a token of grace.

In Petersburg the Beketovs knew the family of the famous chemist Mendeleev, and they renewed their acquaintance with him and his daughter Ljubov' when the Mendeleevs spent their summers in a village near Shakhmatovo. The love between the two young people was born from their participation in amateur theatricals, in which Ljubov' shone, being seemingly as gifted as an actress as Aleksandr was as a poet. Blok married Ljubov' in 1903, while he was still a student at the School of Law (which he left for the School of Letters, from which he graduated several years later). Blok and his wife remained good friends almost always, although Ljubov's career as an actress led them to live separate lives, and in spite of the fact that in later years the poet found solace and oblivion in other loves. Shortly after their wedding, he published in book form the best of the several hundred poems he had been composing from his early youth, or, as he said, *ante lucem* and *post lucem*, by which he meant before and after the revelation of his love for the girl who was then his bride. That collection, which appeared in 1905 under the title of *Poems on the Beautiful Lady*, proves better than any other the truth of the author's later statement that his poetry was written, and should be read, as a long, single personal diary. From the earliest of its manifestations Blok's lyricism impressed readers as a unique blend of talent and temperament. His youthful muse was the least stylish and literary of all the muses of the time, and her voice sounded stranger and newer for speaking in familiar and old-fashioned accents, for striking up again that "song of innocence" which Russian verse had already sounded in the poetry of Zhukovskij, Fet, and Solov'ev.

If Blok was primarily, although not exclusively, a poet of sensibility, it was perhaps because nature had endowed him with an eerie psychic insight, an uncanny sense of the changes which were bound to occur in the world within and outside of him. It was as early as 1901, at the time when his soul brimmed with faith and hope, that he felt the first pangs of doubt, and that he closed with this avowal a poem addressed to the Beautiful Lady: "I fear you will change your countenance." In 1904 he went further, even if he reaffirmed her reality and grace, by claiming in the final apostrophe of another poem that the Beautiful Lady had left him without pledging her protection or return: "You withdrew forever afar. Be hallowed your name." Such unauspicious forebodings were accompanied or followed by shattering private and public events. In 1904 Belyj fell in love with "Ljuba," creating a rift in the poet's circle and a difficult situation in his household. The following year Ljuba's desire to follow an independent career on the stage forced husband and wife to live as strangers to each other. Starting then Blok often led a life of dissolution and dissipation, spending his nights in drinking orgies, or pursuing the "Russian Venus" in her dens or haunts. And it was shortly afterwards that he heeded for the first time the call of passion, entering into a liaison with the actress Natal'ja Volokhova, to whom he was to dedicate later the lyrical cycles *Faina* (1906–1908) and *Snow Mask*.

At the same time, like all thinking and feeling Russians, Blok underwent the traumatic historical experience of the year 1905 and its aftermath. Unlike some of his friends, he was unable to recover from the tragic disappointment of the "little revolution" and the hopes its had raised. He had sincerely believed in the good tidings of a Second Coming, in the imminent advent of a new society, ruled by the cult of Sophia and the religion of love. The defeat of this dream left in his heart a wound that never healed, and he felt that from now on his poetry should not sing but weep. Yet, before he abandoned forever his belief in an impending palingenesis, he passed through a transitional phase, dominated by a mood not yet hopeless, but no longer hopeful. This phase and mood are expressed by the collection of poems which he published in 1907 under the title *The Unexpected Joy*: a title supplied by a phrase in the narrative poem *The Night Violet* (1905), which was included in that book.

Perhaps because he was not yet ready to convey a negative or cynical view of life in lyrical form, Blok chose the vehicle of drama, which allowed him to express criticism of his old beliefs in tragicomic terms. Thus, from 1906 on, he wrote three plays, which were staged by the young director Vsevolod Mejerkhol'd, and acted by the company led by the famous actress Vera Komissarzhevskaja. It was the time when Maeterlinck's influence was felt everywhere, affecting in Russia, among others, even Leonid Andreev. Certainly the plays of the two Russians are as "symbolic" as Maeterlinck's but less "symbolistic," precisely because they were born not out of faith but out of despair. Their aim was to prove, not the presence in, but the absence from, life of those metaphysical values in which the Belgian poet never ceased to believe. While Andreev's plays, which are perhaps more allegorical than symbolical, are written in prose, Blok's mix prose with verse. Moreover, even when regularly divided into five acts, Blok's plays are sketchy and brief, and must be considered closet dramas rather than regular theatrical pieces. These three plays, all composed and performed during the same period of time, are *The Puppet Show* (or *The Show Booth*, 1906–1907), *The King in the Square* (1907), and *The Unknown Lady* (1907–1908).

In 1908, the poet gathered these pieces into a small collection entitled *Lyrical Dramas*. The adjective in the title may seem to question the theory that Blok had chosen the technique of the stage because of his inability to express at that time his new, negative view of life in lyrical terms, but such a doubt will be easily dispelled by a reading of the brief preface, in which the author clearly and simply explained his own artistic intent as a "lyrical" playwright: "These little dramas . . . are lyrical dramas, that is, dramas in which the experiences of an individual soul . . . merely happen to be presented in dramatic form. . . ." In other words, since that individual soul is evidently the poet's own, what they represent dramatically is but a series of personal allegories. The single theme of their fables or parables is the poet's loss of faith, which they evoke through the double perspective of self-pity and self-criticism; and this is the reason why they are ruled by a spirit of bitter humor, and even of grotesque parody. "All these dramas," says Blok, "are united by a mocking tone which perhaps makes them more akin to that 'transcendental irony' of which the Romantics spoke." In reality, even more than by any "romantic irony," they are distinguished by the sarcastic scorn by which the poet treats the "great expectations" of his mystical youth. Despite the subjective quality of his indictment, Blok thought that he was expressing in those plays more than a personal view; but he was soon proved mistaken by the scandalized protest of his friends, who felt shocked by them. The very first of those plays, *The Puppet Show*, caused Sergej Solov'ev and Andrej Belyj to see in Blok a traitor and a renegade, and intensified the private feuds and doctrinal quarrels which were already rending their little church. Blok's fellow believers could not stand the caricatural tone with which the poet had characterized in that play the gatherings of their quaint sect; they also resented one of his first essays, written at the same time, condemning the leading intellectuals of his generation for their vain "religious quests." But, above all, the still faithful worshippers of Sophia could not forgive him for the blasphemous metamorphosis of the Beautiful Lady into a cardboard doll.

It would be difficult to summarize the content and the message of these plays better than the poet did in another passage of his preface. After stating that "all these dramas are linked together by the unity of their principal characters," Blok sums up in this way the special and general traits of their protagonists: "The grotesquely luckless Pierrot in *The Puppet Show*, the morally weak Poet in *The King in the Square*, and the other Poet who . . . dreams away his vision in *The Unknown Lady*, all these are, as it were, different facets of one man's soul. . . ." As for the three plots, the poet concisely conveys their common symbolic meaning by contrasting the magnificence of the dream with the hollowness or vanity of its outcome. The ideal of all the heroes of those plays is, the poet says, "an incarnation of the image of the Eternal Feminine: for the first, it is Columbine, the radiant bride whom only the sickly and nasty imagination of Pierrot could turn into a 'cardboard bride'; for the second, the Architect's Daughter, a beauty who cherishes a Biblical dream and perishes together with the Poet; for the third, the Unknown Lady, a star that fell from the sky and took on flesh, only to disappear again, making fools of the poet and the Astrologer."

In later years, Blok wrote a few more dramatic pieces, almost all of which, along with the previous ones, were collected in 1916 under the title *Theater* in one of the volumes of his collected works. The most important of them, and the longest he ever wrote, is *The Rose and the Cross* (1913–1914). While the action of the preceding plays had taken place in a kind of anonymous nowhere and timeless present, the action of *The Rose and the Cross* takes place in the thirteenth century, in Languedoc and in Brittany. There is no doubt that the poet made some archaeological and philological studies in order to give a feeling of authenticity to the epoch and the locale. Yet its climate is more legendary than historical, and the poet himself denied that the play's chronological and geographical background had any importance per se. He made use of the exotic colors of the story, and of its remoteness in time, only in order to suggest some permanent or modern equivalents for the "merry wisdom" of Provençal poetry, and for what has been called "Celtic magic" or "Celtic twilight."

The story is a pathetic romance: Bertran, the shapeless warden of Count Archimbault's castle, is equally loyal as a feudal vassal and as a servant of love, spending his life in the active service of his lord and in the passive adoration of his lady, Isora, the count's wife. In the course of a single day he proves his fidelity to his lord by shedding blood in battle for him, and shows his devotion to his lady by helping the handsome page Aliscan spend the night with her. He dies during the watch, but his death prevents the suspicious husband from surprising the two lovers. Isora's desire to live fully and joyfully is represented by the symbol of the rose; Bertran's "gladness in suffering," his readiness to sacrifice his life for an ideal of loyalty and love, is represented by the symbol of the cross. As for the poor old knight Gaetan, the minstrel from Armorica, he personifies the spirit of poetry: it is his voice, and the echo of his songs, that fill the play with a sense of mystery and awe.

The Rose and the Cross is generally considered the masterpiece of Blok's drama. It is certainly more elaborate but also more conventional; more fantastic but less imaginative; more constructed, but also more mannered, than his earlier dramatic pieces. Less subjective than usual, it is the only play of Blok's which aims at being a poetic drama rather than merely a poet's drama. Its relative success is perhaps due to the fact that in it Blok's youthful beliefs were revived and redeemed. Yet the previous plays, especially *The Puppet Show* and *The Unknown Lady*, are more interesting and varied, both as personal documents and literary works; they remind the reader not only of Maeterlinck, but also of Strindberg's "dream plays" and of Ibsen's "symbolic" dramas (see, for instance, the similarity of the theme of *The Unknown Lady* to that of *Solness the Masterbuilder*). What is even more striking is that these two pieces re-echo Ibsen and Strindberg with an irony akin to Laforgue's. *The Rose and the Cross* seems instead to be written in the spirit of an all-too-refined and almost bloodless Rostand. All the heroes of Blok's dramas are "puppets," but at least in the earlier plays they are aware that the world they live in is a "puppet show," and for this very reason they are more real and more poetic than the characters of *The Rose and the Cross*.

It was before writing *The Rose and the Cross*, which was his most ambitious undertaking as a playwright, that Blok tried his hand at *Retribution*, a long narrative in verse by which he sought to rival Pushkin himself. He worked at it from 1910 to 1911, but all that is left is an opening canto, a torso of the second, and a prelude to the third. The psychological motivation of *Retribution*, which Blok started composing after the death of his father, was his sense of guilt as a son, and also as a Russian, toward that Poland where his father had lived and died alone. From its fragments, as well as from its title, we realize that the poet intended to deal with the notions of biological heredity and historical nemesis, with that chain of being to which he was tied by the links of life and death. The literary aims are even clearer: Blok wanted to make of *Retribution* a *confession d'un enfant du siècle*, as well as a "novel in verse" like *Evgenij Onegin* and a legendary tale like *The Bronze Horseman*. Blok's genius was neither epic nor fabulous, and it is easy to understand why he failed to complete the work after the initial spark flagged. Yet that unfinished rhapsody contains passages of great power and insight.

Those very passages reflect all the changes of mind and heart which Blok had undergone since the publication of his second book. After his first experiments in the field of drama, a genre he had cultivated as a pretext for venting his private angers and griefs, Blok had returned to lyrical poetry as if he were a changed artist and a new man. For almost a decade, starting with 1907, there issued from his pen a constant flow of cycles, poems, and lyrics, which include most of his highest achievements and almost all his supreme *réussites*. Prince Mirskij rightly considers the production of these years "the greatest body of poetry written by a Russian poet since the middle of the past century." Blok had become a master; and one of the signs of this mastery may be seen in the attention he was now paying to all the classics of Russian poetry, to all those who had shaped the instrument he was now wielding with what seemed to be inborn grace, rather than acquired skill. At this point he could take as his models not only the "romantic" Lermontov and Tjutchev, but also Pushkin the "classic" and Nekrasov the "realist." At the same time this poet seemed to be able to use for his purpose even the imaginations of such masters of Russian prose fiction as Gogol' and Dostoevskij.

The work which opens the most fecund phase of Blok's lyrical creation is *The Snow Mask* (1908), a series of poems written after the pattern of a musical suite, both exalting and lamenting the perdition of the soul in the whirlwind of passion and winter. Immediately after its appearance this series was incorporated in Blok's third book of poems, *Earth in Snow* (1908). Three years later this book was followed by a fourth, *Nightly Hours* (1911); and in the same year, when he published for the first time a full collection of his verse, the poet merged both books in a single volume with the synthetic title *The Snowy Night* (1911). In 1913 Blok issued separately his verse tale *The Nightingale Garden*, almost exceptional in his work, being inspired by a melancholy not devoid of serenity. But generally the poems of these years are dictated by the tragic pathos of the poet's experience; they are the poetic account of his passions and vices, the lyrical confession of his sense of temptation and sin. This pathos finds a peculiarly poignant expression in the gypsy songs which were suggested to Blok by the reading of the forgotten poet Apollon Grigor'ev, whom in 1916 he was to edit in a selection that revived his fame. The highest culmination of this aspect of Blok's art must be seen in *The Snow Mask* and in other poems of the same period, but some traces of the same inspiration are visible in the cycle *Carmen*, composed in 1914 to celebrate the love of the poet for the opera singer L. A. Delmas, a renowned interpreter of the heroine of Merimée and Bizet. This cycle was to enter the canon of Blok's poetry with the publication in 1916 of a second edition of his complete lyrical work. Soon afterward the creative powers of Blok seemed to be on the wane; during the war and its aftermath the most he produced was translations, editions, and prose works. Yet the poems written in this period made the bulk of his fourth and last book of poetry, which was to appear under the sad title *The White-Haired Morning*, as late as 1920, just one year before the poet's death.

The last years of Blok's life were affected by the historical ordeal which was ushered in by 1914 and 1917. Even before the Russian Revolution, even before the First World War, Blok's sensitive mind had felt that catastrophic events were approaching, both in Russia and in Europe; and it was perhaps under the impact of this feeling that, in 1909, 1911, and 1913, he had made his three journeys to the countries of the West. Besides Belgium and Holland, he visited Germany, France, and Italy: Germany seemed to him the land of life, Italy the land of death. Perhaps for this very reason, it was the latter that left a stronger impression on his poetic imagination, causing him to write a beautiful series of *Italian Poems* (1909), which includes a splendid piece on Ravenna. As for France, more than her cities or countryside, he loved her wild Atlantic seascapes, from Brittany to the Bay of Biscay. But, like so many other Russian writers, each time he returned home a more loving son.

Even before those travels, Blok had reflected deeply on Western culture and the destiny of his homeland. More and more often he chose to put down these thoughts in the form of meditative prose, rather than translate them into poetic intuitions. As a matter of fact, it was from 1907 on, up to the Revolution itself, that he wrote all the essays in which he tried to face what he thought was the most critical issue of the epoch. The issue itself may be conveyed in a nutshell by the title *Russia and the Intelligentsia*, which the poet gave in 1918 to an almost complete collection of these essays. Their merit is not very great, yet they are relevant testimonials of the poet's spiritual development. What is even more important is that they help to explain the reasons that led their author to feel sympathy for the Revolution and to write the most extraordinary of all revolutionary poems.

Blok's "political" and "ideological" pieces are apocalyptic and messianic tracts, which seem to be written by a decadent Populist or a modern Slavophile of the Left. In the preface accompanying their publication in book form, the poet defined their over-all intent as a double attempt to view Russia as the incarnation of "the spirit of music," and to prove "the anti-musicalness of the concept of intelligentsia." That the mythical idea of "the spirit of music," which is the leitmotiv of the entire series, derives from Nietzsche's *Die Geburt der Tragödie* is formally indicated in the final passage of one of the essays included in that book. Yet Blok's "spirit of music," although conceived as the Dionysian force of vital change, bringing chaos in order to create a new cosmos, is understood by the poet in a sense very different from Nietzsche's. The writer's outlook or message is already evident in the most important of the earlier pieces, "The people and the Intelligentsia" (1908), which begins as a defense of Gor'kij, discusses at length the schism separating the Russian intellectuals from the Russian masses, and ends with a note of despair about that schism. Equally important among the later essays is "The Intelligentsia and the Revolution" (1918), which condemns the revulsion of the elite against the cruelty and harshness of revolutionary reality. "A revolution is akin to nature. . . . Like a whirlwind, like a snowstorm, it always brings the new and the unexpected. . . . This rumbling is always about great things. . . ." Therefore, says Blok, "the business and duty of the artist is . . . to listen to that music in which thunders 'the thrashing of the tempest.' " The essay closes with this final appeal to his fellow intellectuals: "But the spirit is music. The demon once commanded Socrates to obey the spirit of music. With every cell of your body, with every striving of your conscience — listen to the Revolution."

Written in the same vein is "The Downfall of Humanism," which was read as a lecture in 1919, and which belongs to the same series in spirit, if not in fact. In this, which is the last of Blok's essays, the prophet of doom seems to see the flicker of a new hope. According to Blok the humanistic heritage, which triumphed in the West from the Renaissance to the age of Schiller and Goethe, had failed to achieve its mission in our epoch. Using, almost at the same time as Spengler, the favorite terms of that German thinker, although in the opposite sense, Blok claims that modern humanism had built a "culture" based on individualism, but that, by its inability to understand the collective, unconscious will of the masses, it had failed to build a real "civilization." Humanism's sensitivity to "calendar time" had been accompanied by its insensitivity to "musical time": in other words, to the metaphysical needs of a new historical situation. But "the guardians of the spirit of music become just those elements to which music always reverts. . . : namely, the people and the barbaric masses." Devoid of "historical memories," untouched by the humanistic tradition of individualistic culture, Russia will perhaps be able to help the establishment of a new society and "the birth of a new man."

Before glimpsing the flash of a new light in the dark fire of the Revolution, Blok had seen his worst fears confirmed by the war which had suddenly raged all over Europe. Although he was a neutralist and a pacifist, late in the conflict he volunteered to join a detachment of civilian auxiliaries, helping to build fortifications in the rear of the front. After the fall of tsarism, he returned to Petrograd, where the Provisional Government named him secretary to a Commission of Inquiry investigating the vices and crimes of the ancient regime. Later on, his report on the last days of imperial power was published in book form. He welcomed not only February, but even October, as an epiphany and a triumph. He accepted the new order, and the chaos it brought with it, with religious enthusiasm, and with a strange kind of revolutionary patriotism.

In those days Blok had fallen under the influence of the second-rate political leader and literary critic, R. V. Ivanov-Razumnik, who belonged to that group of Social Revolutionaries who shifted their allegiance from their own party to the Bolsheviks. To his messianic vision of the Russian masses as the barbaric builders not only of a new society but also of a new religion, of a new city of man and a new city of God, Ivanov-Razumnik had given the name "Scythianism." His doctrines affected other poets, like Belyj and Esenin, and influenced the writing of such poems as the former's *Christ Is Risen* and the latter's *Inonija*. Under the same influence, Blok wrote and published in 1918 *The Twelve* and *The Scythians* (both of them appeared originally in *The Flag of Labor*, an organ of the Social Revolutionaries of the Left wing). The poet wrote the first poem to follow his own commandment "to listen to the music of the Revolution," and composed the second as a warning to the Allied Powers, which were then contemplating intervention against the Bolsheviks. *The Scythians*, inspired also by an old allusion to the "yellow peril" made by Solov'ev in one of his poems, took the shape of an ode, where the "barbaric lyre" of the poet sang a resounding appeal to the West to make peace with Russia, and threatened, if the appeal went unheeded, that the new "Scythians" would again open their gates to the hordes of the East. While *The Scythians* is now regarded as merely a splendid piece of pathetic eloquence, *The Twelve* still appears to be not only the single outstanding creation of the closing phase of Blok's career, but also one of his supreme masterpieces.

In spite of the fact that the Bolsheviks tried to be as generous as possible toward him, the hardships of the times, his declining health, and, above all, his growing disappointment with the regime made the last years of Blok's life a long torture. He was able to survive during the worst periods of the crisis by translating and editing for "Universal Literature" (a collection which Gor'kij had founded to help writers in distress), only to succumb later to a moral and physical breakdown. It was in this same period that Blok published in book form his literary essays (the first of which had originally appeared in 1910), under the title *About Symbolism* (1921). With the addition of a few more pieces, such as the lectures on Solov'ev and Strindberg, that book forms the entire body of Blok's criticism, while a few translations and editions, and, above all, the letters and diaries, published posthumously, complete his literary heritage. To this heritage the poet could add very little during the last three years of his existence. If the last lines he wrote, inscribed to Pushkin's great name, read like a moving appeal to the shades of a glorious past, his last public words sounded like a warning for the future, like the foreboding of an enslavement of the mind which would doom man's creativity, and ruin his soul. In 1921, at the very moment of his passing, Blok perhaps felt that not only the old world, but also the hope of a new and better one, was perishing with him.

II

THE POETRY OF BLOK'S YOUTH

As we already know, the young Blok dedicated himself to the celebration of the cult of the Eternal Feminine. That cult had first entered European culture by way of the mysticism of the East, making its appearance in both Christian heresies and pagan myths. Yet it also frequently merged with philosophical visions and orthodox creeds. Thus, while the Gnostics had represented their notion of divine wisdom in the holy image of Sophia, the new religion in time elevated Mary to the place occupied by the Trinity. Medieval poetry, insofar as it was neither barbarian nor popular, exalted both the Virgin Mary and the *domina*, an idealized lady who remains of this world. This dual worship is to be seen in the lyrics of Provence, in the various branches of the *gai saber* within and outside the Romance world, among the *Minnesänger* and the poets of the *dolce stil nuovo*. Humanistic Platonism, at once pagan and Christian, dreamed of reconciling sacred and profane love within one of the highest artistic versions of that cult. Petrarch's verse had humanized his love for woman without humanizing its object: while the Renaissance, by taking his poetry as a code of elegance and a canon of forms, turned the cult into a worldly fashion and a literary convention. The final secularization and profanation of the worship of woman is to be seen in the replacement of the Beatrices and the Lauras, who are quasi-saints, with the Astrées and the Célies, who are quasi-nymphs. At this point both the cult and the image were finally discarded, the one being reduced to a travesty, and the other to a mask.

It was only after the emergence of the Romantic spirit, with its sense of mystery and awe, that the myth revived again. Goethe restated the principle of the Eternal Feminine in the closing words of his masterpiece. The early poets of German Romanticism, especially Novalis, had already devoted to the exaltation of that principle a significant part of their work. As for the Belles Dames Sans Merci, celebrated with other names by other poets than Keats, or the all-too-many Blessed Damosels invoked within and outside of the Pre-Raphaelite Brotherhood, they were but new versions of the same erotic mystique. Yet no modern poet has ever consecrated to that cult so vast a body of poetry as the youthful Aleksandr Blok, who had rediscovered it in the recent metaphysical speculations of his native tradition and had recognized one of Sophia's latest avatars in the esoteric poetry of one of his masters, the philosopher Vladimir Solov'ev. Blok called the being whom his poetry evoked, or rather invoked again, by the designation of Beautiful Lady, which is deceivingly simple, being at once mystical and courtly, as well as chivalric and popular, in both sense and tone. Blok adored the Beautiful Lady with a humble devotion, as if she were not only a heavenly fiancée but also, to use the words of a famous love poem by Baudelaire, a "Guardian Angel," a "Muse," and a "Madonna."

Blok's first collection of poems takes its name from that icon and is entitled *Poems on the Beautiful Lady*. The book is divided into three cycles, the first being called, in Latin, "Ante Lucem," which might be, quite appropriately, a general title for the more than three hundred poems in the whole collection. For the spiritual atmosphere throughout is one of expectation and initiation rather than of mystical revelation. The Beautiful Lady is surmised, rather than seen: she is not so much a presence as a dream or a longing, a hope or a desire. All too often the poet has no visions but forebodings; occasionally, he sees, or better feels, portents and signs.

From a psychological, and perhaps also an aesthetic, standpoint, one might find natural the poet's inability to envisage the ideal figure after which he strives. It is obvious that Blok fails in the attempt to project and to reshape into reality the phantasm he carries within himself. That phantasm is perhaps but a reflection of the femininity of his own psyche; yet the fantasy itself is rooted in innocence and purity. It would be unfair to accuse Blok of perversion or morbidity; ghostly as she is, the Beautiful Lady never takes such ambiguous and perfidious forms as the Morellas and the Ligeias resuscitated by the poetic necromancy of Edgar Allan Poe. A psychoanalytical critic might well see in the Beautiful Lady the sublimation of a Narcissus complex. But the diagnosis would be wrong, at least in literary terms: the childish naïveté of Blok's mystical *Sehnsucht* is such as to dispel the suspicion that his youthful muse is affected by decadent vices or decadent ills. Yet the very paradox of his first collection of poems may be seen in the poet's failure to grasp or reach that feminine image, to embody in the outside world what Jung would call his *anima*, or the womanly archetype which is rooted within his soul.

The whole of Blok's early verse is a realm of gleams and shadows, flickers and *frissons*, resonances and hints. Its mood and taste are not so much symbolistic as neoromantic. Allegory appears only seldom; even "symbols" in the manner of Baudelaire and Mallarmé make rare apparitions in the poetry of the young Blok.

The *Poems on the Beautiful Lady* recalls the book of a non-Russian poet which appeared in the same year, Rainer Maria Rilke's *Stundenbuch*. For both poets ritual seems to count more than faith itself: the experience they convey is the training and testing of the soul, rather than the ecstasy it strives for. This is why in Blok's first book the poet's art tends more to suggestion than to realization: what counts is not the "theme" but its "variations." For these reasons, the impressionistic critique of Chukovskij and the stylistic analysis of Zhirmunskij are far more relevant than the allegorical exegesis of Andrej Belyj for both the interpretation and appreciation of this work. The reader of the *Poems on the Beautiful Lady* has really no need to know much about the significance of its "symbolism," to learn that the Beautiful Lady is a hypostasis of Sophia, or to be told how she is related to the "religion of the Holy Ghost." The real concern of the reader is, and should be, with the poet's inner vision, and with the voice that bodies it forth.

Blok does not fix the intellectual content of his inspiration into firm images: rather, he dissolves that content into reverie and fantasy, into the vague and fluid atmosphere of fancy and dream. In this book he is the poet of the indefinite, rather than of the infinite: even when he feels the presence or the proximity of the Beautiful Lady he merely says that "somebody," or even "something," is beside or near him. Blok sees shadows, not creatures or things: what he contemplates is above all the reflection of his own dream. His psyche is constantly in a state of trance, which never turns into full rapture or transport. In brief, what motivates this poetry is not a manly will to believe, but a sentimental impulse, a naïve mystical wish. If Blok rests his faith mainly on ritual and liturgy, it is because the ultimate grace of religious belief is denied to him. Most of the poems of this book are gestures of adoration rather than acts of love. Often the poet prays not as one who expects a miracle, or at least a sign, but as one afraid that the miracle will fail, that the sign will never come. Sometimes he seems to believe that genuine prayer arises not from faith but from suspicion and doubt.

The development of Blok's early poetry may be described as a crescendo of incertitude and distrust. It is doubt, and doubt alone, that dominates the inspiration of the poems closing his first book, and their presence there finds its aesthetic justification in the fact that they, too, are poems of presentiment and foreboding. What the poet now foresees and foretells reflects no longer the rays of hope, but the shadows of fear. What he now anticipates is not the presence but the absence of the Beloved, not an imminent revelation but an impending failure.

The *Poems on the Beautiful Lady* ignores the concrete world of reality, and evokes in its place an unsubstantial aura, a rarefied atmosphere. The images do not stand in clear and firm outline against the sky, but waver and hover, bodiless and shapeless, at mid-air. When we pass to Blok's second book, *The Unexpected Joy*, however, we witness a change of locale and climate, of vision and imagery. The change itself is well suggested by the title of the opening cycle, "Earth's Bubbles," which Blok took from the words by which Banquo tries to explain away to Macbeth and himself the witches who have just appeared and disappeared before their eyes. In this book, and especially in that cycle, the realm of shadows and fitful cross lights is thus replaced by a landscape which is a recognizable part of this earth, even if it is inhabited by creatures which are inhuman or nonhuman, by a spectral flora and a bloodless fauna.

The new landscape is but a transfiguration of the delta of the Neva, of that Petersburg countryside which looks like a Northern *campagna*, a desert spotted with marshes and lakes. Everything here is grassy and watery, humid and misty, fading and formless. From the unearthly Paradise of the first book we have now descended into a kind of limbo, halfway between life and death. Dreamland is now a marshland. Here, for the first time, the poet foreshadows the human and the worldly through animal legends and floral myths. The first creature which the poet finds in this purgatory of being is not so much a spirit as a sprite, that "little priest of the bogs," who prays not only "for the reed that bends" or "for the ailing leg of a frog," but even "for the Pope of Rome."

Nothing could be more natural for the poet, as soon as he enters this world of fens and pools, to embody the Beautiful Lady in a vegetal fetish, in a pale flower of the bogs. Such a metamorphosis, which is also a metempsychosis, takes place in the long poem *The*

195

Night Violet. Perhaps "the unexpected joy" of the book title refers to the pale and languid epiphany of this poem, which is part of that book. *The Night Violet* is so typical of what one might call the second manner of Blok that it deserves being treated in detail. A study of this piece may also show Blok's method in using for his own purpose alien sources and myths not of his own making. In its theme the reader will easily recognize reminiscences from the Arthurian romances, and a replica of the legendary episode of Percival's entering the castle of Camelot only to find that the King and his retinue of knights are sleeping their century-long sleep.

The full title of *The Night Violet* defines the poem as "a dream," while a poet's note claims that the poem is "the exact reproduction of an actual dream." The oneiric vision begins, however, as soon as the poet abandons the metropolis which appears at the beginning of the poem, and enters what is at once a marshland and a dreamland. The marshland itself exists also on this earth, not just in the geography of the mind: it is a real landscape as well as a mirage. There is no doubt that the subtitle of the poems alludes not only to the content of the vision, but also to the style of the composition, to the lullaby quality of its rhythms, to the poet's obvious intent to transcribe verbally the state of the psyche between sleeping and waking. Metrically, *The Night Violet* is one of Blok's most successful experiments in the field of free verse. Yet, despite its varying length, the line keeps an even and regular beat: hence the poem's impression of insistent monotony, like the sound of water dripping or the tick-tock of a clock.

The background of the opening lines is not so much the metropolis as its outskirts: a street or avenue where two men walk silently together. One of them is the poet, seeking escape from the prose of life, from the world of the city and of people, in that marshland that he apprehends as a dreamland. In a symbolic or mystical sense, one could say that the poet's is only a "vegetative soul." His companion is a wretched creature, consumed by blind impulses of the senses, and, as such, an "animal soul." Soon enough, he disappears alone into somewhere and nowhere, probably to play the beast. Allegorically speaking, these two figures are but a single person, and represent two parallel and different aspects of man. In a sense the poem presents from its very beginning one of Blok's main themes, that of the *dvojnik* or Alter Ego, which he derives from the interpretations that two masters of Russian fiction, Gogol' and Dostoevskij, had given of the German and Romantic notion of the *Doppelgänger*, one of the earliest variants of that myth. The myth itself seems to teach that man has no better friend (or enemy) than himself, and the poet seems glad to have rid himself of that companion who represents the inferior powers, the "animal spirits" of the self.

No sooner does the poet reach the region of the bogs than the metropolis suddenly fades away, with all its lights and shadows, from the horizon. It is now that the poet really enters that marshland which is also a dreamland: and he considers his entry therein not as a fancy of the mind or an illusion of the senses, but a spiritual awakening, as the sudden bestowal of a "second sight." Blok tells us that the revelation took place "when consciousness unclosed itself." Yet the new revelation does not imply a denial of the real world, the world of the city and daily life. The poet's attitude seems to be that of a double quixotism, now viewing the castles as if they were more real than the inns, and now the inns as if they were more real than the castles.

The dual vision of the poet distinguishes the two opposite spheres of his experience not only through the category of space, but also through the category of time. The city stands for "today," for a present from which to escape; the marshland, a "yesterday," or a past to go back as to a refuge. The symbolism of language describes the future as an ascent and the past as a descent in time. In the *Poems on the Beautiful Lady*, the dream was a beyond, an after, an *ultra*. Here the dream is rather a before, or an *infra*. One of the conscious motifs of this poem may well be the Platonic doctrine of knowledge as recollection and reminiscence, and its very locale brings to mind on the one hand Plato's cave, and, on the other, the Russian folk legend of the underwater city of Kitezh. Mystical clairvoyance here turns into a retrospection, into a sort of backward glance; while the sphere where archetypal ideas enjoy their eternal life is lowered from the luminous world above into a dark underworld.

This descent into the abyss of time is symbolized by the sudden discovery on the part of the poem's protagonist of all his remote ancestors, grouped together in a mysterious hut. Those ancestors are Nordic or Scandinavian, and it may well be that the poet thus meant to allude to the presumed Baltic origins of his family. Thinking perhaps of both heredity and fate, the poet calls back from a buried and submerged past the creatures in whom his destiny and fate, his passions and dreams, were already sealed. In the little, wooden cottage he finds and meets all those who in the darkness of his previous lives had been his brothers in spirit and flesh. The first to be seen is a royal couple, an old king and queen, sitting in the center of the room, flanked by a troop of warriors, their body-guard. The second is a young hero sitting in a corner, seemingly absorbed in a single idea, an all-pervading thought. The poet recognizes in him his spiritual Alter Ego, his "intellective soul." The young warrior is immovably chained to his ageless meditation, with "limbs made wooden by time. . . ."

Wood is but a petrification of vegetal life, and it represents here a form of being which endures by losing its very vitality. A dream which survives itself is like flesh ossified. Yet here too there is a living creature, who, in a world like this, cannot be but a flower. That creature is indeed both woman and flower. She is another incarnation of the Beautiful Lady: the only sort of incarnation possible in this underworld. The flower is colorless, and the woman without glamor. Here the Beautiful Lady is neither beautiful nor ladylike, but, as the poet says, "a homely maid, with an invisible face." It is through the very invisibility of her countenance, as well as through her name, Night Violet, that we recognize in this creature the nature or essence of a flower. Blok probably created his floral symbol with the help of Novalis' "blue flower" and that "white lily" in which Solov'ev once allegorized the figure and idea of Sophia. Yet the originality of Blok's creation cannot be denied; by stripping the traditional attribute of beauty from this new version of the Eternal Feminine he transfigures her into a strange and novel vision. The transformation of the Beautiful Lady into the Night Violet, into a flower of the bogs, is a concrete and literal metamorphosis, not merely an abstract allegory.

Such a metamorphosis, which reflects the poet's changed view of dream and reality, carries within itself a sad and a lucid message. What the poet seems now to imply is that dream-life too may be shallow and mean, vulgar and ugly, formless and faceless; that it may be a gray and dark prison no less than waking life. Dreamland itself may well be but a part of what Dostoevskij would call the "underground" of the soul. Even dreaming partakes of that reality which the poet will soon define as "the terrible world."

III

THE POETRY OF BLOK'S MATURITY

Blok's subsequent poetry was largely consecrated to the theme of man's existence within the walls of his modern prisons of stone and brick. To this theme he devoted an entire cycle of poems entitled *The City* (1906–1908). The celebration of urban civilization had already been introduced into modern poetry by Verhaeren's *Les Villes tentaculaires*; Blok proceeded from him, in the wake of Brjusov's translations from that book, and from other works of the Flemish writer. Blok's city poems, however, remind us rather of Baudelaire's *Tableaux parisiens*. It must be also borne in mind that the capital of which Blok was to sing was not an ordinary metropolis, but Petersburg: that unnatural, artificial capital made of granite and "white nights," which the will of Peter the Great had built as a challenge to nature and history, in an epic and tragic feat which Pushkin had been the first to celebrate in *The Bronze Horseman*. But even more than Pushkin's Petersburg, Blok's metropolis recalls the Petersburg of Dostoevskij, that "unreal city" where the "underground man" lives in shame, dejection, and suffering. It is a city ruled by the Northern winter, covered not with an immaculate cloak of snow, but with sleet contaminated by human footprints.

Blok describes the city not with the nebulous abstraction of a Symbolist poet, but with the fluid vividness of an impressionistic painter. He represents it as if it were a living organism, weathered by atmosphere and climate; he paints it in the predominantly gray tones of mist and rain, when its buildings, monuments, and landmarks dissolve into a fog as dense as a cloud. He seems also to treat its dwellers as if they were not human beings but natural phenomena, parasitic plants born from the human spores of the city, diseases of cement and plaster, of stone and brick. Thus the metropolis, too, becomes a sort of dreamland-marshland, where other "night violets" wither or sprout.

Like a character from Dostoevskij's fiction, Blok now pursues the ideal of the Eternal Feminine among the creatures of the city, among the daughters of Eve, the slaves of fashion and sin. They too are flowers: flowers of evil. But in order that he may learn to rediscover his ancient ideal in those vessels of perdition and grief, the poet must first pass through the stages of another initiation; he must achieve that visionary state which Rimbaud sought to attain through le *dérèglement de tous les sens*. Blok achieves this state of grace through the cheapest and basest of all "artificial paradises": alcohol. It is alcohol that enables the poet to recognize for an instant a new incarnation of the Beautiful Lady in a feminine figure who momentarily appears before his bleary eyes in a public place, in a cheap café on the outskirts of the capital.

The transcription of this experience constitutes one of the most beautiful and perhaps the most popular of his lyrics, "The Unknown Lady" (1906), which has nothing to do with the play by the same title. Using a metric form made fashionable by Brjusov, a strophe of four iambic tetrameters alternating rhymes with triple and single endings, Blok successfully expresses, even in the rhythm, that psychological state which Dostoevskij called *nadryv*, that feeling of "laceration" experienced by the human heart when torn between opposite forces, good and evil, foul and fair. The vulgar, impure atmosphere of the place is suggested with such evocative power that it brings to mind the art of Van Gogh, the greatest of the *fauves*, and especially such paintings as his "Café in Arles." Suddenly the apparition occurs. This time the woman is not a phantom or a vision, but a warm, living creature both hiding and revealing her soulless and sinful nature under her fashionable veils and ostrich feathers. But again, as in the case of the Night Violet, her countenance cannot be clearly seen. Yet we feel the presence of beauty, and it is in an attempt to capture that loveliness that the poet cries out, in a despair which is a longing to see and believe: "I know it: truth is in wine."

In the ensuing collections, Blok is the poet of the soul's perdition in what he calls, by the title of one of his new cycles, "The Terrible World" (1909–1916). The "terrible world" is still primarily the world of the city. Wine and love cease to be means of experience and search, and become instruments of oblivion and sin. No longer do they raise Blok to that state of grace which for a moment enabled him to identify the Beautiful Lady even in a woman who walks the street. Like many a Dostoevskian character, he now seeks redemption through degradation, by that mercenary love which is only the defilement of the self. There is no doubt that one of the poems dealing with this theme, "Humiliation" (1911), found its inspiration in a Dostoevskian reminiscence, and more precisely in an episode from *Notes from Underground*. One of the poem's lines, "Is this what we call by the name of love?" echoes the very words and thoughts of the "underground man," when he asks himself in a house of ill-fame: "Is this how one loves?" The poem also brings to mind Baudelaire, especially those pages of the *Journal intime* where the French poet likens sexual love to a surgical operation. It is indeed hard to find in modern poetry a text equally capable of translating into the purest lyrical language a *tranche de vie* which would seem appropriate only to the most prosaic naturalism.

The poem opens with an outdoor scene, haunted by a somber sunset that gives the feeling of an almost cosmic agony. The same feeling is reflected in the gloomy despair of the interior: the four walls of the brothel seem to enclose not a house but a tomb. All sounds and voices are muffled; the colors are a filthy gray and a mourning black. Finally the two sinners meet. The woman, pale and bloodless, looks like a corpse. The man is overcome by perversion and lust, as well as by shame and guilt. Yet here we are confronted not with a clinical, pathological, or social document, but with a moral vision, and spiritual truth. What the poet wishes to express is once again the Dostoevskian *nadryv*: this poem is indeed a song of torture, like the tune which its wretched Magdalene hisses between her teeth.

Every so often oases appear even in Blok's "terrible world." Such is certainly the case with *The Nightingale Garden*, a long poem which was inspired by the poet's sojourn in Biarritz, and which is pervaded by a Southern, even a Mediterranean, light. The poem is a kind of legend or fairy tale, at once wise and naïve, designed for children and grown-ups alike. The action takes place in the dazzling splendor of summer: even the mysterious and occult are here bathed in the sunny radiance of *plein air*. Here the protagonist finds his own Beautiful Lady in a woman both loving and loved, in a being who is both body and soul. This time too we are unable to see her countenance: only the whiteness of her garments is visible through the gate of the garden. In this case the man in love is, however, more than an undisguised image of the poet, and his experience is evoked not in lyrical, but in narrative, terms. He is no longer an inactive dreamer, but a workingman, a quarrier who transports his load of stones, with the aid of a faithful donkey, from a cave near the seashore.

Like all fables, *The Nightingale Garden* has its moral, although in remains unuttered. This charming apologue reveals that moral through the simple allegory of the worker's falling in love, neglecting his work, betraying and losing his donkey. Without daring to affirm that a work of art as pure as this contains a social message, one may still claim that here Blok translates poetically some of the ideas he had been expressing in his essays on the conflict between the Russian intellectuals and the Russian masses. By writing this poem Blok wished perhaps to proclaim that the homecoming of the artist was overdue, that the poet should finally return to earth and the world of man. This charming tale seems to say that the poet too is an artisan and a worker, and that he should not abandon for the sake of any dream, or even of love, that little donkey which symbolizes, not with irony but with charity, in a spirit of Franciscan naïveté and Christian humility, the poor, good-hearted Russian people.

The poet is now on the road that will lead him to the pieces which from the title of a later collection may be called the *Poems about Russia;* some of them are genuine songs of love for a fair and gentle motherland, sound and simple as a woman. It is Russia herself that now replaces Night Violets and Unknown Ladies, and with them all the other incarnations of the Eternal Feminine. But in other poems Blok sees Russia also as an angel and a demon, as a monster of nature and a spirit of the Earth, as a direct manifestation of "the terrible world." She too becomes an object of both blasphemy and adoration. Yet, as a fond child, the poet loves Russia as she is, despite all her sins and faults. Nothing expresses better the poet's attitude toward his native country than the lines by which he closes a poem which is but a list of all the wrongs of Russian life: "dearer to me than any land — are you, my Russia, even so."

It is to this image of Russia that the poet relates one of the themes ruling his inspiration during the years preceding the First World War. That theme might be defined, in medieval terms, as the "triumph of death." Blok evokes through that theme what Turgenev once called "Russian death." Yet Blok's "Russian death" is not the death of the body but that of the spirit: it is that death-in-life which had obsessed Gogol' and inspired his masterpiece. It is in the world of the living, and among the people around him, that Blok, like Gogol', finds his "dead souls." Now the music of his verse turns into a trampling of skeletons and gnashing of teeth, into a Sabbath of skull and bones. His men and women are corpses rather than demons and witches; their cavorting is a *Totentanz*, not a *Walpurgisnacht*. There is no doubt that Blok was thinking of Baudelaire's *Danse macabre* when he wrote the first of his "Dances of Death." What inspired his lugubrious vision was, however, not a satanic fury or a decadent fancy, nor the morbid hallucination of a *poète maudit*. What he wished to convey in terms of ghoulish horror was not man's mortality, but the lifelessness of his way of living and manner of being. As the proper occasion for the *danse macabre* by which he wishes to represent his own "triumph of death," the poet selects a modish reception and a fashionable ball in modern dress. He thus replaces the provincial officials and landowners of Gogolian fiction with the capital's *beau monde* or "smart set." The snobbish elegance of the dancers' behavior and attire intensifies that effect of tragic grotesqueness which is the aim of the poem. The repulsive absurdity of the picture is made even sharper — almost intolerable — by the presence, among dead people who seem alive, of live people who seem dead. The living seem indeed more puppet- or mummy-like than the dead; and this may well be the reason why a lovely girl falls in love with her partner, who is but a skeleton in formal dress. Enraptured by music and passion, she fails to hear the rattling of the bones.

The second of the "Dances of Death" is a very short piece, impressionistic and expressionistic at the same time. Here the poet turns the dim sight of a winter evening and the dull outline of an empty urban landscape into tragic emblems of the absurdity of life. This eight-line piece begins and ends with inverted refrains, listing all the elements and objects that mark the scene. Both figuratively and literally (the poem is almost devoid of verbs, and consists simply of a series of brief and sharp phrases), Blok treats all those objects and elements as the eternal attributes of a senseless and tedious universe. The direct allegory of night and winter joins with the all-too-real symbols of the street and the lamppost to convey the frozen desolation of our existence.

This poem seems to turn the homely tableau of a wintry evening in a modern city into a vision of the glacial era, into a new Cimmerian Night, thus exemplifying the inspiration of the late Blok, who is indeed the poet of Northern darkness and of polar ice. In the poetry of his last years the everyday experience of a cold climate and a dusky light takes on a cosmic significance, and represents the cruelty of creation and the horror of being. Blok treats our whole planet as if it were, like the center of earth in the Dantesque conception of the world, the frozen heart of the universe. Yet ice symbolizes for him not only the curse of existence but also its only reward, which is the unique solitude of human grief. This perhaps is what the poet meant in a lyric without title, which was probably inspired by Baudelaire's *De Profundis Clamavi*. Blok's poem is an *invitation au voyage* turning the dream of escape into a nightmare. All you hold dear will either leave or betray you, says the poet: if you then wish to savor another sweetness, look at the cold polar circle. Take your boat, continues the poet, sail toward the Pole amid ice walls, and forget in silence how down here they used to love, fight, and die. Forget the bygone land of human passions. And in the shivers of the tingling cold accustom your tired soul not to need anything *here* when the rays spring forth from *there*.

The poem's ending reveals that ice and winter were for Blok more than symbols of negation or allegories of nothingness. This is the reason why later he employed the same images to represent the new Russia and the great Revolution of 1917. He did so in *The Twelve*, which was his swan song. There snow and frost become the fabulous metaphors of an epic ordeal, of a historical drama which Blok was bound to view as the conflict of inhuman powers, of telluric and theogonic forces.

IV

THE TWELVE

Technically speaking, *The Twelve* is one of Blok's most perfect and mature works. A supreme harmony is achieved by way of a chaotic confusion, by means of an uninterrupted series of dissonances. Structurally, the poem is a succession of fragments of unequal length, varying greatly in meter, diction, and tone. In this complex composition rhythm and style shift between the opposite extremes of advance-guard art and popular poetry. Many a section is constructed like a mosaic, with the insertion and juxtaposition of factory songs, political slogans, and revolutionary refrains. The beginning is descriptive and evocative, but the central section is chiefly narrative in character. A series of sketches and vignettes acts as a prelude, producing the black-and-white effect of the opening scenes. A set of figurines appears and disappears in pantomimic tableaux, culminating in gestures and words that are in themselves diminutive dramas, microcosmic catastrophes. Everything seems to contribute to an impression of cinematographic technique, from the harsh chiaroscuro of the vision to the foreshortening of the perspective, from the interplay between backgrounds and foregrounds to the tempo of the action, from the sharpness of the images to the brutality of the plot.

From another viewpoint the naturalism of certain parts of *The Twelve* might be likened to that of historical reportage or sensational journalism. Much of the poem consists of the evocation of things, men, and events which the poet remembers with the same vividness as he once saw them. The fidelity with which he reshapes the impressions which his memory has so clearly and fully preserved could not be proved better than by comparing Blok's revolutionary scenes with the testimony which John Reed gave about the same historical happenings in *Ten Days That Shook the World*. The American newspaperman and the Russian poet seem to have seen the same places, persons, and incidents, and to have given in different literary vehicles similar graphic accounts of the same experience. Such a coincidence between poetic testimony and documentary journalism suffices by itself to demonstrate the realistic immediacy of Blok's poetic statement: a quality not to be denied even by the mystical visitation which is both the ending and the climax of the poem.

One of the differences between these two accounts is that in the chorus of *The Twelve* there appear more victims and antagonists of the Revolution than in Reed's book. The poet pays more attention than the foreign observer to the people who represent the *ancien régime* and looks at them with dual feelings, with a mixture of compassion and scorn. He may feel a human pity for their human plight; but toward the crumbling society of which they are still part he takes a merciless attitude of total contempt. Trotskij, who in the Blok chapter of *Literature and Revolution* commented shrewdly on this poem, keenly recognized this fact: "*The Twelve* is a cry of despair for the dying past, but a cry of despair transforming itself into hope for the future."

The central episode is a typically Russian tale. It seems almost a popular, even melodramatic rendering of the plebeian riots occurring at the end of Dostoevskij's *The Devils*. The story's protagonists are indeed not "people" but "mob": they are part of what Marx called the *Lumpenproletariat*. They are not toilers, but hooligans, outlaws, and outcasts. On the moral and psychological plane they must be viewed as another variant of the Russian conception of the criminal as the victim of a curse, who carries the guilt of all, as well as a promise of redemption for his fellow men. This is why the twelve militiamen turn unknowingly into twelve apostles. This is why they will go on marching, like gray shadows, bringing both death and life, between the darkness of night and the whiteness of the snow.

Thus for Blok the Revolution is not so much a messianic vision as an apocalyptic one. The poet views that upheaval not as a social and human catastrophe but as a cosmic cataclysm. This is the reason why he does not symbolize the Revolution in the traditional image of fire, of a flame that burns and destroys but also lights and warms. Ice alone is the proper emblem for the demonic and the monstrous, for all those blind and chaotic forces which are neither divine nor human. Trotskij guessed all this when he wrote: "Blok conceived of the Revolution exclusively as an element: because of his temperament, as a cold one." In many of the poems he had written in the preceding years Blok had already asserted that life was identical with cold and winter. Now he tells us that history is prehistory: that in the natural history of man we are still in the ice age. Hence the symbolic significance of Russia, which becomes a Siberia of the spirit. Like Sleeping Beauty, Russia lies in a desert of frost, under a quilt of snow.

It is evident that even the final appearance of Christ reflects the same vision of life as a frozen wasteland. Here the Saviour manifests Himself as a kind of Snow Guest. Blok may have been led to such an image or intention by the heterodox theology of Rozanov, who saw in the Father a solar god, and in the Son a lunar deity, pale and cold, virginal and sterile. But the Christ of *The Twelve* is Blok's unique creation, even though he may recall the Jesus of Tjutchev, treading on the soil of Holy Russia and blessing that soil with His hand. This identification of Christ with Russia may well explain why the Son of God is here but another embodiment of Blok's feminine conception of the divine: a novel mask or disguise for the Beautiful Lady, or at least for the "Virgin of the Snows."

Any disrespectful interpretation of this feminine metamorphosis of the figure of Christ would be not only in bad taste, but also false. It is true that here the Saviour wears a wreath of white roses rather than a crown of thorns. And it is also true that the halo surrounding His head is made not of bright rays, but of pale snowflakes. But man always conceives of the divine in his own image, and the poet has mirrored himself and his sense of life in the sacred image painted by his hands, in this icon of a bloodless and frozen God. Yet by doing so Blok simply reveals his ability to turn to his advantage some of the traditional details of the Orthodox iconography of the Saviour. The image so produced is distorted; yet in this case we have to do not with the "deformation" of Decadent or advance-guard painting, but with the stylization of Gothic or Byzantine art. The femininity of His effigy gives the person of Christ a feeling of immaculate purity, a sense of inaccessible spirituality. The Redeemer is here not the Lamb but the Dove. The complexity of this figure tends to prove that Christ's final appearance is no mere *deus ex machina.* Jesus does not intervene in order to calm the troubled waters: here He too is wind and storm. What His visitation means is that Jesus is present everywhere, in nature and history, even where and when men hoist flags which do not carry the sign of the Cross. Yet by marching before the Red flag He seems to say *In hoc signo vinces* to every man of good will. He is the great fisher of souls; behind Him, blindly and unknowingly twelve Red Guards become his vicars on earth. No man except the poet is aware of His presence, yet the artist, like Leonardo painting the Last Supper, was unable to draw the face of the Lord. The reason for this failure may well be that the poet could not avoid putting even this last epiphany to the test of doubt. During one of the moral crises of the last years of his life, Blok alluded to the Christ of *The Twelve* in words that reveal his awareness of the ambiguity of that figure: "sometimes that feminine ghost is deeply hateful even to myself. . . ." In this avowal there is also the acknowledgment that the feminine being, half-divine and half-human, that had haunted him all his life, from beginning to end, had been a nightmare as well as a dream.

V

BLOK'S ART

Blok had started his career with the almost Dantesque ambition of singing only the praises of his Lady, and of saying of her "what was never told of any other woman." Yet not even his first book had turned out to be another *Vita Nuova*, or a second *Canzoniere*. Not even when his faith was freshest and purest had the poet been willing or able to fix forever his ideal dream into a real person or figure, rather than into a mere image. Perhaps the young Blok did not even wish to transform Sophia or the Beautiful Lady into a Laura or a Beatrice; he preferred to reduce his vision to a shadow, which would remain in a state of continuous flux, which would constantly dwell in a kind of limbo: morally, in what Rozanov would have called "the world of the uncertain and the undecided"; aesthetically, in the realm of the Verlainian *imprécis*, in the vagueness of "the condition of music." For this, and for other reasons, Blok failed in his "pilgrim's progress," and, after having started with a kind of modern *Vita Nuova*, he followed a path opposed to Dante's. Soon enough, he disbelieved in the reality of the Beautiful Lady or in her godlike essence, even though he could not live without being haunted by her image. But later he grew tired of living only with a phantasm, and tried to give that phantasm a lifelike existence by incarnating it into earthly beings, into creatures made of living matter, if not always of flesh and blood. Thus, in *The Night Violet*, he reduced his Beloved to the state of a flower, while in "The Unknown Lady" he transmuted her, with the help of alcohol, into a fashionable streetwalker. Finally, turning the old idolatry into a new sacrilege, he gave some of her attributes to the Christ of *The Twelve*. Yet even in this final metamorphosis the ghost remained only a ghost.

For a while Blok hoped to be able to glimpse the mysterious effigy of the Beautiful Lady in the dark mirror of nature, in the stormy sea of the elements. Then he transformed her into the "Virgin of the Snows," into a spirit of the tempest. Even this identification was an illusion which could not last, yet it left within his heart an eternal sense of cold, and within his soul the roaring echo of the wind. For ten years, from *The Snow Mask* to *The Twelve*, the sovereign ruler of his poetry was the North wind, a symbol of evil and chaos, a primordial destructive force, sweeping the plains of Eurasia and changing Holy Russia into the land of the white death. For a while, Russia herself took for him the role of the Beautiful Lady, and revealed herself, too, only as a cruel and bloodless spirit. The best poems of Blok were thus inspired by his nihilistic conviction that every faith will be denied, that the last hope will be betrayed, that man's ultimate destiny is to dream away even his dreams. Slowly but surely his poetry turned into a prophecy of doom. Blok was the Cassandra of the coming snowstorms in the history of Russia and the world, and, like Cassandra, he died the victim of the unheeded prophecies that a god, or a demon, uttered through him.

Blok was always aware of the tragic fatality of his own gift. Yet is was an awareness full of humility, devoid of the romantic or titanic pride which taints so many modern carriers of the Word. He was perhaps the only poet in his epoch to consider the poetic calling not as a noble curse, but as a mark of frailty, foredooming the poet to a destiny of ineffectuality and powerlessness. In one of his poems he described himself as "merely a poor poet, one who calls everything by its name, and steals its perfume from a living flower." The paradoxical quality of his symbolic vision resided exactly in the urge that led him to call things by their real, rather than by their ideal, names, and to find lower, rather than higher, truths through the insights of the soul. His mystical vision enabled him to discover that creation is chaos, that life is discord. For him, the task of the poet was to mirror the horror of being, and once he stated that only "in the reflections of art" can man see that destroying flame which is called life.

Because of the inborn inertia of his will, Blok often felt that poetry was a violence committed by unknown forces on the poet and within the poet himself, who is both their tool and their victim. Creation is not joy, but torment; poetry, as he said, is "a burden on one's shoulders." In one of his lyrics he addressed the Muse only to say that, while for others she was both "Muse" and "wonder," for him she was instead "torture and hell." Yet, as shown by the line which defines the poet as one who steals its perfume from a living flower, Blok was sometimes tempted to view the making of poetry not merely as a state of passive agony, but also as an act of violence, which the poet unwillingly perpetrates against reality and life itself. In giving form to his experience, the poet destroys the authenticity and immediacy, the human content and the organic vitality, of that very experience. Blok developed this idea in the poem "The Artist," which may be considered his *ars poetica*. There the poet described his own sense of frustration during the fruitless wait for an inspiration still to come. He compared that state to the watch of a hunter on the lookout for a bird he wants to catch, and likened the finished poem to a cage where the imprisoned bird sings "alien songs."

Perhaps the cage stands for life, and the bird for the poet himself. Yet of Blok no one could say that he ever sang "alien songs." This is true even of his early apprenticeship, when he had not yet discovered his true poetic self. At that early stage he still viewed his poetic destiny in Romantic and Symbolistic terms and saw in the poet an angel exiled on this earth. His youthful poetry had been a quest after a twin angelic soul, and that quest remained a permanent aspect of his work. But as soon as the poet acknowledged the failure of his search, the angel became a man. After all, as Rilke said, *ein jeder Engel ist schrecklich*: and what seemed to be degradation was instead a rebirth. The failure of the "pilgrim's progress" was the beginning of the poet's progress, which consisted in the replacement of the naïve idealism of his mystical youth by a lucid and even cynical vision of life, and a mature even though negative sense of the realities of this world. Thus the poet who had failed to fulfill his youthful dream of a metaphysical harmony was able to create a new music out of the chaos of being and the discord of the soul.

CHAPTER SEVEN

THE NEOPARNASSIANS

I

CLARISM AND ACMEISM

IN December 1909, assured of having successfully achieved the task he had set out to accomplish, Valerij Brjusov ceased editing and publishing the Moscow literary review he had founded four years before. The name of that review, *The Scales*, had proved to be inadvertently symbolic, since the policies of its *de facto* editor had been discriminating but not partisan, and its pages had represented with fair balance not only the writers of his tendency and age group, but also the Symbolists of the second generation, and even those younger apprentices who were seeking, but had not yet discovered, a path of their own. These apprentices, along with many of their elders, soon found a new rostrum in another review, which started appearing the same year in Petersburg. It chanced that this review was also to receive a name charged with emblematic significance. That name was *Apollo*, which seemed almost to hint that the Apollonian spirit was about to rule Russian poetry again, after the Dionysian frenzy of the Decadents and the Symbolists.

As the first of its many programs and appeals, *Apollo* published in 1910 a manifesto which was meant to sound the death knell of the old poetry and the reveille of a new one. Its author, the writer Mikhail Kuzmin, raised the banner of a new movement, which failed, however, to materialize, or hardly lasted beyond the echo of the words announcing it. Yet the manifesto was the timely symptom of a genuine and widespread discontent on the part of Russian youth with the kind of poetry which was still being written

by the masters of the old generation. As for the name which
Kuzmin chose as his emblem, Clarism, it anticipated, although a
little too vaguely, the direction toward which the new poetry was
later to move. In short, with a brief manifesto and a simple slogan,
Kuzmin paved the ground, two or three years in advance, for the
foundation of Acmeism, which coincided with the publication of
two other manifestoes, one by Nikolaj Gumilev and the other by
Sergej Gorodetskij, both of which appeared in 1913 in the same
review. Unlike Clarism, Acmeism attracted many enthusiastic followers, and fought a valiant battle in the years to come. Kuzmin
failed to join the new movement, which in the course of time took
other roads, although it might not have even started unless Kuzmin
had pointed the way to it.

As shown by the very title of his proclamation, "On Beautiful
Clarity," Kuzmin took a stand against the poetics of Symbolism,
with its predilection for the evocative and the allusive, for the
obscure and the occult, and recommended instead a new taste and
style, based on clarity and light, on firm shapes rather than on
vague contours. After having sacrificed for too long to the esoteric,
poetry had to pay again its tribute to the exoteric. Art had to leave
the transcendental for the immanent, and return from heaven to
earth. If Symbolism had been a romantic revival, the new poetry
was to be a classical reawakening; and as such it had to reject that
formal eclecticism, or aesthetic syncretism, which Decadents and
Symbolists had carried so far. After disorder, order; after unre-
strained inspiration, planned and controlled composition; after
dreamy and hallucinated abstractions, concrete visions and solid
forms. Kuzmin's manifesto ended with this eloquent appeal: "If
you are a conscientious artist, pray that your chaos (if you are
chaotic) be clarified and reorganized. . . . I beg you, be logical —
forgive me for this cry from the heart — logical in your plans, in
the structure of the work, in your syntax. . . . Be skillful builders
in the lesser details as well as in the whole. . . . Even the most
formless and anguished conception must be executed in the most
deliberate and legitimate way. . . . One must tell a story in fiction,
unfold action in the drama, keep lyricism for the lyrics. Love the
word like Flaubert; employ your means economically; use words

sparingly; and you will discover the secret of something splendid, beautiful Clarity, which I would like to call Clarism."

As shown by these words, Kuzmin's program was exclusively literary, and this limitation alone prevents us from comparing it to an English proclamation which was partly political, T. H. Hulme's *Classicism and Romanticism*, written more or less at the same time as Kuzmin's piece but published posthumously many years later. As for the manifesto by which Gumilev founded the school he was later to lead, it was more than a denial of the old poetics and the affirmation of a new, even though it was simply entitled "Symbolism's Legacy and Acmeism." Gumilev condemned Symbolism not merely as a specific literary phenomenon, but also as a world view. In brief, his criticism was philosophical in temper, although he avoided too strictly formulating another creed. His definition of Acmeism was a simple one: "To take Symbolism's place there comes now a new movement, whatever its name might be, either Acmeism (from the word ἀκμή, signifying the supreme degree which a thing may attain, its peak or bloom), or Adamism (a firm and manly vision of life) — but which at any rate demands a greater balance of powers and a more precise notion of the tie between subject and object than was the case with Symbolism. . . ."

Gumilev's main accusation against the most brilliant and recent poetic tradition of his nation and time was that "Russian Symbolism had turned its best energies toward the unknown, and had alternately joined hands with mysticism, theosophy, and occultism." Gumilev was willing to concede that by doing so the Russian Symbolists had at times succeeded in creating genuine metaphysical myths, and that they had thus gained the right to ask of the newcomers how they would deal with the problems of the unknown. Yet Gumilev claimed that such a question would be merely rhetorical and settled the issue by maintaining that by its very definition the unknown remains a problem without solution. Accordingly, while contemplating with awe the mysteries of life and death, the new poets would never try to raise the veil hiding those secrets from the eyes of men: "to be always aware of the unknown without corrupting its images with likely or unlikely guesses: this is Acmeism's tenet." This skeptical, and yet not cynical, attitude toward the supernatural and the other-worldly implied a change of outlook toward reality and human experience. Subject and object could no longer part their ways; intelligence had to reconcile itself with man's moral and material universe, without trying to reshape it into a reflection of itself. Harmony had to be restored between nature and man: man could no longer deny his physical destiny and earthly task, and was bound to consider as blasphemous Ivan Karamazov's refusal to accept God's creation while still accepting the idea of God.

It is to that refusal (which Vjacheslav Ivanov had been reinterpreting in a mystical key) that Gorodetskij alluded in his own manifesto, which was entitled "Some Currents in Contemporary Russian Poetry," and in which he restated, in simpler thought and clearer speech, denials and affirmations identical to Gumilev's: "What is primarily at stake in the contention between Acmeism and Symbolism is this resounding and colorful world of ours: this world made of time, volume, and form, this planet the earth. After so many refusals to accept it, the world is now accepted without reservations, in all its varying aspects, either beautiful or ugly." That the target of Gorodetskij's onslaught was indeed the ultra-mystical Symbolism of Vjacheslav Ivanov is made plain by the closing allusion to that "tower" where Ivanov had been living and acting as a priest of the Word: "It is harder to be an Acmeist than Symbolist, just as it is harder to build a cathedral than a tower."

In brief, the Acmeists were men "for whom the exterior world does exist," to use the phrase which sums up the creed of Théophile Gautier, whom Gumilev honored as his master and raised to the status of one of the patron saints of his movement. It was indeed with accents highly reminiscent of Gautier's restatement of his poetics in the famous poem "L'Art" that Gorodetskij called for a poetry molded in noble metals or engraved in hard rock: "Art is solidity, while Symbolism has only exploited the fluidity of the word." And it was in the same spirit that Gorodetskij preached a verbal craft which could make durable the ephemeral and fix eternally the passing instant. The avowed aim of the new school was simply beauty, literally and objectively understood, a beauty to be wrought out of the substance of things rather than out of the shadow of dreams. With words which recall Gertrude Stein's claim that "a rose is a rose is a rose," Gorodetskij declared that "for the Acmeists the rose *had* newly become lovely for itself, for its petals, color, and scent, not because of its mysterious analogy with mystical love. . . ."

It has been said, not without reason, that Clarism and Acmeism played in the Russian poetry of the twentieth century a role analogous to that played by the *Parnasse*, or more generally, by the "art for art's sake" movement in French nineteenth century poetry. Yet one ought to keep in mind the obvious fact that while in France "art for art's sake" and *Parnasse* preceded, and, at least in part, unconsciously prepared for, the developments which were later to be called Decadence and Symbolism, these Russian Parnassians came instead after them. As the immediate successors of the Decadents and the Symbolists, Kuzmin, Gumilev, and company were strongly influenced, or conditioned, by their predecessors' example. Some of the very reactions of the younger poets toward their elders were part of the state of mind against which they raised a voice of protest.

There is, however, a notable difference between the two lines represented respectively by Kuzmin and Gumilev. Kuzmin, as we shall see later, transposed into a new, minor key some of the specific inheritance of the Decadents. His art, charming and fatuous, tended toward miniature forms, and one could say that in the Russian variant of the *Parnasse* he holds a position very similar to that which Théodore de Banville occupied in the original one. Yet Kuzmin is nearer to Henri de Régnier and other forgotten poets of the so-called second generation of French Symbolism, who claimed to be the heirs of Baudelaire, Verlaine, Rimbaud, and Mallarmé, while acting toward the tradition represented by those names in a way not too different from the way Kuzmin and other Russian poets of his tendency reacted against Bal'mont or Brjusov, Ivanov or Blok.

If the parallel with the French *Parnasse* should be extended also to Gumilev, one could say that he performed, with far less influence and prestige, a task comparable to that which Leconte de Lisle had performed in his own place and time. Yet, as in

Kuzmin's case, Gumilev's position and function would be better understood within a more recent frame of reference. Part of what Gumilev did in Russia did not differ greatly from what a lesser French master, Jean Moréas, had done at the very peak of the Symbolist movement, which he deserted to form a school of his own. This does not imply a comparison between the creative achievements of these two poets, greatly varying in quality as well as in degree, but simply suggests that they turned back toward similar poetic precedents and literary models. Moréas gave his school the name of *école romane* precisely because he tried to revive through it the preclassical tradition of French poetry, from the late Middle Ages up to the early Renaissance. Gumilev did almost the same and counted among his ideal masters at least two (Villon and Rabelais) whom Moréas had held equally dear: "The names pronounced oftener than all others in the circles close to Acmeism are those of Shakespeare, Rabelais, Villon, and Théophile Gautier." These four are strange bedfellows, as Gumilev himself seemed to realize, since he tried to justify the incongruity of such a *rapprochement*: "The choice of these names is not arbitrary: each one of them is a cornerstone for the construction of one or another fundamental element. Shakespeare has bared the inner world of man; Rabelais has pointed at the body and its joys, and taught physiological wisdom. Villon has revealed a life never questioning itself, and yet aware of everything, of God and immortality, of vice and death. And Théophile Gautier has found the means to clothe that life with fitting garments of impeccable shape. To harmonize these four moments: such is the ideal that joins together the men boldly calling themselves Acmeists."

Kuzmin shared what one might call Gumilev's "Romanism," although his Pantheon was broader and varied, at once more classical and more modern. Both of them rejected the Gothic and Northern taste of Russian Symbolism, preferring instead a Mediterranean clarity of light and a Southern purity of line. Kuzmin found his favorites in the literatures of Rome, France, and Italy, which offered him themes and images, patterns of language and style. All the writers whom he chose as his models from among those three literatures were, however, so to speak, *petits maîtres*:

Catullus, Petronius, Goldoni, Marivaux, Parny; to these he added from other more or less extravagant traditions the *poésie légère* of the early Pushkin, Hellenistic poetry, and even folk takes and medieval legends. This variety of sources is not the sign of a profound catholicity of taste, since it derives from that decorative eclecticism which was practiced in Russia in Kuzmin's time, especially in the visual arts, where it took the name of "stylization" (*stilizatsija*), and performed the same task that *Jugendstil* and *art nouveau* were then performing in the West. The common denominator of that tendency was simply the attempt to clothe any sort of inspiration or subject matter with the same close-fitting, neoclassical elegance which Kuzmin's real master, Henri de Régnier, had imposed on French poetry after the decline of the great Symbolist tradition.

Gumilev, however, found his ideal poetic example in another, and older, French poet, Théophile Gautier, with whose name he had purposely closed the list of his models. Gautier, by a strange coincidence, was destined to influence at the same time, belatedly and effectively, such different writers as the Russian Acmeists, led by Gumilev, and the Anglo-American Imagists, led by Pound. The coincidence may look less surprising when we consider that both Acmeism and Imagism represented, within two different traditions, the same shift of taste, or at least a similar change of literary emphasis. In both cases the new poets felt the need to submit pathos and inspiration to the control of form, and to replace the musical with the plastic. Yet both Imagists and Acmeists were unable to repudiate in full the heritage of Symbolism. This was especially true of the Russian poets of that tendency and generation, as shown by the second of the chosen designations of their school, which was Adamism. That term implied among many other ideas the dream of a new Adam, "giving new names to all things."

II

MIKHAIL KUZMIN

Mikhail Kuzmin was born in Jaroslavl' in 1875, into a family which on his mother's side claimed a French ancestry. He considered Moscow his home town, although he divided his time between Moscow and Petersburg. It was in the latter city, which had lost its capital status and been renamed Leningrad, that he died in 1936. He spent the last twenty years of his life, if not in silence (he managed to publish a few new books of verse and prose up to 1928), at least in obscurity, solitude, and distress. In a minuscule autobiography, written in 1907, he had mockingly composed the inscription he would have liked to see engraved on his tomb, with words which seem to echo Stendhal's *scrisse, visse, amò*, and which may be read as a prophecy of the early decline of his fame and fortune: "He lived thirty years, sang and mused, loved and smiled."

Kuzmin at first thought of becoming a musician, and studied composition under Rimskij-Korsakov. Later he set to music poems by himself and others, and collaborated enthusiastically on Djagilev's Russian Ballets. His literary career, the beginning of which was greeted by the acclaim of Valerij Brjusov, started rather late, at about the time of the "little revolution" of 1905. In all the verse he wrote he proved to be a craftsman and a virtuoso, and showed great abilities also in his prose works. It is perhaps worth remembering that he gained his first success as a prose writer with the tale *Wings*, which appeared in 1906, although it was a *succès de scandale*, since what the author preached in that story was the cause of perverted love. Kuzmin's fiction is even more elegant and refined than his poetry: this is especially true of the novel *The Adventures of Aimé Lebeuf* (1907), set in eighteenth-century France, and relating the life story of an adventurer who looks very much like Casanova or Cagliostro, and *The Deeds of Alexander the Great*, a sophisticated version of the French medieval romance by the same title. The fastidious delicacy of Kuzmin's taste is no less evident in a later collection of critical essays, fittingly entitled *Conventions* (1926). Yet the best part of his literary production is to be seen in the half-dozen collections of lyrics he published up to the First World War, of which the most important are *Alexandrian Songs* (1906), *Nets* (1908), *Lakes of Autumn* (1912), and *Clay Doves* (1914). To these one may add two later collections, *Unearthly Evenings* (1921) and *Parabolas* (1923), and an earlier composition, unique in his work, *The Carillon of Love* (1906), a charming pastoral in eighteenth-century setting, for which he composed the music himself.

All those books presented to the Russian public a graceful, minor poet, who hailed with delight the concrete reality of daily experience, and who seemed to liberate Russian poetry from the daydreams and nightmares of Symbolism, as well as from its visions and wonders. Kuzmin was aware of the novelty of his task, and in one of his most significant poems he described himself as "alien to all obedient miracles and faithful to your flowers, O gay earth." With him poetry appeared once more to touch solid ground; yet, being a light balloon, Kuzmin could do so only thanks to a heavy ballast of literature.

A genuine, although a slight, artist, Kuzmin worked at his best when he could give weight to the light product of his talent with matter taken from the creation of other writers and poets. This applies not only to the structure and style, but even to the themes and the imagery of his work. In the poem mentioned above there is a stanza portraying one of those ephoebic figures which haunt all too often the effeminate fantasies of this poet. To convey the effect of meretricious charm which that face provokes, Kuzmin finds no better way than to compare it to such aesthetic impressions as those produced by the *lazzi* of a gay farce, by the capricious quill of Marivaux, and by Mozart's *Mariage de Figaro*. The very choice of these literary and artistic references reveals Kuzmin for what he is: a connoisseur who extends his connoisseurship from the field of life to that of art as well as vice versa. In the opening of the same poem, which may be considered his *ars poetica*, he asks himself where one might find the style best suited to describe all those small delights which a more pretentious poet would choose to ignore, and which Kuzmin exemplifies in a morning walk, a few slices of toasted bread, a plate of ripe cherries, a bottle of chilled Chablis wine. The modesty implied in that rhetorical question is a false one, since Kuzmin knows very well that, better than any other artist or poet, he had found the ways and means to represent all the "magic trifles" or "merry levities" which brighten and enliven the days of a hedonist endowed with a refined taste and eager to enjoy all the good things of life. Kuzmin, however, is not only a hedonist, but also an aesthete, and as such he indulges all too often in artificial, as well as in natural, pleasures. He likes not only the fruits and flowers which grow spontaneously from our earth, but also those which man may nurse in his hothouses, or manufacture out of alabaster or even papier-mâché. In brief, Kuzmin is a Decadent of a new kind and perhaps of a lesser brand. As such, he is a unique figure within the Russian poetry of his time, where he acts as the single representative of a minor, and yet widespread, trend, which considerably affected the development of Western poetry during the first decade of the century. That trend is little known, perhaps because there is not yet a general term by which to identify it. Yet one could easily define and designate it by extending to other literatures the name given in Italy to the local representatives of that trend.

It was the critic G. A. Borgese who coined the label "twilight poets" (*crepuscolari*) for a group of secondary poets who flourished immediately before the First World War, and who transposed into a minor key the themes and attitudes which D'Annunzio had expressed in his *Poema Paradisiaco*. In that book D'Annunzio had replaced the barbaric and panic vigor of his early inspiration with the sickly languor of a convalescent soul, morbidly enjoying the fading beauty of a neglected garden or of an abandoned villa, as well as the pale charm of old-fashioned objects and things. The *crepuscolari* translated the same vision from its still aesthetic and aristocratic background to a more prosaic and vulgar one, or more precisely, to a provincial, bourgeois, and domestic milieu. The best of them, Guido Gozzano, sang of all those "good things in bad taste" which are the strange and familiar signs of bourgeois status and bourgeois psychology. Thus Gozzano and his peers became the pathetic ironists of a petty bourgeois aestheticism, of a middle-class Decadence, both comfortable and uncomfortable in its mediocrity.

Few poets expressed more typically than Gozzano a mood which he shared with many other poets of his time, and which he had not been the first to express. That mood had already appeared in the work of two French poets whom the Italian *crepuscolari* later treated as their models and masters, Francis Jammes and Jules

Rodenbach. Jammes' and Rodenbach's example, joining with the belated influence of two extravagant masters of early Symbolism, Jules Laforgue and Tristan Corbière, spread the same sensibility to other literatures, making possible the appearance in Germany of the poetry of Franz Werfel, and adding in Poland another chord to the lyre of Julian Tuwim. The mood ruled for a while even Anglo-American poetry, as shown by the early works of T. S. Eliot, whose youthful poems, especially *Prufrock*, were at once a pathetic manifestation and a detached satire of the same mood. In brief, all the poetry written in that key was but an attempt to portray the softness, emptiness, and weakness of the modern soul; to convey and to condemn at the same time that bourgeois decadence which is the spiritual disease of the modern world.

There is no doubt that Kuzmin is the only Russian poet who represented that trend, and it is equally certain that he expressed it in a manner all his own. He faced the little world of Decadent twilight without bourgeois ambiguity; he accepted its reality with a feeling of sympathy, rather than with indulgent compassion, or with mocking irony. An aesthete and Decadent in miniature, he felt at home within that mood, which he depicted in lines both subtle and firm. Thus he stands out among the poets of the Decadent twilight not only for the fluid limpidity of his style, but also for the directness with which he treated the literary materials which fed that mood. While Gozzano or Jammes submitted those materials to the acid test of parody, Kuzmin preferred to imitate and recreate his own precedents or models in a spirit of lively gaiety, of innocent fun. It is highly significant that his little, yet exquisite, masterpiece is but the pastiche of a pastiche: the free and original reworking of an amusing literary mystification of the beginning of the century. This is the cycle of poems entitled *Alexandrian Songs*, written after the pattern of Pierre Louÿs' *Chansons de Bilitis*, which purported to be translations of the newly discovered lyrics of a *hetaira* of ancient Alexandria. The persons speaking in the first person in the poems of Kuzmin's cycle are a young man or a girl, an old poet or a poor scribe, all singing the praises of pleasure and desire, of love and youth. Elegant but not precious, exquisite in rhythm and delicate in sound and speech, literary but not pedantic, these pieces reveal Kuzmin's ability to give a new moving voice to that commonplace philosophy of life which had already found classical expression in such poets as Horace, Anacreon, or Omar Khayyâm.

The French eighteenth century, as reinterpreted by the Goncourts, or as expressed in such works as *Les Liaisons dangereuses* and in such figures as Manon Lescaut and the Chevalier de Faublas, is another of the cultural backdrops against which Kuzmin likes to fix his miniature view of life in the filigree patterns of his art. In his attempt to re-evoke that age and milieu, Kuzmin found his master and model in the Verlaine of *Fêtes galantes*, which conveys the sentimental futility and the frivolous elegance generally associated with eighteenth-century life in a series of scenes which look like a pastoral dumb show. Kuzmin is often fully aware that his own creations or recreations are lacking in vital power; and he confesses as much in the title piece of *Clay Doves*. The poet portrays himself first in the act of shaping, with assiduous hands, little doves of blue clay, and then in the attempt to infuse life into them with his breath. Of a sudden, says he, they rustlingly moved. But their flight was a short-lived illusion, since they were made of water and mud, not of flesh and blood. "And I felt," the poet concludes, "that my mysterious handicraft was lifeless." This may be all too true; yet it is only fair to remember that in the world of culture there is place not only for the imitation of nature and the representation of life, but also for artifice and for the imitations of art. Thus, in the gallery of modern Russian verse, there is also a place for the charming showcase of Kuzmin's poetry, with its Rococo or Biedermeier artifacts.

III

NIKOLAJ GUMILEV

The son of a navy doctor, Nikolaj Gumilev was born in 1886 in the arsenal city of Kronstadt. He started his literary career very early, and when he was twenty-two he had already published two collections of poems, *The Way of the Conquistadors* (1905) and *Romantic Flowers* (1908). He briefly studied Romance philology at the Sorbonne, and in 1909 he was one of the founders of the Petersburg literary review *Apollo*, which a few years later became the organ of Acmeism. The acknowledged leader of that movement, Gumilev also helped to establish in Petersburg a "guild" of young poets. It was in that period of time that he married the poetess Anna Akhmatova (from whom he was divorced in 1918) and published the most important collection of his youth, *Pearls* (1910). Obsessed by a spirit of adventure, and perhaps influenced by Kipling (as he was to be later influenced by D'Annunzio, to whom he addressed an ode during the Fiume affair), he dreamed of an African empire for Russia. After an earlier voyage, he returned in 1913 to Somaliland and Abyssinia, this time at the head of an ethnographical and geographical expedition organized by the Russian Academy of Sciences. He reflected his experience of the dark continent in many of his ensuing books, starting with *Foreign Sky* (1912), which contained, among many other things, a series of Abyssinian songs.

Gumilev was the only Russian poet of stature who fought in the war of 1914, volunteering as a private and then serving as an officer in a cavalry unit. The bravery he showed in the East Prussia campaign earned him two Saint George crosses, or, as he said in "Memory," speaking of himself in the third person, "Saint George touched twice his breast untouched by bullets." Soldiering did not prevent Gumilev from writing and publishing new volumes of verse, such as *The Quiver* (1916) and *The Pyre* (1918), the first of which includes most of his war poems. The February Revolution caught him in Paris, on his way to join a Russian corps fighting on the Macedonian front. He returned home the following spring, and upon his arrival he publicly declared himself a supporter of the monarchy. As shown by the words of another poem ("I shall not die in bed between a doctor and a lawyer"), he had always known that his destiny had marked him for an out-of-the-ordinary death. Accused of counter-revolutionary activity and implicated in the so-called Tagantsev conspiracy, he was shot by the Bolsheviks on August 25, 1921, barely thirty-five years of age, just after the publication of another book of poems, *The Tent* (1921), mostly inspired by his experiences and adventures in Africa.

The most important of his posthumous collections, *The Pillar of Fire*, appeared the next year, to be followed by *Poems* (1922) and *To the Blue Star* (1923). *The Pillar of Fire* remains his masterpiece and shows how the poet had grown and matured at the very time of his death. None of these or of Gumilev's earlier books was ever reprinted in Soviet Russia, and this is why there is not yet a complete edition of his writings, which include not only poems, but also plays and tales in prose and verse. Even outside Russia many of these items and other fragments have appeared in print only recently in a volume edited by Gleb Struve, entitled *The Unpublished Gumilev* (1952). What remains still important in Gumilev's literary legacy is the fruit of his varied activity as a translator, which enriched Russian literature with splendid versions of Villon's ballads, Gautier's *Emaux et Camées*, Coleridge's *Rime of the Ancient Mariner*, and the Assyrian epic of *Gilgamesh*. Also his critical essays, collected posthumously in the volume *Letters About Russian Poetry* (1923), have more than a purely historical value, and may still be read with great interest.

The emergence of Gumilev was for Russian poetry an event not too different in kind (although far less in degree) from the earlier appearance in England of Kipling, and in Italy of the martial and patriotic D'Annunzio. Gumilev's sudden rise on the horizon of Russian poetry was viewed at first as a novel miracle, as a wonder of youth. Gumilev came to the fore in the shape of a new David, a gay rogue who relied on his arm and eye no less than on his God, and the weary spirit of the giant, Russian Symbolism, seemed to collapse under the shot from his sling. Gumilev was aware of the novelty, or rather, of the timeliness of his message. He felt that he had come to restore to manliness and health a poetry which had degenerated into the vices opposed to those two virtues. Thus, in the poem entitled "My Readers" he prided himself for sparing them from all those morbid, effete, and mystical impressions which the poetry of his elders tried to achieve: "I do not offend them with neurasthenia," said the poet, "I do not humble them with a soft heart, nor do I bore them with complex symbols about the shell of a sucked-out egg."

The Decadents had viewed poetry as if it were a descent into the underworld of the senses; the Symbolists, as an ascent toward the heaven of the soul. Gumilev refused to explore both the forest of symbols and the cave of our dreams, since the path going through them may lead to what is either too base or too lofty for the heart and the mind of man. He rejected the temptation to wander into the ghostly realms of the metaphysical and the occult, and ventured instead into the material and physical world. His quest was not for Eden or Hell, but for a remote oasis or a lonely island, an unbeaten desert or a virgin continent. What spurred him was not the external urge of literary exoticism, but a romantic and passionate nostalgia for the venturesome discovery of new worlds. The frequence in his poetry of Southern and Eastern landscapes may remind us of the Parnassian predilection for the same distant countries and faraway seas. Yet one must not forget that for the Parnassians those landscapes were hardly more than ornamental frames or decorative backgrounds, while in Gumilev's poetry they are direct illustrations of his states of mind. This may serve as a further proof that, all appearances to the contrary, Gumilev's conception of poetry is hardly Parnassian in the real sense of the term. The Russian poet cannot accept the Parnassians' detachment and indifference, as well as their outright denial of any sense of order in the universe beyond the sphere of art. It is against both Parnassian nihilism and Symbolistic mysticism that Gumilev proclaimed, in strongly moral accents, that "religion and poetry are but opposite sides of the same coin." For the Parnassians poetry is but the triumph of a lucid eye and a firm hand on a brute and blind matter, and such a triumph is possible only when no subjective concern affects the artist, at least while he is shaping his object. This is the doctrine of poetic impersonality, which the French Symbolists had inherited from the Parnassians, and were later to impose on many of their followers outside of France. The doctrine, as we well know, had little effect on the Russian disciples of French Symbolism, except on Brjusov, and Gumilev reacted perhaps against the only one among his elders whom he respected as a master when he restated the Romantic belief that "poetry is for man one of the means by which to express his personality." It is to poetry, not less than to religion, that

Gumilev assigns the task of educating mankind, or, as he says, of "raising man to the level of a higher type."

Gumilev also took a middle position toward some of the main poetic issues of his time, protesting equally against the Parnassian tendency to treat the word as a mere object and the Symbolist one to treat it almost as pure spirit, and choosing to treat it as if it were a living thing: "poetry, as a living organism, has its anatomy and its physiology; and it is primarily in word combinations that we see what one might call its flesh." He viewed the word also as an instrument of action, through which man makes, or remakes, the world. Once, said he in the poem "The Word," men used words to stop the sun, or to lay a city in ruins. For primitive man, even numbers were endowed with the magic power of words. But modern man has mechanized and materialized both numbers and words, and the latter lie now like dead bees in the empty hive of modern life.

It is with words which are both complex and simple that Gumilev sings his main themes, war, danger, and adventure. He celebrates a free life in a wild world, and praises among men only those with whom one can share a common undertaking or the same risk. It is in such men, "strong, wicked, and happy, loyal to this planet," that he sees his ideal readers. Like them, Gumilev respects the body, which he deifies. In his poem "Memory," as a matter of fact, he reverses the doctrine of reincarnation by assigning a series of different souls to a single physical being. It is perhaps this ability to understand in all its complexity the problem of personality that enables this imperialist to understand and admire the "lesser breeds." Gumilev feels himself the friend and the equal of any native, of a decrepit beggar in Beirut or of an old Ethiopian outlaw. An uncanny feeling of the ties between physical and psychic forces allows him to describe animals, especially wild beasts, in a light of poetic and natural innocence, avoiding at once the pitfalls of sentimental idealization or emblematic stylization, as can be seen in many pieces, especially in the lovely poem "The Giraffe."

Conscious of being born a leader, Gumilev knows that he has the right to excel and to command: he considers his own poetry as an example of courage, as a lesson in self-discipline. In "My Readers" he defines his own poetic task as that of teaching all his peers "not to dread, and to do what must be done." In brief, Gumilev's ethos is a martial one, and rests on the warrior's acceptance of fate and death. There is no better proof of this than the poem "The Worker," written during the war, describing a little, old, German workingman in the act of shaping the bullet destined to pierce the poet's heart. The poem remains prophetic, although we know that that bullet was molded, or at least fired, by Russian hands. Later the poet dared to face again the vision of his own death in "The Derailed Streetcar," the nightmarish poem he composed shortly before the end of his life.

Gumilev's early work perhaps lacks the visionary power which distinguishes such poems as these. Born too late in a world too old, the youthful poet had felt too much the anguish of living in a shrunken space: and this is why he had tried to find not only escape, but also self-realization, in the faraway corners of this all-too-narrow planet of ours. Yet it would be a mistake to define the early Gumilev as merely "the poet of geography," as the critic Julij Ajkhenval'd did, with the intent of praising him. In reality, even the early Gumilev searched not so much for new lands as for the tree of life; and that tree spreads its roots in depth, not in width. This is why he changed from a geographer and an explorer into an ethnographer and an archaeologist. Perhaps what he sought was to be found in the caves of prehistory, rather than in the broad expanse of a geographical world. Hence the importance of a poem such as "The Stellar Fright," which evokes the terror felt by primitive man at the vision of the star-filled sky. This sense of awe before the sacred mystery of nature is perhaps one of the most vital strains of Gumilev's inspiration. It is from that sense that the poet derives his belief that man's destiny is ultimate defeat, and that his duty is to accept that destiny readily, with heroic resignation and silent stoicism. In this Gumilev recalls Vigny, from whom he drew the epigraph for one of his books. Such an attitude is obviously Romantic: yet Gumilev's is a vigorous and virile Romanticism, impatient of all sentimental vagueness and moral perplexity. What he called Acmeism was but a projection of the lit-

228

erary side of his personality, which he expressed, at its best and most directly, in the book which he prepared for publication just before his death. The muse which dictated that book was life rather than literature: and this is why the figure of its author seems still to stand and shine before our eyes like "the pillar of fire" of its title.

IV

ANNA AKHMATOVA

Anna Gorenko, who was born in Kiev in 1889, and who took Akhmatova, the surname of her mother, as her own pen name, was bound to Acmeism by subtler bonds than those of her short-lived marriage to its leader. Discovered by Vjacheslav Ivanov, she was presented to the Russian public by Mikhail Kuzmin, to whose conception of poetry, as a matter of fact, she was nearer than to Gumilev's. Without the theoretical pretensions of both, and with a more genuine gift than either of them, Anna Akhmatova showed with at least equal effectiveness that poetry should turn toward earthly, and yet unbeaten, paths. Her reaction against the un-worldly mysticism of the Symbolists was a feminine one: she reas-serted the right of a private and intimate inspiration, of a personal and autobiographical lyricism. Her success was naturally greater than that of either Kuzmin or Gumilev. Her earliest books, *Evening* (1912), *Rosary* (1914), *The White Flock* (1917), were to be seen in all the parlors of prerevolutionary Russia, and her popularity was deserved, although it was due perhaps more to the passionate subjects of her poems than to the refined perfection of their form. Her poetry, as a matter of fact, survived even the war and the Revolution, at least for those few years during which she composed the lyrics of *Wayside Grass* and the narrative poem *On the Very Sea*, both of which appeared in 1921. Both *On the Very Sea* and *Wayside Grass* (the generic and etymological meaning of the original title word, which in Russian, however, stands for the English "plantain," or a specific herb) were included by Akhma-tova in the last collection of her creative period, *Anno Domini MCMXXI* (1922), where there are a few simple poems inspired

229

by the historical ordeal she had witnessed, and of which she was herself a tragic victim.

In 1921 the poetess' former husband, from whom she had been divorced since the end of the war, was executed as a counter-revolutionary. The poetess was deeply affected by the violent and cruel death of the father of her son, but she refused to leave Russia, where she remained for more than twenty years, lonely and silent, with no other voice and company than that of her grief. Except for a few translations and a couple of literary studies, she failed to appear again in print until 1940, when she published a collection of new poems, *The Willow*, and a selection of old ones, entitled *From Six Books*. Her fame revived in the favorable climate created by the victorious war, during which her grown-up son had fought valiantly with the Soviet Air Force. But in the year 1946, after having had published a few new lyrics in *Star*, a Leningrad literary review which was edited by Nikolaj Tikhonov and had been equally hospitable to Zoshchenko's satirical sketches of Soviet life, the poetess became the target of the wrath which those publications aroused in the late Andrej Zhdanov, who was then the dictator of Soviet cultural life. Zhdanov condemned Akhmatova with harsh, insulting words, describing her as "the typical representative of a poetry devoid of substance and alien to the Russian people." The poetess was expelled from the Union of Soviet Writers and re-entered a new period of silence. After several years she again broke the spell, and the few poems which she published in 1950 and 1956 in Soviet literary journals proved her renewed mastery and the lasting attractiveness of her voice.

Except for a single verse tale and a few longer pieces, Akhmatova's poems are as brief as Chinese or Japanese lyrics, as madrigals or epigrams, as album verses or *Lieder*. She is one of those poets for whom the word "inspiration" seems to reacquire its traditional meaning, but since inspiration works within her only when stirred by an inner emotion or an external happening, one could say that anything she writes is, in the Goethean sense of the term, an occasional poem. Each one of her lyrics recalls sketchily, and yet vividly, not only a unique, real-life experience, but also its precise location in space and time, so that the scholars of the future will probably be able to refer each one of her poems to a precise event within her biography. In brief, the muse of Anna Akhmatova is memory, a memory incredibly near in quality, if not in time, to the incident she records from the exclusive viewpoint of her "I." Yet in what the poetess reports there is no afterthought nor hindsight: one would say that she represents objectively a past which has only a subjective reality. It is quite significant that she chose as a title for her best book, simply and eloquently, a mere date; yet not only *Anno Domini MCMXXI* but each one of her collections is a lyrical diary. In this Akhmatova follows the great tradition of feminine poetry, which, from Sappho to Louise Labé, from Gaspara Stampa to Marceline Desbordes-Valmore, has always tried to tell, in rhapsodic or fragmentary form, and from the viewpoint of its feminine partner, a single and simple love story, at once old and new.

The eternal theme of the poetry of love, when sung by a woman, is the fealty of a loving soul, the loyalty of a passionate heart. Thus the secret of Anna Akhmatova's poetry could be summed up in a single word: fidelity. Fidelity to her man and her passion, as well as to nature and life; above all, fidelity to the glories and miseries of her sex. Hence the strange harmony reconciling the opposite strains of her poetry, made at once of candor and modesty, of spontaneity and discretion, of passion and restraint. All the images employed by this free and capricious lover are feminine in the familiar sense, motherly or housewifely, homespun or domestic, as in the beautiful metaphor by which a smooth liquid surface becomes "the tablecloth of the water." The main theme of her poetry is passion, yet she sings of love in the humble tone of the elegy, rather than in the lofty mode of the hymn. Hers is not the soul of a maenad or a nymph, but of a pious Christian woman, or of a modern, bourgeois lady, simple and direct. She finds love beautiful and terrible for being an all-day reality, an everyday thing: the most intimate of all habits, the daily bread of the soul. The poetess savors the experience of love in all its recurring phases, meeting and separation, distance and absence, desire and longing, jealousy and remorse. Each one of these feelings or events is projected outside, within the visible, objective world and finds forever a local habitation and a name in the place to which it is still connected in the poetess' memory, which turns that place into a kind of private shrine.

The poetess represents every emotion and every person, even the smallest detail or the most insignificant object, with guileless innocence, with almost virginal shyness. Under her gaze, the realities of love seem to appear at once veiled and naked. Each human being, even during the embrace, remains forever enclosed within the shell of its own integrity, for, as Anna Akhmatova says with words which seem to recall Emily Dickinson's poetry, "near each creature is drawn a line, which neither love nor passion can trespass." This perhaps is the reason why Anna Akhmatova never describes her lovers except as half-seen: as if she would never look openly into their faces, or would do so only stealthily, or with half-shut eyes. What we are shown are details pertaining more to the lovers' clothing than to their persons; all we see of one of them is "a red tulip in the buttonhole." The poetess herself seems to feel the presence of her lover mainly through other senses than that of sight, by feeling the fire of his gaze, or the caress of his voice. Blind and unprotected, she yields to the vocal or mute language of seduction without will to resist, but without self-deceit: "In vain I cautiously wrap my shoulders and breast in furs. . . . In vain you speak softly of the first love. How well I know your piercing, greedy glances!"

The poetess is so overwhelmed by love that she can do hardly more than observe with fascinated absorption what is taking place within and outside of herself. How feminine and ladylike is the detail she chooses to convey her feeling of embarrassment during the last meeting with her lover: "I stuffed on my right the glove of my left hand." And in another poem how simple and pure are the words by which she describes a daring gesture of love: "Once again he touched my knees, lightly, with untrembling hand." If the poetess seems almost never able to see the face of the beloved, it is perhaps because the beloved is but a means or pretext for the passion agitating the soul of his loving partner. Anna Akhmatova, like Stendhal and Proust, not only learns this lesson when the fire of passion is spent ("how heavy is the memory of love"); she also

seems to be aware of its truth even in the moment of expectation or desire. This can almost be felt in the lovely lyric in which
the poetess dreams not so much of the meeting, but of herself while
waiting for it. She imagines rising at dawn in the cabin of a steamship, going in furs on deck, waiting there for her rendezvous, and,
during the wait, "being made younger by the spray and the wind."
Here there is *amour-passion* and *amour-vanité*, a woman's fondness
for elegance and beauty, the intoxication of happiness and youth.

This, and other poems of this kind, are eloquent proofs that
Anna Akhmatova sings at her best not of the present moment, but
of the moment just past, or of the moment about to come: in
brief, of the moments when she is alone with no other company
but her fantasies and daydreams. Sometimes she seems to be alone
even when she has a companion beside her, as in the lovely poem
where she describes herself at night, by a lake, with a man who
remains silent and invisible, and whose presence is revealed only
by the "we" of the closing line. They look together at the moon;
yet the poetess gives us only her own thoughts and feelings, the
melancholy forebodings which fill her all-too-womanly soul. Even
in that vast outdoor scene she projects her superstitious fears in
personal and domestic terms. Thus the full moon hanging over the
lake becomes for her a window mysteriously lighted at night, as
if to announce the sudden discovery of a misfortune afflicting the
family of the house, such as the flight of the husband, or the
death of a child.

This sense of an impending calamity, which threatens to engulf the earth with all its creatures, fills the whole of *Anno Domini
MCMXXI*. We do not know what the calamity means; we know
only that it is already bringing violence and bloodshed among men,
and that plague and famine will follow that violence and bloodshed. As a patient and suffering woman, the poetess neither judges
nor condemns; she merely asks herself "why our century is more
cruel than ages past." Is it because, she wonders, "our time has
placed its finger on the blackest of all wounds without being able
to heal it?" Even before facing the tragedy of modern history,
Anna Akhmatova seems to have always conceived of woman's
destiny in terms of the expectation of love and of the visitation of

death. This is, after all, the theme of the beautiful verse tale *On the Very Sea*, which tells in legendary vein the story of a Crimean girl who has been dreaming of a fairy-tale lover, and who, just after having found the prince of her dreams, loses him forever when he drowns "on the very seashore." Yet, despite her dreams of happiness, the soul of the girl is always filled with the sense of an imminent misfortune, foreshadowed by such simple and natural happenings as a sudden changing of the season, a sounding of bells, the flickering of a lamp, or the barking at night of stray dogs: all signs, as the poetess says, that "it was a time of sorrow for the heart." For a poetry of this kind there is perhaps no more fitting epigraph than those Latin words in James Joyce's *Portrait* by which Stephen Dedalus suddenly welcomes within his soul the sudden echo of an unseen woman's song: "mulier cantat."

v

OTHER POETS

Sergej Gorodetskij (born in 1884) was for a while considered Acmeism's second in command. As a poet, he failed to fulfill his early promise, and his reputation still rests on a single book, which he published even before the foundation of Acmeism. That book, which appeared in 1907, was entitled *Jar'*, a root suggesting the notions of sap and light, and which according to Roman Jakobson is associated with Jarilo, the name of an ancient god of the Slavs. If not this title, at least that of Gorodetskij's second volume of verse, which he issued in the same year and named *Perun* after the Zeus or Thor of the Slavic Pantheon, bared the poet's liking for a mannered and decorative mythology, as well as his attempt to replace the ghostly mysticism of the Symbolists with a neopaganism of his own. It was, however, folk poetry, rather than mythology or paganism, which inspired Gorodetskij's most famous cycle, "Spring in the Monastery." There the daughter of a convent's bellringer sings of her love, and her singing is accompanied by a refrain of church bells. After his early success, Gorodetskij gradually lost his youthful gift and lowered himself as an artist by writing erotic fiction in the worst taste. After the Revolution, he degraded himself as a moral being by his servile acceptance of the new regime and by a public condemnation of Gumilev, who had been his teacher and friend.

The leaders of Acmeism had the great merit of uncovering new talent, and of giving a helping hand to budding poets in need of guidance or support. It is precisely to Gorodetskij that the credit must go for turning the attention of Velimir Khlebnikov, when the latter was still a youth, to the mysterious and rich treasure of Slavic mythology and Russian folklore; and for revealing the peasant poet, Sergej Esenin, who had started as Kljuev's disciple, to the literary circles of Petersburg. Kljuev is the only one of these poets to be treated here, if for no other reason than that there is some kinship between his work and Gorodetskij's, although as a poet the latter is quite inferior. This kinship lies in the artificial quality of Kljuev's inspiration, which he derives not from Slavic paganism, but from Russian peasant Christianity, which retains many traces of pagan rites and beliefs.

Nikolaj Kljuev was born in 1885 in the Lake Onega region, then still preserving the tradition of epic singing and the memory of the heroic tales of old. It was perhaps this origin that prevented Kljuev from becoming merely a new Kol'tsov, a simple singer of peasant toil, of the joys and sorrows of a way of life close to nature and the earth; and that made of him a far more conscious and skillful artistic interpreter of Russian folklore. His poems translate popular themes and motifs into highly stylized forms. The air of naïveté in his work is frequently a mannerism: its effects of simplicity and primitivism are often produced by deliberate and elaborate devices. Kljuev's images, scenes, and visions tend at the same time toward the rustic and the emblematic, toward the opposite patterns of an ancient icon or a popular print. This is particularly true of his first book, *Chimes of Pines* (1912), where the poet was able to join in surprising harmony the decorative rigidity of his formal patterns with freshness of vision and purity of song. The moral center of Kljuev's poetry is the Russian peasant hut, the *izba*, which he idealizes through the perspectives of decoration and fancy, and projects into the eerie world of fairy tales, legends, and myths.

In the collections he published after the Revolution, Kljuev became the high priest of an agrarian messianism, which he announced with turgid declamations and oracular speech. At first, he believed that the Revolution would bring in its wake the embodiment of his ideals, the fulfillment of his dreams. Soon enough he realized, however, that the Revolution would not only fail to keep its promises to the peasantry, but would even destroy its way of life. The poet vented his wrath at this tragic turn of events in words both private and public, in his writings as well as in his talks; and it was as a "mad *kulak* of poetry" that, like millions of other prosperous peasants, he was deported to Siberia, where his traces were soon lost, although it is presumed that he died in 1937.

No assessment of the contributions of Acmeism would be complete without mentioning that the movement attracted two beginners who were destined to occupy important places in the history of Russian poetry. The first of them was Osip Mandel'shtam, who will be treated at length in another chapter. The second was Georgij Ivanov, of whom I shall speak briefly here. Born in 1894, he started his literary career while still a youngster, under the double spell of Severjanin's Ego-Futurism and Kuzmin's Clarism. It was the latter's example that inspired Ivanov's first booklet, *The Embarkation for the Island of Cythera* (1912), which, as its title indicates, found its theme in the masterpiece of Watteau, one of those eighteenth-century artists of whom Kuzmin was such an ardent devotee. In the years that followed, from the war to the Revolution, Ivanov took his cue directly from the Acmeists, and published several collections of poems conveying with fresh objectivity the charms of the physical world. The best book he produced during this phase is *Gardens* (1921), where, perhaps under the influence of Anna Akhmatova, he reflected the experiences of the senses in the mirror of feeling.

Ivanov left Russia in the early twenties, and settled in Paris, failing for almost a decade to write, or at least to publish, anything new. In 1931 he issued the collection *Roses*, which is undoubtedly his masterpiece, as well as one of the highlights of Russian *émigré* verse. At this stage the poet had not only broken forever with his Acmeist past, but had found new models, or rather ideals, in

Annenskij and Blok. As Gleb Struve has remarked, Ivanov, after having been a neoclassicist in his youth, was to become a neoromantic in his maturity: by ceasing to seek the wonder of form in the outside world, he discovered the higher miracle of music within his soul. Yet, unwilling to rest on his laurels and unable to imitate himself, the late Ivanov was perhaps all too eager to heed the morbid appeal of the muses of dejection and rejection, of despair and cynicism. Just before his sudden death, which occurred in 1959, his inspiration seemed to take a new and better turn: yet there is no doubt that at least *Roses* will preserve Ivanov's reputation as the rival and successor of Vladislav Khodasevich. As long as he lived, the latter was the king of all Russian poets in exile; still, there are many critics and readers who claim that Ivanov deserved to wear that crown even before Khodasevich's death.

CHAPTER EIGHT

THE POETS OF THE ADVANCE GUARD

I

FUTURISM

THE twenty-year period between 1910 and 1930 witnessed the gradual appearance, the short-lived triumph, the sudden decline, and the final death of the Russian literary advance-guard movements. The foremost of them, and also the most representative and lasting, was Futurism. The second was Ego-Futurism, which was only slightly connected with Futurism proper, and which perhaps could be hardly called a movement, since it lasted *l'espace d'un matin* and was confined to the activity and production of almost one single poet, whose advance-guardism was, moreover, rather superficial and doubtful. That poet, whose pen name was Igor' Severjanin, will be briefly dealt with at the proper place. The third movement, Imaginism, also identified itself with the work of a young and lonely master, Sergej Esenin; yet it was a manifestation of greater authenticity and significance, partly deriving, and partly diverging from the mainstream of Futurism.

Historically, these three movements may be differentiated according to their respective stands, before, during, and after February and October, toward the Revolution. Ego-Futurism could hardly adjust itself to the new order, and its leader Severjanin survived in exile the success of his youth. In spite of their anti-bourgeois pose, the cheap hedonism and vulgar aestheticism of Severjanin and company had been the fashionable expression of the ideals of the *nouveaux riches*, and the movement disappeared with them. The slogan of Ego-Futurism had been modernism, but the only kind it cared about was the modernism of the drawing room. Futurism, too, preached modernism, but not only in the arts, whether they were applied or not; at least some of its followers aimed at destroying the past and at molding the present after the pattern of the future, not merely in the field of culture, but also in the historical and social realm. Thus its reaction against the art and culture of the past was in part also a revolt against the *ancien régime*, or at least against the new bourgeoisie. Futurism prophesied the coming revolution and joined hands with it. Later it tried to become the moral and artistic interpreter of the new order, and for a while the attempt seemed, at least in part, to succeed. Finally, as soon as its leaders realized that the Communist Party had chosen not to recognize their movement as the official representative of poetry and art within the new society, Futurism ceased to exist.

Imaginism was founded in 1919, to flourish and wither within a two-year span. Although it was in sympathy with the destructive spirit of the age, it rejected any tie of solidarity with the Revolution as soon as it felt that the latter was being institutionalized; and from this standpoint, it manifested a more authentic advance-guard temper than postrevolutionary Futurism. Such an attitude, along with other factors, condemned Imaginism to a short life and a rapid end; that school could not survive the time of the Civil War and War Communism, nor last beyond the end of that period, during which, on both the external and the internal fronts, the party had been forced to a policy of compromise and retreat, and for a while had to wait and see.

The treatment of a fourth movement, Constructivism, must be postponed to our survey of Soviet poetry, of which that movement was part. Here it will suffice to say that Constructivism was the only literary advance guard destined to appear at the very moment when the revolutionary advance guard, confronted by a new political reality, had begun to give way to a new ruling elite: and thus Constructivism was fated to follow, belatedly and even more pitifully, the example and the destiny of the late Futurists.

239

Moreover, the ideas expressed by the Constructivists in their artistic struggle were to be literal translations into cultural terms of the ideological slogans of the party on the political and industrial fronts; and this casts some doubt on the advance-guard character of the movement. Such a lack of theoretical independence was not even sufficient to save its existence as an organized group, and Constructivism disappeared, leaving fewer traces than Futurism and even Imaginism.

Distinct as it was from all the other variants of the same international trend, the movement which shortly after its formation took the name of Russian Futurism would have developed altogether differently without its Franco-Italian precedent. Besides this, it would have had to find for itself a tag probably far less effective than the one provided ready-made by F. T. Marinetti. Almost everywhere the idea of Futurism was already in the air; Marinetti had the great merit of inventing the right word, which he launched at the proper time as a stirring slogan and a ringing call. In matters like this questions of priority are harder to decide than questions of primacy: even an all-too-literal chronology may hardly help to settle the issue. Yet dates must be given, even though they should not be taken at their face value. What they tell is simply that Marinetti published his first Futurist manifesto in *Le Figaro* of Paris in 1909, and that in the same year a group of Moscow poets issued an almanac to which they gave the nonsensical and, in Russian, alliterative title of *Hatchery of Judges* (*Sadok sudej*). The members of the group, following the advice of their youthful leader Khlebnikov, who was paradoxically a purist and an archaist in matters of language, thought of calling themselves *budetljane*, a word coined from *budet*, the third person singular of the future tense of the verb "to be," and which sounds in Russian like "those who will be," or "the men of the coming age."

Almost at the same time the same poets accepted as their own the label of Cubo-Futurists, seemingly supplied by an outsider, the critic Kornej Chukovskij. It is difficult to say whether its adoption indicates acquaintance on the part of those poets with the Cubism of Braque and Picasso, then just starting to revolutionize the visual arts of the West. After all, it was only some time later that Guillaume Apollinaire turned into a flag and a program the outcry of *cubisme!* — the laconic stricture which the *fauve* Matisse had flung at the new style, when it had made its first appearance in a Braque painting exhibited in 1908 at the *Salons des Indépendents*. But it was probably in order to emphasize their independence from any parallel Western development that the Moscow Futurists employed for a while as their own trademark the place name *Gileja*, which belongs to a small region on the coast of the Black Sea.

There is no doubt that the first genuine poetic manifestations of Russian Futurism appeared in 1910, the very year Marinetti made his first visit to Russia, lecturing in both capitals. Yet the movement affirmed itself with due deliberation and authority only with the publication of its full-fledged manifestoes in 1913. The most productive phase of Russian Futurism lasted from 1911 to the war, a period closed by Marinetti's second *tournée*, which was a partial failure, while the first had been an unqualified success. This time the Franco-Italian poet disappointed and even offended both the literati and the public with the martial overtones of his speeches, already inspired by a kind of bourgeois imperialism. Yet the Moscow Futurists were at least disingenuous when on that occasion they declared in print that even two years earlier they had felt "to have nothing in common with the Italian Futurists except the name."

The memoirs that Kruchenykh, Kamenskij, Livshits, and other members of Russian Futurism were to publish fifteen or twenty years after the event show an equal lack of candor and reveal an excessive touchiness in regard to the question of the dependence or independence of their movement. In these and other similar documents a wrongheaded attempt to prove an unjustified and irrelevant claim of precedence has produced some juggling of dates and dissembling of facts. All such quibbling was altogether unnecessary, since every unbiased observer will easily admit that Russian Futurism was a highly original movement, far more seminal than its Italian counterpart in both theory and creation, particularly in the art of verse.

Yet there is no denying that, especially from the viewpoint of their aggressive tone and caustic style, at least the early declarations of Russian Futurism read almost like those of its Italian counterpart. While diverging in aesthetic purpose, Russian and Italian Futurists shared the same negative ideals, and this is why their polemical declarations often differ only in the names of those representatives of tradition whom each national group chose to pillory and to repudiate. To prove this point it may suffice to quote from a proclamation which David Burljuk, Kruchenykh, Majakovskij, and Khlebnikov signed in December 1912, and printed shortly afterward at the head of the pamphlet *A Slap to Public Taste*: "To those who will read us: the New, the Primordial, the Unexpected. We are the face of the new time. Time's trumpet blares in ourselves and in our verbal artifice. The past suffocates us. The Academy and Pushkin are more incomprehensible than hieroglyphics. Throw overboard Pushkin, Dostoevskij, Tolstoj, etc., from the steamship Modernity. . . . All those Kuprins, Bloks, Sologubs, Remizovs, . . . Kuzmins, Bunins want is a villa on the river. . . . From the top of our skyscrapers we look at their meanness. . . . Even if our writings still preserve traces of your 'common sense' and 'good taste,' yet they shine for the first time with the flashes of a new beauty to come. . . ."

As in the case of Italian Futurism, the Moscow group included not only men of letters but also artists, and frequently men of letters who were also artists. Almost all of the Burljuk brothers, David, Nikolaj, and Vladimir, led by David, the oldest (born in 1882), were poets and painters at the same time. The connections between the new poets and the new painters were at any rate very close, and one could even claim that the Futuristic spirit emerged and triumphed later and more slowly in the sphere of letters than in that of the arts. Even in the field of painting the center of the Russian advance guard of those years was the old city of Moscow: it was there that Burljuk and others had founded the "Jack of Diamonds," a group of experimental artists, already trying their hand at what would later be called objective, nonrepresentational, or abstract art. It was also there that Larionov and Goncharova, who then were more interested in the decorative distortion of neo-primitivism (they were as fond as Rimbaud of what he had called *peintures idiotes*, and the like), joined with Tatlin and Malevich, two future Suprematists or Constructivists, to establish together the painters' club which took the grotesque name of "Donkey Tail." Besides writers and artists, the movement attracted even men of action, either adventurers or sportsmen, like the poet Vasilij Kamenskij, who was one of the first Russians to try to fly an airplane. But Russian Futurism was not merely a meeting ground for eccentrics; it was also a breeding ground of new talents, as shown by the presence in its ranks of two real masters, Khlebnikov and Majakovskij, and of a few minor but authentic craftsmen of the word, like the woman poet and artist, Elena Guro, whose early death (1910) prevented her from developing the exceptional gifts she manifested in two slim collections of prose and verse, *The Street Organ* (1909) and *The Little Camels of the Sky* (1912).

Naturally, the activity of the movement expressed itself, at least as much as in works of art, in printed declarations and in public manifestations, even in public scandals; above all, in the irregular but constant publication of a series of arbitrary and challenging anthologies, miscellanies, almanacs, collecting the best of the minor members of the movement and often some of the most interesting pieces left by Khlebnikov, the most finished literary artist produced by early Russian Futurism. The titles of some of these collections are highly indicative of the paradoxical taste of the group: *Hatchery of Judges* (I and II, 1909 and 1913); *A Slap to Public Taste* (I and II, 1912 and 1913); *The Roaring Parnassus* and *The Cadaverous Moon* (1914). Even a cursory reading of these publications shows how Russian Futurism was, theoretically and technically, less superficial than its Italian equivalent and far more interested in problems of language and style, in questions of versification and form. The elaboration of a Futurist poetics was primarily due to Velimir Khlebnikov, who contributed to it both brilliant insights and interesting experiments; to Aleksej Kruchenykh, born in 1886 and still living in Russia, whose contribution was more valuable in the field of theory than in that of creation; and finally, to the painter and poet David Burljuk, the real organizer of the movement during its heroic years and its outstanding propagandist, who barely survived as an artist after he left Russia in the early twenties to settle in New York.

Its concern with theory was a peculiar trait of prewar Futurism, so well represented by its outstanding figure, Velimir Khlebnikov. The postwar movement, more political and practical, found its standard-bearer in Majakovskij, who was supported by a host of followers, the best known of whom were two poets who had already joined the earlier group. These two were Nikolaj Aseev, who was to become an important Soviet author, and Benedikt Livshits, the only former Futurist to perish in the great purges of the thirties. Majakovskij himself had foreseen the future changes of the movement from the very beginning of the First World War, in the article "A Drop of Tar" published in the pamphlet *Vzjal* (1915), the title of which is the past tense form of a Russian verb meaning "to take" or "to seize." That piece contained a double foreboding, announcing the parallel triumphs of the Revolution and of Futurism, and claiming that the latter had already "seized Russia in its grasp."

After October 1917, the concerted effort by the Russian advance guard to gain official recognition as the single representative of the Revolution in the aesthetic realm met with an unexpected, if ephemeral, success in the field of the arts. With the support of Anatolij Lunacharskij, the Commissar for Instruction, an old Bolshevik who was a mediocre and pretentious man of letters, the new painters were able for a while to control the museums, the academies, and the galleries, and to spread their doctrines through an organ of their own, *The Art of the Commune*. The advance guard was, however, confronted from the very beginning with the inborn diffidence of the Red leaders toward its endeavor to gain the upper hand in the sphere of the written word, even within the limited scope of the literary press. It was to foster the cause for which they strove that the new poets led in the foundation of an organization called LEF, an abbreviation of *Levyj Front Iskusstv*, or "Left Front of the Arts." LEF gathered around itself not only the new Futurists, but also the Constructivist poets, as well as the Formalistic critics and such outstanding screen directors as Èjzenshtejn and Dziga Vertov, the latter the great theorist and practitioner of the documentary film.

It was as editor-in-chief of *LEF* (the organization issued from

1923 to 1925 a journal by the same name) that Majakovskij waged his campaign for the cultural and literary monopoly which his movement failed to obtain from the Soviet regime. At the same time, Majakovskij helped to make the movement more normal and more popular, succeeded for a while in keeping it in a state of uneasy balance between the taste of the public and the demands of the party line, and did his best to defend his own brand of Futurism from the attacks against it from the opposite quarters of the cultural Right and political Left. When he began to lose his control over the movement, he founded *The New LEF* (1927–1928), which he described as being "to the left of *LEF*": but finally, shortly before his death, confronted with the hard facts of Soviet reality, he resigned his post in disgust, with the practical effect of hastening the dissolution of the movement to which he had given the best years of his life.

Owing to the poetic achievement of Majakovskij, and to the psychic bond that existed for a while between his inspiration and the new state of mind, enthusiastic and heroic, which dominated Russian youth during the early phase of the Revolution, the second period of Russian Futurism may seem more important than the first. But as seekers after new forms and techniques, as pioneers in yet unexplored fields, thanks to Khlebnikov's tireless quest, the Futurists of the old guard left a far deeper imprint in the soil of Russian letters. The two generations of Russian Futurism differed equally from the Italian Futurists by being more aggressive toward the national tradition itself; on the other hand, their exaltation of modern life was less subordinated than that of their Western rivals to what the latter called "the aesthetics of the machine." In Russia, the glorification of the values of our modern mechanical civilization became prominent only later, with Majakovskij and his group, and in connection with the Communist idolatry of technology and industrialization.

According to the letter of their statements, and sometimes even according to the spirit of their deeds, the Russian Futurists, who had never been dominated by an egotistical and tyrannical leader like Marinetti, and who in some cases had been actively sympathetic to the ideal of a social revolution, were less individualistic than their Italian colleagues, and acted with more consistency and discipline as a group. They constantly opposed any Decadent *culte du moi*, stating in the most important of their manifestoes that they would "stand fast on the rock of the word 'we' amidst an ocean of hisses and indignation." As a matter of fact it was this distrust of any form of self-idolatry by the artist, as well as their concern for formal values, that marks the difference between the Cubo-Futurists of Moscow and the Ego-Futurists of Petersburg.

The Ego-Futurists were interested only in disguising old feelings and moods under fashionable dresses or clever masks, but the Cubo-Futurists were really interested in creating new forms. While the posthumous example of Mallarmé's *Coup de dés* had suggested to Marinetti the doctrine, which remained little more than a slogan, of the *mots en liberté*, the Russian Futurists developed instead the theory and practice of a complete metamorphosis of poetic language, and tried to enact a radical revolution of the word. In this attempt they went further than any other offshoot directly derived from Futurism, and anticipated experiments performed in the West by later advance guards. They failed in their search, yet they had the merit of pushing it to its extreme consequences, without being satisfied with wishful or boastful advertisements of unrealized programs.

After all, Marinetti's doctrine of the *mots en liberté*, while proclaiming the dissolution of all syntactical ties, had merely achieved the abolition of punctuation and had done little more than develop minor external or material effects, like onomatopoeia and "typographical relief." At least some of the Russian Futurists aimed instead at creating a new kind of poetry, based on a language invented anew, consciously constructed for this very purpose. Their intent was to transcend the traditional and conventional meaning of each word, and to devise words morphologically new, and therefore devoid of any pre-established connotation. The language thus created took the name of "transmental tongue" (*zaumnyj jazyk*). It was Kruchenykh who in the pamphlet *Trio* (1913) stated the theory of "transmental" poetry with the following words: "Before us no art of the word ever existed. Up to now it has been maintained that it is poetry that rules the word, rather than contrariwise. We have bared this mistake. . . . A word is wider than its meaning. . . . Each letter, each sound, has its relevance. . . . Why not renounce ideas, why not write with idea-words, with words freely made? . . . . There is no need for such intermediaries as symbol and thought, and we prefer uttering our truth anew. . . ."

Khlebnikov's method was more original and complex, and his poetic experiments cannot be reduced merely to arbitrary exercises in the medium of the "transmental tongue." We can therefore safely assert that the only poet of some reputation among the few using the new medium was Kruchenykh. His "transmental" poems are generally made of newly coined monosyllabic words, joined together in series or lines based on the associative power of either phonetic suggestions or etymological allusions; the content of the poems, if any, is hinted at only by their titles. These pieces are among the many poems of early Futurism belonging to the metrical experiment of *vers libre*, which their authors often adorned with casual rhymes and fashioned after the rhythmical pattern of the folk song. Except for this formal aspect, and against the best intentions of its authors, "transmental" poetry ended, however, by achieving effects similar to those produced by nonsense verse. This does not mean that Kruchenykh's attempts, or that the far less superficial experiments of Khlebnikov, which went into many other directions, are devoid of interest.

Despite the strong polemical attitude which Futurism took against Symbolism, it is evident that "transmental" poetry is directly related to some extreme Symbolist trends and is similar in nature to some of the experiments which were undertaken at the end of his life by such a Western master as Mallarmé. Both the suggestive verbalism of the Symbolists and the sensuous verbalism of the Decadents, with their emphatic cult of a musical language, were bound to open the way to developments in the directions mentioned above. Furthermore, some of Kruchenykh's ideas seem to anticipate even the doctrines of the Surrealists who, in spite of their protest to the contrary, are but the children or grandchildren of the Symbolists. Kruchenykh anticipated, for instance, the very hypotheses on which the Surrealists based their conceptions of

247

"oneiric poetry" and of "automatic writing," as the following statement may easily show: "Psychic motions and changes of mood may originate strange combinations of letters and words, devoid of any articulate meaning."

Khlebnikov was perhaps the only Futurist, in either Russia or the West, who clung to the traditional idea that verse writing naturally brings poetic diction along with itself, even though he submitted that principle to new and iconoclastic norms. He had a strong sense of the formality or artificiality of literary language, and this is why, unlike Majakovskij, he sharply differentiated "poetic speech" from "colloquial discourse." At least in this connection Khlebnikov and his wing failed to break their ties with the Symbolist tradition as fully as did Majakovskij and his band. The proof of this may be seen in the very emphasis by which the former had developed their own theory of the Word. Yet, instead of viewing the Word as Logos and Symbol, as a reflection of the poet's spirit, or as a mirror of the world's soul, they viewed it as an entity which was both absolute and unique, as *Ding an Sich*.

Khlebnikov himself spoke of the "autonomous" or "self-sufficient word" (*samovitoe slovo*), inspiring and probably writing the manifesto significantly entitled *The Word as Such* (1913). It is in that manifesto that we read the resounding statement: "We, Futurist poets, have been thinking far more about the Word than about the Psyche, which our predecessors have mercilessly abused. Rather than by our experiences, let us live by the word per se." Such a notion of the autonomy of the word may be viewed as the literary version of the idea which had brought about Cubism and like-minded trends in the visual arts. For the Cubists and their allies art should not represent an objective, external reality, but create an inner reality of its own, which in painting and sculpture should consist of formal patterns, of an interplay of lines and masses of volumes and colors. The Russian Futurists maintained likewise that poetry should consist of a verbal pattern, made not of word-ideas or of word-images, but of pure words. Rather than suggesting "pure poetry," as this was to be understood by the *epigones* of French Symbolism, that view advanced the more daring hypothesis of poetry as the verbal parallel of abstract art.

It is chiefly their scorn for passion and eloquence that differentiates Khlebnikov and the Cubo-Futurists not only from the Symbolists, but also from the Futurists of the Italian school. The most significant of all Marinetti's ideas was perhaps the one he summed up in the famous slogan "the aesthetics of the machine." The first thing to keep in mind is that Marinetti preached that idea not as an aesthetician, but as an aesthete: if he found the machine beautiful, it was because he viewed it as a function of man's *élan vital*, not as a formal model or a technical structure. Thus, despite their rejection of academic realism, and, up to a point, of representational art, Marinetti and his followers ended by accepting a canon of beauty offered by man's vital experience, and even by the external world. In brief, they continued to see the creative process as a sort of mimesis, as the imitation not of natural objects, but of man's mechanical artifacts. While some of the Russian Futurists shared the admiration of their Italian colleagues for the products of modern technology, the most thoughtful among them were interested not so much in the aesthetics of the machine, as in the mechanics of art.

One could even say that Russian Cubo-Futurism found its visual and plastic equivalent nearer home than in French Cubism: in a group of native artists who worked in Russia from 1913 to the early 1920's, and who called themselves first Suprematists and then Constructivists. These artists, who included Kazimir Malevich, Vladimir Tatlin, Anton Pevsner, and Naum Gabo (the last two, who are brothers, are still active in England), proclaimed and put into practice a new plastic art, using as its own raw material the stuff our mechanized civilization is made of, namely, steel. They sought to shape that medium not into machinelike molds, but into a three-dimensional design, into pure spatial forms. In brief, they tried to turn engineering into the handmaid of architecture, thus reversing the modern trend, which is to submit architecture to engineering. The theorists and practitioners of Cubo-Futurism aimed at attaining similar results by reducing language to the status of a sound-object, and by building artistic structures out of a linguistic matter made, to use Rabelais' fabulous image, of *paroles gelées*, or "frozen words."

While Suprematists and Constructivists must be viewed as their ideal allies in other artistic fields, the poets and prophets of Russian Futurism found from the very beginning their most active and convinced supporters in the members of a new critical school which took the name of Formalism. The two centers of that school were the Society for the Study of Literary Language in Petrograd, and in Moscow, the Linguistic Circle, founded by a group of the university's philology students. The two groups appeared between 1913 and 1917. The first was headed by a gifted man of letters, Viktor Shklovskij (1893), who made a joint plea for the new linguistics and the new poetry in *The Resurrection of the Word*, a book he published in 1914. The most brilliant member of the second group was Roman Jakobson, born in 1896, who in 1920 settled in Czechoslovakia, becoming one of the outstanding members of the Prague Linguistic Circle and one of the leaders of modern linguistics (at present, he is Professor of Slavic at Harvard University). Formalists and Futurists reacted at first almost equally against the psychologism and the subjectivism of the Symbolist movement; and the Formalists could have subscribed to the Futurists' claim that it was better to think "about the Word" than "about the Psyche." Yet both Formalists and Futurists learned from the Symbolists to pay attention to problems of literary, and especially poetic, craftsmanship, and in a sense their strongest protest was directed against the Russian critical tradition, which, in its social and radical, as well as in its mystic or religious, currents, had always taken too seriously the content of literature, its message or idea, its purpose or intent. Thus, at the beginning, the polemical aim of the new school was paramount and inspired Shklovskij's accusation against the lay saint of the Russian intelligentsia, which to many ears must have sounded like blasphemy: "I hate . . . the assassin of Russian literature . . . the *raté* Belinskij."

The best-known members of the Formalist school, besides Shklovskij and Jakobson, were Boris Èjkhenbaum (1886) and Jurij Tynjanov (1894–1943), while Boris Tomashevskij (1890–1957) and Viktor Zhirmunskij (1891) may be considered the fellow travelers of the movement. All these critics, philologists, and theorists developed or applied a doctrine which can be summed up in the following aphorisms: art is style; style is *métier*, technique; technique is both the method and the object of artistic creation. Technical and formal media are thus at once the means and the goals of art. When speaking of media and means, the Formalists seemed almost to speak of conscious stratagems or deliberate tricks; and this is why they raised to the level of a key concept the word and notion of *priem*, which, at least in the sense they used it, can be translated as "device," although it also means "grasp" or "grip." They treated literary composition as if it were an operation both cerebral and mechanical; hence Shklovskij's statement that " a work of art is equal to the sum of the devices used in it." Jakobson developed the same notion when he affirmed that "if literary scholarship wants to be a science, it must acknowledge 'device' as the single hero of literature." While criticism is essentially an internal study of artistic devices, literary history is essentially historical poetics, or an analysis of the constant changing of old sets of devices with new ones.

This in practice meant an emphasis on the problem which Brunetière had called *évolution des genres*, and which Shklovskij reformulated in the following terms: "new forms are simply the canonization of lower genres." Shklovskij himself applied the principle by declaring, for instance, that "Pushkin's lyrics come from album verses; Blok's from gipsy songs; Majakovskij's, from funny-paper poetry." The evolution of a genre was envisaged as being a formal process even when dealing with ideas, subject matter, characterization, or plot; "if art develops through the understanding of its own technique," then even characters are by-products: "the technique of the novel creates personages; Hamlet is engendered by stagecraft."

Formalism flourished in the mid-twenties, to languish a few years more, up to the early thirties, when it died a non-natural death. Its influence, like that of Futurism, managed to survive only scantily, in hidden channels and disguised forms. At first the Formalists' view of the man of letters as an artisan, or as an engineer of words, seemed to fit within the framework of the Communist exaltation of man's control over matter and the physical world, but later the Soviet authorities were led to dissolve a school which seemed to be an offshoot of Bohemia and the advance guard, and whose very ideological indifference made it look suspiciously bourgeois. In brief, Formalism met the same end as Futurism, to which it was connected by the same spirit of iconoclasm and by the same paradoxical conception of form: a form no longer tied to the static idea of beauty, but connected instead to such dynamic notions as operation and function. This is why it would be more proper to call the members of this school not "formalists," but "morphologists," since they were less interested in the essence or finality, than in the phenomenology, or more simply, in the machinery, of art.

II

IMAGINISM AND EGO-FUTURISM

Even more extravagant than those of both Futurists and Formalists were the theoretical claims made by the poets who banded together to form the movement to which they gave the pretentious name of "Militant Order of the Imaginists." As we already know, thanks to that very militancy, which often was sheer hooliganism, the movement itself lasted only from 1919 to 1921. As is shown by the borrowing of the label, Russian Imaginism had a vague connection with Anglo-American Imagism, which, however, developed the program implied in its choice of the same name far less literally than its Russian counterpart. As a matter of fact, it seems that Russian Imaginism originated as the wholly independent offspring of American Imagism: or rather, as the offshoot of an article by Zinaida Vengerova, which appeared in 1915, and reported an interview with Ezra Pound, under the misleading and yet significant title of "English Futurists."

As we have already remarked, Imaginism was the last poetic school that tried to remain apolitical, and that affirmed the right of the writer to swim alone, even if not necessarily against the revolutionary current. Thus, its founders defined the movement as a "neo-idealism," anarchic and individualistic in character; and from this standpoint, Imaginism represented even better than other

252

similar groups the function that so many Marxist critics consider typical of the advance guard: namely, that of representing the final phase of the degeneration of bourgeois art. The first manifesto, or *Declaration*, of the Imaginists appeared in 1921 and was signed by the poets Sergej Esenin, Rjurik Ivnev, Anatolij Mariengof, and Vadim Shershenevich, who shortly afterwards were joined by Aleksandr Kusikov. The *Declaration* defined the image as "the naphthalene preserving a work of art from the moths of time"; and this idea of the poetic primacy of the image was destined to remain the leitmotiv of the proclamations of Shershenevich, who, often without the approval of his colleagues, acted as the theorist of the group.

Shershenevich had started his career as a disciple and supporter of Severjanin's Ego-Futurism, and from this experience had derived a cheap brand of Decadent mysticism. At the same time he had flirted with the "transmental" poetry of the Cubo-Futurists, and his noisy statements betray the frivolous eclecticism of his mind. Thus, he proclaimed "the victory of the image over the sense and the emancipation of the word from its content"; maintained that "the image must swallow its own meaning"; and finally recommended "the overturning of the word: from its reversed position, which is the natural one, there will later arise the novel image." Vadim Shershenevich, who was born in 1883 and died in 1942, was primarily a salesman and an advertiser, and only secondarily a poet, and a very minor one at that. To give a sample of his taste, it may suffice to cite the titles of two of his books: *The Extravagant Vials* (1913) and *Automobile's Stride* (1916). Yet Shershenevich's statements about the autonomy of the image or, as he used to say, its "autocracy," still have some relevance and significance, and they may help us to understand better some aspects of the poetry of Esenin and even Majakovskij, as well as the dependence of their work on the ideas of the Symbolist masters of the preceding generation, whom they affected to deny or to ignore.

Before becoming the theorist of Imaginism, Shershenevich had also been the theorist of Ego-Futurism, and this is perhaps the place to speak briefly of the man who had been the leader, and the minor master, of that short-lived school. This man was Igor'

Lotarev, who was born in 1887 and who died in 1942, after a long exile in Estonia, just as soon as the Soviet Army overran the little Baltic republic. This poet, who took the pen name of Severjanin (derived from the word *sever*, "north" and meaning, therefore, "man of the North"), had been at first in touch with the Moscow Futurists, to the point of signing one of their earliest proclamations. Soon enough he decided, however, to beat his own path and founded in 1912 the movement which he called Ego-Futurism. He gathered around himself and "The Petersburg Crier" (the name of the press of the new group) a handful of young poets, including Shershenevich and Georgij Ivanov, who shortly after was to transfer his allegiance to the Acmeist school. About a year later Severjanin published his first collection of poems, the title of which was taken from a line of the great Romantic poet Tjutchev: *The Thunder-Seething Cup*. This book, which earned for its author a laudatory preface by Sologub and an enthusiastic review by Brjusov (in brief, public recognition of its merits by two of the main literary leaders of the older generation), made the name of Severjanin very popular, and it is perhaps the only one of his works still worth mentioning. The poet, however, followed it by dozens of other booklets of inferior value, among which we shall single out, for the snobbish eccentricity of their titles, *Pineapples in Champagne* and *Victoria Regia*, both of which appeared in 1915. Severjanin's gusto for cheap verbal novelties can be seen also in his labeling of his poems as "poèzy" (the plural of *poèza*, a word coined by him).

Severjanin and the other poets of the same group were more modernists than Futurists, and their modernism consisted merely in the attempt to evoke those aspects of contemporary life which had been neglected by their immediate predecessors. It is true that Aleksandr Blok had seen those aspects, but he had evoked them from a negative, even tragic, standpoint. Only one of the older poets had sung of the urban and mechanical civilization of our time in order to glorify it; that poet had been Brjusov, when he fell under the spell of Emile Verhaeren. But the truly epic theme of the modern metropolis was to be developed especially by Majakovskij and the second generation of Futurism. Severjanin and his followers, however, were interested not so much in what was modern, but in what was merely up-to-date. Their world was the world of vogues, styles, and fashions; their society was the "smart set." Among the by-products of our technological culture, they appreciated only luxury and comfort. Their ideals were "high life" and "high living," which they considered the best ways to satisfy and realize the self.

The early success of Severjanin was enormous, and in part it was also due to the conventionality of his effects, which popularized, in the form of *clichés*, the innovations already introduced within Russian poetry by the masters of Symbolism. But, as in all cases of this kind, the short-lived triumph of Severjanin was due even more to nonliterary factors; above all, to the appeal which his poetry had for the rising bourgeoisie, for the cultural and social *parvenus*, for the provincial youths seeking pleasure and fortune in the capital; in other words, for all those people ready to interpret the pseudo-futuristic slogan of Shershenevich — "Learn to appraise the beauties of the world, which are only two: the beauty of form and the beauty of speed" — as an advice to modernize their home furnishings and to buy a new car.

It may seem that there is some similarity between the poetry of Severjanin and the poetry of Kuzmin, who had already changed the mystical and dreamy longings of the Symbolists into a yearning for frivolous and worldly things. But while Kuzmin is artificial, Severjanin is mere "arty"; if the former is refined, the latter is mannered. If Kuzmin is an *arbiter elegantiarum*, Severjanin is a mannikin. The poetry of Kuzmin aims at being a conscious pastiche, while Severjanin's becomes, unwillingly, a kind of parody. If Kuzmin's craftsmanship produces the effects of applied art, Severjanin's tricks give the impression of commercial art. All this is evident in the very composition of Severjanin's language, an international mosaic predominantly derived from the *lingua franca* of cosmopolitan tourism. It is true that neologisms and barbarisms also abound, for instance, in Majakovskij's poetry, where, however, they are used for broad realistic and caricatural effects, not as exhibitions of the poet's snobbery.

III

VELIMIR KHLEBNIKOV

It would be impossible to find a greater contrast, in tone and in quality, than the one dividing the poetry of Severjanin from the poetry of Khlebnikov. We may go even further and safely assert that the leader of Cubo-Futurism had little in common not only with the vulgar modernism of Severjanin, but with Futurism itself as it was understood in Italy by Marinetti, and even in Russia by Majakovskij. Yet, along with Majakovskij, and even before him, Khlebnikov was the most important figure which Russian Futurism produced. Majakovskij acknowledged more than once the merits of Khlebnikov. Immediately after the latter's death, Majakovskij described him as "the most magnificent and blameless knight in our poetic struggle . . . the Columbus of new poetic continents later settled by us"; and subsequently paid many other similar tributes to the memory of that master. Even writers of very different literary and political tastes qualified their critical reservations with an unbounded admiration for the originality and integrity of the work of Khlebnikov. For instance, "several of his lines," said Nikolaj Gumilev, "seem like the fragments of an unwritten epic."

Viktor Khlebnikov, who chose as *nom de plume* the Slavic, pagan name of Velimir, was born in 1885, in a little town in the province of Astrakhan'. He spent his youth in Simbirsk and studied at the University of Kazan'. When he was twenty-three, he went to Petersburg and began writing his first poems, under the influence of the Symbolists and other older poets of that time. It is noteworthy that he was especially affected by the "Byzantinism" of Vjacheslav Ivanov and the "mythologism" of Sergej Gorodetskij; what is still more remarkable is that even then his verse had a ring of its own. Later he settled in Moscow, where, first with the Burljuk brothers, and then with Majakovskij and Kruchenykh, he founded and led Russian Futurism. He helped to write almost all of the movement's manifestoes, and contributed to most of its publications. Finally he collaborated with Kruchenykh in framing the doctrine of the "transmental tongue."

Drafted into the army during the war, Khlebnikov was caught

by the Revolution in uniform, and the Civil War left him stranded in Kar'kov. Without becoming a member of the Communist Party, he served the new regime in many places and on many fronts. He saw in the Revolution a messianic Utopia, and it is doubtful whether his vague Communist sympathies would have lasted long. He died suddenly in 1922, of starvation and hardships. He left an important, but uneven, body of work, scattered in pamphlets, leaflets, periodicals, anthologies, and almanacs. The most important titles which he published in his lifetime are *Creations* and *A Book of Selections*, both of 1914; *Night in a Trench* and *Zangezi*, of 1921 and 1922. These and other of his writings were collected and reprinted after his death. Yet, even though his work never fell into neglect, the official mistrust for any form of experimental poetry and advance-guard art prevented Khlebnikov's example from influencing effectively the main lines of development of Soviet verse.

In spite of its label, the poetry of Khlebnikov is not Futuristic in the literal sense of the word. This is no less true from the standpoint of ideas and feelings than from the standpoint of form and technique. Khlebnikov looked at modern life with a sense of aversion, and worked hard at his experiments and research, while the other Futurists were often satisfied with announcing the most radical innovations in resounding manifestoes, or in rhetorical proclamations. Khlebnikov's indifference toward modern themes, toward the most attractive or repulsive aspects of contemporary existence, is proved by contrast by his deep interest in Slavic mythological lore, which inspired several of his poems; or more generally, by his longing for all those forms of primordial or ancestral life which are the field of study of the archaeologist and the anthropologist.

In Khlebnikov's work there breathes a kind of pantheistic inspiration à la Walt Whitman, but his own is an escapist pantheism, out of tune with the present, going backward into the past, and trying to find the regained paradise of primitive innocence in the darkness of prehistory. Also from this viewpoint his poetry has little to do with the international movement to which he gave his allegiance. One should suppose that Futurism was bound to unfold in Russia as one of the last and most extreme literary manifestations of the Westernizing tendency, while in the West it was nothing else than an unconscious variation of the nineteenth-century idea of progress, from which it derived the myth symbolized by the very term "Futurism." Yet, despite such expectations, Russian Futurism turned out to be a uniquely Russian creation. As for Khlebnikov himself, he was from his very beginnings one of the most consistent Slavophiles in the history of Russian poetry: he even anticipated the ideology built up after the Revolution by a group of *émigré* scholars on the claim that Russia and Siberia are an ethnographic and geopolitical unit, forming the sixth continent of Eurasia.

Khlebnikov's utopia is regressive and retrospective, and it repudiates our own steel or iron age for a mythical age of gold, even for a stone or wooden age. His sentiment and imagination constantly turn back to the time when the forests and plains of European and Asiatic Russia were still inhabited by the spirits of the trees and the waters. This nostalgia is expressed in pieces like "Woodland Anguish" or "The Vila" (the Slavic name for a wood nymph); or even in the poem entitled "The Shaman and Venus," which combines barbaric and classical mythology, and in which the goddess of love offers herself not to a hero or demigod, but to a Mongol, to a Siberian sorcerer. And Khlebnikov's repudiation of modern life is tragically stated in the poem "The Crane," with its monstrous mechanical bird wrecking the world as a vengeance of the machine upon man.

It would be wrong to interpret too literally the numerous poems which Khlebnikov devoted to historical subjects: their themes are never ends in themselves, but rather media through which the poet turns our attention toward what is archaic and prehistoric in life and man. This effect is generally produced by employing anachronisms, because, as we read in one of the poet's tales, "there are no barriers within time . . . ; consciousness joins together the different ages. . . ." These violations of chronology, this conversion into other categories of the dimension of time, are applied by Khlebnikov not only to the collective experience of mankind, but to the individual himself. That tale is "The World Upside Down," reversing the biography of the protagonist, and rehearsing his life from grave to cradle.

As shown by the judgment of Gumilev, quoted above, the impersonal, almost choral solemnity of Khlebnikov's poetry has led a few critics to assert the epic character of his inspiration. But in the poet's imagination the mythical element is stronger than the heroic one; and his conception of nature as in a state of permanent flux, as a steady renewal of the first day of creation, as an everlasting conflict between the human and the cosmic, between creatures that are like things and things that are like creatures, suggests, rather than the epic, the theogonic character of his inspiration. This character can be easily recognized also in the poems which Khlebnikov wrote under the impact of the war and the Revolution. Except for one piece or two written in the spirit of Majakovskij's "marches," all these poems look at those two historical events as if they were cosmic catastrophes, elementary cataclysms. The military and revolutionary struggle is seen as a new Titanomachy, as a conflict between upper and nether gods, as the eternal warfare between the animistic forces of the universe. History, again, is reduced to prehistory; war, to a telluric outburst; the Revolution, to a metamorphosis. The tragic breath of the gods of destruction and death transforms the cosmos into chaos, and the earth into a Gehenna.

Sometimes Khlebnikov seems to conceive of revolution as a palingenesis, as in the poem "Liberty for All": but even here, significantly enough, he asks for the resurrection of the natural deities of the primitive mythology of the Slavs. In "Death Feast" he describes the burning of the corpses on a modern battlefield as if it were an ancient ritual, an archaic funeral pyre, while the uncontrolled forces of nature, symbolized by two great Russian rivers, are considered as more powerful than that fire which man has learned to use and to control. Thus, in Khlebnikov's poetry the fragile order of man is forever upset by the revolt of the elements. This can be seen in the beautiful poem describing a fusillade in the dark streets of a city, in the autumn or early winter of 1917. We do not see the people who are killing, but only those who are being killed; we hear only the voice of the guns. The shots themselves, rather than a man-made curse, are a wind of fire, a rain of lead. The bullets are like cruel sprites engendered in the obscure recesses of the material world. Human beings are either their blind victims, or their blind instruments, never their conscious agents. The very act of slaughter is described as the cutting down of a poplar tree's branches and trunk.

Nothing is more significant than this identification of war and murder with the falling of leaves, with the felling of a tree; in brief, with autumn and winter. Here Khlebnikov shows once more his tendency to translate the events of human history into the phenomena of natural history, to interchange epochs and seasons, to introduce within the microcosm the laws and proportions of the macrocosm. The methods mentioned above, tending toward indifferentiation and anachronism, the same attempt to establish metaphysical and metahistorical categories, are to be found also in his linguistic revolution, in his verbal reform. In this, too, he remains independent of the mainstream of the literary movement to which he belongs. While the average Futurist starts from the traditional vocabulary to shape his strange words, and from conventional grammar to postulate his final denial of syntax, Khlebnikov looks into the storehouse of popular and national speech in order to find ancient and eternal roots and to rebuild a new tongue on the ideal chain of pure forms and perfect words. The neologisms and barbarisms so frequent in normal Futurist idiom are replaced in this poet's work by archaisms and Slavonicisms, more often reinvented than found anew. It is by means like these that Khlebnikov seems literally to fulfill the poet's task as defined by Mallarmé: *donner un sens plus pur aux mots de la tribu.*

As a philologist, Khlebnikov is especially interested in the primitive stage of the linguistic evolution. It is there that he tries to find the embryo or the shell, the secret of the genesis of language, or even of creation itself, since he is one of those who believe that "in the beginning was the Word." He states his purpose in the following terms: "Without breaking the links of the roots, to find the philosopher's stone of the reciprocal interchange of all Slavic words, freely dissolving them into each other; such is my conception of the word. The Word per se, outside of life, and beyond its vital uses." The notion of the poetic word as an entity completely divorced from history and culture, this reversal of the idea of language as a token conventionally accepted and exchanged by man, are conceptions that may be found also in Mallarmé, although it is quite probable that Khlebnikov was unaware of the relationship.

The poet tried to put into practice the doctrines of the theorist, by testing them in the crucible of his art. This is what he did with a poem like "Incantation [or "Conjuration"] by Laughter," by which he sought to achieve the lyrical catharsis of an etymological unit. In this poem, where one does not find even one of the forms of the verb "to be," all words are without exception derived from the Russian and Slavic root meaning "to laugh." This root is used in all its existing forms or possible variants: nouns and verbs, adjectives and adverbs, cases and aspects, tenses and moods, derivatives and compounds; and also in new words convincingly invented by the poet with the aid of several prefixes and suffixes. Because of this reduction of the poem to only one word-idea, the experiment from the linguistic standpoint has an exclusively phonetic and morphological character. As a work of art, it aims successfully at achieving a poetic equivalent of that kind of musical composition called "theme with variations." As a psychological or anthropological document, the poem is, however, as Roman Jakobson has observed, also an act of verbal witchcraft, working, as its title indicates, like a charm or spell.

Khlebnikov's linguistic and experimental interests relate his work to the critical theories of the Formalist school. But the poet, besides being a born philologist, was also an arbitrary and mystical one, as was the case with some of the Symbolists. He was obsessed by the ancient myth of the universal tongue, of an adamic or edenic language, which he dreamed of reaching again through methods reminiscent of those employed by the French René Ghil. Valerij Brjusov had been the only one in Russia to pay any attention to René Ghil and his "scientific poetry," which, rather than scientific, was cabalistic. Khlebnikov thought, however, of poetry as a means for discovering the secret of language itself, and stated his position in the following terms: "After having realized that the roots are but ghosts hiding the alphabet's strings, to find the universal identity of all tongues: this is my second conception of the word."

It is evident that by letters of the alphabet Khlebnikov meant not only the sounds, but also the signs representing them; like many poets of his time, he wanted not only to speak or sing, but also "to paint with words." This led him to experiment not only with merely verbal, but also with nonverbal, signs; his research in the field of general symbolism is a poetic anticipation of modern semantics. His early verbal exercises had been a clever manipulation of the doctrine of the "transmental tongue," as shown by the predominance of phonetic values, if not of onomatopoeic effects. But while we have been led to compare the compositions of other "transmental" poets to a kind of nonsense verse, we must say that these experiments by Khlebnikov are charged, even overcharged, with meanings of every sort, not merely verbal, but graphic and ideographic too. They are dominated by a system of allusions in which there also appear, like hieroglyphics, historical references and iconic symbols. Yet even these are reduced to the common denominator of linguistic structure, playing at the same time the roles of grammatical functions and of myths.

Thus, in the opening lines of a short piece without title, which begins with the words "Villa by night," Khlebnikov takes three proper names belonging to the cultural and historical tradition (Genghis-Khan, Zarathustra, Mozart) and treats them as if they were the roots of three verbs. By a sleight-of-hand change of the closing letter of each, he turns those names into three imperatives; and, along with the three noun-objects of the lyric's landscape (the villa, the nocturnal darkness, the blue sky), he throws those verbal forms into the chaos of the poem as agents of that mythopoeic metamorphosis which is the ultimate aim of his art. The strangeness and arbitrariness of such methods may be equally approved or reproved, and their importance may be too easily overrated. But we must not stop at the technical details per se. What counts is that by means of a given device the poet has shown us an insight into a world of his own, where human reality and historical events become qualities of things, where life and history are lowered, or raised, to the condition of nature itself. It is for visions of this kind, not only for his daring use of language, that the poet Khlebnikov, far more than Andrej Belyj, whose novels have been so often compared to such a work as *Ulysses*, reminds us of Joyce and of his creations, especially of *Finnegans Wake*.

IV

VLADIMIR MAJAKOVSKIJ

The peculiarity of Khlebnikov's gifts, along with his early death, prevented him from realizing in full the promises of his talent, and from giving more power and meaning to the move-ment which he was the first to lead. This task was to be ac-complished by the man who took over the leadership of Russian Futurism even before Khlebnikov's death. The son of a forest ranger, Vladimir Majakovskij was born in 1893, in a small Cau-casian hamlet. He lost his father when he was ten years old, and moved with his family to Moscow, where, while still a youth, he was jailed for revolutionary activity. In 1910 he enrolled in the local Academy of Fine Arts, but David Burljuk, whom he met then and there, persuaded him to exchange the brush for the quill. He joined the Futurist movement almost as soon as it began; and when he settled later in Petersburg, he became one of the most popular and picturesque figures of the Russian Bohemia, wearing as a kind of uniform on his giant frame a yellow blazer that shocked the bourgeosie of the two capitals, as much as the red vest of Théophile Gautier and the green gardenia of Oscar Wilde had scandalized the burghers of Paris and London. His tempera-ment was boisterous and mischievous; it is worth noting that in his make-up there was a strain of wild humor, a gusto for the cari-catural and the grotesque, to which the young Majakovskij gave vent in his contributions to a prewar humorous periodical, *The Satyricon*. As a matter of fact, as we have already seen, Viktor Shklovskij maintained (and the statement was meant as praise) that Majakovskij's mature poetry was but a sublimation of the humorous verse of his youth.

As a serious poet, Majakovskij broke into print immediately before the First World War, and became famous during the early years of the Revolution. His first two books were a collection of lyrics and a tragedy to which he gave, significantly, the respective titles of *I* (1913) and *Vladimir Majakovskij* (1915). These two works were followed by a series of long poems, which are perhaps the best works of his youth: *A Cloud in Trousers* (1915), *Flute-Spinal Cord* (1916), *Man* (1917), and *War and the World* (1916). The title of the latter is a pun on the title of Tolstoj's masterpiece, since in Russian the words for "world" and "peace" are homonyms, once differing only in the spelling of their single vowel sound.

During the civil war Majakovskij wrote a series of Communist hymns, to which he gave the name of "marches," as well as many appeals to his fellow writers and artists, inviting them to join in the revolutionary struggle, and which he named "commands." Among the former the most important is "The Left March," written during the Polish-Soviet War, to which the Polish poet Slonimski answered with a "Right March"; among the latter, the "Command to the Army of the Arts." The following years were taken up by travels to the West and even to America; by his strange *ménage à trois* with Osip and Lilija Brik; by the editing, with the help of Brik, who was a gifted critic, of *LEF* and *The New LEF*; and by the production of a rich but uneven series of poetic works.

Majakovskij did not hesitate to write poetic tracts supporting not only the main policies of the regime, but even some of the minor educational drives concerning such matters as water purification and public health. He celebrated the new order even in his major works: in 1921 he published the long poem *150,000,000* (the figure indicated the population of Soviet Russia), which is both a Communist epic and a satire on the West; and in 1924, immediately after that leader's death, he wrote the heroic narrative in verse, *V. I. Lenin*. His ironical and comic talent found expression in a series of dramatic grotesques, which opened in 1918 with *Mystery Buff*, followed in 1928 and in 1929 by *The Bedbug* and *The Bathhouse*. In 1926 he wrote the famous poem "To Sergej Esenin," commenting on the latter's suicide and condemning it. In one of the most insensitive passages of that piece, after alluding to the fact that Esenin had been forced to write his last lines with his blood in the hotel room where he killed himself, Majakovskij asked in verse that the Soviet light industry be directed to produce more ink.

Yet, at that very time, the literary watchdogs of the party had already started persecuting him; and the persecution did not stop even when, shortly before his death, he abandoned the very groups he had helped to found, and joined the association of proletarian writers. This, in conjunction with an unhappy love affair, led the poet to a nervous breakdown and a moral collapse. Unable to find a way out of his ordeal, the poet killed himself in 1930. Like Esenin, he left a farewell poem in the final letter he wrote for his relatives and friends. The meaning of this tragedy, so personal and impersonal at the same time, was to be conveyed, a few years later, by Boris Pasternak in his tale *The Safe Conduct*. The regime chose to forget that Lenin had disliked Majakovskij's poetry (to the point of leaving a theatrical performance he was attending, merely because he could not bear to hear to the end the recitation of "Our March"); even more, it chose to ignore that Majakovskij's suicide had been a sign of protest. While the reprinting of Pasternak's *The Safe Conduct* was forbidden, the party encouraged the study and publication of Majakovskij's literary heritage, as well as the build-up of a legend which made him *the* poet of the Communist revolution and of the Russian proletariat. It was then, said Pasternak in his recent *Sketch for an Autobiography*, that "Majakovskij began to be propagated compulsorily, like potatoes in the reign of Catherine the Great. That was his second death. For that he was not to blame."

From the technical standpoint, Majakovskij's greatest contribution to Russian poetry consisted of making a working instrument of *vers libre*. While that medium had made its appearance in France with that second generation of Symbolist poets with whom Brjusov had been well acquainted, Brjusov himself had publicly denied that the Russian modernists would or could follow too slavishly the example their French colleagues had set in that field. Some of the Symbolists had introduced into Russian prosody not only the equivalent of what the French had called *vers libéré*, or, in other words, a slightly irregular verse pattern, but even a kind of free verse called *dol'nik*, still avoiding an excessive looseness of rhythm. Yet, up to Majakovskij's time, all the many compositions in free verse which had already appeared seemed to be part of one of the marginal currents of modern poetry, rather than of its mainstream. This applies in part even to the Cubo-Futurists, who adopted the new medium, but never to the exclusion of other metrical forms.

Majakovskij himself preferred to use conventional strophic schemes in his lyrics, especially those having the character of odes and hymns, and used free verse only for his longer poems, in which he never completely renounced the ornament of rhyme. As a matter of fact, Majakovskij treated rhyme with full freedom, from the viewpoint of its richness and frequence, as well as from the viewpoint of its position and quality. Hypermetric, compound, and equivocal rhymes abound in his poems, where they produce striking, and often grotesque, effects. Majakovskij stretched the traditional rhyming freedom of Russian verse to the point of changing the identical endings into distorted echoes, vague phonetic approximations, consonances and assonances. If by doing this he followed the example of the popular songs of his time, generally urban or proletarian in origin, in the matter of rhythm he based his metrical reform on his unerring instinct, rather than on theory and experiment; the method which his insight made him choose was merely the spontaneous imitation of the accentual versification of the ancient Russian folk song.

Despite his keen sense for all the values of language and meter, Majakovskij was temperamentally the least interested, among the leading Futurists, in questions of craft and technique. A born poet, he conceived of his art as a medium toward an end, rather than as as end in itself. From this viewpoint he played within the Futurist movement a role not dissimilar to the one Blok had played within the Symbolist school. That obscure and often impure power which goes under the name of inspiration again took hold of Russian poetry in his person and work. Despite all appearances to the contrary, his muse, like Blok's, was a muse of disaster: and the poet acted like an echo reproducing and repeating the noise of the storm then raging over Russia and the world. Majakovskij, however, was not content to remain a passive echo, and joined his voice with that of the storm. And unlike Blok, who almost against his will turned even the discord of the elements into a harmony and melody of his own, Majakovskij based the rhythms of his poetry on what he called "the cacophony of wars and revolutions."

The wordless music of Blok's poetry is better felt by the inner ear, while Majakovskij's verse is written to be read aloud, in a resounding voice. As such, it is the perfect verbal instrument of an inspiration which may be defined, without derogatory intent, and without contradiction of what has just been said, as essentially declamatory in character. In a certain sense, this is the fatal destiny of that tradition of modern poetry which since Walt Whitman has chosen looser metrical structures as its vehicle. But the peculiar quality and pathos of Majakovskij's medium was appropriately suggested by the poet's self-definition as the "crier" and the "drummer" of the Russian Revolution. That extraordinary historical event was, at least at its beginnings, perfectly suited to the temperament of Majakovskij, so full of exuberance and exhibitionism. The October upheaval made not only compulsory, but even necessary, what was later called "agitation" and "propaganda," and these two activities justified the use of loudspeakers in the fields of both eloquence and poetry.

The poems of Majakovskij must always be shouted, rather than recited or chanted, "at the top of *one's* voice," to use the title of his last, splendid, and unfortunately unfinished composition. In later years Majakovskij was forced to recognize that when a poet uses a loudspeaker, he is bound to utter alien words, and to speak, rather than with his own, with "his master's voice." One could even say that this revelation led him finally to his ordeal, and to his very death; yet it remains undeniable that there existed, for a brief span of time, an authentic affinity, and a kind of kinship, between the climate of the Revolution and the inspiration of its greatest poet.

This does not mean that his muse was anonymous or collective. Majakovskij paid only lip service to the early slogans of both Futurism and proletarian poetry, always being unable to replace the Romantic or Decadent "I" with the "we" of the group, or of the masses. A stentorian voice is not necessarily a choral one: it may be the voice of a heroic ego, or of a virtuoso singing solo his own tunes. Thus Majakovskij's poetry was public merely in the sense that it was often performed publicly, and with great effect. He was not so much a proletarian poet as an urban one, loving the open, and yet walled, spaces, of the metropolis, with its squares and avenues, alleys and streets. In other terms, he was a city poet, rather than a civic one; not a popular, but a plebeian artist. He was aware of this fact, as is shown by a passage in his last poem, in which he describes himself as "a street cleaner and water carrier, drafted and called to the colors by the Revolution." This is why his language is so full of vulgarities; this is why bad taste is as frequent in the poetry of Majakovskij as in that of Severjanin. But the bad taste of the latter is unconscious, since Severjanin was a snob, longing, like all snobs, for *bon ton*, while Majakovskij's bad taste is nothing but his own sense of reality, directly conveying the healthy coarseness of the raw material of life.

Yet, as has just been stated, Majakovskij's poetry is as highly individualistic as Bal'mont's or Severjanin's, especially at the beginning of his career. His lyricism, always obsessive, becomes often sentimental and even pathetic. Even his humorism, when directed toward the self of the poet, is like the humorism of a suffering clown, producing grotesque effects, such as those in his youthful poems devoted almost exclusively to the unhappy love affairs of their author. In them self-irony may lower itself to the level of an unconscious self-parody. In one of those early pieces, the poet sings of his own passion by accompanying himself on the "flute" of his own spinal chord; in another one, he mirrors his own mood of love and despair in the self-image of "a cloud in trousers." These two metaphors show that the states of mind dominating his inspiration are exasperation and paroxysm. The poet cultivates and expresses his own psychic urges by employing two typical media of advance-guard poetry, the "hyperbolic" and the "iconoclastic" image, which are both the symptoms and the symbols of his own poetic pathos. The first type of image is directly derived from the poet's megalomania; yet it is sometimes able to sublimate itself into a kind of cosmic vision. The second type derives equally directly from his nihilism and cynicism; yet, not infrequently, it transcends the very ugliness of the experience it intends to convey.

The poetic practice of Futurism influenced Majakovskij's imagery in both form and matter, as is proved by its frequent reference to the world of machinery. Like Khlebnikov, Majakovskij looks at the machine as an instrument of war and death, rather than as a working tool; yet this view is not derogatory in character, as is shown by a famous passage in *At the Top of My Voice*, in which he compares the series of his lines to rows and weapons, to armed ranks. This mechanistic imagery is nihilistic in essence; and one could say that Majakovskij exalted the Revolution as an engine of destruction, rather than as a machine helping to construct a new world. Although ideologically a Marxist, psychologically he was an anarchist; and this may help to explain certain aspects of his art, the crisis of his life, and the tragedy of his death.

V

SERGEJ ESENIN

Unlike Majakovskij, whose destiny it was to become the poet of history and of "October," Sergej Esenin remained forever the poet of nature and of the decaying season, as if fated by his own family name, derived from a Slavic root meaning "autumn." Yet for a while he too wanted to be, like Majakovskij, the poet of the new era. But the man who in *Inonija* defined himself as "the prophet, Sergej Esenin," projected into the image of the Revolution hopes and fears undreamed of by his rival. Majakovskij had learned his craft from early Futurism, Westernizing in tendency if not in effect, and his political ideology derived from the workers' movement and Marxism. This orientation, as well as his temperament, had made of him an urban poet, the singer of the metropolis, the glorifier of city life. Esenin, instead, had begun his literary career as a pupil of the peasant poet, Nikolaj Kljuev. Even though he surpassed, in artistry as well as in inspiration, the achievements of his master, he constantly hesitated between the contrasting attractions of the modernistic trends and the traditions of folk poetry. At the end of his career he felt that he had failed to rec-

269

oncile within himself the old and the new, as shown by his famous complaint: "I am the last peasant poet; rough is the wooden bridge of my songs."

So, while Majakovskij accepted, almost beyond his will, the task of celebrating the "edification of Socialism," Esenin remained always the poet of "wooden and vegetable Russia." Politically, he had always felt closer to the Social Revolutionary Party, an off-shoot of the Populist movement, which interpreted in radical terms the messianic view of an agrarian Russia, thus acting as an un-conscious Slavophilism of the Left. While the Marxists exalted the working class, the Social Revolutionaries idolized the peasantry, in which they saw the whole of Russia. Besides being affected by this political ideology, Esenin had been subjected from his child-hood to the eschatological mysticism still alive in the countryside among the sectarian groups which had left the mother Church at the time of the great schism. It was this combination of doctrines and beliefs that led the poet to see at first in the Revolution both a new Zion and a modern Arcadia, bringing Christian peace, pastoral happiness, and utopian justice to the men of good will, who were the toilers of the earth.

Actually, except for the accident of his birth, Sergej Esenin was never a tiller of the soil. Yet, in a moral sense, he remained until his death a child of the Russian countryside. He was born in 1895 in the village of Konstantinovo, in the province of Rjazan'. The father and mother of the future poet went to work in Mos-cow, and the boy was raised by his maternal grandparents, who were prosperous farmers, and who instilled in him a love for the old faith and the simple legends of the Russian people. He started studying to become a country teacher, but while he was at school the mysterious magic of poetry was revealed to him through his reading of Pushkin. He joined his father in Moscow, where, among other jobs, he worked in a bookshop and in a printing press, dream-ing of a literary career, and writing his first poems. In 1914, he settled in Petrograd, where he became a protégé of Sergej Gorodets-kij. There he also met Kljuev, with whom he led for a while a group of poets of peasant origins. In 1916 he published his first collection of poems, to which he gave, as to many other of his books and works, a title so peculiarly Slavonic as to be practically untranslatable: *Radunitsa* (the word designates a quasi-pagan spring ritual for the dead).

Shortly afterward, Esenin was drafted into the army, but served in the courtly town of Tsarskoe Selo. By then his name was already well known, and it is reported that he was once invited to read his poems to the Empress. At that time, like Belyj and Blok, he fell under the influence of R. I. Ivanov-Razumnik and his national-social messianism. It was perhaps because of his leftist leanings that in 1917 the poet was sent to the front, where he was surprised by the Revolution. Like millions of other Russian soldiers, he deserted and returned home, settling later in Petrograd, where he married Zinaida Rajkh, and published the poems he had written under the spell of Ivanov-Razumnik's "Scythianism," *Inonija* (1918) and *Transfiguration* (1919).

Later on, in Moscow, he tried to show his independence not only from Kljuev, but also from even the brightest stars of the Russian poetic firmament, such as Blok and Majakovskij, by founding, along with other younger writers, the movement called Imaginism. It was then and there that he started his *vie de bohême*, leading a life of orgies and scandals. Sometimes Esenin would spend a night in jail: once the poet and his companions were arrested while painting their names on the signposts of the main thoroughfares of the capital. The psychological experiences of those years were to be forcefully conveyed in the poems of *A Hooligan's Confession*, published in 1921 (the title piece had already appeared in 1918); and in the cycle entitled *Moscow of the Taverns* (1922). The metaphoric technique of Imaginism found expression as early as 1919 in the lyrics of *Trerjadnitsa* (another untranslatable title!), and later in the poetic drama *Pugachev* (1921), which is centered on the heroic and romantic figure of that eighteenth-century rebel. This verse play, or rather, dramatic poem, is theatrically very weak, and, as far as I know, was never staged; yet the poet poured into its lines some of the most powerful streams of his lyricism. One of its high points, which is also one of the peaks of Esenin's poetry, is the scene where the young Burnov, one of Pugachev's hounded followers, and perhaps one of his betrayers, sings of the splendor of life and of the horror of death in a magnificent passage which re-echoes, through the intermediary of Pushkin's imitation in *Angelo*, Claudio's famous speech in Shakespeare's *Measure for Measure*.

It was in 1921 that Sergej Esenin first met the famous American classical dancer, Isadora Duncan, who by then had already reached middle age. They became lovers and married in 1922. Unable to speak each other's tongue, they found a common experience in high living and heavy drinking. Impoverished by her lavish style of living, Isadora Duncan decided to make a *tournée* abroad, and Sergej accompanied her in a long journey through Western Europe and the United States. It was a shabby odyssey, full of misadventures and failures. Esenin felt cruelly disappointed in the West and drowned his despair in alcohol. When he returned to Russia, his mental and physical health was fatally impaired. He broke with Miss Duncan and in 1925 married a descendant of Lev Tolstoj, who nursed him and after his death became the custodian of his literary heritage and the vestal of his memory. Fearing that his creative powers were forever gone, on December 27, 1925, the poet hanged himself in a Leningrad hotel room. The night before, since there was no ink on his desk, he slightly cut a vein in his wrist and wrote in his blood a brief farewell poem, ending with the famous lines: "to die is not new, but to live is not newer." As we already know, Majakovskij answered those lines with a poem condemning Esenin's act, without knowing that within five years he would come to the same willful end.

There is at least a minor vein in the poetry of Esenin which is not too different from certain aspects of Majakovskij's work. This is the apocalyptic vein which appears in *Transfiguration* and *Inonija* (the latter is a word coined by the poet, meaning "Other-Land"). In both pieces the poet condemns the dying old world, while exalting the Revolution as a kind of cosmic rebirth. Here Esenin's verse, like Majakovskij's, overflows with "hyperbolic" and "iconoclastic" images, which in this case, however, derive from a morbid and perverted mysticism, often turning into heresy and blasphemy, into a parody of Christian hopes, myths, and beliefs. In these two poems Esenin became the secular apostle of a new

Gospel, the announcer of a new earthly kingdom, the seer of the Revolution as the earthly paradise of the peasant and the shepherd. These two pieces greatly differ from the long poems of the later years, predominantly autobiographical in character and expressing the disappointment of the poet with the Revolution, as well as the complaint of a peasant's son uprooted from the countryside, and living as an outcast in the alien world of the city.

Both the early revolutionary pieces, which are the weakest part of his work, and the later autobiographical poems may all too often seem to a foreign reader the most important fruits of this poet's talent. Certainly nobody can deny their significance as human and social documents. Yet the most genuine of Esenin's masterpieces are to be found among his shortest, least ambitious lyrics, written in the pure and simple modes of the elegy and the idyll, devoid of any rhetorical and anecdotal structure, and lightly woven as a cobweb of transparent words around the cluster of a few bright and striking images. Each one of these songs may be reduced to a landscape and to the mood it evokes within the soul of the poet. Although the narrative element is lacking, or hardly present, such poems partake of the magic aura of the legend and the fairy tale. They recreate a private and intimate universe, domestic and rustic, where all things are humanized by a naïve animism, by a pathetic anthropomorphism. The ingenuousness of Esenin's vision is evident in the central image of each one of these lyrics, defining its object by a kind of childish puzzle, which follows or accompanies its name.

It is from the same simplicity of outlook that Esenin derives his gusto for the colorful, the vivid, the picturesque. His favorite color is the color of the sky, in all its shades; and he loves it so much as to attribute it to his native land, to his "blue Russia." But his poems are equally full of white and yellow patches, so enameled as to give the effect of gold and silver, and to remind us of icons and miniature painting, of Byzantine mosaics and popular prints or cuts. This chromatism is not merely a decorative, but also a compositional, element and intensifies the stylization of the poet's vision, so evident in the stillness of the landscapes, with their motionless figures and timeless moods. But almost always this stillness is broken by a sudden burst of song, by a hidden stream of music, changing the stasis into ecstasis, and flooding the entire scene with a melodic grief which makes a vibrant chord of every fiber.

This feeling of cosmic pain is suggested through a constant parallelism, a continuous identification between men, beasts, plants, and stars. For Esenin there is no difference between our tears and the tears of all other creatures, and even of things. Since only the humble may be exalted, the poet celebrates even the heavenly creature he loves most, the moon, through a series of animal metamorphoses: by converting it, metaphorically, now into a bear, now into a frog. In the same spirit, when wishing to express his own sorrow at the passing of time, he changes himself into an old maple; or when wishing to declare his love for a girl, he addresses instead a young birch.

It is the beasts that play a central role in the poet's belief that there exists a universal, brotherly and mystical bond, joining together the human and the nonhuman, the animal and vegetable kingdoms, the organic and inorganic worlds. Animals are for Esenin the most human and humane of all the creatures of God. Thus, in one of the most beautiful and moving poems of his later years, he projects the horror of the Revolution through the vision of animal, rather than human, slaughter: through the ordeal of starvation and famine, when human beings are forced to kill their domestic animals, and to eat of their flesh. This poem is "Mare Ships," in which the tragedy of Revolution is reduced to the tragedy of hunger, symbolized by a fleshless carrion abandoned in a city street.

As the poet of wooden Russia, Esenin also protested against the invasion of the Russian countryside by the technological monsters of modern civilization: the telegraph poles and the electric cables, the steam engines and steel derricks demanded by the Soviet drive for industrialization. This theme is fully developed in "Requiem," especially in its final scene, describing a foolish colt that vainly challenges to a race the train crossing the Russian plains as a ghostly and awful "iron guest." The two themes of the sacrifice of the animals and of the countryside's martyrdom dominate the poetry of the late Esenin, in which they merge with a more individual note, with the poet's lament about his plight as a man and an artist. Such a lament and the poet's foreboding of his own ruin reflect in personal terms the cruel destiny of any uprooted villager, living as an exile in the foreign and harsh world of the city. The peasant's son had become a successful writer, even a public figure; yet he remained forever obsessed by a sense of failure and guilt. The disease of modern life had tainted his body and his soul, and there was nothing that could cure him. Esenin conveyed this feeling of alienation and corruption in "Soviet Russia," a poem describing a visit to his native village, and vented his indignation against a way of life he could neither reject nor accept by acting, in both imagination and reality, as a bohemian and a hooligan, as an eccentric and an outcast.

As we know, he also sought escape in the artificial paradise of alcohol, in the hell of "firewater," and this is the main motif of *Moscow of the Taverns*. Yet the only way out he could find was self-inflicted death, and the double misery of his brief existence and of his violent end proves the truth of his statement that "the poet came on earth to understand everything, but to take nothing." The lesson we may learn from his fate, as from the fate of Majakovskij, is that in no country do poets find it harder to live or survive than in that Red Russia which they once saluted as a promised land.

CHAPTER NINE

THE POETS OF YESTERDAY

I

THE TWILIGHT OF POETRY AND ART

THE emergence and the triumph in Russia of the peculiar phenomenon which takes, in a strict and emphatic sense, the name of Soviet literature, brought along with itself, among other things, the decline of the art of writing and the decay of the poetic form. Soviet literature is certainly not a proof of Edmund Wilson's claim that in the modern literary condition "verse is a dying technique," precisely because, through an immense quantity of verse writing, rhythmical speech has survived in postrevolutionary Russia, if not as an art, at least as a craft. To be sure, when we speak of Soviet letters, we do not think primarily of poets or writers of verse, but of a swarm of mediocre writers of fiction, who, unlike some of their predecessors in prerevolutionary times, cannot even find an excuse for the vulgarity of their own work in the nobility of their ideals, or in the courage of their moral or social protest. In Soviet Russia even literature serves not the cause of the Russian people, but the interests of the Russian state, or, rather, of the regime. While the chosen task of the Russian novelist of the nineteenth century, as personally stated by Turgenev, was to bare the lie which was at the base of Russian life, the forced duty of the Soviet storyteller is to glorify, as if it were a new truth, the new and far worse lie which has replaced the old one. This is no less true for the Soviet poet, who must reduce poetry to the condition of prose, to the rhymed or versified lingo into which he translates the gross oratory of his leaders, the coarse slogans of

276

their political posters, the catchy phrases of the party press. One could say that in Soviet Russia the poet's pen has become a bureaucrat's quill; and from this standpoint the Soviet writer may appear to have been forced back to the status and function which were the lot of the Russian man of letters two or three centuries ago.

The most recent and sophisticated interpreters of the Russian literary tradition give a very high aesthetic evaluation of the authors who rose on the literary horizon at the very time tsarist Russia emerged from her long slumber, and became a great European power. Yet there are even now many old-fashioned and traditional literary historians, raised in the atmosphere of nineteenth-century liberalism and progressivism, who still look at Russian literature as it developed in its "imperial age," which opened with the reign of Peter the Great and closed with that of the great Catherine, as if it were a transplanted flower, the growth of which was entirely dependent on the autocrat's good or ill will. In this those historians share the view of Vasilij Rozanov, a representative of the reactionary camp, who once remarked, not without disgust, that the whole of Russian seventeenth- and eighteenth-century literature had practically been impressed into government service. Yet the first who asserted that almost all the writers of that age had acted, directly or indirectly, as the mouthpieces of autocracy, working in behalf of a single cause, which was the glory or the benefit of a hardly enlightened despotism, were the radical critics of the nineteenth century, who left the legacy of that view to their modern disciples, the Marxist critics.

In its most extreme form this view is but a manifestation of "vulgar Marxism," and is based on a misinterpretation of Marx's literary theory. The misinterpretation itself is related to a doctrine which in the earlier revolutionary years the Futurists fostered for their own misguided purposes, when they coined the term and developed the idea of "social command." Then the Futurists thought of themselves as the artistic interpreters of the Revolution's "general will," and they could not foresee that their own formula would be soon turned against them. The official spokesmen of Leninism and Stalinism on the literary and cultural front took up the formula and enforced their interpretation of "social command" as an ideological directive or a political prescription from above, which the artist and the writer could not disregard without risk. Thus, when applied to the present, the formula produced in practice a truthful description of the actualities of the Soviet literary and cultural scene. Yet, notwithstanding its universal claims, when applied retrospectively, that formula failed to account for most of the historical and aesthetic variants of the same problem. The ways and means by which artists and writers may serve the state or society to which they belong are manifold; and we shall understand better such variety and multiplicity if we remember that Marx's critical ideas, from which both the Futurists and the theorists of Marxism-Leninism drew the notion of "social command," besides being broader and subtler, were meant to apply primarily to the social conditioning of bourgeois literature and art. If it wants to become less ideological and more scientific, Marxian literary and cultural history should rest not on the concept of "social command," but on that of "social demand," where the adjective ought to be understood as a synonym of "sociological," and the noun as an extension into the cultural field of the economic notion of "demand."

From such a perspective the Russian man of letters of the seventeenth and eighteenth centuries will appear far more of a free agent than he was supposed to be. From the same perspective the literature of Russia's "imperial age" will seem to diverge far less than expected from that of France and of the Frenchified West in the same epoch, since that literature, like its Western counterpart, was primarily motivated by the demands, aesthetic as well as practical, of a ruling elite. Its chief distinction, or most peculiar shortcoming, besides its relative limitation in both range and quality, is to be seen in the failure on the part of its writers, a failure fully understandable on the grounds of Russia's political and cultural lag, to act as the critics as well as the spokesmen of the society of which they were part. The Russian authors of that age could not turn from courtly poets and official writers into *philosophes* and *Aufklärer*, into Russian equivalents of the French *encyclopédistes* and *illuministes*. Yet in the age that followed, in that nineteenth century which was not only the golden age of Russian literature, but also its *siècle des lumières*, that function was to be brilliantly performed by most of the great masters of Russian fiction under the labels of "classical" and "critical realism."

In contrast with this, the main public task of the official literature of the "imperial age" had consisted of composing formal odes celebrating such lofty occasions as the anniversary of a great military triumph, the impending ceremony of dynastic marriage, or the recurring date of the sovereign's birth. Sometimes that literature would allow, through the interested indulgence of the throne, the composition, publication, or performance of either a satire or a comedy pillorying the minor vices of the upper classes, all too often unwilling to change themselves into the bureaucratic or technical elite required by reasons of state or the monarch's will. The great Catherine went so far as to fulfill that task with her own hands, with compositions in both Russian and French. What counts most is, however, that the obscurantism, the conformity, and the cultural backwardness of old tsardom did not prevent the appearance, even in the preclassical age of Russian literature, of such exceptional and unfettered talents as those of Gavriil Derzhavin and of the dissident clergyman, the Archpriest Avvakum. If the latter was able to produce such a masterpiece as his *Life* by merging within its prose the two ancient traditions of popular lore and religious culture, and by turning apologetics and hagiography into autobiography in the modern sense of the term, the former succeeded in forging a native equivalent of the aulic poetry of the West by fusing Baroque imagery and classical diction within the crucible of an original talent.

Yet it remains true that at least under the reign of Peter the Great a good deal of the literary production was motivated, as is often the case also in Soviet Russia, by the criterion of practical or technical utility. Much of that production was, for instance, made of translations of foreign materials and of compilations of useful handbooks, the purpose of which was to contribute to the reorganization of the Russian Empire after the model of the great states of the West. From this viewpoint, one could assert, although with many reservations and qualifications, that the task of many Russian writers of the seventeenth century, not excluding that of such a major figure as Lomonosov, was similar to the task which Arnold Toynbee attributes in general to the class he named "intelligentsia" by expanding and distorting for his own benefit the original and genuine Russian meaning of that term. For Toynbee the function of the intelligentsia is to help a backward country to advance rapidly on the road of technological progress. Such a definition hardly applies to the Russian intelligentsia of the nineteenth century, which went to the school of the West not to serve the interest of the state and its rulers, but to educate a generous audience, which was willing to hear and eager to learn. Despite the fact that the linguistic definition of the original term admits professionals and specialists to the membership of that class, the real calling of the Russian intelligentsia was, its godless ideology notwithstanding, a religious one. The Russian *intelligent*, although a radical and a rebel, was also a moralist and an idealist, always ready to bear witness and to set an example, turning his sacrifice into an act of faith and his martyrdom into an act of protest. Thus Toynbee's redefinition and reinterpretation of the term seems far better suited to the Soviet intellectual class, which exalts within itself the technician and the expert, to the point that even writers find it flattering to be called, in Stalin's words, "engineers of the human soul." Since in Communist Russia even engineers are public servants, this means in practice that the Soviet man of letters must act or behave like a party or state functionary, working in the fields of indoctrination and propaganda, of mass education and applied psychology.

If this is true, then the Soviet writer belongs to a type without historical precedent. Nothing will emphasize better the peculiarity of his function and the uniqueness of his situation than to contrast him with the Russian writer of the nineteenth century. The latter felt alienated from the political order of which he was an unwilling part; yet he felt in tune with the most advanced social and cultural groups of his nation and time, to which he offered intellectual and moral leadership, getting in exchange their admiring attention and reverent respect. A few representatives of the same type are still to be found in the Western literatures of our day, and their presence makes the task and condition of the Soviet writer even more exceptional. The Soviet writer enjoys a greater official prestige and a far more secure social status than does his contemporary Western colleague, who all too often feels in strong disagreement with the bourgeois order, which in its turn may publicly condemn that dissent without, however, legally silencing it. Yet, despite all this, the Soviet writer is all too often inclined to indict as a "lackey of capitalism" that Western writer who enjoys more freedom but fewer rewards, and to forget all too easily that he must pay himself for his own privileges and advantages, for the position of honor if not of influence he holds within the Soviet order, with the heavy price of conformity.

If the Western writer complains vocally and publicly of being isolated, of feeling estranged from his society, the Soviet writer may silently suffer or lament privately for being integrated so fully that his creative personality is almost obliterated. The Polish poet Czeslaw Milosz, who "chose freedom" and re-evoked the slavery from which he fled in a book entitled *The Captive Mind*, makes in this regard an observation which fits the Soviet case no less well than that of the so-called people's democracies. The former, after all, is but the necessary and exemplary precedent of the latter. "Poetry as we have known it," says Milosz, "can be defined as the individual temperament refracted through social convention. The poetry of the New Faith can, on the contrary, be defined as social convention refracted through the individual temperament." What these words imply is simply that in Soviet Russia and her satellites the personality of the writer or the artist is no longer a creative factor, but merely a receptive or assimilative one.

What Milosz calls social convention means something both broader and subtler than an orthodoxy enforced by institutional pressure, something more pervasive than the direct influence of a fixed system of dogmas and beliefs. We must undoubtedly admit that history knows of many societies which produced great artistic achievements by a single-minded allegiance to a universal world view, as well as by a purely instrumental conception of the finality of art. The medieval artist worked within the limits as well as within the range of such a framework: yet, as Meyer Schapiro has pointed out, there is no need to suppose that he had to be a literal believer to perform as effectively as he did what was at once his given and his chosen task, namely, to celebrate the glory of the faith and the grandeur of the Church. What really mattered was that his fealty was primarily a psychological and cultural fact; that, even if he was an unbeliever or a heretic, he could not conceive of art except in religious and communal terms. The Soviet artist is, however, a modern man in more senses than one, living in a society which is both more totalitarian and less stratified than many societies of the past. Like his contemporary Western colleague, although in a different way, the Soviet artist, too, is torn by contrasting public and private demands, equally tempted by the will to doubt and the will to believe. Precisely because of this we must avoid underrating the appeal that Marxism, this new scholasticism secular in temper and materialistic in content, seems to have, even outside of Russia, for the modern mind. Milosz acknowledged this paradox when he stated that "the Method, the *Diamat* — that is, dialectical materialism as interpreted by Lenin and Stalin — possesses a strong, magnetic influence on the men of the present day."

This is certainly one of the motives which lead the Soviet artist to accept without too many qualms the official culture the regime imposes on him from above. If he complies all too readily with the mandate which such acceptance implies, it is also because the authority he serves provides him with both a ready-made style and a custom-made world view. Such is the double effect of the theory and practice of what takes the name of Socialist Realism, a fact which Milosz recognizes with keen insight. "Socialist Realism," says the Polish poet, "is not, as many think, merely an aesthetic theory to which the writer, the musician, the painter, the theatrical producer is obliged to adhere. On the contrary, it involves by implication the whole Leninist-Stalinist doctrine. If writers and painters are not forced to become members of the party, that is because such a step is unnecessary."

Socialist Realism thus supplies the writer and the artist with an ideology and an aesthetics at the same time. Yet the former, although it may sometimes become a spring of faith, hardly ever turns into a source of vision. As for the latter, while determining the over-all technique of Soviet art, it seems wholly unable to inspire a sense of form. This double failure might be summed up by saying that Socialist Realism prevents the artist from attaining the very values he should constantly seek, which are those Goethe once named "poetry" and "truth." It was for the second of these defects, which may well be the more important, that Ignazio Silone indicted the literary system which claims to express the ideality and reality of the Soviet way of life. A socialist and a realist himself, Silone found that in that system there was neither realism nor socialism. The Italian writer pointed out this deception and anticlimax in the last of a series of letters he exchanged in 1957 with Ivan Anisimov, the editor of the Soviet journal *Foreign Literature*: "In my opinion, your 'socialist realism' usurps the name; 'state realism' would be a more 'realistic' term, and would render its true meaning more accurately. How else can one define an aesthetic canon which demands from the writer an optimistic picture of a society whose beings are oppressed and terrorized?" As if such a question, more eloquent than rhetorical, would admit of no reply, Silone closed his verdict of guilt with the taunting mockery of this parting remark: "There exists to my knowledge only one work by a Russian author that might, at a pinch, be catalogued under the heading of 'socialist realism' — the secret report of Khrushchev; but it was the Americans who published it, and moreover there are rumors that the author now intends to disclaim it."

As for the other fault or sin of Socialist Realism, which is to hinder the artist from seeking "poetry" or "beauty" as well as "truth," we shall understand it better if we keep in mind that even Soviet culture is not devoid of standards of taste, of aesthetic norms of its own. The point is, unfortunately, that such standards and norms act in a restrictive and negative sense, rather than in a formative and positive one. There is no social structure which does not entail a cultural order of its own; to any set of social conventions there corresponds a parallel set of literary conventions. In brief, every society, especially if culturally and institutionally centralized, enforces its own sense of value even in matters of form. It should not be surprising that the Soviet regime has its say in the domain of style as well as in the realm of thought. If this surprises us, it is only because the very opposite happens in that bourgeois culture of which we are part. Sartre remarks that the bourgeois is the first social order without a style of its own. It would be more exact to say that bourgeois culture has no single style, since it admits many, even those most alien to its taste, or offensive to it. Of all of them, the only style that deserves being called bourgeois is the one which the artists of bourgeois society hold unworthy of being considered a style at all. That style, dominating all inferior cultural activities of our epoch, especially what we now call "mass culture" or "popular arts," may be defined as a conventional and academic realism. Paradoxically, it is this inferior brand of bourgeois realism that Soviet society has taken as a single and official standard of style, and has imposed on all genres and arts, from poetry to fiction, from the drama to the film, from painting to music. By doing so, Soviet culture has leveled both genius and taste and has reduced Russian creative and spiritual life to an immense flatland. By their outright rejection of what they label "formalism," the bureaucrats of Russian literature are enforcing not only a political orthodoxy, but also a formal one. When deprived of the heavy clothing of its ideological program, and reduced to its bare bones, Socialist Realism reveals itself to Western eyes simply as a glorified variant of what might be termed the realism of the Philistines and the lowbrows. It is this aesthetic or pseudoaesthetic quality which is its most important constant. Propaganda slogans and political tenets may vary with the party's "general line," as so many Russian writers, too slow to feel in time the change of the wind, have learned too late and at their loss: yet no sensible change has affected Socialist Realism as literary doctrine or technical practice.

We do not need to reconstruct the tedious and devious process by which the Soviet regime has succeeded in submitting all creative activities to a control without precedent in essence as well as in degree. It will be enough to say that its cultural strategy is constantly aiming at the same goal, even though, as Gleb Struve, the foremost authority on Soviet literature, once remarked, tactical considerations may force it sometimes to follow a zigzag line rather than a straightforward path. Nor can we describe in any detail the highly organized instruments or complex devices which enable Russia's rulers to enforce their will in the cultural domain: a domain they manage directly, or through overseers who pay dearly for the slightest oversight. Those instruments and devices are many and manifold, varying from the *ukazy* of the ruling elite to the literary plebiscites of the official congresses, from the pronouncements of party functionaries to the self-policing of the writers' association, from the public recantations of deviant artists to the *auto-da-fés* of unrepentant heretics, or at least of their works. The system itself could thus be described as a combination of deadly terrorism and of deadening bureaucratism. The second of these factors is perhaps the more effective, as is shown by the fact that no writer can have his work printed except through official channels, since publishing is in Russia a centralized state monopoly, like all communication and entertainment industries.

What should strike more the Western observer is then not so much the murderous results of the system in extreme or exceptional cases, as the normal and average consequences of its current operations and routine procedures. To realize what such consequences can be, it may suffice to think of the sterilizing effect of an organization of this sort on the most vital springs of cultural change, or on the quest for new ideas and the search for new forms. The search for new forms is made impossible by the practical disappearance in Soviet Russia of any advance guard, which bourgeois society may well push to the periphery of its own culture, but never tries to banish forever, or to repress in full. The implicit, and even explicit, veto against the cultivation of what the French once used to call *art d'exception* is quite consistent with the Marxist conviction that that kind of art is but a cultural symptom of the decay of capitalism. This is why even such an open- and broad-minded Marxist critic as Georg Lukács has found it fit in his recent essay *The Present Significance of Critical Realism* (which up to now has appeared only in an Italian version) to brand again the advance guard as a form of Decadence, as a variant of bourgeois Bohemianism.

As for the quest for new ideas, it is made impossible by the rejection of any cultural influence from abroad, by the prevention of any meaningful intellectual exchange between the Communist and the non-Communist worlds. Soviet Russia can hardly tolerate any free trade in the market of thought, or the free flow of such commodities as foreign books. Thus, from the time when Karl Radek warned Soviet writers from yielding to the dangerous attraction of such wicked seducers as Proust and Joyce (who were represented as a single, double-headed monster by the name of Proyce), Soviet literature has more and more shied away from the most innocent and productive of all cultural temptations, which is intellectual curiosity. The culmination of this process is to be seen in the campaign against "cosmopolitanism," by which the regime waxed the ears of the few writers and artists who were still trying to listen, from a distance, to the siren song of foreign muses. The success of that campaign amounted to a final and total secession of Soviet Russia from the Republic of Letters. As far as poetry is concerned, this means in practice that the only link still joining Western and Soviet writing is reduced to that group of foreign authors who are *personae gratae* in the Soviet Union. The group includes some poets from the so-called people's democracies, such as the Pole Antoni Slonimski, the Czech Vitezslav Nezval, and the German Bertolt Brecht (the last two are now dead), and a few others from bourgeois countries who embraced the Communist credo, such as the French Louis Aragon and the Chilean Pablo Neruda.

The combined effect of this double denial of "advance-guardism" and "cosmopolitanism" is the proscription of formal experimentation, which prospers only in a cultural atmosphere open to suggestions from outside, and not too unfavorable to internal dissent. By way of conclusion one could say then that the literature of Soviet Russia, or of a nation and country claiming to be the leader of mankind, is bourgeois in form and provincial in content. Its typical products are long narratives in verse and prose exalting the achievements of the regime; novels glorifying the artisans of the five-year plan and pillorying diversionists or saboteurs; plays extolling the wisdom and bravery of party leaders or the moral political rehabilitation of political misfits. In brief, the Soviet writer has been led to ignore, or at least to neglect, those primary and eternal themes of literature which affected so much the creative imagination of the great Russian masters of the nineteenth century, such as the soul's progress through the ordeal of passion and vice, or its catharsis through love and death. Some of these themes may certainly appear in the work of a Soviet writer, but only as cheapened "assembly-line romance," as Trotskij himself observed in his diary of exile, written in 1935 and published in America in 1958. Even so, the simple and direct account of man's individual experience may reappear in Soviet fiction only as part of its secondary plot, since the main plot deals always with the heroic deeds and superhuman feats of a collective and abstract protagonist, which may be the party or the proletariat, the Revolution or socialism.

The Soviet man of letters has sought and found a few avenues of escape from this obsession with a bright present and a brighter future, to be depicted in both ideal and conventional terms. Yet almost all of them have turned into blind alleys, at least from the viewpoint of art. The first of such avenues of escape is historical fiction, where the writer's freedom is severely hampered by the official outlook. Another one is literary biography, where the author may move somewhat freely, especially if he chooses as his own subject one of those great classical, traditional figures which Soviet official culture affects to respect. Sometimes, to play even safer, the biographer gives up any attempt at interpretation, and turns into a glorified archivist, compiling a so-called *litmontage*, or a mosaic of documents claiming to re-evoke the life of his subject through the mute eloquence of fact. Biography is thus reduced to "factography," a form of writing which from the times of LEF Futurists and Constructivists had unwisely and perhaps not too seriously recommended as a literary equivalent of such an exemplary form as the documentary film. The most effective avenues of escape are, however, editing and translating, especially the latter, which permits greater latitude in the domain of expression and entails fewer political risks. The two fields the Soviet writer prefers to cultivate as translator are on one side the great Western classics, which the regime tolerates with a liberality denied to most of the Western writers of today, and on the other the old or new literatures of the non-Russian speaking minorities of the Soviet Union, such as Armenians, Georgians, and the like.

More recently, especially during those short breathing spells which followed the end of the war and the death of Stalin, verse writing seemed to have found a way out from some of its ideological impasses far more promising than the favorite bypath of Soviet poetry in the late twenties. If the young poets of those years had skirted the dangers of both subjectivity and propaganda by cultivating an arty imitation of folk balladry, the new poets of the late forties dared to withdraw into a corner of their own, to compose what they called "chamber poetry," or an intimate lyricism allowing for the expression of private emotions and individual feelings. Even though Soviet "chamber poetry" can hardly avoid the pitfalls of a quasi-bourgeois sentimentalism, its appearance should be saluted as a symptom of relative relaxation of party and state controls in some sectors of the literary front. No such relaxation has, however, been possible in the area of criticism, which is the central bulwark of the Soviet cultural system. Nothing would be more inconceivable in Soviet Russia than the toleration of a "chamber criticism," or of an interpretation and evaluation of literature and art in terms of individual taste or coterie connoisseurship. Soviet criticism, which defines itself as a public and social activity, is, so to speak, demotic and demagogic: its real function is to educate, or rather, to indoctrinate the reader, while at the same time censoring the writer, or rather censuring, and chastizing him. It is while fulfilling this function that criticism exhibits at their worst two of the main vices of Soviet literary culture, the adulteration of language and the corruption of thought, which manifest themselves in the use of jargon and casuistry, in the practice of what Orwell calls "newspeak" and "double-think."

Of all the forms of Soviet culture criticism is the most directly related to Communist philosophy, which is fully identical with a single school, still taking the old name of dialectical materialism. The mission of Communist philosophy is to strengthen the theoretical foundations of the ideology which is the official faith of the Soviet Union and her satellites. That ideology does not rest directly on the works of Marx and Engels, but on their constant reinterpretation in pragmatic and even opportunistic terms. Thus the pronouncements of Lenin, of Stalin, and of even lesser luminaries of the Red church, may become far more binding for the faithful than the Sinaitic tables Marx himself inscribed with his fiery hand. This explains why the secular religion of Soviet Russia is now more frequently and properly called with the newer name of Marxism-Leninism. While thus avoiding the Scyllas of fundamentalism, Communist thought can hardly escape from the Charybdis of scholasticism. It was Berdjaev who remarked that Communist philosophy, like medieval theology, tends to reduce the complex question of truth and error to a simple dualism of orthodoxy and heresy. We know the tragic consequences such dualism entails for the deviationist (as Soviet lingo calls the thinker who strays from the right path), as well as for the progress of thought. All too often the political situation may demand the rehabilitation of a view once rejected, or the repudiation of a view once officially held: and while in such case the historian is required to write anew the annals of the past, the philosopher is entrusted with the readjustments to be made within the system of which he is mender and keeper, rather than inventor or ruler. To this task he brings uncommon gifts for polemics and controversy, a barbaric pedantry and a Byzantine fondness for sophistries and logomachies. Similar services must be sometimes performed also in the sciences, by the scientists themselves, as shown by the case of Lysenko, who acted much too long as the high priest of Soviet biology. Yet science remains the most free, protected, and productive zone in the Soviet cultural domain; and there is perhaps no more ominous threat for the West than in this paradoxical combination, within Russian society, of scientific creativity and of spiritual sterility.

No "chamber art" is practically possible, even if it were tolerated, in the nonliterary realm. This is particularly true of the most public of all arts, the theater and the film, which have been unable to produce in the Russia of Stalin and his successors anything comparable to the memorable achievements which earned the Russian stage and screen of the early revolutionary years the enthusiastic approval of an international audience. As a matter of fact there is no sorrier tale in the history of Soviet culture than the degeneration of these two arts. For what happened to the glorious tradition of Russian stagecraft, it will be enough to refer to the disgrace and disappearance of the greatest of all the theatrical innovators of our time, Vsevolod Mejerkhol'd. For what happened to the less brilliant, but no less noble tradition of Russian playwriting, it will suffice to quote what the storyteller and dramatist Evgenij Zamjatin had to say in a lecture he gave in Prague just after he left Russian soil: "What has taken place may be described as an enormous literary miscarriage. A series of embryonic monsters, atrophic and amorphous, is now flooding the stage. Like premature or stillborn babies, they have a head disproportionately huge, crammed with first-class ideology, and a weak and rickety body, unable to support such a heavy head." As for the Soviet cinema, which Lenin himself considered the outstanding cultural manifestation of the new order, after releasing the creative energies of such masters as Vsevolod Pudovkin and Sergei Èjsenshtejn, who forged such masterworks as *Storm over Asia* (1929) and *The Battleship Potemkin* (1925), it was bound to become in the following years one of the chief vehicles of Communist jingoism and Soviet Babbitry. The great Èjsenshtejn himself agreed to produce and direct such a patriotic and archaeological monstrosity as *Ivan the Terrible* (1944–1946), not too different in taste and style from the "blood and soil" sagas or Roman epics manufactured before the war by the film industries of Nazi Germany and Fascist Italy.

The Soviet regime does not favor the development of "chamber art" even in music and painting because, like other despotic societies, it tends to view them as celebratory arts. This is even truer of sculpture and architecture, which after all now hardly admit of private patronage even in the capitalistic world. The task of the Soviet sculptor and architect is merely to glorify the regime by erecting huge academic monuments to its leaders, or colossal buildings for its institutions or bureaus. The sculptor is not allowed to seek new materials or new forms, while the architect is unable to harmonize the decorative and the functional elements in structures which look half like temples and half like barracks. As for the Soviet painter, who is even more bound than the sculptor to respect some of the taboos of Communist life (for instance, the almost puritanical proscription of the nude), he is suspected if he works at a landscape or a still life, or more generally if he chooses other subjects than revolutionary or proletarian ones. Because of the painter's medium, Socialist Realism is able to exact from him even a greater conformity to its representational norms than from the writer himself. Painting is then the art where Soviet culture manifests its own vulgarity and mediocrity at their worst. The proscription not only of abstractionism, but even of representational distortion, or of any divergence from the canon of academic realism, all of which the Soviet order, like the Nazi regime, considers parallel manifestations of "degenerated art," reduces the whole painting of Communist Russia in the best cases to a kind of photographic impressionism, and, in the worst, to unadulterated *Kitsch*.

In Soviet Russia music stands at the opposite pole of painting, precisely because the nature of music permits that art to resist more successfully official encroachments, or to elude them. After all it was from music that there derived the very concept of "chamber art." Yet there is hardly any "chamber music" in Soviet Russia. As a matter of fact, the regime chose music itself as a test case in its own condemnation of "formalism": a verdict which such an old master like Sergej Prokof'ev accepted with less grace and more defiance than the younger Dmitrij Shostakovich, all too eager to beat his breast and bow his head. After all, like poetry and paintings, music is a creative art, and a totalitarian society is highly suspicious of creation precisely because it resists any form of planning and control.

The Soviet regime has no reason to feel likewise, however, in regard to artistic activities based on execution and interpretation rather than on creation and invention. Thus the only realm which permits a free development of the artist's genius and an unfettered schooling of public taste is that of the performing arts. It is not surprising, then, that Soviet culture has achieved its highest and most deserved triumphs in this field. There is no doubt that Soviet society has produced outstanding actors, singers, musicians, dancers, who from the viewpoint of both quantity and quality have few peers in the world of today. From this we must infer that, like other despotic orders, Soviet society tends to favor the development of the virtuoso, or of the artist who limits himself to serving or exploiting his craft. Lukács and the other Marxist critics who have read Balzac's *Les Illusions perdues* as an indictment of the bourgeois corruption of art, and of the corruptibility of the bourgeois artist, will never recognize that Communism has far better succeeded than capitalism in destroying all illusions in its Luciens de Rubempré, in changing them into mere producers and sellers of artistic commodities, into hawkers and hucksters, or into entertainers who perform at best in gorgeous dumbshows. What a comedown from the prerevolutionary ideal of the socialist artist as a critic of life and as a breaker of new paths! Perhaps nothing tells more about the realities of a so-called proletarian society than the fact that Soviet culture has attained unsurpassed perfection in such an art form as the classical ballet, stylized and premeditated like a chess game, and which had been originally invented as an aristocratic amusement of courtiers and kings.

The widespread acceptance on the part of the Russian public of such a form as the classical ballet may on the other hand suggest that Soviet society is, up to a point, able to cultivate more sophisticated variations of our own "mass culture" and "popular arts." The effect of this is perhaps to raise the Soviet lowbrow to the level of our own middlebrow. This, however, is no great consolation for the artist in search of new spiritual avenues, or simply of new practical outlets. While the Western "highbrow" writer or artist may once in a while do some free-lancing for radio or television, for Hollywood or the popular press, his Soviet counterpart in effect is bound to work all his life only for a highly organized opinion-, communication-, and entertainment-industry, which is a state monopoly as well. It would be hardly candid to deny that we are witnessing similar developments, even though on a smaller scale, also in the West: after all, advertising and propaganda may differ in aims, but not in means. It would be likewise unfair to refuse to admit that Soviet mass culture may contribute more effectively than ours to the education, as well as to the indoctrination, of the average man. Yet, unlike our own pluralistic society, the Soviet order prevents the artist's withdrawal into a secluded corner, where he can live and work in solitude, producing in toil and hardship works which may please only himself and the happy few.

The Soviet artist may often delude himself that his real patron is the Russian public, which certainly offers him a far more homogeneous audience than the one our society supplies to the artist in our midst. Yet his real patron is the state, and this prevents him from achieving in full both his artistic and his moral tasks. Once in a while, even when he is an aesthete or a hedonist, a mystic or an individualist, the Western artist may stop listening to the muse, and heed the call of a cause, which he will serve in words as well as deeds. The new faith to which he commits himself, which all too often is an ideal and naïve Communism, very different from that unto which the Soviet artist is born, may soon tire and disappoint the convert, who is then free to change his mind and to discard his newly acquired beliefs. The Soviet artist begins, however, his career by joining forever, as passive servant rather than as an active partner, a moral and social order he has neither the power to change nor the right to judge. By committing himself to a compulsory, rather than to a spontaneous, *engagement*, he condemns himself to a rigid and life-long conformism. What he gets in exchange is status, prestige, and economic security: yet, while being denied freedom, he remains accountable for all his acts and thoughts. In brief, he is granted patronage but refused protection; as a matter of fact, he must carry the burden of a limitless liability and of an unpredictable responsibility, which all too often entail retroactive guilt. In this the Soviet intellectual shares the destiny of the Soviet political leader, although the latter has the advantage of leading, at least as long as he is at the helm. It is the political leader who decides at any instant what the "general line" really is, or who changes it at a moment's notice, thus affecting not only the present and the future, but the past as well. The Soviet writer, painter, or musician, as Max Eastman put it, is then an "artist in uniform," liable to pay for the mistakes or the crimes of his superiors, as all subalterns are likely to be. Acting, as he does, under battle conditions, he is trained to expect neither truce nor respite on the cultural front. He cannot free himself from this servitude without grandeur except by breaking his soldier's oath, and we know all too well the consequences of such an act. The entire history of Soviet culture does not list a single case of successful desertion; the only clamorous gesture of defiance that escaped full retribution is perhaps the publication abroad of *Doctor Zhivago*, by which, taking a chance no one had yet dared to take, Pasternak declared his "objection of conscience" before the world.

It is evident that Soviet planning, so successful in the industrial, technological, and scientific sphere, in the long run cannot but fail in the domain of the arts. It fell upon Evgenij Zamjatin, a writer trained as an engineer, who in his youth had been sympathetic to the revolutionary cause, to foretell this failure from the very beginning of the Communist double attempt to foster literature and to control it. "A genuine literature," said Zamjatin, "can exist only where it is produced by madmen, hermits, heretics, dreamers, rebels, and skeptics, not by painstaking and well-meaning officials." When he spoke these words, the officials, whether well-meaning or not, were far less powerful than they would later become; and the writers were not yet a fully tamed breed. Most of them, even those who had appeared on the literary scene before 1917, still thought they had found a new voice after February and October, in the ordeal of the early revolutionary years. The chief center of Russian literary life was at that time the very city where the Revolution had fought and won its main battle; and a poet, a storyteller, and an essayist have left us moving documents of the ordeal which man's body and his spirit had to undergo in the Petrograd winters of those years. The poet is Sergej Esenin, who evoked in "Mare Ships" the horrors of famine, symbolized by a swarm of ravens despoiling a carrion abandoned in a city street. The storyteller is Evgenij Zamjatin himself, who in his tale *The Cave* intimated the horrors of cold by depicting the existence of his fellow citizens in those years as a return to a trogloditic way of life, as the recurrence of a new Ice Age. The essayist is Viktor Shklovskij, who recalled in a famous chapter of his memoirs, self-consciously but not too ironically entitled *A Sentimental Journey*, the literary chronicles of those winters, and celebrated the survival of the creative spirit beyond all calamities and hardships.

During the early revolutionary years it was almost impossible to publish books and journals, yet Esenin and Majakovskij, who wrote their best poems in that period, would read them in the literary cabarets before a brave and eager audience which was worthy of its poets. Many young prose writers, who took as their patron saint the hermit Serapion, a character from Hoffmann's tales, after whom they named themselves "Serapion Brothers," chose the time of foreign intervention to follow the advice of one of the youngest members of their group, the storyteller and playwright Lev Luntz, whose *Westward!*, a manifesto he had written just before his death, recommended relearning the craft of writing fiction and of unfolding plots from the masters of the West. Some of this vitality and freedom survived even the end of the period which took the name of "War Communism." Up to the midtwenties, and even later, a few writers succeeded in emancipating themselves from the compulsion to sing in chorus the nauseating eulogy of the building of socialism. Most of them did so by going back to the glorious and tragic memories of the recent past, and recorded, from the standpoint of their leftist allegiance, but without partisan blindness, the years of turmoil during which the Revolution was born. This trend received only a grudging blessing from above, under the quasi-official label of "revolutionary romanticism," which Gor'kij had once invented as a political justification for some aspects of his work. Yet the trend itself attracted many gifted literary artists who had taken an active part in the great upheaval, but who were not party members, and felt no longer in tune with the new state of things, although they were still moved by the bloody chronicles of October and the Civil War. This is the reason why Trotskij, who was endowed with a keen critical and literary sense (as shown by his very denial of the idea of "proletarian literature"), designated all the members of that group with the label of "fellow travelers," or rather, "companions of route" (*poputchiki*). The best which was written under the Soviet regime came from such "fellow travelers," or from the fewer ones who went even further and chose to convey their dissatisfaction with the new order by criticizing the socialist present rather than by idealizing the revolutionary past. It may be worthwhile to cite briefly the few names or titles which deserve being remembered in the annals of Soviet writing.

A book hard to forget, although proscribed in Soviet Russia since the purges of the thirties, which claimed its author among their victims, is *The Mounted Army* by Isaak Babel' (1926), better known in English as *Red Cavalry*. This book, a reprint of which was allowed to appear in 1957, consists of a series of miniature rhapsodies in prose recalling the campaigns of Budennyj's riders against the Poles and the Whites, from the Ukraine to the Caucasus. Another good story of the same period and kind is Vsevolod Ivanov's *The Armored Train No. 14–69* (1922), dealing with the obsessive vision of that mechanical monster crossing and raiding the Siberian steppes during the Civil War. The most classic work of fiction produced in Soviet Russia, after the model of Tolstoj's *War and Peace*, is Mikhail Sholokhov's *Silent Don* (1928–1933), an epic narrative dominated by the great, quiet river, and by the strife and turbulence ruling over the Cossack land. Among older writers, we must name again Evgenij Zamjatin, who chose the road of dissent, and whose novel *We*, written in 1920 and published abroad without the author's consent, opened the way in the West for a series of similar works, including Huxley's *Brave New World* and Orwell's *1984*. By writing *We* Zamjatin thus determined the creation of a new literary genre, taking as its own form that of the utopian novel, but using that form to indict the present reality of an inhuman social order, rather than to dream of an ideal society still to come. Among the younger writers who found inspiration in the spirit and style of Zamjatin's earlier example, one should mention Boris Pil'njak, who turned back from the nightmare of both the present and the future to the mirage of the ancient Russian way of life, not yet fully washed away by the new flood. In his novel *The Bare Year* (1922) and in other works, he looked back, with the nostalgia of a new Slavophile of the Left, at those archaic and patriarchal survivals from primitive Russia which the regime could not accept. Other writers of the same generation chose straighter but not easier paths: so, for instance, Mikhail Zoshchenko turned his exclusive attention toward contemporary Soviet life, which he portrayed through the petty chronicle of the daily existence of an average Soviet citizen, satirizing the new society from the viewpoint of its manners, rather than of its morals. The most naïve and pure of all these rebels was, however, a writer of the following generation, Jurij Olesha, who wrote a charming psychological novel, *Envy*. Published in 1927 (and allowed recently to reappear after a proscription of almost thirty years), *Envy* relates with comic pathos the "sentimental education" of that rare variant of *homo sovieticus*, the man who despite his good will toward the regime remains congenitally unable to conform.

Many of these authors, as well as other writers of fiction, paid in person, sometimes all too dearly, for the small liberties they took in their work. The harmless satirist of Soviet daily life, Mikhail Zoshchenko, was publicly condemned, and had to apologize publicly for his wrongdoing. Zamjatin, often branded as an "inner" *émigré*, but who had enjoyed a situation of privilege for being both Gor'kij's protégé and a highly prized *spets* or "specialist" by trade (as a naval engineer he had designed a few icebreakers and was still lecturing in technological institutions), was the only writer permitted to leave Soviet Russia as late as 1931 and to settle in Paris, where he died in 1937. Both Babel' and Pil'njak fell victims to the great purge; whether they were deported or summarily liquidated, we know they died all-too-untimely deaths. To the martyrology of the writers of fiction we must add the even more tragic one of the poets. We know already that Blok died of a broken heart; that Gumilev was shot as a counter-revolutionary; that Kljuev was banished and persecuted; that Akhmatova was silenced twice in her life; that Pasternak was insulted and humiliated; that Mandel'shtam died in, or on his way to, a forced labor-camp. Yet the destiny of them all is not so poignantly cruel as that of those poets who could find escape only in self-inflicted death. The tragic annals of Russian poetry list the suicides of Sergej Esenin, Vladimir Majakovskij, and Marina Tsvetaeva: each one of whom could be truly defined, in a far more proper sense than that formula had when Antonin Arthaud coined it to convey the pathos of Van Gogh's end, as a "suicide of society." And the horror of their martyrdom is not diminished, but rather increased, by the consideration that their fate was shared by the mediocre novelist Aleksandr Fadeev, who put an end to his life after having hounded his brethren as one of the regime's literary watchdogs.

Of all these self-immolations the one which seems the most

tragic in public as well as in private terms was perhaps that of Majakovskij, not only because he had been the only poet constantly in tune with Soviet life, but also because he had enjoyed more than anyone of his fellow writers some indulgence on the part of the regime. Yet what makes Majakovskij's suicide even more significant is that it coincided with the disappearance of the last vestiges of creative freedom, with the agony, or at least the paralysis, of poetry itself. It was "during the last years of Majakovskij's life," says Pasternak in his recent *Sketch for an Autobiography*, which has been published only abroad, that "poetry ceased to exist." Majakovskij killed himself in 1930, and it was at that time that "literature stopped," since real literature has always been poetry, whether in prose or in verse. Such had been the case, Pasternak remarks, with the best products of Soviet fiction, all of which appeared in the twenties, from the first works of Babel', Pil'njak, and Vsevolod Ivanov to the early part of Sholokhov's *Silent Don*.

II

THE LITERATURE OF EMIGRATION

No survey of the effects of Revolution and Communism on Russian literary culture can be complete without a brief reference to the literature of emigration. Of the poets of the old generation who survived the great upheaval, Brjusov accepted the new order and Belyj chose to return. A few, like Sologub, Kuzmin, or Voloshin, were unable or unwilling to leave. But all the others, led by Merezhkovskij, Gippius, Bal'mont, Bunin, and Ivanov, sooner or later took the path of exile and settled in the many unstable centers of the Russian diaspora, of which the main were Prague and Belgrade, Paris and Berlin, but which included also other havens, such as Riga, New York, Shanghai, or Kharbin. Despite the lack of resources, the *émigrés* founded journals and publishing houses, which attracted beyond the borders of many lands, and for a while even across the frontier of Red Russia, a little, scattered public of their own.

Most of these literary exiles already had given their best before

298

the Revolution; and they contributed to the emigration press primarily as polemists and memorialists. With no significant exceptions, all the old exiled authors who were primarily writers of verse withered, like transplanted flowers, all too soon. More active and fortunate than they were a few storytellers of the old school. Thus Mark Landau, better known under the pen name of Aldanov (1882–1957), gained an international reputation with a series of novels topical in substance although historical in form, while Ivan Bunin scored the highest triumph for the culture of the emigration when in 1933 he became the first Russian to receive the Nobel Prize for literature. Unlike Thomas Mann, whose realistic imagination, after a long severance from German experience, felt more and more the attraction of symbols, visions, and myths, Bunin remained deeply attached to Russian life through the bonds of longing and memory, and it was through the perspective of a nostalgic reminiscence that he wrote *The Life of Arsen'ev* (1930), a long semi-autobiographical rhapsody which is one of the last fruits of the tradition of Russian realistic fiction, and the best to ripen on foreign soil.

The seeds of verse found a little too barren the alien ground on which they fell, and no new poetic flora was able to grow outside Russian land. What this means is that despite their great individual contributions, the *émigré* poets of the younger generation, which included such outstanding talents as Vladislav Khodasevich, Georgij Ivanov, and Marina Tsvetaeva, failed, not as individuals, but as a group, to develop trends not anticipated by the prerevolutionary tradition of Russian verse. This is even truer of the poets who rose directly from the ranks of the emigration, the most gifted of whom was perhaps the lamented Boris Poplavskij (1903–1935), still remembered for the single collection of poems he published in his lifetime, *Banners* (1931), as well as for a couple of posthumous books. The seeds of fiction seemed better able to fructify and even prosper from transplanted roots, and allowed the almost spontaneous generation of fresher and freer forms. It was from the emigration that there emerged the original and strange talent of Vladimir Sirin. Sirin began his career as a poet (he published a collection of Russian verse as late as 1952), yet he was destined to become first an outstanding novelist in his native tongue, and then, under his real name, Vladimir Nabokov, an exceptional writer in English, gaining world-wide renown with such a masterly novel as the recent *Lolita*. If the work of the late Bunin represents the best contribution of the first generation of the Russian *émigrés*, the early writings of Nabokov-Sirin represent the highest achievement of the second one, and it is quite significant that at the height of his maturity the latter chose to break through the ghetto walls of a literary culture without future.

The Russian is not the only *émigré* culture our epoch has seen, but certainly it is the one which has lasted longest, without, however, outlasting the political order from which it fled. The exodus from Fascist lands of a few Italian, many German, and almost all Spanish writers followed the exodus of their Russian brethren from the land of Communism. But the Italians and the Germans have returned home, while most the Spaniards have found havens in faraway countries still graced by the Castilian tongue. Yet forty years have passed, and the Russian *émigrés* who have survived are still in our midst. There is no end in sight for the Russian diaspora, for which the "ingathering of the exiles" is no longer even a dream. This is the very reason why the culture of that diaspora is fated to die all too soon. One has already witnessed the sunset of two of its generations, without seeing the dawn of a third one. The generation of the grandfathers managed to keep alive the uprooted plant it brought away with itself. The generation of the fathers sought to revive and nurse that plant in a hothouse of its own. The grandchildren have failed, however, to form a third generation devoted to the same task. Both contingency and necessity now force those of them who were born with the writer's gift to choose as their literary vehicle the tongues of their adopted countries. One could hardly blame them for this since more than once some of their elders had already taken the same path. By doing so they did not so much impoverish the literary culture of the emigration as they did enrich that of their new homeland. This is particularly true of two authors, Prince Dmitrij Svjatopolsk-Mirskij (1890– ?) and Vladimir Vejdle (1895), who made brilliant contributions to English and French criticism, the first with his outstanding *History of*

Russian Literature (1926–1927), and the second with many lively aesthetic essays, the most important of which is *Les Abeilles d'Aristée* (1936). Such examples suffice to prove that what still remains to be said about the literature of the Russian emigration, even if couched in the present tense, is but a tale of the past or a story about to close.

While the Soviet writer has a mind that is "captive" and closed, the *émigré* author has a mind that is open and free. In literary terms this means that he may be acquainted with Soviet culture, and even affected by it, while the Soviet writer is impervious to any outside influence. Yet a free mind must walk alone, without the help and comfort which the captive mind receives from the herd spirit. All Russian men of letters in exile are keenly aware of this fact and feel a deep concern about it. This is particularly true of one of their leaders, Georgij Adamovich (1894), who started his career as the youngest of the Acmeists and who was to collect his late poetry in a single, little book of great charm, *In the West* (Paris, 1939). In 1955 Adamovich published in New York a volume of criticism under the no less significant title of *Solitude and Freedom*. That title suggests that it is with the predicament of isolation that one pays for the privilege of liberty. With the passing of time the predicament becomes more and more real, and the privilege far less so. In the long run even self-imposed exile turns, always and everywhere, into a kind of Babylonian captivity. A foreign country, even the most hospitable, remains forever a land of infidels, which either alienates or corrupts the stranger in its midst. That sense of alienation may lead the exile to react unfavorably toward what seems to him an unfriendly, if not hostile, environment; to idealize all too fancifully his own cultural background; to exasperate the feeling of his own ethnical peculiarities. It is quite significant that in the early thirties a long and disappointing contact with the West sharpened in a group of old or mature scholars the sense of the uniqueness of their tradition to the point of claiming that the spirit of their nation was more Eastern than Western, that Russia embodied the historical destiny of an immense geographic unit they called Eurasia and viewed as a sixth continent.

Similar psychological motivations were to inspire into many of the very young, at the time of the Second World War, a newly born sense of loyalty toward the land of their ancestors, or what took the name of "Soviet patriotism." If in the main the thinking elite of the emigration rejected between the two wars the temptation of Fascism, a few of its members were less able to resist the double seduction of a return home and of a conversion to Marxism. The trauma of emigration, which often joins a sense of mission with a sense of guilt, led Prince Mirskij, for instance, to embrace the Communist creed and to retrace his steps toward the land of his birth. There, shortly after his return (1932) he was first banished to a remote province, and then sacrificed, as an innocent scapegoat, in one of the many Stalinist slaughters of "saboteurs" and "diversionists," thus adding his name to the martyrology of Russian literature.

The artist who remains in exile is not exposed to shocks as tragic as these; yet he must undergo a daily ordeal, not only as a man, but also as an artist. The artist, and especially the writer, who must live as a stranger, must also work with traditions which the people around him ignore, misunderstand, or despise, and which he is himself unable to preserve or change according to their inner nature. Language and style, the media of the writer's creation, are not hardened tools, but delicate instruments, which an excess of either insulation or exposure may put forever out of tune, making them issue false notes. Excessive insulation may lead a transplanted culture to lean too much in the direction of what Toynbee terms "archaism"; excessive exposure, in the opposite direction, toward what the English historian names "futurism." In short, an émigré culture tends to become a culture of decadence, as happens all too often with the spiritual heritage of a dispossessed elite.

This is perhaps the foremost of the many reasons why the manifest literary consequences of the condition of exile differ so greatly, both psychologically and otherwise, from the far less evident effects produced by the state of mind which both friendly and unfriendly observers define metaphorically as "inner emigration." The young critic Vladimir Markov, now living in America as one of those refugees from Soviet tyranny whose influx seemed for a while to give a new lease of life to Russian writing in exile, has recently published in this country an anthology of the "inner emigration" for which he has chosen the moving and fitting title of *Suffocated Voices*. If such voices are hardly audible, those of the writers in exile are calls in the wilderness; and the comparison between the literature of the "inner" and that of the "outer" *émigrés* is valid insofar as one can hardly hear the echo of either. Yet it is worth remarking that if the "suffocated voices" of the "inner" *émigrés* sing in soft discord with the noisy chorus of Soviet poetry, they do so far more in moral than in literary terms. From this one might draw the paradoxical inference that the Soviet cultural condition prevents even more successfully the formation of aesthetic deviants than of political or religious ones. Even the greatest of all "inner" *émigrés*, the most modern and European of all the poets living in Soviet Russia, Boris Pasternak, exhibited, by publishing abroad what appears to be the most significant document of Soviet dissent, a far greater concern for a spiritual revival than for an artistic one.

If this is true, then the most useful function which Russian *émigré* literature will perform, perhaps a long time after its death, may well be to set a precedent and an example for the reintroduction of Russian literature and poetry within the mainstream of the tradition of modern art. The heritage of the poets who worked and died in exile may thus contribute to the restoration of beauty, as well as of truth, in the future revival of Russian verse. Perhaps the poets to come will learn useful lessons also from the work of two masters whose talents were able to flourish even after being transplanted on foreign soil. The first of these two figures was Georgij Ivanov, of whom I have already spoken in another context; the second was Vladislav Khodasevich, of whom I am about to speak.

III

VLADISLAV KHODASEVICH

When compared to the *epigones* of prerevolutionary lyricism, or to the *neoteroi* of Soviet verse, feebly and briefly glimmering, like will-o'-the-wisps, in the darkening sky of Russian poetry, Khodasevich shines like a bright star, the light of which seems to come from another heaven or from another era. The poet, after starting his literary career in Russia, settled abroad, where he was hardly influenced by the social and cultural changes affecting Russian life. Yet, at least at the beginning of his exile, through his association with Gor'kij and Belyj, who had either accepted or tolerated the Soviet regime, and with whom he co-edited in Berlin, from 1922 to 1925, the important journal *Table Talk*, he kept in touch with his homeland, and was thus able to reflect there some of the rays of his poetry. That poetry, however, remains, historically and critically, hard to classify. Khodasevich began his career at the apogee, or rather at the early decline, of the Symbolist movement; and while taking its achievements for granted, he felt rather detached toward its aesthetic creed. Formally and chronologically, his poetic ideal is more obviously related to that of the followers of both Acmeism and Clarism; yet, despite this connection, his imaginative and moral world greatly differs from Kuzmin's, Gumilev's or Akhmatova's. His work escapes the pitfalls of Kuzmin's verse, all deriving from the whimsical fatuity of the author's caprice, to which Khodasevich opposes the high seriousness, and even ponderosity, of his own inspiration. Khodasevich showed that he was aware of this quality by defining his own poetry, in the title of his best collection, as a "heavy lyre." Gumilev's *engagement*, based on his view of art as action and of life as adventure, was equally foreign to Khodasevich, who treated both art and life as private and subjective experiences. Although nearer in spirit to Akhmatova than to any other poet, Khodasevich differs from her in his ability to submit emotion to the shock of reflection and to a detached contemplation of things and events.

Despite other, and perhaps more important, divergences, Khodasevich must be placed in the triad he ideally forms with Mandel'shtam and Pasternak. It matters very little that he was hardly ever connected with the one or the other: his mature poetry, though so independent and distant, belongs with theirs. With Mandel'shtam, whose point of departure was the quasi-Parnassian reaction of Acmeism, Khodasevich shares, for instance, a classical taste and a spirited wit. With Pasternak, whose work proceeds from a neoromantic interpretation of the Futurist creed, he has in common a "rage for order," an urge to find some sense and design in the chaos of immediate experience. If there is something which sets him aside from Mandel'shtam and Pasternak, it is his dependence on tradition, which for him means in practice almost exclusively Pushkin's example. In this he followed precedents already established by Brjusov and Blok. For those two older poets, however, the Pushkinian tradition had been a point of arrival, while for Khodasevich it was a point of departure. And the Pushkin whom the latter chose as his model was the Pushkin of *Evgenij Onegin* rather than the romantic lyricist: in brief, the master who had captured the fleeting magic of feeling in the prosaic syntax of neoclassical verse.

Vladislav Khodasevich was born in 1886 in Moscow in a modest family of Polish descent. He left Russia after the Revolution, and was forced to spend the most creative years of his life in exile, mainly in France, where he died in 1939, the leading figure among all *émigré* poets. With the exception of a few translations from Polish fiction and neo-Hebrew poetry, an abundant crop of critical writings, and a few other compositions in prose, the whole of Khodasevich's published output is contained in the following volumes of lyrics: *Youth* (1908), *The Happy Cottage* (1914), *The Grain's Way* (1920), all of which appeared in Russia; *The Heavy Lyre* and *Collected Poems*, which were published respectively in Berlin and Paris in 1922 and 1927. Of all his minor works, one should at least mention a book of literary memoirs, suggestively entitled *Necropolis* (1935); *Derzhavin* (1931), an outstanding monograph on the great Russian eighteenth-century poet; and the brilliant critical essay on "Pushkin's Poetic Economy" (1929).

This best of all Pushkin's modern disciples seems to have understood as well as his master the secret of poetic economy. In his case, this means the deliberate choice of the speech of reflection to express a state of constant emotional tension. Formally and externally, his poetry takes well-beaten paths; it follows the standards of tradition and observes the norms of common sense. This does not imply a tendency toward the conventional and the commonplace; without indulging in either the gnomic or the epigrammatic, Khodasevich's poetry produces the effect of a mature wisdom and achieves an astonishing mastery of both imagery and thought. Classical in temper, always keeping his inspiration under control, Khodasevich is one of those rare modern poets who treat with prudent skepticism the very poetic power which is their birthright. He never exalts the muse or the artist within himself. He looks with great awe at the mystery of life, which may well "make vain all thoughts and words." A prosaic kind of verse seems to him a fitter tool than a high-flown poesy to convey his impersonal and objective vision of men and things. The poet sees himself as a man among men, as a bourgeois like everybody else, or, as he says in the poem "Noon," "a passer-by, a citizen, in a brown coat and a derby, the same as all the others. . . ." Yet it is not without irony that in the same poem he magnifies his own physical size to convey the impression it makes on a boy playing at his feet. Still, instead of suggesting that contrast by comparing himself to Gulliver in the land of Lilliput, he prefers to describe his own person in terms of an inanimate and inarticulate landmark, as a huge and aged stone which has survived from an immemorial past.

This emphasis on the relative disproportion of things is one of Khodasevich's favorite motifs. Elsewhere he assigns a precarious and provisional greatness to modest domestic objects, while reducing to their mean size and scope cosmic and elemental things. This reciprocal metamorphosis occurs in the central image of "Ballad," a poem in *The Heavy Lyre*, when the poet fixes his gaze on a lamp hanging from the ceiling, to contemplate, as he says, "a sixteen-watt sun in a stucco sky." Such an interplay between the domestic and the cosmic does not imply that the poet fails to distinguish between the different levels of man's experience of himself and of the world. As a matter of fact, Khodasevich keeps strictly separate the spheres of emotion and reflection from those of creation and life. His inspiration is often sparked by a recurring awareness of transcendental and metaphorical antinomies, of the external dualism ruling man's existence and the whole universe. Yet the very task of his poetry seems to be to reconcile those antinomies, and to bridge the gap that separates opposite realms of being. This is why he often bases his images on a witty and systematic antithesis of different philosophical categories, as when he describes the process of living as "breathing the space of time"; or when he defines hope as a "sweet memory of the future." In another poem he develops a simile of perfect symmetry, by treating time as if it were the fifth element, the unique medium of human life, where men live as naturally as birds in the air, fish in the water, worms in the earth, and salamanders in fire.

The poet views the universal dualism of all forms of being as a natural feature of the human condition, as a mysterious grace leading our body and our mind in contrary directions, which, as he says in the poem "Ballad," turns our feet toward the underground fire and our head toward the sky and its stars. It was on the premise of such a view that the poet wrote one of his best poems, "Episode," where he re-evoked in the first person what a psychiatrist would call a case of split personality. There Khodasevich reworked in his own way the Romantic theme of the Alter Ego, which had so deeply fascinated the imagination of many Russian writers, from Gogol' and Dostoevskij to Blok. The novelty of Khodasevich's treatment of this theme lies in the detachment with which he looks at his own double, whom he catches in the act of sleeping, and whom he describes with calm objectivity, as a purely material image rather than as a spiritual vision.

Despite his longing after a cosmic order, the poet feels the powerful attraction of the forces of destruction and disaster, which endanger the integrity of both life and the self. Thus, in a poem highly reminiscent of the so-called "President's Song" in Pushkin's play *The Feast During the Plague*, Khodasevich avows that he feels the pathetic seduction of all historical catastrophes or elemental cataclysms, since, as he says, "the heart of man sports as playfully as a child just awakened when revolt or plague crash upon us, throwing time as wide open as the sky." Khodasevich recognizes the presence of chaos not only in the world of history, but also in the narrow sphere of private, ordinary life. Nothing is more significant in this respect than the highly original "Ballad," which voices the tragedy of being within the four walls of a room. The highest grace of Khodasevich's poetry, in contrast with the transcendental ambitions of the Symbolists, is to be seen in this ability to express the pathos of life in small proportions, engraving it on matter as hard as a mosaic.

A poetry of this kind requires a frugal use of words and a

sober employment of the poet's craft. Its double necessity is to open the way for introspection, and yet to restrain the flow of emotion. The poet achieves this difficult feat by adopting a moral attitude made of both candor and modesty. He may share the Decadent notion of poetic experience as a descent into a lower world; or the Symbolist conception of the poetic imagination as the soul's reminiscence of an earlier and higher existence. Yet his vision is neither apocalyptic nor mystic; Khodasevich ignores devils, angels, and even gods. He may treat man's life on earth as an exile of the soul, but by doing so he makes no less real either that life or this earth. It is this emphasis on the concrete that gives an objective quality to the revelations of his art, which, even more than spiritual, are ethical epiphanies. Such is the case with the beautiful poem "The Monkey," where the poet tells how once he discovered the signs of supreme moral nobility in a monkey's hand, which, in a joking gesture of friendship, he shook as if it were a human one; and how, by a tragic chance and an ironic twist, all this took place on the very day when time got out of joint for all men: "That was the day that they declared the war." The contrast between the central vignette and the finale of this piece (probably inspired by "The Navigation," one of Turgenev's prose poems) is eloquent proof that Khodasevich's chamber music may achieve effects as magnificent as those of a church organ.

IV

OSIP MANDEL'SHTAM

Osip Mandel'shtam was born in the Jewish quarter of Warsaw, in 1892, and spent his mature years in the two capitals. He died still relatively young, in faraway banishment; we do not know exactly when and where. It is rumored that in 1932 he was denounced for having imprudently recited a lampoon against Stalin in the house of a friend; that he was jailed and punished for this; that several years later he was released and then rearrested; and that in 1938 (other authorities give far different dates) he died in Vladivostok, in, or on his way to, a forced labor camp. The memory of his personality is vividly engraved in Viktor Shklovskij's *Sentimental Journey*, in the brilliant pages re-evoking the living conditions of a few young Russian writers during the early revolutionary years in Petrograd. Indifferent to both hunger and cold, oblivious of his bleak surroundings, Mandel'shtam is portrayed there while working at his poems, like a splendid "fly of marble," as Shklovskij puts it. It was also by taking such a stance toward life that Mandel'shtam fulfilled the literary ideals of the Acmeist movement, of which he had been an active and brilliant exponent in his youth.

Mandel'shtam's literary output is a small treasure, which originally was contained in four little books. The major part of his poetic production appeared at first in two slender volumes, the earlier of which, *Stone*, was issued before the First World War (1913). The other one was published in Berlin in 1922, under the Ovidian title *Tristia* (which is also that of its opening piece), but was reprinted the following year in Russia and renamed *A Second Book*. Both volumes were included in *Poems* (1928), the only full collection of Mandel'shtam's verse to appear in his lifetime. His prose, too, was originally contained in two volumes, partly containing the same materials, *The Noise of Time* of 1925, and *The Egyptian Stamp* of 1928. No line of Mandel'shtam, either old or new, ever appeared in print in Soviet Russia after the poet's political disgrace and subsequent death: and it is only thanks to the labors of two *émigré* scholars (Gleb Struve and Boris Filippov) and to the care of an *émigré* concern (Chekhov Publishing House) that we possess what up to now is the only edition of his *Complete Works* (New York, 1952) in both verse and prose. Yet it seems that the poet left important manuscripts which were not lost, and which all the friends of Russian letters hope to see some time in print.

Mandel'shtam's is a poet's prose, without being a poetic one. It is written with the rigor of verse, but with a music of its own. It is only in this sense that it has the virtues of his own poetry. Although couched in fictional shape, Mandel'shtam's prose leans toward the form of the essay, toward a personal but not autobiographical mode. Its aim is to recollect in obsessive tranquillity, through the perspective of fragmentary memories or episodes, the forlorn and chaotic atmosphere of our era. The sense it conveys is tragic, although the perspective is that of a closet drama. Thus, in a sort of lucid hallucination, with a quasi-cinematographic technique, *The Egyptian Stamp* brings before our eyes the so-called "Kerenskij summer," the interval before the uprisings of February and October. The writer recalls that brief and confused period not as a historical event, but as a metaphysical experience, perceived through the metamorphosis of memory and the metempsychosis of things: "The centrifugal force of time has dispersed our bentwood chairs, and the Dutch plates with the blue flowers. . . ." It is not the odyssey of a city or a people which forms the theme of the story's fragmentary visions, but rather the melancholy rhapsody of the soul, the private chronicle of daily life, ancient and timeless as the past of the race: "We reckon in years, yet in reality in each apartment on dim Kamennoostrovskij Alley time is divided into centuries and dynasties."

If Mandel'shtam's prose amounts to a limited number of pieces, in the main quite short, and all belonging to a short-lived phase of his career, the whole of his published poetry amounts to about two hundred lyrics, most of which were composed within a ten-year span, from 1910 to 1920. And, in contrast to his prose, it is a novel and strange sense of history which seems to have given inspiration to many of his lyrics. As had been the case with many older masters, either Decadent or Symbolist, such as Brjusov and Ivanov, and as was still the case with such younger craftsmen as the Acmeists Kuzmin and Gumilev, Mandel'shtam seems to have chosen historical erudition and literary learning as a mainspring of his poetic work. As a matter of fact, in his ability to recognize and to fulfill the imaginative potential of a cultural or scholarly subject, Mandel'shtam has, with the exception of Vjacheslav Ivanov, no rival among his peers. And like Ivanov, who was a classical philologist by trade, Mandel'shtam prefers in history the themes still offered to us by the glories which were Greece and Rome. Truly enough, Ivanov tends to translate classical and Hellenic myths in mystical terms, rendering them almost medieval or Byzantine in character, while trying at the same time to give an ancient, pagan dignity even to his poems on Christian or modern themes. In brief, the classical strain remains a permanent aspect of Ivanov's historical and religious syncretism.

Mandel'shtam's preoccupation with the classical and the Hellenic is not as exclusive and as serious as Ivanov's: generally he prefers to project his philological and archaeological reconstructions into an ironic atmosphere, as if he would place them in the cold and abstract light of a museum. All his learned poems are conversation rather than period pieces, and yet they typically convey the static and abstract quality of Mandel'shtam's vision. Hence the significance of the title of the poet's first collection, *Stone*; hence his predilection, rare in Russian poetry, for composition and architecture, for the "frozen music" of pure design. Thus, even when minuscule in scope, Mandel'shtam's art is monumental in quality, and it tries to transform the historical and the temporary into the untimely and the timeless. The poet once affirmed, paradoxically, that the poetry of the Russian Revolution should be classical in temper, and he saluted its advent with a neo-Pindaric ode, not devoid of an elegiac strain, which he entitled "Liberty's Twilight." Yet, as we already know and as T. S. Eliot averred, a modern poet can be classical only in tendency. That Mandel'shtam must have been aware of the same truth is shown by his splendid poem on Racine, expressing the poet's impossible longing for an art really able to separate, like a stage curtain, the opposite worlds of imagination and reality, of creation and experience. Beyond that curtain, Racine's heroes and heroines are frozen forever in their inflexible stage attitudes. Mandel'shtam yearns likewise for the absolute perfection of a vibrant, and yet motionless, pose, for the fixing of passion in a gesture both conventional and unique. For Hegel, the task of Greek art, especially of Greek sculpture, was to express life in the moment of habit, rather than in its instant of tension, or in its exceptional phases. Mandel'shtam's neo-classicism is a similar, all-too-modern, attempt to treat stasis as if it were no less a state of grace than ecstasis itself.

Mandel'shtam also likes to treat themes other than purely classical ones. Many of his poems deal with such divergent and extravagant topics as the poetry of Ossian and the architecture of Saint Sophia, or with such topical or fashionable subjects as Dickens' fiction, a game of tennis, or the projection of a moving picture. In general, he handles modern themes with caricatural mockery; or, when approaching such subjects in a more serious mood, he reinterprets them in classical or mythological key. This is what he does in the poem "Tristia," written in 1918, to convey the peculiar fate of modern man, which is to die or to kill. The scene of the poem is Petersburg, which the poet calls Petropolis and transforms into a mythical city, where he finds again the footprints of Proserpine. The central scene evokes the Russian popular, superstitious rite of fortune-telling according to the figures shaped by melting wax. The girl performing that rite assumes the proportion and likeness of a Sibyl. As for the men going to war, for whom the horoscope is read, they will meet their destiny in battle, without guessing, as the poet says, about "the Erebus of the Greeks."

The artists to whom Mandel'shtam may be likened are to be found in fields other than that of the verbal arts. He recalls Giorgio de Chirico, at least in the latter's attempt to represent classical landscapes or old Italian squares as both tragic and melodramatic décors. He recalls also the Picasso of the classical period with his ability to reduce human flesh to the heavy rigidity of inorganic matter, making it both plastic and lifeless. Mandel'shtam's figures are less huge and solid, and they are molded in plaster, although they look as if they were made of alabaster. In one of his most magnificent lyrics the poet offers to a friend the image and the gift of a chunk of honey which changes itself into sunlight after the creatures which produced it are turned into a necklace of dead bees. Yet the sense of his art is more genuinely conveyed by a far different metaphor or process: by this artist's attempt to embalm forever the worm of life within that amberlike matter which is the very substance of his poetry.

V

MARINA TSVETAEVA

One of the most gifted of the Russian poets of yesterday was a woman, who, like Khodasevich, was able to nurture the plant of her art on foreign soil, but who, forced to return to Russia, was fated to die, like Mandel'shtam, the victim of a social order which was not made for spirits like theirs. Endowed with a talent as genuine as Khodasevich's or Mandel'shtam's, it was her destiny to play in the annals of Russian poetry the role of Anna Akhmatova's antagonist, of whom she was the chief rival and only peer.

This woman, whose name was Marina Tsvetaeva, was born in Moscow in 1892, or, according to other authorities, in 1894. In 1921 she left Russia, to spend abroad twenty years of her life, mainly in Prague and Paris. Before emigrating she had already published two collections of poems, *Evening Album* (1910) and *Magic Lantern* (1911). The most important books she published in exile were the fairy tale in verse *King-Maiden* (1922) and two collections of lyrics, *Craft* (in the sense of French *métier*) and *Psyche* (1922 and 1923). During the Civil War, while her husband, Sergej Èfron, was fighting with the counter-revolutionary army in Southern Russia, she became, as has been said, the "chronicler" of the White movement and the "herald" of the White Guard. She did so in a collection of poems significantly entitled *The Swans' Camp*, which she might have published during her long exile. Yet, quite strangely, she failed to do so, and that collection appeared only posthumously, and as late as 1957, when the manuscript found an editor and publisher in Gleb Struve, one of the leading critics among the *émigrés*.

It seems that in the thirties Sergej Èfron became a Soviet agent. After being involved in a political murder, the poetess' husband disappeared without leaving any trace: it is rumored that he fled back to Russia, and that eventually he was shot. In 1941, for unknown reasons, the poetess, too, decided to return to her native land; for a while she lived in Moscow, where she worked at translating Georgian poetry, but at the height of the German invasion she was evacuated to a little town, where, one year and a half after her return, she hanged herself (1942). It was only in 1956 that Il'ja Èrenburg published an article making public her tragic end, and intimating that a selection of her old and new things would soon appear in print. The article, which was read as if it were an official "rehabilitation" of the poetess, was presented as a preface written for the forthcoming volume: but the promise so made has not yet been kept. We know that the poetess left a rich crop of poems, and that "their publication" (as Pasternak says in his *Sketch for an Autobiography*) "would be a great triumph and a great find for Russian poetry."

Marina Tsvetaeva learned her *métier* (we have seen that she took a Russian synonym of this term as the title of one of her books) from two very different sources. One was the "grand style" of the eighteenth century, as exemplified by Derzhavin, with his lofty rhetorics and weighty archaisms. The other was the popular tradition of the heroic or lyric folk song. Yet she learned also from her contemporaries, for instance Khlebnikov, whose example perhaps she followed when she freely reinterpreted in *King-Maiden* ancient Russian myths and old folk motifs. But the poet of her time who taught her most was the early Pasternak, whom Tsvetaeva resembles in her romantic temper, as well as in her expressionistic technique. As in Pasternak's case, the marks of her style are a tight syntaxis and an elliptic imagery, a discordant sound pattern and a rigid metrical design.

Tsvetaeva's poetry is deeply feminine, but of a femininity which is neither soft nor weak. Unlike Akhmatova, who cannot express her experience except personally and directly, by means of poems which read like fragments from a private diary, Tsvetaeva is often able to convey her vision of life through historical or legendary "masks." It is from the Biblical and the Christian tradition, as well as from mythological and literary lore, that she takes all the exalted figures of saints and knights, lovers and poets, heroes and heroines whom she turns into objects of praise: David and Saint George, Phaedra and Hippolytus, Don Juan and *Manon Lescaut's* Chevalier de Grieux, Pushkin and Byron, Napoleon and Marina Mniszek, the Polish princess who married the Pseudo-Dmitrij to seize with him the Russian crown. Tsvetaeva does not hesitate, however, to seek her idols or *personae* even among the women and men of her circle, paying her homage in verse to Anna Akhmatova or Aleksandr Blok. To the latter she consecrated a lyrical cycle full of loving admiration and of lucid psychological insight.

If Akhmatova speaks only with the voice of a fiancée, bride, or mistress, Tsvetaeva speaks also with the voice of wife, mother, and sister. Woman is in her poetry the equal of man, not in a modern, but in a primitive, almost heroic sense. So it is only natural that in *The Swans' Camp*, when re-evoking her ordeal as the wife of a man fighting faraway for a lost cause, she chose to echo the most famous passage in the *Lay of the Host of Igor'*, the complaint of Jaroslavna, waiting with trembling and fear for her princely husband, threatened by all the curses of war. Yet even in her less subjective and more elegant pieces, often written on ancient Greek themes, Tsvetaeva looks at life with primordial and barbaric simplicity, with a kind of rebellious fatalism. Like a tribal mourner, she both laments destiny and condemns it. She expresses the ferocious absurdity of the human condition, especially in times of storm and stress, with an almost stuttering diction, with sobbing, often monosyllabic words, with sharp masculine rhymes that rend the ear and tear the heart.

Sometimes Tsvetaeva conveys all the cruelty of life with the eloquence of an accusing finger, of a wordless and tearless grief. Nothing proves better the poignant power of her art than the closing stanza of a poem inspired by the Civil War, where, despite her partisan sympathies, she looks with equal terror and pity at the youths who fell on either side of the barricade. There the poetess produces a sense of tragic irony with a conjuring trick and with a verbal conceit: by inverting the emblematic colors of the two party flags and converting them into the all-too-real hues of blood and death. In those haunting lines the poetess projects a single horror within a double vision of the same lethal metamorphosis, reflecting and reversing itself into two parallel metaphors: "he from white turned red, blood coloring him; he from red turned white, death discoloring him." Unlike the Whites and Reds who fell in open battle or before an execution squad, Marina Tsvetaeva died by her own hand: yet even so, she perished as a belated victim of the same hecatomb.

CHAPTER TEN

POETS OF TODAY

T HE literary fashions or trends which conditioned technically the early, or even the later, writing of the poets who came
to the fore during the first decade after 1917 were part of the
vital inheritance left by both Acmeism and Futurism. From the
latter school came Nikolaj Aseev, born in 1889, who before the
First World War joined the "Centrifuga" group, of which Pasternak was also a member. This Moscow group was an offshoot of
Cubo-Futurism, and in this early stage of his career Aseev was
strongly affected, as shown by the poems of *The Night Flute*
(1914), by Khlebnikov's example. Soon afterward he chose, however more facile paths, merging in *The Steel Nightingale* (1922)
the cult for modern life with a rather old-fashioned sentimentality,
or with a romantic lyricism. The poetry of his maturity, more
ideological and partisan in temper, opened with a series of political
pieces, *October Songs* (1925), and with a few narrative poems in
revolutionary setting. From that period on, Aseev followed in the
footsteps of Majakovskij: and after the death of the latter he became his continuator, as well as his disciple. In 1940 he published
Majakovskij Begins, the first part of a verse biography of his teacher
and friend. The merits of Aseev's poetry, which is direct and
simple, are to be seen in its fresh treatment of current themes and
conventional motifs. The main task of this poet has been to adjust, without vulgarity, the diction and imagery of Futurism not

so much to the demands of official propaganda as to the conditions of Soviet culture and to the taste of a large audience.

A far more genuine and considerable poet of the same generation, at least in his early works, was Nikolaj Tikhonov, born in Petersburg in 1896, who drew instead on the Acmeists' doctrine and example. A volunteer in the First World War and a Red soldier during the Revolution, Tikhonov published his best pieces in two collections of verse, *The Horde* (1922) and *Hydromel* (1923), and in a volume of tales, *The Daring Man* (1932). Yet it was the topical and patriotic pieces in verse and in prose which he wrote during the Second World War that earned him a belated official recognition, as well as the presidency of the Union of Soviet Writers, a short-lived honor which did not survive Zhdanov's condemnation of Akhmatova and other Petersburg authors.

Tikhonov was one of the few poets who after the Revolution joined the "Serapion Brothers" and succeeded in putting into practice their literary doctrines in the medium of verse. Like them, he envisioned an art unsophisticated in content and sophisticated in form, the secret of which he sought to learn from the masters of the West. Thus in both *The Horde* and *Hydromel* Tikhonov chose as his own vehicle a modern type of "ballad," partly inspired by Kipling's poems of military life. The main theme of his poetry is war, as felt and seen by a man who goes through it with open eyes and a willing heart. His tone is martial and manly; his style, lucid and sober; the ring of his diction and meter, almost metallic. The poet views danger as a test and challenge by which the soul proves its mettle, using the body as a sword and a shield. His favorite word-image is "nail": he praises his comrades in arms by describing them as "hard as nails"; rejoices in the military experience which has made him "as simple as an iron nail"; and entitles as "Ballad of the Nails" a poem celebrating a naval crew on a suicide mission. Tikhonov's poems recall the tales of Babel', although they are less "poetic" than the latter, and never indulge in meditative asides or lyrical doubts. This does not mean that Tikhonov treats war as a theatrical and glamorous spectacle; far from it. The virile realism of his vision of war is evident in the best, most famous, and most significant lines he ever wrote, where enumeration and hyperbole emphasize the perplexing complexities involved in war itself. When war came, says the poet, "fire, rope, bullets, and axe greeted and followed us like footmen; a deluge slept in each drop; from pebbles mountains grew. . . ." Then "lies ate and drank with us; coins lost weight and ring; children were not scared by the dead." It was then, concludes the poet with a line that reads like his *ars poetica*, "that we learned magnificent, bitter, terrible words."

It is quite significant that the younger poets who grew to manhood after the Revolution followed the examples of both Aseev and Tikhonov, and merged the lessons of the Acmeists and the Futurists, vainly trying to embody them in a new school of their own. The attempt took place with the founding of Constructivism in 1924. Constructivism, being prevalently literary, was not directly connected with the movement by the same name which a group of Russian painters, engineers, and architects had launched in 1920 to bring abstraction and modern design into the visual arts. The lack of formal connection does not deny the existence of an ideal tie between later and earlier Constructivism. The leaders of the latter, however, had left Soviet Russia to continue working and experimenting abroad. The writers who took that name as their label remained at home, to see their movement, after a brief and feeble life, easily quenched by official disfavor in 1930, and to realize only too late the impossibility of reconciling literary novelty and artistic experimentation with the rigid dogmas of the Soviet creed. Like many other advance guards, Constructivism fought a rear-guard action, covering not so much a retreat as a rout.

Constructivism sought to formulate in literary terms the technological myth which the Soviets were to enforce on the Russian people with the Five-Year Plans. The man primarily entrusted with such formulation was Kornelij Zelinskij, the theoretician of the group, who stated the aim of the movement in the following sociological terms: "Constructivism, by applying to literature, and above all, to poetry (for the Constructivists are primarily poets), the same demands which the building of Socialism imposes in all cultural domains, expresses the cultural aspiration of the new Soviet intelligentsia. . . . One could say that Constructivism is the symptom of the birth of a new Soviet intelligentsia, which in its ideology and world view greatly differs from the old Russian intelligentsia, either mystic or nihilistic, affected, Oblomov-like or Onegin-like, by an impotent idealism." What all this meant in practice was that the group made its own, and adapted to present Soviet conditions, the Futurists' mystique of the machine and their worship of technology. The movement took a leaf also from the Formalist school of criticism, equally fated to premature death, and reduced poetic composition to a skillful manipulation of devices by which one could refit into new shapes traditional material or conventional forms. If Constructivism corrected or reversed in any way the Formalists' viewpoint, it was in the sense that instead of viewing subject matter as an aspect of formal structure, it often viewed formal structure as an aspect of content. The very term Constructivism was understood from an engineer's, rather than from an architect's, viewpoint: or at best, from the viewpoint of functional architecture, for which form is determined by the building's function, or by the criteria of material convenience and practical utility. Zelinskij pushed the analogy so far as to claim that poetry must be ruled by the standards of economy and efficiency, both of which he understood so literally as to make them meaningless. The motives which inspired this doctrine were mixed ones and included certainly the desire to court the favor of the regime, and to raise the writer to the honored status of a technical specialist in the field of ideas and forms. Thus there was both tragic irony and poetic justice in the fact that the regime cracked down on the Constructivists as hard as it had done with far greater literary heretics than they could ever be.

The poets of Constructivism were spared the unpleasant consequences of the liquidation of their movement, perhaps because their poetic practice had little connection with Zelinskij's doctrines. This certainly applies to its two leading masters, Sel'vinskij and Bagritskij, who had started their literary careers with a group of Odessa Jewish writers, of which Isaak Babel' was also a member. In their ambitious verse tales those two poets aimed at a vivid combination of popular storytelling and modernistic imagery. Their lyrical work is more independent, although it wavers between the extremes of a conscious absurdity and an unsophisticated naïveté. Il'ja Sel'vinskij, born in Simferopol' in 1899, began his career in 1924 with the advance-guard experiments of *Records* (the Russian *Rekordy* is an Anglicism, and has the meaning of the original word when used as a sport term), and with the humorously autobiographical *Notebook of a Poet* (1927), which contains amazing parodies of other poets. His "gypsy" poems are the best pieces he ever wrote, and they recall E. E. Cummings' work, with the peculiarities of their punctuation and syntax, and their admixture of graphic signs and technical symbols. The favorite form of Sel'vinskij's later work is the verse tale, which he used in *The Story of Uljalaev* (1927), relating the adventures of a band of marauders during the Civil War; and in *Pao-Pao* (1932), which has as its protagonist an overly anthropomorphic ape who ends by becoming an adept of Marxism.

Far more gifted than Sel'vinskij was his colleague Eduard Bagritskij (born in the Ukraine in 1896, with the surname of Dzjubin), who served as a Red soldier in the Civil War, translated Robert Burns, and died prematurely in 1934. His early collection *Southwest* (1928) looks almost like the work of a jejune Pasternak. Like Sel'vinskij, he adopted the verse-tale form and produced the best work of this kind in the *Lay of Opanas* (1925), relating the adventures of a Ukrainian peasant who joins the Greens, the agrarian anarchists led by the rebel Makhno, who fought with the Red against the Whites, and with the Whites against the Red. The story ends with the death of the protagonist, excuted for killing a commissar sent into the countryside to seize wheat. As indicated by its title ("lay" renders the *duma* of the original, which means "folk ballad" in Ukrainian), this poem is patterned after the heroic rhapsodies of old Little Russia, and it is quite significant that its author chose the form of the popular epos to sing of those who fought not for the Revolution, but against it. It is equally significant that Bagritskij was one of the many poets of his generation that were ultimately led to abandon these pure lyrical forms which, for giving expression to private feeling and personal experience, seemed to the regime even more dangerous than the semipopular narrative poems by which the same poets were evoking the picturesque and pathetic figures of some of its defeated enemies. By choosing to sing of outlaws and outcasts, Bagritskij and his companions attempted the only kind of romantic escape which was still possible at that time; yet by doing so they reduced poetry to a picturesque fancy, episodic and anecdotal, superficial and fragmentary, in brief, almost to a parody of itself.

It was by following the line of least resistance that these and other would-be pioneers of Soviet poetry were led into bypaths without issue. Starting as *neoteroi*, they ended as *epigones*, precisely because they failed to realize that the great achievements of art are attained only by those who stay on the royal road, which is often the hardest to travel on. No living Russian author seems to have known this as well as a poet slightly older than they, who became the master he was born to be by never deviating from the path marked for him by his star.

II

BORIS PASTERNAK: HIS LIFE AND CAREER

This poet is Boris Pasternak, who was born in Moscow in 1890. His mother was a gifted pianist, his father a well-known painter, who illustrated Tolstoj's novel *Resurrection*, and taught at the local Academy of Fine Arts. The young Pasternak devoted himself to the arts cultivated by his parents, especially music, which he studied under no less a master than the famous composer Skrjabin. He also studied philosophy at the Universities of Moscow and Marburg. In the latter, under the guidance of Hermann Cohen, he came into contact with the neo-Kantian and neo-Hegelian schools. He began his poetic career at a precocious age, in that feverish advance-guard atmosphere which marked the first prewar era. He was one of a special group of Moscow Futurists who were connected with Khlebnikov, but who also went back to other models, as recent as Ivan Konevskoj or as remote as Jazykov. That group took its name from the almanac *Centrifuga*, published in 1913, to which Pasternak contributed his earliest poems. The young poet was destined to keep a loose association with the Futurist movement, and later contributed to the *LEF* of Majakovskij. In 1914, he published his first volume of verse, *The Twin in the Clouds*, which remained unnoticed. His second book, *Above the Barriers*, appeared in 1917, and was already the work of an expert craftsman, although it did not bear the imprint of his more mature genius.

It was to be Pasternak's two succeeding volumes that would reveal the rarity and novelty of his gift. In 1922, when the poems collected under the title *My Sister, Life*, which had been written in 1917 and circulated for years in manuscript, finally appeared in book form, they marked the emergence of a major talent. In 1923, Pasternak published his second important collection, *Themes and Variations*, in which his style became at once more sober and more extreme. The best work from these two volumes, which exercised a perceptible influence not only on younger poets but also on the more established writers, was afterwards collected in *Two Books* (1927). After a long interval, Pasternak returned to lyric poetry with *Second Birth* (1933), which was followed in the same year by *Poems*, the first full collection of his verse.

It was in that period of time that the poet's ordeal began. He remained steadfastly loyal to his calling within a social order admitting no other loyalty than to itself. He had to fight single-handedly a sustained rear-guard action in order to avoid surrendering unconditionally to the political pressure of the regime, augmented by the vicious attacks of sycophantic critics, by the whispering campaigns and the outright calumnies of enemies and rivals. The main accusations leveled against him were that he had committed the unspeakable crimes of individualism and formalism, and that he had shown indifference, and even hostility, to Marxist ideology. His stubborn refusal to obey the party's "general line," and to change his poetry into an instrument of propaganda, was branded as a betrayal. The literary press treated him as an outlaw; the writers' association, as an outcast.

Yet, in a spirit not of compromise but of humility, Pasternak tried to give poetical expression to his desire to connect himself with the will of the Russian people. He did so by trying to understand the Russian present through the perspective of history, and in 1926 he published his poem *Spektorskij*, in which, following similar experiments by Belyj and Blok, he used the protagonist's character, whose name gives its title to this work, as an autobiographical mirror, reflecting not only the poet's personality, but also the society and the age out of which he had come. In the same years Pasternak wrote and published (1927) a cycle of lyrical fragments, re-evoking, under the title *The Year 1905*, the political turmoil of that year. That rhapsody was followed by a long, simple episode, *Lieutenant Shmidt*, more epic in tone and content, retelling the story of the mutiny of the battleship *Potemkin* in the Black Sea, with a naked power reminiscent of Èjzenshtejn's film.

It was in the same period that Pasternak composed his prose tales, which he collected twice, under the titles *Stories* and *Airways*, in 1925 and 1933. The most important of them is the opening piece, "The Childhood of Ljuvers," written originally in 1918, in a tone and style that Western critics have compared to Proust's, although it is more reminiscent of *Malte Laurids Brigge* by Rainer Maria Rilke. (The Austrian poet had remained a lifelong friend of the Pasternak family from the time of his journeys to Russia, when the elder Pasternak had painted his portrait.) The theme of this story is feminine puberty, the foreshadowings of womanhood in the body and soul of a young girl, which the writer evokes with psychological subtlety and poetic insight. In 1931 Pasternak published his literary and intellectual autobiography, which he entitled, with enigmatic irony, *The Safe-Conduct*. The narrative is written in the first person, yet the ego of the narrator never intrudes and often retires into the background, giving way to a detached representation of persons and places, of ideas and things. The last part of the book is dominated by the figure of Majakovskij, acting like a mask or a ghost. In the finale, which recalls the official funeral of that poet, the palpable, almost bodily presence of that monstrous abstraction, "our Russian state," haunts the scene. Quite understandably, the authorities never permitted a reprint or a new edition of *The Safe-Conduct*.

In the following years, Pasternak managed to evade the required lauding of the regime and still function as a writer by devoting almost all his energies to translating. In his youth he had translated many foreign writers, especially German, from the Romantics to the Expressionists, but later he was attracted to more exotic models, and in 1935 published a rich anthology of poets from that Caucasian region which is called Gruzija in Russia, and Georgia in the West. More recently he tried his hand at the tragedies of Shakespeare, producing splendid versions of such plays as *Hamlet, Macbeth, King Lear, Othello, Romeo and Juliet,* and *Antony and Cleopatra.* Yet even then he never gave up his own writing, although very little of his appeared in print after the publication of his *Collected Poems* in 1932 and 1936. A decade later he took advantage of the short-lived calm after the Second World War to publish two slim collections (the second is but an expansion of the first), entitled *On Early Trains* (1943) and *The Vast Earth* (1946). They were followed by a long, silent spell which the poet broke by issuing his translation of Goethe's *Faust* and later by publishing a few new poems in literary periodicals, during the brief thaw following Stalin's death.

III

BORIS PASTERNAK: HIS POETRY

Despite its native originality and independent growth, Pasternak's poetry still seems to preserve the traces of its early connection with Futurism. What ties his poetry to the Futuristic experiment, and especially to the manner of Khlebnikov, is his conception and treatment of the word. While the typical Decadent or Symbolist poet seems to control the music of language by yielding to it, Pasternak masters his medium by doing violence to the very nature of poetic speech. His idiom is like a mosaic made of broken pieces. The fragments are shapeless, and if they finally fit within the pattern of a line, or within the design of a poem, it is only because of the poet's will. The cement holding them together is either syntax or rhythm; more frequently, both. From his early beginnings, Pasternak tightened the syntax of Russian poetic speech as no modern poet had ever done. At the same time, in reaction against both the vagueness of late Symbolistic verse, which was a kind of *vers libéré*, and the declamatory effusions of *vers libre*, characteristic of Majakovskij and his followers, he chose to use, with strictness and rigor, duly regular and even closed metrical forms. In doing so he succeeded in reconciling within his poetry the demands of both the old and the new. Like all the most successful figures of the advance guard, Pasternak (who is its only surviving representative in Russia today) was thus able to prove that tradition also must play a role in the revolutions of art.

There is an obvious parallel between this historical function and the internal structure of the poetry of Pasternak. With terms taken from the vocabulary of our "new critics," one could say that his verse constantly aims at tension and paradox. His poems are equally ruled by passion and intelligence, or rather, by a reciprocal interplay of emotion and wit. This is why Prince Mirskij compared him to John Donne, by which that critic probably meant that Pasternak's poetry is "metaphysical" not in the original, but in the modern and revived, sense of that term. Yet his work is better understood if placed within the immediate and local tradition from which it sprang. If we do so, we may find that the concept of "transmental poetry" is the frame of reference we need. We know already that in their attempt to create a poetry purely verbal in essence, some of the so-called Cubo-Futurists wrote poems in what they named "transmental tongue," or in newly coined words without meaning, and with no other semantic value than that of their sound effects. The experiment was bound to fail; poetry can never become, at least in the sense that painting or sculpture can, an abstract art. Poetry cannot but be either expressionistic or ideational, and Pasternak made poetry nonrepresentational, so to speak, by forcing it to be both things at once. One could say that he succeeded where the Cubo-Futurists had failed, by using, instead of nonsense language, a highly complex linguistic mosaic, made of an interplay of denotative and connotative values: or, more simply, by employing a diction ruled at once by mental balance and emotional stress. It is only in such a context that one might define his style as a modern Baroque, reducing to sense and order a verbal matter apparently incongruous and absurd.

Pasternak's poetry, to quote a line from his favorite foreign master and friend, Rainer Maria Rilke, seems thus to lead *zum*

Arsenal den unbedingten Dinge. Yet in the process it changes all the nondescript objects cluttering the world of experience not into abstract symbols, but into living, suffering, humanlike creatures. The anthropomorphic pathos of Pasternak's imagination brings him closer to the Romantics than any other of his immediate predecessors with the exclusion of Blok. The poet must have been aware of this since, unlike his great and distant contemporary, Khodasevich, who found a master in Pushkin, he sought a model in Lermontov, the Russian poet who felt and understood better than any other the tears of things, and who would perhaps have approved of Pasternak's claim that "one composes verses with sobs." It is equally significant that in recent times Pasternak has shown some interest in Shelley, whose vision he finds akin to that of Blok. Yet Pasternak's neoromanticism is strange and novel: so strange and novel that it can be compared only to some of the most novel works of modern art. To use a double musical analogy, properly drawn from the field of Russian modern music, one could say that while Khodasevich is as neoclassic as the Prokof'ev of the *Classical Symphony*, Pasternak is as neoromantic as the Stravinskij of *The Rite of Spring* or of *The Firebird*.

The artistic game of Pasternak consists in a sort of balancing act: or in the attempt to fix in a precarious, and yet firm, equilibrium, a congeries of heterogeneous objects, of vibrant and labile things. His poetry seems to pass, almost at the same time, through two different and even opposite phases. The first is a moment of eruption and irruption, of frenzy and paroxysm; and second, which often overlaps the first, is the moment when matter seems to harden and freeze. Burning rivers of lava congeal at a nod. The sound and fury of lightning suddenly become, as in the poem so named, "a thunder eternally instantaneous." Fires are extinguished at a breath. Showers and thunderstorms abruptly stop; floods suddenly dry up. Often the same poem seems to be written now in hot, now in cold, blood. This dualism may perhaps be traced in, or symbolized by, the early education of the poet, which was both philosophical and musical. Yet, while his music ends in dissonance, and his logic leads to dissent, such a double discordance resolves itself into a harmony of its own.

The raw material of Pasternak's poetry is introspection. Yet Pasternak treats the self as object rather than as subject. Thus, in a nonmystical sense, one could apply to him Rimbaud's formula: *Car je est un autre.* Sometimes he seems to treat the psyche as a neutral and an alien being, to be seldom, and if possible only indirectly, approached. Hence the negative hyperbole by which he claims, in one of his poems, to have appealed in prayer to his soul only twice in a hundred years, while other men do so at every instant. Pasternak, with the firm hand of a hunter or tamer, always holds his own spirit in his power, like a fluttering, wounded bird, and often encloses it in the solid cage of a stanza, from which the winged prisoner vainly tries to escape through the broken mesh of a rhyme.

Many critics have remarked that Pasternak looks at the world with the eyes of one newly born. It would be better to say that he looks at it with *reborn* eyes. As suggested by the title of one of his books, poetry is for him a "second birth," through which man sees again the familiar as strange, and the strange as familiar. Yet, whether strange or familiar, every object is unique. To give the effect of this uniqueness, the poet paints every single thing as if it were a monad, unwilling or unable to escape from the rigid frame of its own contours. Such an effect is primarily achieved through the harshness and hardness of his imagery, through the frequent ellipses of his speech, through the staccato quality of his meter. Rhythmically, he prefers a line heavily hammered, where no stress is blurred, and every beat is pounded as in a heel dance. He fails, however, to extend this rapid, metallic quality to rhyme, which he treats with the negligence and freedom of Majakovskij, and which he describes, echoing perhaps Verlaine's famous definition (*ce bijou d'un sou*), as a "checkroom ticket."

Though some of his poems are romantically set against the lofty mountains of the Caucasian landscape, Pasternak usually prefers a restricted, bourgeois, and prosaic scenery, such as a city park, a country orchard, a home garden, or a villa in the suburbs. Yet even "back-yards, ponds, palings" are not mere backdrops, but, as the poet says, "categories of passions, hoarded in the human heart." His poetry thus leans toward a highly personal version of the pathetic fallacy, involving in his case not only nonhuman creatures, such as animals and plants, but also inanimate things, or manmade objects. For many of his poems Pasternak chooses, like Mallarmé in his *poèmes d'intérieur*, indoor settings. Yet, unlike the French poet, the Russian introduces within the four walls of a room cosmic powers and elemental forces. This is especially true in the cycle "Themes and Variations," which is part of the book by the same title. In the third piece of this cycle Pasternak describes the now empty study where Pushkin has just finished writing his famous poem "The Prophet." Great geographical and historical landmarks, from the arctic city of Archangel to the river Ganges, from the Sahara to the Egyptian Sphinx, seem to witness in silence, along with the molten wax dropping from a burning candle, the drying of the ink on the manuscript.

In this, as in other poems, Pasternak surprises not only by a violent association of disparate elements, but by the even more violent dissociation of each one of them from the frame of reference to which it naturally belongs. The ripe pear which one of his poems describes while falling to the ground along with its leafy stem and torn branch can be taken as an emblem of his art. Hence the frequency in his verse of such words and ideas as "fracture" or "breach." At the end of the closing poem of the cycle "Rupture" (meaning here a lovers' quarrel, or their break), even the opening of a window is equated with the opening of a vein. In the same piece the poet transfers the trauma of life to an uncreated thing: for instance, to the piano, which "licks its foam," as if it were a human being in an epileptic fit. Yet even in metaphors like these the poet transcends both pathos and bathos, reshaping the disorder of experience into a vision of his own. If he succeeds in doing so, it is because in his poetry (as he said in *The Safe-Conduct*) the author remains silent and lets the image speak. In this ability to infuse words with passion, rather than passion with words, Pasternak has no rival among his contemporaries, and, among the poets of the previous generation, he yields only to Aleksandr Blok.

While Majakovskij's imagery is hyperbolic and iconoclastic, as it tries either to sublimate reality or to degrade it, Pasternak's is dramatic and pathetic, aiming at conveying the poet's vital experience in psychic terms. His metaphors tend to express the shock and wonder of being in abridged and concentrated form. In his recent *Notes on Translating Shakespearean Tragedies* (1954), the poet bases his theory of metaphor on the truth which the old saying *ars longa vita brevis* seems to have stated once for all; "hence metaphors and poetry," says Pasternak, and concludes: "imagery is but the shorthand of the spirit." As hinted in these words, Pasternak views metaphor not as an emblem or symbol, which suggests and conceals, but as a graphic scheme or a sketchy outline of the experienced thing. This may well be the reason why this artist has never indulged, like so many modern poets, in the false mystique of his own calling and craft. Poetry is for him not the revelation of a higher harmony, but simply the direct expression of "the dissonance of this word."

A poetry so understood gives the immediate sense of a reality endowed with no other glamor than that of being reality itself; poetry, as Pasternak says, is "a suburb, not a refrain." The dreams of such a poet are made of the stuff life is made of. One could then say that this artist has always unconsciously followed the principle which he has recently uttered through the fictional protagonist of his last book: "Art never seemed to me an object or aspect of form, but rather a mysterious and hidden component of content." Such a statement indicates the importance of that book, which is worth discussing at length, even though the medium in which the poet chose to write it is not lyric verse, but narrative prose.

IV

BORIS PASTERNAK: THE CASE OF DOCTOR ZHIVAGO

It was in April 1945 that Pasternak announced in the Leningrad literary journal *The Banner* the imminent completion of a work in progress, entitled *Doctor Zhivago*. The author defined it as "a novel in prose," an obvious play on the subtitle "novel in verse" of Pushkin's *Evgenij Onegin*. The announcement was followed by a series of poems, supposedly written by the novel's protagonist. (The series failed to include those of Doctor Zhivago's poems which are

Christian in tone and religious in content.) Although the poet declared that the series was destined to close the novel as a fictitious appendix of posthumous papers or documents, through which the reader would understand better the personage to whom the writer attributed their authorship, everybody read those pieces as if their real author had written them in an autobiographical vein rather than in a fictional key. Later on, when the "thaw" which followed Stalin's death was already over, Pasternak submitted the complete draft to the Moscow literary monthly *New World*, but its editors (including such well-known writers as Konstantin Fedin and Konstantin Simonov) rejected the novel with a letter which convinced Pasternak that his book could never appear in Soviet Russia without changes so radical as to disfigure it. Shortly afterward the author handed the manuscript to a scout of Giangiacomo Feltrinelli, an Italian publisher with left-wing leanings. Notwithstanding his political sympathies, and despite official Soviet protests, Signor Feltrinelli managed to issue in 1957 an Italian translation of the original text. This was followed a year later by versions in French, English, and other languages, many of which became best sellers shortly after they appeared, making of the book a world-wide success. As for the original text, it appeared in the early months of 1959, under the imprint of the University of Michigan Press. It was in the wake of this triumph that Pasternak was also able to publish abroad in 1959 his *Sketch for an Autobiography*, originally written for a project which failed to materialize, a new, complete edition of his poetic works.

Doctor Zhivago, this new and challenging product of Pasternak's talent, is huge in size and broad in scope. The narrative rehearses the life and fate of its hero from his childhood to his premature death on the eve of the great Stalinist purge. Raised in the idealism of the early part of the century, Zhivago trains himself to become both a doctor and a poet, thus following the double call of charity and grace. He marries, but the Revolution forces him to settle in the Urals, where he is forever separated from his family and is made to serve as a medical officer in a Red guerrilla unit during the Civil War. His only consolation is his love for Lara, an old Moscow acquaintance, who represents in the novel the intuitive wisdom of life. When the crisis is over, he returns to Moscow, and in 1929 he dies there of a heart attack.

The narrative of Dr. Zhivago's existence merges with that of other, numberless characters, originally connected as neighbors, relatives, or friends, and who, in the course of the story, meet again in the most surprising circumstances. Although traditional in structure, the novel lacks a well-made plot: coincidence works beyond the limits of verisimilitude, taxing the credulity of the reader, and failing to raise the whims of chance or the writer's fancy to the level of either destiny or providence. Deprived of an epic or tragic design, the narrative unfolds as a rhapsody: and this explains why all its beauties are but fragmentary ones. There are many memorable episodes, but the novel's high point is the section describing the hibernation of the Red partisans in the wilderness of the far North, and the attempt by some of their wives to reach them by cutting a path through the snow and ice of a primeval forest.

The protagonist survives many physical trials, besides that of winter; yet he dies still young, worn out by an inner ordeal, wasted by the fever of life. Up to the end he faces each test with both the passive compliance of his will and the active resistance of his conscience. He acts at once like a witness and a victim, never like an avenger or judge. His mind often says "yea" to the reality to which his heart says "nay." Ivan Karamazov accepted God while rejecting the world He had created; Doctor Zhivago similarly accepts the postulate of the Revolution while rejecting many of its corollaries. From this viewpoint there is no doubt that the protagonist represents the author's outlook. The writer refuses, however, to intervene directly in the narrative; he thinks only with the thoughts of his characters, and speaks with no other words than theirs. Yet we hear his unique voice in the descriptive passages, and especially in those vivid images by which he constantly suggests to the reader that man, as well as time, is out of joint.

Perhaps the only characters who speak solely for themselves are those representing the younger generation in the novel's epilogue. The latter projects Russian life as seen now, twenty years after the death of the protagonist, in the immediate aftermath of the Second World War. There we meet again also some of the novel's main characters. The regime has recalled them before their term from deportation and exile; and they have rehabilitated themselves politically by defending the fatherland against the German invaders. It is difficult to say whether Pasternak considers these men and their sons as the children of the old bondage or the harbingers of a freer covenant. In a sense they seem to turn more toward the past than toward the future: perhaps they are also, as the author says of many others, naïve and innocent slaves who cannot help idealizing the slavery which is still their lot. Survivors of one upheaval, they may well disappear in the next one.

Despite all appearances to the contrary, it is this perplexing epilogue, more than any other parallel, which reveals that Pasternak wrote *Doctor Zhivago* — as other readers have already remarked — on the pattern of *War and Peace*. It is well known that Tolstoj at first conceived of his great novel as a long introduction to the homecoming, after thirty years of Siberian exile, of an old "Decembrist." The conception was discarded, but its residues are still visible in the epilogue of Tolstoj's masterpiece, which projects the Romantic liberalism and the naïve political idealism of Pierre and Nikolinka, the young son of Prince Andrej. In the light of his historical knowledge, the Russian, if not the Western reader knows that both tutor and ward are marked for sacrifice by their political dreams. Yet, despite its strong ties with Tolstoj's masterpiece, *Doctor Zhivago* is not a historical novel in the sense of *War and Peace*, since it deals with the contemporary age, an epoch not yet closed. Hence its epilogue is problematic rather than prophetic. Yet this difference is not important; whether or not it is a historical novel, *Doctor Zhivago*, like *War and Peace*, is written against history. What really matters is that Pasternak's protest rests on other grounds, and may well contain a message just the opposite of Tolstoj's. In *War and Peace* all the violence and cunning of history ultimately yield to the law of nature, to the universal principles of life and death, to the wars and peaces of being, which reduce strategy and diplomacy to senseless games, vainly attempting to shape the destiny of the human race. In Tolstoj's view mankind survives the ordeal of history in the wholeness and singleness of the species. The immortal cell of human life is the family, which triumphs, always and everywhere, over the destructive force of that monster which men call "reason of state." In Tolstoj's novel the issue is simplified, since the "reason of state" is symbolized by the aggressive imperialism of a foreign power; hence patriotism coincides with the moral and practical interests of that patriarchal household which for Tolstoj represents an ideal way of life.

Pasternak, however, sees the perfection of human existence in the person, in the inviolate integrity of its inner conscience. Such a form of being implies the refusal of all constraints, including the ties of blood and the bonds of the heart. This is why his hero must go his way even though against his own will, never to rejoin his wife and offspring; and perhaps his almost fleshless love for Lara should be seen as the sign of a personal destiny which must unfold itself in a cold and distant solitude, far away from the comforting warmth of the fireplace, from the charmed circle of the family nest. *Doctor Zhivago* differs from *War and Peace* in its view of the human condition; it differs, also, in its interpretation of the function of history. In Pasternak's novel history manifests itself as civil war and domestic strife, in a "permanent revolution" which is at once material and spiritual warfare, a total struggle without quarter or truce. Through technology, ideology, and social planning, history is now able to submit to its will the nation, the class, and the family — perhaps the world itself. But its weakest victim may be also its most elusive enemy, and that victim and enemy is the single person, the individual soul. Hence the voice protesting here is the one that says not "we," but "I." Here it is not Mother Russia, but one of her orphan children, who, like a fairy-tale Kutuzov, defends the homeland of the soul, the little realm of personal dignity and private life, first by trading time for space rather than space for time, and then by withdrawing into other dimensions than those. Such a stubborn retreat of the spirit, or, if we wish, the passive resistance of an inflexible soul which repels the temptation as well as the threat of all violence, is *Doctor Zhivago*'s main motif, perhaps its only one; and it is the exceptional nobility of this theme that turns Pasternak's novel, if not into a masterpiece, at least into a spiritual document of great significance, which brings to us a very different message from that of *War and Peace*. Nothing conveys better the sense of this difference than the two plants symbolizing the "tree of life" in each novel. In one we have the old oak which Prince Andrej suddenly sees rejuvenated by the sap of spring, with its once bare trunk and despoiled limbs covered by a crown of new leaves; in the other we have that evergreen thicket, almost buried by ice and snow, holding high a branch full of berries in the heart of the Siberian winter. Pasternak's "golden bough," unlike Tolstoj's, is thus a burning bramble that shines and consumes itself mystically and ecstatically in the desert of the self, in the cold land of the spirit.

Despite the urgency and immediacy of its message, *Doctor Zhivago* must be viewed as an old-fashioned novel even if looked at from a less superficial perspective than that of its conventional structure. Its spiritual quality may be conveyed by saying that Goethe's definition of the novel form as a "subjective epos," hardly fitting for *Madame Bovary* or *War and Peace*, seems to suit *Doctor Zhivago* almost as well as *Werther*. As for the limitations of Pasternak's novel, they may be hinted at by remarking that *Doctor Zhivago* is unable to become a new *Wilhelm Meister*: that there the "subjective epos" fails to grow and ripen into a *Bildungsroman*. The reason for this is that its main character, who acts as if he were both accepting and refusing the lesson of history, seems already to know all too well the lessons of life. The novel treats all events or experiences as if they were not dreams or crises, but tests or ordeals, which the protagonist undergoes more like a martyr than like a hero, and which he overcomes with the help of a grace which is not of this world. This, as well as the fact that all its figures are not painted in the round but drawn like abstract, allegorical outlines, turns *Doctor Zhivago* into a kind of morality play. It is this quality of the novel's vision that fully justifies Pasternak's use of religious imagery and Christian symbolism. Such imagery and symbolism need not be explained as polemical devices, or as the signs of the author's conversion to another creed. Like many a poet raised in another faith, or who lost his religious beliefs, Pasternak seems to have found no better language than the one which the Christian imagination shaped forever to convey the sacraments and the redemptions of the soul.

In an article published in *Partisan Review* immediately after the Italian edition of the novel, Nicola Chiaromonte described *Doctor Zhivago* as "a meditation on history, that is, on the infinite distance which separates the human conscience from the violence of history, and permits a man to remain a man. . . ." This is true, and well said, and it is no less true that the extension and depth of such a meditation represents something new in Pasternak's work. There is no doubt that in such poems as *The Year 1905* and *Lieutenant Shmidt* the poet had tried to come to terms with historical reality, rather than to face it as a critic and a judge. Only once did he express his sense of alienation from Soviet society: in that page of his long autobiographical essay *The Safe-Conduct* where he described Majakovskij's funeral, haunted by the weird presence of that state power which the dead poet had served only to be crushed by it. As for Pasternak's lyrical poems, they had often expressed in passing (and not without a sense of guilt) the poet's attempt to shun or to transcend the historical experience of his nation and time. Nothing exemplifies better such an attempt than an early piece dealing with the secluded workings of the poetic imagination, where the poet's voice suddenly bursts out with the question: "Children, what century is it, outside in our courtyard?" That question, both sophisticated and naïve, hints that the poet was then convinced that the artistic mind is innately indifferent to the dimension of time, to the category of history. Later, however, Pasternak seemed to realize that such an indifference is impossible, and that the self was bound to merge, whether willingly or unwillingly, with the historical process. He once conveyed the sense of this awareness in a famous line where he significantly spoke in the first person plural, although that plural refers to a few, rather than to the many: "We were people: we are epochs now." But it is true that in another poem he claimed that the poet could at least evade contemporary history by projecting himself into the future, or, as he said, by escaping like steam, through the chinks of fate, from the burning peat of dead time.

Many similar statements could be quoted from Pasternak's earlier and later verse: yet, taken together, all of them sound like apologies which the poet addressed not so much to the regime as to public opinion, or rather, to an elite able to understand equally the reason of poetry and the reason of state. Yet the poet seemed to know, at least in the depth of his heart, that any reconciliation between art and politics was fundamentally impossible. Hence that sense of both pride and shame in all of Pasternak's statements on the subject: the pride of his unconquerable loneliness, and the shame of being unable to pay the Revolution the tribute which all pay, and which may well be justly due it.

Pasternak continued to grapple with these questions during the long years of a silence which was at least in part self-imposed; and at the end of that period he reached the conclusion that lyrical poetry had become too limited and subjective a vehicle to allow him to express what was no longer a purely private attitude toward the problematics of revolution and the dialectics of history. After presenting his poet's case in verse, he felt that now he should present the case of man in prose. The writer was still in an apologetic mood, but the apology he now wanted to make was a far more universal one; and he wished to address it, beyond official Russia, to the Russian people, and even to his Western brethren. He felt that the proper vehicle for such an apology, which was also to be a protest, could be only fictional and narrative prose, the traditional tool of the Russian literary genius, which has found the master road of its ethos and art in that "classical" and "critical" realism of which Socialist Realism was but a monstrous caricature. If Pushkin's "poetry" had never denied "truth," so the "truth" of the "classical" and "critical" realists had never denied "poetry"; and this may help us to understand why, the first time Pasternak spoke in public of the novel he was then writing, he called *Doctor Zhivago*, with a formula which was not a mere pleonasm, a "novel in prose."

The poet himself recently explained this new aesthetic and moral view in a reply to a series of questions submitted to him by a South American magazine: "Fragmentary, personal poems are hardly suited to meditations on such obscure, new, and solemn events. Only prose and philosophy can attempt to deal with them. . . ." Here Pasternak seems to re-echo, unknowingly, Sartre's statement that prose, unlike poetry, should always be *engagée*; nor does it matter that *engagement* for Pasternak involves different, and even opposite values: not social obligations but moral ones. Pasternak seems to feel that such an *engagement* was impossible while he was only a lyrical poet; and this is why the author of *Doctor Zhivago* spoke disdainfully of his poetic work in his reply to that questionnaire. By doing so he merely underscored something at which he had hinted in the novel itself. Nothing in *Doctor Zhivago* has a more autobiographical ring than the comment on the literary career of the protagonist. According to his creator, Doctor Zhivago "had been dreaming of writing a book on life, in which to express the most wonderful things he had seen and understood in the world. Yet for such a book he was too young, and meanwhile he went on writing poems, like a painter who all his life draws studies for a painting still in his mind."

Yet if these words apply to the author himself, as the latter undoubtedly meant them to do, then what dictates the truth they may contain is not insight, but hindsight. It would be unfair to Pasternak both as man and writer to accept his retrospective claim that his poetic production was but a gradual preparation for *Doctor Zhivago*, which is a moral act and a psychological document of great value, but not the single culmination of his work. His poems are more than simple preludes to the novel; and though *Doctor Zhivago* towers over all Soviet fiction, this is due not only to Pasternak's stature as a novelist but also to the mediocrity of his rivals. What I prefer to emphasize is that this "novel in prose" proves more passionately and eloquently, yet in a less spirited and witty way than his poems, the same truth: that even in Communist Russia there are moral "corners" or spiritual "pockets" permitting the cultivation of the most bourgeois of all psychological activities, which could be defined in literary terms as the "sentimental education" of the soul.

In his poetry and his earlier prose, no less than in this novel, Pasternak had asserted and defended the private rights of the spirit in a forthright manner, without a wrong idealization, or a false mystique. Pasternak has never uttered to history, revolution, or society any ecstatic *noli me tangere*, any aesthetic *noli tangere circulos meos*. He has always known, as he says in one of his poems, that when in contact with reality human passion cannot heed the warning which reads "Fresh paint: do not touch." In short, Pasternak has never longed after a purity which is not of this world. He is one of those who feel that the soul is too rooted in life to be disinfected, as if it were merely a wounded limb. We may "purge" the soul, rather than "cleanse" it; and this is the catharsis which *Doctor Zhivago* in the end finally achieves. Perhaps after such an act of purgation, the author might feel free to publish poetry again. Like a Jonas delivered from the whale, he may now walk again on the mainland of his art. If we must hope that he will do so, it is because Pasternak's poems are more vital and exciting than this novel, which lacks the inner tension of his previous works in verse or prose, so challenging in their inborn advance-guardism. Sooner or later Pasternak may heed once more the command he once uttered to his muse: "Hurry, my verses, hurry; never have I so needed you before."

In view of this, it is perhaps worth remarking that when the Swedish Academy decided, in October 1958, to crown Boris Pasternak with the second of the two Nobel Prizes ever granted to Russian writers, it chose to honor him as poet as well as novelist. That, after having gratefully accepted that deserved honor, Pasternak was forced by the vilifications of the Soviet press, and by such official acts as his expulsion from the writers' association, first to reject the greatest of all international literary awards, and then to address a pathetic and noble petition to Khrushchev, lest the regime deprive him of his birthright, of the privilege to live, work, and die on his native soil, is another story. There is no doubt that it was this scandal, even more than the circumstances that had led the writer to publish his novel abroad, that stirred in the West the heated controversy now going under the name of Pasternak's case. Sad as it is, the tale cannot be forgotten, and should be retold again and again, not only in admiration, to bless the gift of the poet, but also in anger, to curse that party or state power which, like another Moloch, demands every day a new holocaust. Not content with the thousands of nameless victims on which it has built its jails, its fortresses, and its factories, the Soviet regime seems to require the public sacrifice of their life, liberty, or happiness even by those artists, who, like Majakovskij and Esenin, or like Akhmatova and

Pasternak, either remained the loyal friends of the Revolution, or refused to become its active enemies.

V

EPILOGUE

The name of Boris Pasternak, whose most important work had already been written before 1930, gloriously closes the history of modern Russian poetry, if we take that adjective as something more than a mere chronological term. It would be hardly fruitful to bring up to date the chronicle of Soviet verse, since what we have been witnessing after that date is, to speak clinically, but a case of arrested growth. It is true that before that turning point there resounded for a while the mischievous and whimsical voice of Nikolaj Zabolotskij, who was, however, first reprimanded into silence, and then tamed into that parrotry which seems to be the supreme law of Soviet art. It is equally true that more than a quarter of a century later a little anthology entitled *The Day of Poetry* (1956) revealed in a passing glimpse the promising talent of the still unknown but no longer young Leonid Martynov, whose poems seem to join a clever mimicry of Khlebnikov's verbal experiments with a pathos and fancy of their own. Yet one or two swallows do not make a spring: and Zabolotskij and Martynov do not represent Soviet poetry as fully as such a successful mediocrity as the poet and novelist Konstantin Simonov (born in 1915), who gained popular fame and official prestige with the cheap, patriotic, and sentimental songs he wrote in wartime. In such a context, and despite Simonov's failure, it is perhaps worth noticing that some of the best lyrics ever composed in Soviet Russia were inspired by the war, felt as a universal experience, involving all human beings, even beyond the front lines. What is perhaps even more significant is that the most touching notes of this war poetry were struck by two women, Ol'ga Berggol'ts and Margarita Aliger, while living through the siege of Leningrad and watching the agony of their beloved city.

Yet, when all this is said, it still remains true that the curve which Soviet poetry has been following up to now has been, and still is, a descending one. Nor is there any reason to believe that

339

the process will reverse itself in the foreseeable future. Even the most indulgent observers of the Russian literary scene are willing to admit that no new poet worth the name is flourishing on the wasteland of Soviet poetry. After all, despite the two short-lived parentheses which allowed for a slight relaxation of controls (one occurring after the end of the war, the other, after Stalin's death), the pressure of the regime on the artist and the writer, even when discarding its most cruel instruments of coercion, has hardly decreased, in either range or intensity. Nobody can predict whether history will allow for a new thaw, which will melt the frozen landscape of Russian culture and last long enough to restore a milder climate, far more favorable to artistic creation and spiritual growth. Even so, it will take a long time for new talents to appear on the horizon. It is not paradoxical to affirm that the Soviet environment may have been even more lethal for new plants than for some of the old. One could say that Red Russia has fulfilled Shigalev's prophecy (in Dostoevskij's *The Devils*) that revolution would strangle all geniuses in their cradles. Perhaps it would be more exact to say that the Soviet revolutionary order has prevented new geniuses from being born, by creating a suffocating atmosphere where adult organisms may still survive, but where no new germ can grow.

The hope that a radical transformation of the regime will be immediately followed by the sudden apparition of hidden masterpieces, nursed in silence or solitude, is a false one. Masterpieces or exceptional works do not remain hidden, as the case of *Doctor Zhivago* proves so well. Nor must we forget that *Doctor Zhivago* is a nineteenth-century novel written by a twentieth-century poet, who found it easier to transcend Soviet artistic reality by looking backward. What we cannot expect even from the "inner" *émigrés* of Soviet culture is that they look forward, that they shape in secret a future poetry or art. Advance-guard experimentation is possible in the garrets of our Latin Quarters or Greenwich Villages, but not in the attics or cellars of Soviet apartment houses. History has proved vain the expectation that daring and unorthodox works of art would be unburied and come to light in Germany after the Nazi regime crumbled into dust. German art has not yet fully regenerated itself from Hitler's curse of all "degenerate art." As for the good films and novels that appeared in Italy since freedom was restored, they were made or written after, not before, Fascism's downfall. This suffices to prove that a totalitarian society tends to destroy the seed of creation while it is still in the womb.

It seems thus fitting to close this study of the poetry of modern Russia with the generation which came to the fore before the great purge, since the latter made a free spiritual activity definitely impossible. The period which this book has surveyed thus covers a span of time shorter than half a century, from the 1890's to the 1930's. Those forty years went fast, at the all-too-rapid pace imposed by the forced march of history, and consumed three generations in the process. No observer or witness is yet able to say at this stage whether the contributions of those three generations will remain in the annals of Russian culture as the pledge of a brighter future, or as a vain sacrifice. The perennial destiny of art and poetry is either to perish from the memory of man, or to transcend the historical moment out of which they sprang. When they do so, they are reborn from their own ashes, like the phoenix. Hegel foretold that art will die when philosophy becomes the single, universal principle, ruling civilization and history itself. It would be all too tempting to assume that that prophecy has proven true for the very society which claims to have opened a new historical era for all mankind by submitting to the standard of reason and the laws of science even the world of man. In such a case one might also recall, not without irony, that that society is but the issue of the dreams of one of Hegel's disciples, Karl Marx.

Yet man cannot believe in the death of poetry and art. Poetry and art may decline and disappear from sight as the sun at each sunset. But one bright morning they will reappear anew. This will occur sooner or later also in Russia, when her culture will dispel the two plagues still afflicting it. One, the more peculiar of the two, is what Western Communists have termed, with words which for them sound like praise, "party patriotism." The other blight is perhaps more dangerous and lasting, since it plagues all cultures at the difficult moment when they challenge their tradition, and are at the same time challenged by the outside world. Its name is "cultural nationalism," although it could be named "spiritual provincialism" as well. The attitude it fosters and represents prevents a culture from seeking the necessary equilibrium between universal values and particular, local demands. The nemesis of that attitude, as Goethe once said, is to lead a literature to ape its own most obvious image, and ultimately to die of boredom with itself. Yet the Russian literary tradition is too strong and rich to be forever condemned to such an inglorious end.

BIBLIOGRAPHY

INDEX

GENERAL BIBLIOGRAPHY

A. HANDBOOKS AND SURVEYS OF RUSSIAN LITERARY HISTORY

1. GENERAL

Baring, M., *An Outline of Russian Literature*, London 1910; Hofmann, M., Lozinsky, G., Motchoulsky, C., *Histoire de la littérature russe*, Paris 1934; Lo Gatto, E., *Storia della Letteratura Russa*, Florence 1950; also, *Storia della Letteratura Russa dalle origini ai giorni nostri* (6 vols.), Rome 1927–1937; Luther, A., *Geschichte der russischen Literatur*, Leipzig 1924; Mirsky, D. S., *A History of Russian Literature: From the Earliest Times to the Death of Dostoevsky*, New York 1927 (the best handbook in English); Muchnic, H., *An Introduction to Russian Literature*, New York 1947; Setschkareff, V., *Geschichte der russischen Literatur*, Bonn 1949; Slonim, M., *The Epic of Russian Literature: From Its Origins Through Tolstoy*, New York 1950 (a very useful survey); Stender-Petersen, A., *Geschichte der russischen Literatur* (2 vols.), Munich 1957.

2. MODERN PERIOD

Brodskij, N., L'vov-Rogachevskij, V., and Sidorov, N., *Literaturnye manifesty*, Moscow 1929 (a collection of all the Russian literary manifestoes since Symbolism); Evgen'ev-Maksimov, V., *Ocherki istorii novejshej russkoj literatury*, Leningrad 1925; Gorbachev, G., *Ocherki sovremennoj russkoj literatury*, Leningrad, 1926; Ivanov-Razumnik, R., *Russkaja literatura 20 veka*, Petrograd 1920; also, *Russkaja literatura ot 70-kh godov do nashikh dnej*, Berlin 1923; L'vov-Rogachevskij, V., *Novejshaja russkaja literatura*, Moscow 1922; Mikhajlovskij, D., *Russkaja literatura 20 veka, s 90-kh godov do 1917*, Moscow 1939; Nikitina, E., *Russkaja literatura ot simvolizma do nashikh dnej*, Moscow 1926; Rozanov, I., *Russkie liriki*, Moscow 1929; Sajanov, V., *Ot klassikov do sovremennosti*, Leningrad 1929; Vengerov, S. (ed.), *Istorija russkoj literatury 20 veka* (3 vols.), Moscow 1914–1916; Volkov, A., *Ocherki russkoj literatury kontsa 19 i nachala 20 veka*, Moscow 1955; also, *Poèzija russkogo imperializma*, Moscow 1935.

Arseniew, N., *Die russische Literatur der Neuzeit und Gegenwart*, Mainz 1929; Lo Gatto, E., *Storia della letteratura russa contemporanea*, Milan 1959 (with rich bibliography); Mirsky, D. S., *Contemporary Russian Literature*, New York 1926 (the best survey in English); Pozner, V., *Panorama de la littérature russe contemporaine*, Paris 1929; Simmons, E., *An Outline of Modern Russian Literature*, Ithaca, N.Y. 1944; Slonim, M., *Modern Russian Literature*, New York 1953 (a useful handbook); Tvorgevsky, I., *De Gorki à nos jours. La nouvelle littérature russe*, Paris 1945.

B. ANTHOLOGIES OF RUSSIAN POETRY

I. GENERAL

Baring, M., *The Oxford Book of Russian Verse*, Oxford 1925 (1948 edition revised by D. P. Costello, with notes by Prince D. S. Mirskij); Bogolepov, A., *Russkaja lirika ot Zhukovskogo do Bunina*, New York 1953; Éliasberg, A. and D., *Russkij Parnass*, Leipzig 1921; Mirskij, D. S., *Russkaja lirika*, Paris 1925.

Beckhofer, C., *A Russian Anthology in English*, London 1917; Bowra, C. M., *A Book of Russian Verse*, and *A Second Book of Russian Verse* (translations by several hands), London 1943 and 1946; Cornford, F., and Polianowsky-Salaman, E., *Poems from Russian*, London 1943; Coxwell, C. F., *Russian Poems*, London 1929; David, J., *Anthologie de la poésie russe*, Paris 1948; Deutsch, B., and Yarmolinsky, A., *A Treasury of Russian Verse*, New York 1949 (translations by several hands); Elton, O., *Verse from Pushkin and Others*, London 1935; Plank, R., *Russische Dichtung*, Karlsruhe 1946; Rais, E., and Robert J., *Anthologie de la poésie russe*, Paris 1947; Roellinghoff, E., *Russlands Lyrik in Uebertragung und Nachdichtung*, Vienna 1920.

2. MODERN PERIOD

Ezhov, I., and Shamurin, E., *Russkaja poèzija 20 veka*, Moscow 1925; Mel'nikova-Papoushkova, N., *Antologija russkoj poèzii 20 stoletija* (2 vols.), Prague 1920.

Chuzeville, J., *Anthologie des poètes russes traduits en vers français*, Paris 1914; Günther, J., *Neuer russischer Parnass*, Berlin 1911; Lindsay, J., *Russian Poetry 1917–1955*, London 1957; Naldi-Olkienizkaia, R., *Antologia dei poeti russi del XX secolo*, Milano 1924; Poggioli, R., *Il Fiore del Verso Russo*, Turin 1949; Ripellino, A. M., *Poesia russa del Novecento*, Modena 1954; Robin, A., *Quatre poètes russes* (*V. Maïakovsky, B. Pasternak, A. Blok, S. Essénine*), Paris 1949; Selver, P., *Modern Russian Poetry*, London 1917; Shelley, G., *Modern Poems from Russia*, London 1942.

C. RUSSIAN LITERARY JOURNALS AND MISCELLANIES

I. BEFORE THE REVOLUTION

Apollon (Apollo), Petersburg 1909–1917; *Fakely* (The Torches, misc.), Petersburg 1906–1908; *Grif* (The Griffin, misc.), Moscow 1903–1914; *Mir Iskusstva* (The World of Art), Petersburg 1899–1904; *Novyj Put'* (The New Road), Petersburg 1903-1904; *Pereval* (The Divide), Moscow 1906-1907; *Russkaja Mysl'* (Russian Thought) Moscow 1880-1918; *Severnye Tsvety* (Northern Flowers, misc.), Moscow 1901-1911; *Severnyj Vestnik* (The Northern Herald), Petersburg 1882-1898; *Shipovnik* (The Wild Rose, misc.), Petersburg 1907-1917; *Sirin* (Siren, misc.), Petersburg 1913-1914; *Vesy* (The Scales), Moscow 1904-1909; *Voprosy Zhizni* (Questions of Life), Petersburg 1905; *Znanie* (Knowledge, misc.), Petersburg 1903–1914; *Zolotoe Runo* (The Golden Fleece), Moscow 1906–1909.

2. SINCE THE REVOLUTION

Krasnaja Nov' (Red Virgin Soil), Moscow 1921–1940; *LEF* (*Levyj Front Iskusstv*, The Left Front of the Arts), Moscow 1923–1925; *Na Literaturnom Postu* (On Literary Guard), Moscow 1926–1932; *Na Postu* (On Guard), Moscow 1923–1925; *Novyj LEF* (The New *LEF*), Moscow 1927–1928; *Novyj Mir* (The New World), Moscow 1925 —; *Oktjabr'* (October), Moscow 1925 —; *Skify* (The Scythians, misc.), Moscow 1917–1918; *Zapiski Mechtatelej* (Notebooks of Daydreamers), Petersburg 1919–1922; *Znamja* (The Banner), Moscow 1931 —; *Zvezda* (Star), Leningrad 1924 —.

3. IN EMIGRATION

Beseda (Table Talk), Berlin 1923–1925; *Èpopeja* (Epopée), Berlin 1922–1923; *Grani* (Facets), Frankfurt a.M., 1946 —; *Novosel'e* (The New Homestead), Paris-New York 1942 —; *Novyj Zhurnal* (The New Review), New York 1942 —; *Opyty* (Experiments), New York 1951 —; *Sovremennye Zapiski* (Contemporary Annals), Paris 1920–1940; *Versty* (Mileposts, misc.), Paris 1926–1928; *Volja Rossii* (The Will of Russia), Prague 1922–1934; *Zveno* (The Link), Paris 1923–1928.

SPECIAL BIBLIOGRAPHY

CHAPTER ONE: THE MASTERS OF THE PAST

I. PROLOGUE

Berdjaev, N., *Dukhovnyj krizis intelligentsii*, Petersburg 1910; Fedotov, G. P., *Novyj Grad*, New York 1952; also, "Tragedija intelligentsii," *Versty*, 1927, 2; Vejdle, V., *Zadacha Rossii*, New York 1955; *Vekhi: Sbornik statej o russkoj intelligentsii*, Moscow 1909 (essays by several authors).

Baring, M., *The Russian People*, London 1910; Berdiaev, N., *The Russian Idea*, London 1947; Gobetti, P., *Paradosso dello spirito russo*, Turin 1926; Masaryk, T. G., *The Spirit of Russia* (2 vols.), New York 1954; Mirsky, D. S., *Russia: A Social History*, London 1931; Vernadsky, G., *Ancient Russia*, New Haven, Conn. 1943; Weidlé, W., *Russia Absent and Present*, New York 1952.

II. EARLY RUSSIAN LITERATURE

Cizevskij, D., *History of Old Russian Literature: From the 11th to the 19th century*, The Hague 1958; Gudzij, N., *A History of Early Russian Literature*, New York 1949.

POETRY OF THE EIGHTEENTH CENTURY

Blagoj, D., *Istorija russkoj literatury 18 veka*, Moscow 1945; Gukovskij, G., *Russkaja literatura 18 veka*, Moscow 1939.

Gukovskij, G., "Von Lomonosov bis Derzhavin," *Zeitschrift für Slavische Philologie*, 1925, II.

Bowring, J., *Specimens of the Russian Poets*, Boston 1822 (translations from Derzhavin, Zhukovskij, Batjushkov, and others).

LOMONOSOV

Berkov, P., *Lomonosov i literaturnaja polemika ego vremeni*, Moscow 1936.

Martel, L., *Lomonosov et la langue littéraire russe*, Paris 1933.

DERZHAVIN

Èjkhenbaum, B., "Derzhavin," *Skvoz' literaturu*, Leningrad 1924; Khodasevich, V., *Derzhavin*, Paris 1931.

ZHUKOVSKIJ

Veselovskij, A., *V. A. Zhukovskij: Poèzija chustva i serdechnogo voobrazhenija*, Petersburg 1904.

Ehrhard, M., *Joukovski et le préromantisme russe*, Paris 1938.

348

BATJUSHKOV

Vengerov, S., "K. Batjushkov," *Istorija russkoj literatury 19 veka*, edited by D. Ovsjaniko-Kulikovskij, I, Moscow 1908.

III. PUSHKIN

Brodskij, N., *A. S. Pushkin*, Moscow 1937; Èjkhenbaum, B., *Problemy poètiki Pushkina*, Petrograd 1921; Gershenzon, M., *Mudrost' Pushkina*, Moscow 1919; Grossman, L., *Pushkin*, Moscow 1939; Veresaev, V., *Pushkin v zhizni*, Moscow 1936; Vinogradov, B., *Jazyk Pushkina*, Leningrad 1935; also, *Stil' Pushkina*, Moscow 1941; Zhirmunskij, V., *Bajron i Pushkin*, Petrograd 1924.

Cizevskij, D., "Pushkin und die Romantik," *Slavische Rundschau*, 1937, 2; Cross, S., and Simmons, E. (editors), *Centennial Essays for Pushkin*, Cambridge, Mass. 1937; Hofmann, M., *Pouchkine*, Paris 1931; Mirsky, D. S., *Pushkin*, London 1926; Simmons, E., *Pushkin*, Cambridge, Mass. 1937; Wilson, E., "In Honor of Pushkin," *The Triple Thinkers*, New York 1938.

The Poems, Prose and Plays of Pushkin, edited by A. Yarmolinsky, New York 1936 (translated by several hands); *Evgenij Onegin*, the Russian text edited with introduction and commentary by D. Cizevskij, Cambridge, Mass. 1953; *Evgeny Onegin*, translated by O. Elton, London 1937; *Three Russian Poets: Selections from Pushkin, Lermontov, and Tyutchev*, translated by V. Nabokov, Norfolk, Conn. 1944.

IV. ROMANTICISM

Cizevskij, D., *Gegel' v Rossii*, Paris 1939; Gershenzon, M., *Istorija molodoj Rossii*, Moscow 1908.

Bem, A., "Über die Romantik in der russischen Literatur," *Slavische Rundschau*, 1939, 3-4; Setschkareff, V., *Schellings Einfluss in der russischen Literatur*, Leipzig 1939.

KOL'TSOV

Kallash, V., "A. V. Kol'tsov," *Istorija russkoj literatury 19 veka*, edited by D. Ovsjaniko-Kulikovskij, II, Moscow 1909.

BARATYNSKIJ

Gofman, M., *Poèzija E. A. Boratynskogo*, Petrograd 1915; Setschkareff, V., "Zur philosophischen Lyrik Boratynskijs," *Zeitschrift für Slavische Philologie*, 1947, XIX.

LERMONTOV

Èjkhenbaum, B., *Lermontov*, Petrograd 1924; Kotljarevskij, N., *Lermontov*, Petersburg 1909; Shuvalov, S., *Lermontov*, Leningrad 1927.

Duchesne, E., *M. I. Lermontov: sa vie et ses oeuvres*, Paris 1910.

The Prophet and Other Poems, translated by E. M. Kayden, Sewanee, Tenn. 1944; *A Song About Tsar Ivan Vasilievich*, translated by J. Cournos,

SPECIAL BIBLIOGRAPHY

New York 1928; *A Hero of Our Times*, translated by V. and D. Nabokov, Garden City, N.Y. 1958.

TJUTCHEV

Cizevskij, D., "Tjutchev und die deutsche Romantik," *Zeitschrift für Slavische Philologie*, 1927, IV; Strémoukhoff, D., *La poésie et l'idéologie de Tioutchev*, Strasburg 1937.

Tjutchev: Izbrannye stikhotvorenija: Poésies Choisies, translated by Ch. Salomon, introduction by N. Otsup, Paris 1957.

V. ALEKSEJ TOLSTOJ

Lirondelle, A., *Le poète A. Tolstoï*, Paris 1912.

NEKRASOV

Chukovskij, K. *Nekrasov kak khudozhnik*, Petrograd 1922; Evgen'ev-Maksimov, V., *Zhizn' i dejatel'nost' Nekrasova* (2 vols.), Moscow-Leningrad 1947.

Poems by Nekrassov, translated by J. Soskice, London 1929; *Nekrassov's Poems*, translated by D. Prall, Berkeley, Calif. 1944.

FET

Ajkhenval'd, Ju., "Fet," *Siluèty russkikh pisatelej*, II, Berlin 1923; Èjkhenbaum, B., *Melodika russkogo liricheskogo stikha*, Petrograd 1922.

CHAPTER TWO: MODERNISM AND DECADENCE

I. HISTORICAL BACKGROUND

1. GENERAL

Florinsky, M. T., *Russia: A History and an Interpretation* (2 vols.), New York 1953; Kluchevski, V. O., *A History of Russia* (4 vols.), New York 1911-1926; Milioukov, P., Seignobos, Ch., and Eisemann, L., *Histoire de la Russie* (3 vols.), Paris 1932-1933; Miljukov, P., *Outlines of Russian Culture* (3 vols.), edited by M. Karpovich, Philadelphia 1943; Pares, B., *A History of Russia*, New York 1926; Pokrovsky, M. N., *History of Russia*, New York 1931; Vernadsky, G., *A History of Russia*, New York 1944.

2. MODERN PERIOD

Breshko-Breshkovskaya, K. E., *Hidden Springs of the Russian Revolution*, Stanford, Calif. 1931; Carr, E. H., *A History of Soviet Russia, I: The Bolshevik Revolution 1917-1923*, New York 1951; Chamberlin, W. H., *The Russian Revolution* (2 vols.), New York 1935; also, *Russia's Iron Age*, Boston 1934; Fisher, G., *Russian Liberalism: From Gentry to Intelligentsia*, Cambridge, Mass. 1958; Florinsky, M., *The End of the Russian Empire*, New Haven 1931; Hedenström, A., *Geschichte Russlands 1878-1918*, Stuttgart 1922; Karpovich, M., *Imperial Russia*, New York 1932; Kornilov, A., *Modern Russian History*, New York 1943; Lyons, E., *Assignment in Utopia*, New York 1937; Nikolaevsky, B. J., *Aseff, The Spy, Russian Terrorist and Police Tool*, New York 1934; Pares, B., *The Fall of the Russian Monarchy*, New York 1939; Serge, V., *From Lenin to Stalin*, New York 1937; Seton-Watson, H., *The Decline of Imperial Russia, 1855-1914*, New York 1952; Souvarine, B., *Stalin: A Critical Survey of Bolshevism*, New York 1939; Tompkins, S., *"Vekhi and the Russian Intelligentsia,"* *Canadian Slavonic Papers*, II, Toronto 1957; Trotsky, L., *The History of the Russian Revolution*, translated by Max Eastman, New York 1939; Venturi, F., *Il Populismo russo* (2 vols.) Turin 1952 (translated into English as *Roots of Revolution. A History of the Russian Populist and Socialist Movements in the 19th Century*, London 1959); Wilson, E., *To the Finland Station*, New York 1940; Wolfe, B., *Three Who Made a Revolution*, New York 1948.

II. THE MODERN MOVEMENT

See General Bibliography, especially A,2, and C,1; see Special Bibliography for this chapter, Section V, and for Chapter Four, Sections II to V.

VOLYNSKIJ

Vengerov, S., "A. Volynskij," *Russkaja literatura 20 veka*, edited by S. Vengerov, II, Moscow 1915.

THE SCALES

Pogorelova, B., *"Skorpion i Vesy," Novyj Zhurnal*, XL (1955).
Reeve, F. D., *"Vesy:* A Study of a Russian Magazine," *Slavonic and East European Review*, 88 (1958).

III. THE WORLD OF ART

Dobuzhinskij, M., "Krug *Mira Isskustva," Novyj Zhurnal*, III (1942); Makovskij, S., "Aleksandr Benua i *Mir Isskustva," Portrety sovremennikov*, New York 1955.

VISUAL ARTS

Alpatov, M., *Russian Impact on Art*, New York 1950; Benois, A., *The Russian School of Painting*, London 1904; Newmarch, T., *The Russian Arts*, London 1916; Réau, L., *L'Art russe*, Paris, 1945; Talbot Rice, T., *Russian Art*, West Drayton, Middlesex 1949; Wulff, O., *Die neurussische Kunst*, Augsburg 1932.

DANCE AND BALLET

Lifar', S., *S. Djagilev i s Djagilevym*, Paris 1939.
Propert, W. A., *The Russian Ballet in Western Europe*, London 1921.

SPECIAL BIBLIOGRAPHY

MUSIC AND OPERA

Abraham, G., *On Russian Music*, New York 1939; Carvocoressi, M. D., *Survey of Russian Music*, New York 1945; Sabaneeff, I., *Modern Russian Composers*, New York 1939.

STAGE AND DRAMA

Èfros, N., *Moskovskij Khudozhestvennyj Teatr*, Moscow 1923; Komissarzhevskij, F., *Tvorchestvo aktera i teorija Stanislavskago*, Moscow 1917; *Kamernyj Teatr*, Moscow 1934 (essays by several authors); Stanislavskij, K., *Moja zhizn' v iskusstve*, Moscow-Leningrad 1931; Stepun, F., *Teatr i kino*, Berlin 1932; Volkov, N., *Mejerkhol'd* (2 vols.), Moscow-Leningrad 1929; Znovsko-Borovskij, E., *Russkij teatr nachala 20 veka*, Prague 1925.

Evreinov, N., *Histoire du théâtre russe*, Paris 1947; Fülöp-Miller, R., and Gregor, J., *Das russische Theater*, Leipzig 1927; Gourfinkel, N., *Le Théâtre russe contemporain*, Paris 1931; Lo Gatto, E., *Storia del Teatro russo* (2 vols.), Florence 1952; Magarshack, D., *Stanislavskij, A Life*, London 1950; Poggioli, R., "Quadrumvirato del palcoscenico russo," *Pegaso* (May 1933).

Stanislavsky, C., *My Life in Art*, translated by J. J. Robbins, London 1924; also, *Building a Character*, translated by E. Hapgood, New York 1950, and *Stanislavsky on the Art of the Stage*, translated by D. Magarshack, London 1950.

IV. NEW TRENDS OF THOUGHT

Florovskij, G. *Puti russkogo bogoslovija*, Paris-Belgrade 1937; Griftsov, B., *Tri myslitelja: V. Rozanov, D. Merezhkovskij, L. Shestov*, Moscow 1911.

Bulgakov, S., *The Orthodox Church*, London 1935; Lossky, N. O., *History of Russian Philosophy*, New York 1951; Zenkovsky, V. V., *A History of Russian Philosophy* (2 vols.), New York 1953.

MEREZHKOVSKIJ

Dolinin, A., "Dmitrij Merezhkovskij," *Russkaja literatura 20 veka*, edited by S. Vengerov, I, Moscow 1914; Gippius, Z., *Dmitrij Merezhkovskij*, Paris 1951; Lundberg, G., *Merezhkovskij i ego novoe khristianstvo*, Petersburg 1914; Terapiano, Ju. "D. S. Merezhkovskij," *Vstrechi*, New York 1953.

Chuzeville, J., *Dmitri Méréjkowsky*, Paris 1922; C. H. Bedford, "Dmitry Merezhkovsky, the Intelligentsia, and the Revolution of 1905," *Canadian Slavonic Papers*, III (1959).

Tolstoj e Dostoevskij, translated by A. Polledro, Bari 1947.

BERDJAEV

Fielding Clark, O., *Introduction to Berdiaev*, New York 1950; Lampert, E., *Nicolas Berdyaev and the New Middle Ages*, New York 1947.

Freedom and the Spirit, New York 1935; *Dostoevsky*, New York 1957; *The Destiny of Man*, New York 1937; *The Origin of Russian Communism*, New York 1938; *Autobiografia spirituale (Samopoznanie)*, translated by G. Donnini, Florence 1953.

MODERNISM AND DECADENCE

SHESTOV

Les Révélations de la Mort: Dostoïevsky, Tolstoï, translated with introduction by B. de Schloezer, Paris 1922; *La Nuit de Gethsémani: Essai sur la philosophie de Pascal*, Paris 1923; *La Philosophie de la tragédie: Dostoïevsky et Nietzsche*, Paris 1926; *L'Idée du Bien chez Tolstoï et Nietzsche*, Paris 1927; *All Things are Possible (Apofeoz Bezphochvennosti)*, translated by S. S. Koteliansky, New York 1920; *Anton Tchekhov and Other Essays*, translated by S. S. Koteliansky and J. Middleton Murry, London 1916.

ROZANOV

Izbrannoe, selections, with an introduction by Ju. Ivask (in Russian), New York 1956.

Poggioli, R., "On the Works and Thoughts of Vasili Rozanov," *The Phoenix and the Spider*, Cambridge, Mass. 1957.

Solitaria, translated by S. S. Koteliansky, London 1924; *Fallen Leaves, Bundle One*, translated by S. S. Koteliansky, with a foreword by J. Stephens, London 1929; *L'Apocalypse de notre temps précedé de Esseulement*, introduction by B. de Schloezer, translated by B. de Schloezer and V. Pozner, Paris 1930.

V. DECADENCE (see also under Chapter Four, Sections II to V)

Apostolov, N., *Impressionizm i modernizm*, Kiev 1908; Gofman, M., "Romantizm, Simvolizm i Dekadentstvo," introduction to *Kniga o russkikh poetakh poslednego desjatiletija*, Petersburg-Moscow 1909; Merezhkovskij, D., *O prichinakh upadka i o novykh techenijakh sovremennoj russkoj literatury*, Petersburg 1893; Stoljanov, M., *Ètjudy o dekadentstve*, Khar'kov 1899; Vengerov, S., "Ètapy neo-romanticheskogo dvizhenija," *Russkaja literatura 20 veka*, edited by S. Vengerov, I, Moscow 1914; Volkov, A., "Poèzija dekadansa," *Ocherki russkoj literatury kontsa 19 i nachala 20 vekov*, Moscow 1952; Volynskij, A. L., *Bor'ba za idealizm*, Petersburg 1900 (see especially "Dekadentstvo i Simvolizm" and "O simvolizme i simvolistakh").

NADSON

Divil'kovskij, A., "S. Ja. Nadson," *Istorija russkoj literatury 19 veka*, edited by D. Ovsjaniko-Kulikovskij, IV, Moscow 1911.

MINSKIJ

Polonskij, G., "Poèzija Minskogo," *Russkaja literatura 20 veka*, edited by S. Vengerov, I, Moscow 1914.

MEREZHKOVSKIJ (as poet and literary theorist)

Volynskij, A. L., "D. S. Merezhkovskogo *Simvoly*," *Bor'ba za idealizm*, Petersburg 1900.

Bedford, C. H., "D. S. Merezhkovsky: The Forgotten Poet," *Slavonic and East European Review*, 86 (1957); Matlaw, R., "The Manifesto of Russian Symbolism" (on Merezhkovskij's *On the Causes of the Present Decline and on the New Currents of Contemporary Russian Literature*), *The Slavic and East European Journal*, 3 (1957).

SPECIAL BIBLIOGRAPHY

CHAPTER THREE: THE DECADENTS

I. BAL'MONT

Anichkov, E., "K. D. Bal'mont," *Russkaja literatura 20 veka*, edited by S. Vengerov, I, Moscow 1914; Annenskij, I., "Bal'mont lirik," *Kniga otrazhenij*, Petersburg 1906; Brjusov, V., "Bal'mont," *Dalekie i blizkie*, Moscow 1912; Chukovskij, K. "Bal'mont," *Ot Chekhova do nashikh dnej*, Petersburg 1908; Èllis (L. Kobylinskij), *Russkie Simvolisty: Konstantin Bal'mont, Valerij Brjusov, Andrej Belyj*, Moscow 1910; Zajtsev, B., "O Bal'monte," *Sovremennye Zapiski*, LXI (1936).

Quelques Poèmes, translated by A. de Holstein and René Ghil, Paris 1916; *Visions Solaires*, translated by L. Savitzky, Paris 1923; (Bal'mont and Brjusov:) *Gedichte*, translated by W. E. Groeger, Berlin 1921.

II. BRJUSOV

Ajkhenval'd, Ju., *Brjusov: Opyt literaturnoj kharakteristiki*, Moscow 1910; Batjushkov, F., "V. Brjusov," *Russkaja literatura 20 veka*, edited by S. Vengerov, I, Moscow 1914; Èllis (L. Kobylinskij), *Russkie Simvolisty: Konstantin Bal'mont, Valerij Brjusov, Andrej Belyi*, Moscow 1910; Gippius, Z., "Brjusov," *Zhivye litsa*, Prague 1925; Grossman, L., "Brjusov i frantsusskie simvolisty," *Ot Pushkina do Bloka*, Moscow 1926; Khodasevich, V., "Brjusov," *Sovremennye Zapiski*, XXIII (1925); Lelevich, G., *V. Ja. Brjusov*, Moscow 1926; Maksimov, D., *Poèzija Valerija Brjusova*, Leningrad 1940; Mirskij, D. S., "Valerij Ja. Brjusov," *Sovremennye Zapiski*, XXII (1924); Pogorelova, B., "Valerij Brjusov i ego okruzhenie," *Novyj Zhurnal*, XXXIII (1953); Zhirmunskij, V., *Valerij Brjusov i nasledie Pushkina*, Petrograd 1922.

Poggioli, R., "Qualis Artifex Pereo! or Barbarism and Decadence" (on Brjusov's poem "The Coming Huns"), *Harvard Library Bulletin*, XIII, 1 (Winter 1959); Raggio, O., "Brjusov e la poesia francese," *Letterature Moderne*, 1956, 5; Setschkareff, V., "The Narrative Prose of Brjusov," *International Journal of Slavic Linguistics and Poetry*, I–II (1959).

(Bal'mont and Brjusov:) *Gedichte*, translated by W. E. Groeger, Berlin 1921.

III. SOLOGUB

Chulkov, G. "Fedor Sologub," *Gody stranstvij*, Moscow 1930; Gippius, Z., "Sologub," *Zhivye litsa*, Prague 1925; Gornfel'd, A., "F. Sologub," *Russkaja literatura 20 veka*, edited by S. Vengerov, II, Moscow 1915; Khodasevich, V., "Sologub," *Sovremennye Zapiski*, XXXIV (1928), (also in *Nekropol'*, Bruxelles 1939); Struve, G., "Tri sud'by (Blok, Gumilev, Sologub)," *Novyj Zhurnal*, XVI (1947).

Cournos, J., "Feodor Sologub," *The Fortnightly Review*, September 1915; Holthusen, J., *Fedor Sologub's Roman Trilogie (Tvorimaja Legenda): Aus der Geschichte des russischen Symbolismus*, The Hague 1958.

The Created Legend, translated by J. Cournos, New York 1916; *The Little Demon*, translated by J. Cournos, New York 1916; *Le Démon mesquin*, translated by J. Leclère, Bruxelles 1947; the same, translated by H. Pernot and L. Stahl, Paris 1949–1950; *Der kleine Dämon*, translated by R. von Walter, München 1909.

IV. GIPPIUS

Adamovich, G., "Zinaida Gippius," *Odinochestvo i svoboda*, New York 1955; Brjusov, V., "Z. Gippius," *Russkaja Literatura 20 veka*, edited by S. Vengerov, I, Moscow 1914; Terapiano, Ju., "Z. Gippius," *Vstrechi*, New York 1953; Zlobin, V., "Z. N. Gippius (ee sud'ba)," *Novyj Zhurnal*, XXXI (1952).

V. BUNIN

Aleksandrova, V., "I. A. Bunin," *Novyj Zhurnal*, XII (1946); Batjushkov, F., "I. A. Bunin," *Russkaja literatura 20 veka*, edited by S. Vengerov, II, Moscow 1915; Nartsissov, B., "Bunin-poèt," *Grani*, 24 (1955); Stepun, F., "I. Bunin," *Sovremennye Zapiski*, LIV (1934); Zajtsev, B., *I. A. Bunin: Zhizn' i tvorchestvo*, Berlin, n.d.

Guershun Colin, A., "Ivan Bunin in Retrospect," *The Slavonic and East European Review*, 82 (1955); Ledré, Ch., *Trois romanciers russes: Ivan Bounine, Alexandre Kouprine, Marc Aldanov*, Paris, n.d.; Nabokov, V., *Conclusive Evidence*, New York 1951 (see chapter on émigré literature); Poggioli, R., "L'arte di Ivan Bunin," *Pietre di Paragone*, Florence 1939; also, "The Art of Ivan Bunin," *The Phoenix and the Spider*, Cambridge, Mass. 1957.

The Village, translated by I. F. Hapgood, New York 1923; *The Gentleman from San Francisco*, translated by B. G. Guerney, New York 1934; *The Well of Days* (from *The Life of Arsen'ev*), translated by G. Struve and H. Miles, New York 1934; *Valsecca (Sukhodol)*, translated with introduction by R. Poggioli, Lanciano 1933.

CHAPTER FOUR: SYMBOLISM

I. SOLOV'EV

Ajkhenval'd, Ju., "Solov'ev," *Siluèty russkikh pisatelej*, III, Berlin 1921; Blok, A., "Rytsar'-Monakh," *Sbornik pamjati Vladimira Solov'eva*, Moscow 1912; Brjusov, V., "Poèzija Solov'eva," *Dalekie i Blizkie*, Moscow 1912; Mochul'skij, K., *Vladimir Solov'ev: zhizn' i uchenie*, Paris 1936; Radlov, V., *Vladimir Solov'ev: zhizn' i uchenie*, Petersburg 1913; Slonimskij, M., "A. Blok i V. Solov'ev," *Ob A. Bloke*, Petersburg 1912; Trubetskoj, E., *Mirosozertsanie V. S. Solov'eva*, Moscow 1913.

Strémoukhoff, D., *Vladimir Soloviev et son oeuvre méssianique*, Paris 1935; Zernov, M., *Three Russian Prophets: Khomiakov, Dostoevsky, Soloviev*, London 1944.

SPECIAL BIBLIOGRAPHY

Conscience de la Russie, edited by J. Gauvain, Paris 1950; *A Solovyov Anthology*, selected by S. C. Frank and translated by N. Waddington, London 1950; *Ausgewälte Werke* (4 vols.), translated by H. Kohler, Stuttgart 1914–1922; *Poesie*, translated with introduction by L. Pacini Savoj, Florence 1949.

II, III, IV, V. SYMBOLISM

Ajkhenval'd, Ju., *Siluèty russkikh pisatelej*, III, Berlin 1921; Anichkov, E., *Novaja russkaja poèzija*, Berlin 1923; Annenskij, I., *Kniga otrazhenij*, Petersburg 1906; also, *Vtoraja kniga otrazhenij*, Petersburg 1909; Bal'mont, K., *Gornye vershiny*, Moscow 1904; also, *Poèzija kak volshebstvo*, Moscow 1915; Belyj, A., *Lug zelenyj*, Moscow 1910; also, *Simvolizm*, Moscow 1910; also, *Arabeski*, Moscow 1911; Blok, A., "O sovremennom sostojanii russkago simvolizma," *Apollon*, 1910, 8; also, *O Simvolizme*, Petrograd 1921; Blok, A., and Belyj, A., *Perepiska*, edited by V. N. Orlov, Moscow 1940; Brjusov, *Dalekie i Blizkie*, Moscow 1912; Chulkov, G., *Pokryvalo Izidy*, Moscow 1909; Chulkov, G., *O misticheskom anarkhizme: Sbornik statej* (introduction by V. Ivanov) Petersburg 1906; Èllis (L. Kobylinskij), *Russkie simvolisty: Konstantin Bal'mont, Valerij Brjusov, Andrej Belyj*, Moscow 1910; Èrenburg, I., *Portrety russkikh poètov*, Berlin 1922; Gippius, Z., *Zhivye litsa* (2 vols.), Prague 1925; Gumilev, N., *Pis'ma o russkoj poèzii*, Petrograd 1923; Ivanov, G., *Peterburgskie zimy*, Paris 1928; Ivanov, V., *Borozdy i mezhi*, Moscow 1916; Khodasevich, V., *Nekropol'*, Bruxelles 1939; also, *Literaturnye stat'i i vospominanija*, New York 1954 (see especially the essay "O Simvolizme"); Kuzmin, M., *Uslovnosti*, Petrograd 1923; Makovskij, S., *Portrety sovremennikov*, New York 1955; Mandel'shtam, O., *O poèzii*, Leningrad 1928; Solov'ev, V., "Russkie Simvolisty," *Sobranie Sochinenij*, VI, Petersburg 1901; Terapiano, Ju., *Vstrechi*, New York 1953; Tynjanov, Ju., *Arkhaisty i novatory*, Leningrad 1929.

Donchin, G., *The Influence of French Symbolism on Russian Poetry*, The Hague 1959; Holthusen, J., *Studien zur Aesthetik und Poetik des russischen Symbolismus*, Göttingen 1957; Laffitte, S., "Le Symbolisme occidental et Alexandre Blok," *Revue des Etudes Slaves*, XXXIV (1957).

CHAPTER FIVE: SYMBOLISTS AND OTHERS

I. BELYJ

Adamovich, G., "Andrej Belyj i ego vospominanija," *Russkie Zapiski*, May 1938; Èllis (L. Kobylinskij), *Russkie simvolisty: Konstantin Bal'mont, Valerij Brjusov, Andrej Belyj*, Moscow 1910; Ivanov-Razumnik, R., "A. Belyj," *Russkaja literatura 20 veka*, edited by S. Vengerov, III, Moscow 1914; also, *A. Belyj i A. Blok*, Petrograd 1919; Khodasevich, V., "A. Belyj," *Nekropol'*, Bruxelles 1939; Mochul'skij, K., *Andrej Belyj*, Paris 1955; Stepun, F., "Pamjati Andreja Belogo," *Sovremennye Zapiski*, LVI (1934); Tsvetaeva, M., "Plennyj Dukh," *Sovremennye Zapiski*, LV (1934); Valentinov, N., "Vstrechi s Andreem Belym," *Novyj Zhurnal*, XLV–XLVII (1956).

Maslenikov, O., *The Frenzied Poets: Andrey Biely and the Russian Symbolists*, Berkeley, Calif. 1952; also, "Ruskin, Bely, and the Solov'yovs," *The Slavonic and East European Review*, 84 (1956).

St. Petersburg, translated with introduction by John Cournos, New York 1959.

II. VJACHESLAV IVANOV

Belyj, A., "V. Ivanov," *Russkaja literatura 20 veka*, edited by S. Vengerov, II, Moscow 1915; also, *Sirin uchenogo varvarstva*, Berlin 1922; Golenishchev-Kutuzov, I., "Lirika Vjacheslava Ivanova," *Sovremennye Zapiski*, XLIII (1930); Makovskij, S., "Vjacheslav Ivanov v Rossii"; also, "Vjacheslav Ivanov v èmigratsii," *Novyj Zhurnal*, XXX–XXXI (1952), (both pieces reprinted in *Portrety Sovremennikov*, New York 1955); Shestov, L., "Vjacheslav Velikolepnyj. K kharakteristike russkogo upadnichestva," *Russkaja Mysl'* (1916), 10; Stepun, F., "Vjacheslav Ivanov," *Sovremennye Zapiski*, LXII (1936).

Deschartes, O., "Vyacheslav Ivanov," *Oxford Slavonic Papers*, V (1954); also, "Être et mémoire selon Viatcheslav Ivanov," *Oxford Slavonic Papers*, VII (1957), (both pieces are followed by unpublished poems); Gancikov, L., "Venceslao Ivanov," *Enciclopedia Filosofica*, III (Venice-Rome 1957); Poggioli, R., "A Correspondence From Opposite Corners," *The Phoenix and the Spider*, Cambridge, Mass. 1957.

Venceslao Ivanov (special issue), *Il Convegno*, XV, 1934; (in collaboration with M. Gershenzon:) *Correspondence Between Two Corners*, translated by N. Guterman, *Partisan Review*, 1948, 9; *Corréspondance d'un coin à l'autre*, with introduction by Gabriel Marcel and a letter by V. Ivanov to Charles Du Bos, Paris 1931; *Corrispondenza da un angolo all'altro*, translation revised by the author, with an introduction by O. Deschartes, Lanciano 1932; *Freedom and the Tragic Life; A Study in Dostoevsky*, translated by N. Cameron, New York 1957; *Das alte Wahre* (essays), translated with an introduction by V. Wittkowski, Berlin and Frankfurt a. M. 1954.

III. ANNENSKIJ

Ivanov, V., "O poèzii Innokentija Annenskogo," *Borozdy i mezhi*, Moscow 1916; Khodasevich, V., "Ob Annenskom," *Èpopeja*, 1922, 3 (also in *Literaturnye stat'i i vospominanija*, New York 1954); Makovskij, S., "Iz vospominanij ob Annenskom, *Novosel'e*, XXXIX–XLI (1949); Mitrofanov, P., "I. Annenskij," *Russkaja literatura 20 veka*, edited by S. Vengerov, II, Moscow 1915; Voloshin, M., "Annenskij," *Apollon*, 1910, 4.

IV. VOLOSHIN

Èrenburg, I., "M. A. Voloshin," *Portrety russkikh poètov*, Berlin 1922;

Ivanov, V., "Voloshin," and Kuzmin, M., "Stikhi M. Voloshina," both in *Apollon*, 1910, 7; Karalin, B., "Zastignutyj posredi dorogi," *Grani*, 4 (1948).

BALTRUSHAJTIS

Èrenburg, I., "Ju. K. Baltrushajtis," *Portrety russkikh poètov*, Berlin 1922; Ivanov, V., "Jurgis Baltrushajtis," *Russkaja literatura 20 veka*, edited by S. Vengerov, II, Moscow 1915; Rozanov, S., *Baltrushajtis*, Moscow 1919.

V. KONEVSKOJ

Brjusov, V., "Mudroe ditja," *Mir Iskusstva*, 1901, VIII–IX; also, "I. Konevskoj," *Russkaja literatura 20 veka*, edited by S. Vengerov, III, Moscow 1916.

DOBROLJUBOV

Makovskij, S., "Dobroljubov," *Portrety sovremennikov*, New York 1955; Mochul'skij, K., "Aleksandr Dobroljubov," *Novyj Zhurnal*, XXXII (1953).

CHAPTER SIX: ALEKSANDR BLOK

Biography: Ashukin, N., *A. Blok v vospominanijakh sovremennikov i ego pis'makh*, Moscow 1924; Beketova, M., *Aleksandr Blok: biograficheskij ocherk*, Petrograd 1922; Belyj, A., "Vospominanija o A. Bloke," *Èpopeja*, 1922–1923, 1–4; Nemerovskaja, I., and Vol'pe, Ts. (eds.), *Sud'ba Bloka*, Leningrad 1930.

Adamovich, G., "Smert' Bloka," *Tsekh Poètov*, III (1922); also "Nasledstvo Bloka," *Novyj Zhurnal*, XLIV (1956); Annenkov, Ju., "Ob A. Bloke," *Novyj Zhurnal*, XLVII (1956); Brjusov, V., "A. Blok," *Russkaja literatura 20 veka*, edited by S. Vengerov, II, Moscow 1915; Chukovskij, K., *Kniga o Bloke*, Berlin 1922; also, *Blok kak chelovek i poèt*, Petrograd 1924; Gippius, Z., "Blok," *Zhivye litsa*, Prague 1925; Medvedev, I., *Tvorcheskij put' A. Bloka*, Moscow 1926; also, *Dramy i poèmy Bloka*, Leningrad 1928; Mochul'skij, K., *Aleksandr Blok*, Paris 1948; Nikitina, E., and Shuvalov, S., *Poèticheskoe iskusstvo Bloka*, Moscow 1926; Timofeev, L., *Aleksandr Blok*, Moscow 1946; Tynjanov, Ju., "Blok," *Arkhaisty i novatory*, Leningrad 1929.

Berberova, N., *Alexandre Blok et son temps*, Paris 1947 (with translations); Bonneau, S., *L'univers poétique d'Alexandre Blok*, Paris 1946; also, *Le drame lyrique d'Alexandre Blok*, Paris 1946; Bowra, C. M., "Alexander Blok," *The Heritage of Symbolism*, London 1943; Gauvain, J., and Bickert, E., *A. Blok, poète de la tragédie russe*, Fribourg 1943; Goodmann, Th., *Alexander Block, eine Studie zur neueren russischen Literaturgeschichte*, Königsberg 1936; Laffitte, S., *Alexandre Blok: une étude* (with translations), Paris 1958; Lednicki, W., "Blok's 'Polish Poem' " (on *Retribution*), *Russia, Poland, and the West*, New York 1954; Lewitter, L. R., "The Inspiration and Meaning of Alexander Blok's *The Rose and the Cross*," *Slavonic and*

East European Review, 85 (1957); Poggioli, R., "Studi su Blok: I *Versi della Bellissima Dama*," *Rivista di Letterature Slave*, 1930, I.
Poemetti e Liriche, translated with introduction by R. Poggioli, Modena 1947; *Gedichte*, translated by R. v. Walter, Berlin 1920; *Gesammelte Dichtungen*, translated by J. von Günther, Munich 1947; *Les Douze*, translated by S. Komoff, Paris 1920; the same, translated by Y. Sidersky, Paris 1923; *The Twelve*, translated by C. Beckhofer, London 1920; the same, translated by B. Deutsch and A. Yarmolinsky, New York 1931; the same, translated by C. M. Bowra, in *A Second Book of Russian Verse*, London 1949; *Die Zwölf*, translated by R. v. Walter, Berlin 1921; the same, translated by W. Groeger, Berlin 1921; *I Dodici*, translated by R. Poggioli, in *Il Fiore del Verso Russo*, Turin 1949; *The Rose and the Cross*, translated by I. Smith and G. R. Noyes, *The Slavonic and East European Review*, 42 (1936); *Rose und Kreuz*, translated by W. Groeger, Berlin 1923; *The Spirit of Music* (essays), translated by I. Freiman, London 1946.

CHAPTER SEVEN: THE NEOPARNASSIANS

I. CLARISM AND ACMEISM

Brjusov, V., "Akmeizm," *Russkaja Mysl'*, 1913, IV; Mochul'skij, K., "Klassitsizm v sovremennoj russkoj poèzii," *Sovremennye Zapiski*, XI (1922); Zhirmunskij, V., "Na put'jakh k klassitsizmu," *Vestnik literatury*, 1921, IV-V.
Strakhovsky, L., *Craftsmen of the Word: Three Poets of Modern Russia: Gumilyov, Akhmatova, Mandelstam*, Cambridge, Mass. 1949.

II. KUZMIN

Èjkhenbaum, B., "O proze Kuzmina," *Skvoz' literaturu*, Petrograd 1924; Gumilev, N., "Kuzmin," *Pis'ma o russkoj poèzii*, Petrograd 1923; Ivanov, G., "Kuzmin," *Peterburgskie zimy*, New York 1952; Ivanov, V., "Kuzmin," *Apollon*, 1910, 7; Znovsko-Borovskij, E., "O tvorchestve Kuzmina," *Apollon*, 1917, 4-5.
Alexandrinische Gesänge, translated by J. Günther, München 1919.

III. GUMILEV

Gumileva, A., "N. Gumilev," *Novyj Zhurnal*, XLVI (1956); Ivanov, G., "O Gumileve," *Sovremennye Zapiski*, XLVII (1931); Khodasevich, V., "Gumilev i Blok," *Nekropol'*, Bruxelles 1939; Makovskij, S., "N. S. Gumilev," *Grani*, 36 (1957); Nevedomskaja, V., "Vospominanija o Gumileve i Akhmatovoj," *Novyj Zhurnal*, XXXVIII (1954); Otsup, N. "N. S. Gumilev," *Opyty*, I (1953); Struve, G. (ed.), introduction to *Neizdannyj Gumilev*, New York 1952 (contains important unpublished material).

SPECIAL BIBLIOGRAPHY

IV. AKHMATOVA

Èjkhenbaum, B., *Anna Akhmatova*, Petrograd 1923; Mochul'skij, K., "Poèticheskoe tvorchestvo A. Akhmatovoj," *Russkaja Mysl'*, 1921, III–IV; Trubetskoj, Ju., "Anna Akhmatova," *Literaturnyj Sovremennik*, Munich, 4 (1952); Vinogradov, V., *Poèzija Anny Akhmatovoj*, Leningrad 1925.

Landolfi, T., "Contributo ad uno studio della poesia di Anna Achmatova," *Europa Orientale*, XIV–XV (1934–1935); Sandomirsky, V., "A Note on the Poetry of Anna Akhmatova," *Poetry* (May 1950).

Poesie, translated by D. D. Di Sarra, Florence 1931.

V. KLJUEV

Filippov, B. (ed.), introduction to Kljuev, N., *Polnoe Sobranie Sochinenij* (2 vols.), New York 1954 (with important unpublished material); Ivask, Ju., "Kljuev," *Opyty*, II (1953); Lo Gatto, E., "Vospominanija o Kljueve," *Novyj Zhurnal*, XXVI (1953), (with the story of how the author succeeded in bringing back from Soviet Russia some of Kljuev's unpublished manuscripts); Menskij, R., "N. Kljuev," *Novyj Zhurnal*, XXXII (1953).

Patrick, G. Z., *Popular Poetry in Soviet Russia*, Berkeley, Calif. 1929.

GEORGIJ IVANOV

Gul', R., "Georgij Ivanov," *Novyj Zhurnal*, XLII (1955).

CHAPTER EIGHT: THE POETS OF THE ADVANCE GUARD

I. FUTURISM

Chukovskij, K., *Futuristy*, Petrograd 1922; Gorlov, N., *Futurizm i revoljutsija*, Moscow 1924; Kamenskij, V., *Put' entuziasta*, Moscow 1931; Kruchenykh, A., *15 let russkogo Futurizma*, Moscow 1928; Livshits, B., *Polutoraglazyj strelets*, Leningrad 1933; Markov, V., "Mysli o russkom Futurizme," *Novyj Zhurnal*, XXXVIII (1954); Shapirshtejn-Lers, Ja., *Obshchestvennyj smysl russkogo Futurizma*, Moscow 1922; Shklovskij, V., "O poèzii i zaumnom jazyke," *Poètika*, Petrograd 1919.

Lehrmann-Gandolfi, G., *De Marinetti à Maïakovski: Destins d'un mouvement littéraire occidental en Russie*, Fribourg 1942.

FORMALISM

Èngel'gardt, B., *Formal'nyj metod v istorii literatury*, Leningrad 1927; Zhirmunskij, V., "K voprosu o formal'nom metode," *Voprosy teorii literatury*, Leningrad 1928.

Ehrlich, V., *Russian Formalism: History-Doctrine*, The Hague 1955 (the most important work on the subject); Goriély, G., *Science des lettres soviétiques*, Paris 1947; Gourfinkel, N., "Les nouvelles méthodes d'histoire littéraire en Russie," *Le Monde Slave*, II (1929); Kridl, M., "Russian Formalism," *The American Bookman*, 1944, I; Setschkareff, V., "Die Theorie des literarischen Kunstwerk nach Viktor Sklovskij," *Lexis*, 1954, 7; Tomashevsky, B., "La nouvelle école d'histoire littéraire en Russie," *Revue des Etudes Slaves*, VIII (1928); Voznesenskij, A., "Die Methodologie der russischen Literaturwissenschaft," *Zeitschrift für Slavische Philologie*, 1927–1928, IV–V; Zhirmunskij, V., "Formprobleme in der russischen Literaturwissenschaft," *Zeitschrift für Slavische Philologie*, 1925, I.

II. IMAGINISM AND EGO-FUTURISM

L'vov-Rogachevskij, V., *Imazhinisty*, Moscow 1921.

SEVERJANIN

Brjusov, V., "Igor' Severjanin, poèt v luchshem smysle slova," *Sbornik kritiki i tvorchestva I. Severjanina*, Moscow 1915.

III. KHLEBNIKOV

Jakobson, R., *Novejshaja russkaja poèzija: Khlebnikov*, Prague 1921; Majakovskij, V., "Nekrolog o Khlebnikove," *Krasnaja Nov'*, 4, 1922; Markov, V., "O Khlebnikove: popytka apologii i soprotivlenija," *Grani*, 22 (1954); Tynjanov, Ju., "O Khlebnikove," *Arkhaisty i novatory*, Leningrad 1929.

Ripellino, A., "Chlebnikov e il Futurismo russo," *Convivium*, 1949, 5.

IV. MAJAKOVSKIJ

Chukovskij, K., "Majakovskij," *Repin, Majakovskij, Brjusov: Vospominanija*, Moscow 1940; Jakobson, R., "O pokolenii, rastrativshem svoikh poètov," *Smert' Vladimira Majakovskogo*, Berlin 1931 (also contains Mirskij, D. S., "Dve smerti"); Khodasevich, V., "O Majakovskom," *Literaturnye Stat'i i Vospominanija*, New York 1954; Pertsov, V., *Majakovskij* (2 vols.), Moscow 1951–1956; Shklovskij, V., *O. Majakovskom*, Moscow 1940; Vinokur, G., *Majakovskij, novator jazyka*, Moscow 1943.

Bachtin, N., "Mayakovski," *Oxford Slavonic Papers*, II (1951); Bowra, C. M., "The Futurism of Vladimir Mayakovsky," *The Creative Experiment*, London 1949; Jakobson, R., "Unpublished Majakovskij," *Harvard Library Bulletin*, IX, 2 (Spring 1955); Marshall, H., *Mayakovski and his Poetry*, Bombay 1955; Muchnic, H., "Vladimir Mayakovsky," *Russian Review*, 1958, 2; Poggioli, R., "Epigrafe per Majakovskij," *Pietre di Paragone*, Florence 1939; Ripellino, A. M., *Majakovskij e il teatro russo d'avanguardia*, Turin 1959; Triolet, E., *Maïakovski, poète russe*, Paris 1945.

Vladimir Mayakovsky 1894–1930 (special issue), *The American Quarterly on the Soviet Union*, 1940, I; *Vladimir Maïakovski, Tragédie, suivie de Poèmes*, translated by A. Lassaigne, Paris 1952; *Mystery-Bouffe*, translated by G. R. Noyes and A. Kaun, in Noyes, G. R. (ed.), *Masterpieces of the Russian Drama*, New York 1933; *Vers et Prose*, translated by E. Triolet, Paris 1952; *Opere* (4 vols.), edited by I. Ambrosio and translated by several hands, Rome 1958.

SPECIAL BIBLIOGRAPHY

V. ESENIN

Adamovich, G., "Literaturnye besedy," *Zveno* (Paris), 1927, I; Khodasevich, V., "Esenin," *Sovremennye Zapiski*, XXVII (1926); Mariengof, A., *Roman bez vranja*, Leningrad 1928; Nikitina, E., *Esenin: zhizn', lichnost', tvorchestvo*, Moscow 1926; Zavalishin, V., "Esenin i Majakovskij," *Literaturnyj Sovremennik*, Munich, I (1951).

De Graaf, F., *Serge Esénine, sa vie et son oeuvre*, Leiden 1933; Pascal, P., "Esénine, poète de la campagne russe," *Oxford Slavonic Papers*, II (1951); Poggioli, R., "La poesia di Sergio Esenin," *Pietre di Paragone*, Florence 1939.

Confession d'un voyou, Paris 1923, and *Requiem, suivi d'autres poèmes*, Paris 1926, both translated by M. Miloslawsky and F. Hellens; *Liriche e Frammenti*, translated by R. Poggioli, Florence 1940; *Poesie*, translated by O. Resnevich-Signorelli and F. Matacotta, Modena 1940; *Poesie* (with original texts), translated by I. de Luca, Florence 1946.

CHAPTER NINE: THE POETS OF YESTERDAY

I. SOVIET LITERATURE

Èrenburg, I., *A vse-taki ona vertitsja. O novom stile v iskusstve*, Berlin 1922; Gorbachev, G., *Sovremennaja russkaja literatura*, Leningrad 1929; Gor'kij, M., *O literature. Stat'i i rechi 1928–1936*, Moscow 1937; Ivanov, F., *Krasnyj Parnas*, Berlin 1922; Kogan, P., *Literatura velikogo desjatiletija*, Moscow-Leningrad 1927; Lezhnev, A., *Sovremenniki*, Moscow 1927; also, *Literaturnye budni*, Moscow 1929; Lunts, L., "Na zapad!," *Beseda*, 1923, 3; Polonskij, V., *Ocherki literaturnogo dvizhenija revoljutsionnoj èpokhi*, Moscow-Leningrad 1929; Selivanovskij, A., *Ocherki po istorii russkoj sovetskoj poèzii*, Moscow 1930; Shklovskij, V., *Santimental'noe puteshestvie*, Moscow-Berlin 1923; Slonim, M., *Portrety sovetskikh pisatelej*, Paris 1932; Tarasenkov, A., *O sovetskoj literature*, Moscow 1952; Timofeev, L., *Russkaja sovetskaja literatura*, Moscow 1952; Trotskij, L., *Literatura i Revoljutsija*, Moscow 1923; Vinogradov, I., *Voprosy marksistskoj poètiki*, Leningrad 1936; Voronskij, A., *Literaturnye portrety* (2 vols.), Moscow 1928–1929.

Antowiak, A. (ed.), *Sowietische Literaturkritik* (anthology), Leipzig 1949; Bonnard, A., *Vers un humanisme nouveau: Réflexions sur la littérature soviétique*, Lausanne 1948; Brown, E. J., *The Proletarian Episode in Russian Literature*, New York 1953; Eastman, M., *Artists in Uniform: A Study of Literature and Bureaucratism*, New York 1934; Egolin, A. M., *The Ideological Content of Soviet Literature*, Washington, D. C. 1948; Flores, A., *Literature and Marxism: A Controversy of Soviet Critics*, New York 1938; Goriély, B., *La Nouvelle poésie en U.S.S.R.*, Bruxelles 1928; also, *Les poètes dans la révolution russe*, Paris 1934; Kaun, A., *Soviet Poets and Poetry*, Berkeley, Calif. 1943; Lo Gatto, E., *Poesia russa della revolutione*, Rome 1923; also, *La letteratura soviettista*, Rome 1929; Lukács, G., *Der russische Realism in der Weltliteratur* (with a section on "Socialist

Realism"), Berlin 1952; also, *Karl Marx und Friedrich Engels als Literaturhistoriker*, Berlin 1953; also, *Il significato attuale del realismo critico*, Turin 1957; Mathewson, R., *The Positive Hero in Russian Literature* (before and after the Revolution), New York 1958; Messina, G., *La letteratura sovietica*, Florence 1950; Milosz, Cz., *The Captive Mind*, translated from the Polish by J. Zielonko, New York 1953; Patrick, G., *Popular Poetry in Soviet Russia*, Berkeley, Calif. 1929; Reavey, G., *Soviet Literature To-Day*, London 1946; Scott, H. C. (ed.), *Problems of Soviet Literature: Reports and Speeches of the First Writers' Congress*, London 1935; Silone, I., and Anissimov, I., "A Troubled Dialogue," *Encounter*, XLV (1957); Simmons, E., "Soviet Russian Literature," *Handbook of Slavic Studies*, Cambridge, Mass. 1949; also, *Russian Fiction and Soviet Ideology: Introduction to Fedin, Leonov, and Sholokhov*, New York 1958; Struve, G., *Soviet Russian Literature 1917–1950*, Norman, Oklahoma 1951 (by far the most important work on the subject); also, *Geschichte der Sowjetliteratur*, Munich 1957 (translation of preceding item, revised and brought up to date); Zavalishin, V., *Early Soviet Writers*, New York 1958.

ANTHOLOGIES OF SOVIET AND EARLY REVOLUTIONARY POETRY

Belov, D., Perstov, B., and Surkov, A., *Russkaja sovetskaja poèzija*, Moscow 1948; Èrenburg, I., *Poèzija revoljutsionnoj Moskvy*, Berlin 1922; Lugovskoj, V., and others, *Antologija russkoj sovetskoj poèzii 1917–1957* (2 vols.), Moscow 1957.

Rodker, J., *Soviet Anthology*, London 1943; Tartakower, *Das russische Revolutionsgesicht, Anthologie moderner russischer Lyrik*, Berlin 1923.

SOVIET ARTS

Freeman, J., Kunitz, J., and Lozowek, J., *Voices of October: Art and Literature in Soviet Russia*, New York 1930; Fülöp-Miller, R., and Gregor, J., *Mind and Face of Bolshevism: An Examination of Cultural Life in Soviet Russia*, London 1927; London, K., *The Seven Soviet Arts*, London 1937.

SOVIET FILM

Eisenstein (Èjzenshtejn), S., *Film Sense* and *Film Form*, both edited and translated by Jay Leyda, New York 1942 and 1948; Pudovkin, V., *Film Technique* and *Film Acting*, both translated by Y. Montague, London 1929 and 1935.

Dickinson, Th., and de la Roche, C., *Soviet Cinema*, London 1948; Moussinac, L., *Le cinéma soviétique*, Paris 1928; Macdonald, D., "The Eisenstein Tragedy," *Memoirs of a Revolutionist*, New York 1957.

SOVIET THEATER

Dana, H. W. L., *Handbook on Soviet Drama*, New York 1938; Evreinov, N., *Le Théâtre en Russie soviétique*, Paris 1946; Gorchakov, N., *The Theatre in Soviet Russia*, New York 1957; Gsell, P., *Le Théâtre soviétique*, Paris 1937; Markov, P. A., *The Soviet Theatre*, London 1934; McLeod, J., *The New Soviet Theatre*, London 1943; Rühle, J., *Das gefesselte Theater*, Cologne 1957; Zamjatin, E., "Il teatro sovietico: poeti, attori, registi" (a lec-

363

ture given in Prague in 1932, translated by R. Poggioli), *Scenario*, May 1932.

EARLY SOVIET PROSE WRITERS:

SERAPION BROTHERS

    Tsetlin, M., "Plemja mladoe," *Sovremennye Zapiski*, XII (1922); Voronskij, "Serapionovy Brat'ja," *Krasnaja Nov'*, 1922, 3.

LUNTS

    Gor'kij, M., "Pamjati L. Luntsa," *Beseda*, 1924, 5.

BABEL'

    Lezhnev, A., "Babel'," *Literaturnye budni*, Moscow 1929; Voronskij, A., "Babel'," *Literaturnye portrety*, I, Moscow 1928.
    Poggioli, R., "Isaak Babel in Retrospect," *The Phoenix and the Spider*, Cambridge, Mass. 1957.
    The Collected Stories, edited and translated by W. Morison, with an introduction by L. Trilling, New York 1955.

VSEVOLOD IVANOV

    Slonim, M., "Vsevolod Ivanov," *Portrety sovetskikh pisatelej*, Paris 1933.
    Armoured Train 14-69, translated by G. Cowan and A. T. K. Grant, London 1933.

SHOLOKHOV

    Lezhnev, I., *Mikhail Sholokhov*, Moscow 1941; Scherbina, V., "*Tikhij Don* M. Sholokhova," *Novyj Mir*, 1941, 4.
    The Silent Don, translated by S. Garry, New York 1942.

ZAMJATIN

    Voronskij, A., "Zamjatin," *Literaturnye Portrety*, I (Moscow 1928).
    Poggioli, R., "Antinomie di Zamjatin," *Pietre di Paragone*, Florence 1939.
    We, translation by G. Zilboorg; introduction by P. Rudy; preface by M. Slonim, New York 1959.

PIL'NJAK

    Voronskij, A., "Pil'njak," *Na styke*, Moscow-Petrograd 1923.
    The Naked Year, translated by A. Brown, London 1928.

OLESHA

    Struve, G., "Olesha," *Soviet Russian Literature*, 1917-1950 (pp. 98-106), Norman, Oklahoma 1951.
    Envy, translated by A. Wolfe, London 1947.

THE POETS OF YESTERDAY

II. LITERATURE OF EMIGRATION

1. SURVEYS AND ESSAYS

Adamovich, G., *Odinochestvo i svoboda*, New York 1955; Gazdanov, G., "O molodoj èmigrantskoj literature," *Sovremennye Zapiski*, LX (1936); Issako, G., "Predvoennaja èmigrantskaja poèzija," *Grani*, 5 (1949); Ivask, Ju., "O poslevoennoj èmigrantskoj poèzii," *Novyj Zhurnal*, XXIII (1950); Struve, G., *Russkaja literatura v izgnanii*, New York 1956 (the only book on the subject); also, "The Double Life of Russian Literature," *Books Abroad*, Autumn 1954; also, "Russian Writers in Exile: Problems of an Emigré Literature," *Proceedings of the Second Congress of the International Comparative Literature Association*, vol. II, Chapel Hill, N.C. 1959.

2. ANTHOLOGIES OF ÉMIGRÉ POETRY

Adamovich, G., and Kantor, M., *Jakor': Antologija zarubezhnoj poèzii*, Berlin 1936; Ivask, Ju., *Na Zapade: Antologija russkoj zarubezhnoj poèzii*, New York 1953; Markov, V., *Priglushennye golosa (Poèzija za zheleznym zanavesom)*, New York 1952 (an anthology of the "inner" émigrés, or, as the subtitle says, of "poetry beyond the Iron Curtain").

III. KHODASEVICH

Belyj, A., "*Tjazhelaja Lira* i russkaja lirika," *Sovremennye Zapiski*, XV (1923); Terapiano, Ju., "V. Khodasevich," *Vstrechi*, New York 1953; Vejdle, V., "Vladislav Khodasevich," *Sovremennye Zapiski*, XXXIV (1928); Vishnjak, M., "Vladislav Khodasevich," *Novyj Zhurnal*, II (1944).

Berberova, N., "Vladislav Khodasevich: A Russian Poet," *Russian Review*, 1952, 2.

IV. MANDEL'SHTAM

Èrenburg, I., "O. È. Mandel'shtam," *Portrety russkikh poètov*, Berlin 1922; Ivanov, G., "Mandel'shtam," *Peterburgskie zimy*, New York 1952; Struve, G., preface to O. Mandel'shtam's *Sobranie Sochinenij*, New York 1955 (an important collection, including materials never published before in book form); Ivask, Ju., review of the same, *Opyty*, VI (1956).

Poggioli, R., "Commento a Mandelstam," *Pietre di Paragone*, Florence 1939; Strakhovsky, L., "Osip Mandelstam, Architect of Words," *Russian Review*, 1948, 1.

Gedichte, translated by P. Celan, Frankfurt a. M. 1959.

V. TSVETAEVA

Èrenburg, I., "M. I. Tsvetaeva," *Portrety russkikh poètov*, Berlin 1922; also, "Poèzija Mariny Tsvetaevoj," *Literaturnaja Moskva*, II (Moscow 1956); Ivask, Ju., "Pis'ma M. I. Tsvetaevoj Ju. P. Ivasku," *Russkij Literaturnyj Arkhiv* (ed. M. Karpovich and D. Cizevskij), New York 1956; Izvol'skaja, E., "Ten' na stenakh (O Tsvetaevoj)," *Opyty*, III (1954); Stepun, F., introduction to Marina Tsvetaeva's *Proza*, New York 1953; Struve, G., preface, and Ivask, Ju., "Blagorodnaja Tsvetaeva," introduction to Marina Tsvetaeva's *Lebedinyj stan*, Munich 1957.

SPECIAL BIBLIOGRAPHY

CHAPTER TEN: POETS OF TODAY

I. ASEEV

Arkhangel'skij, V., "Poèzija N. Aseeva," *Pechat' i Revoljutsija*, 1929, XII; Selivanovskij, A., "N. Aseev," *Ocherki po istorii russkoj sovetskoj literatury*, Moscow 1936.

TIKHONOV

Gorbachev, G., "Nikolaj Tikhonov," *Pechat' i Revoljutsija*, VI (1927); Voronskij, A., "Tikhonov," *Literaturnye portrety*, II (Moscow 1928–1929).

CONSTRUCTIVISM

Arvatov, B., "Iskusstvo i klassy. Teorija Konstruktivizma," *LEF*, 1923; Zelinskij, K., *Poèzija kak smysl*, Moscow 1929.

SELVINSKIJ

Lezhnev, A., "Il'ja Selvinskij i Konstruktivizm," *Pechat' i Revoljutsija*, 1927, I.

BAGRITSKIJ

Postupal'skij, I., "Poèzija Bagritskogo," *Pechat' i Revoljutsija*, 1928, V; Selivanovskij, A., "Eduard Bagritskij," *Novyj Mir*, 1933, 6.

II, III. PASTERNAK

Anstej, O., "Mysli o Pasternake," *Literaturnyj Sovremennik*, Munich, 2, 1951; Antokol'skij, P., "Boris Pasternak," *Ispytanie vremenem*, Moscow 1945; Aseev, N., "Pis'ma o poèzii," *Krasnaja Nov'*, 1922, 3; Lezhnev, A., "Boris Pasternak," *Krasnaja Nov'*, 1926, 8; Selivanovskij, A., "Boris Pasternak," *Krasnaja Nov'*, 1933, 1; Tsvetaeva, M., "Svetovoj liven'," *Èpopeja*, 1922, 3 (also in *Proza*, edited by F. Stepun, New York 1953); Vejdle, V., "Stikhi i proza Pasternaka," *Sovremennye Zapiski*, XXXVI (1928).

Bowra, C. M., "Boris Pasternak, 1917–1923," *The Creative Experiment*, London 1949; Cohen, J. M., "The Poetry of Boris Pasternak," *Horizon* (July 1944); Jakobson, R., "Randbemerkungen zur Prosa des Dichters Pasternak," *Slavische Rundschau*, 1935, 6; Muchnic, H., "Toward an Analysis of Boris Pasternak," *Slavic and East European Journal*, 2 (1957); Wrenn, C. L., "Boris Pasternak," *Oxford Slavonic Papers*, II (1951).

Poesie, translated with introduction by A. M. Ripellino, Turin 1957; *Selected Poems*, translated by J. M. Cohen, London 1946; *Poems*, translated by L. Slater, with foreword by H. MacDiarmid, Fairwarp, Sussex, 1959; *Autobiografia e nuovi versi*, Milan 1958; *Poems*, translated by E. M. Kayden, Ann Arbor, Mich. 1959; *The Poetry of Boris Pasternak, 1917–1959*, translated with a critical and biographical introduction by G. Reavey, New York 1959; *Selected Writings* (verse and prose, including *The Safe-Conduct*, translated by several hands), New York 1949; *Récit*, translated by B. Goriély, Lyon 1958, *L'an 1905*, translated by B. Goriély, Paris 1959.

IV. DOCTOR ZHIVAGO

Abel, L., "Boris Pasternak's *Doctor Zhivago*," *Dissent*, Autumn 1958; Chiaromonte, N., "Pasternak's Message," *Partisan Review*, 1958, 1; also, "Il valore del *Dottor Zivago*," *Il Mondo* (Rome), Dec. 7, 1958; also, "*Doctor Zhivago* and Modern Sensibility," *Dissent*, Winter 1959; Deutscher, I., "Pasternak and the Calendar of Revolution," and Howe, I., "Freedom and the Ashcan of History" (a debate *contra* and *pro* the "politics" of *Doctor Zhivago*), *Partisan Review*, 1959, 2; Editors of *The New World* (*Novyj Mir*), "A Letter of Rejection," *New York Times Book Review*, Dec. 7, 1958; Hayward, M., "Pasternak's *Doctor Zhivago*," *Encounter*, 56 (1958), Herling, G., "Boris Pasternaks Sieg," *Merkur*, XII, 123 (1958); Matlaw, R., "A Visit With Pasternak," *The Nation*, Sept. 12, 1959; Moravia, A., "Entretien avec Pasternak," *Preuves*, 88 (1958); Struve, G., "Russia's Terrible Years: *Doctor Zhivago*," *The New Leader*, Oct. 17, 1958; Wilson, E., "Doctor Life and his Guardian Angel," *The New Yorker*, Nov. 15, 1958; also, "Legend and Symbol in *Doctor Zhivago*," *The Nation*, Apr. 25, 1959 (p. 188); Zolla, E., "Cinque tesi sul *Dottor Zivago*," *Tempo Presente*, 1958, 2.

Il Dottor Zivago, translated by P. Tsvetemirich, Milan 1957; *Doctor Zhivago*, translated by M. Hayward and M. Harari, New York 1958; *Doktor Zhivago* (Russian edition), Ann Arbor, Mich., 1959; *Essai d'autobiographie*, Paris 1958; *I Remember: Sketch for an Autobiography*, translated with introduction by D. Magarshack, with an essay *On Translating Shakespeare*, translated by M. Harari, New York 1959.

V. WAR AND POSTWAR POETRY

Sandomirsky, V., "The Sad Armchair: Notes on Soviet War and Postwar Lyrical Poetry," *Harvard Slavic Studies*, III (1957).

ZABOLOTSKIJ

Tarasenkov, A., "Pokhvala Zabolotskomu" (a negative critique), *Krasnaja Nov'*, 1933, 9.

RECENT TRENDS

Monas, S., "The Private Muse: Some Notes on Recent Soviet Literature," *Hudson Review*, XI (1958).

INDEX

INDEX

371

INDEX

INDEX